Cambridge Studies in Islamic Civilization

Roman, provincial and Islamic law

Cambridge Studies in Islamic Civilization

Titles in the series

ANDREW M. WATSON. *Agricultural innovation in the early islamic world: the diffusion of crops and farming techniques 700–1100*

ELIAS N. SAAD. *Social history of Timbuktu: the role of Muslim scholars and notables 1400–1900*

G. H. A. JUYNBOLL. *Muslim tradition: studies in chronology, provenance and authorship of early Ḥadīth*

BASIM MUSALLAM. *Sex and society in Islam: birth control before the nineteenth century*

SURAIYA FAROQHI. *Towns and townsmen of Ottoman Anatolia: trade, crafts and food production in an urban setting, 1520–1650*

NABIL A. SALEH. *Unlawful gain and legitimate profit in Islamic law*: riba, gharar *and Islamic banking*

SURAIYA FAROQHI. *Men of modest substance: home owners and house property in seventeenth-century Ankara and Keyseri*

Roman, provincial and Islamic law

The origins of the Islamic patronate

PATRICIA CRONE

Cambridge University Press

Cambridge
London New York New Rochelle
Melbourne Sydney

Published by the Press Syndicate of the University of Cambridge
The Pitt Building, Trumpington Street, Cambridge CB2 1RP
32 East 57th Street, New York, NY 10022, USA
10 Stamford Road, Oakleigh, Melbourne 3166, Australia

First published 1987

Printed in Great Britain at the University Press, Cambridge

British Library cataloguing in publication data

Crone, Patricia
Roman, provincial and Islamic law: the
origins of the Islamic patronate.——
(Cambridge studies in Islamic civilization)
1. Islamic law
I. Title
340.5′9 [LAW]

Library of Congress Cataloguing in Publication Data

Crone, Patricia, 1945–
Roman, provincial, and Islamic law.
(Cambridge studies in Islamic civilization)
Bibliography:
Includes index.
1. Islamic law – Roman influences. 2. Roman law.
I. Title. II. Series.
LAW 340.5′9 86–29916

ISBN 0 521 32253 7

WV

Contents

Preface *page* vii

1 The state of the field 1
2 A practical guide to the study of Islamic law 18
3 The Islamic patronate 35
4 The case against Arabia 43
5 The case against the non-Roman Near East: *paramonē* 64
6 The case for the Roman Near East 77
7 Conclusion 89

Appendices
1 The slavegirl's twins 100
2 Goldziher on Roman and Islamic law 102
3 The *muḥtasib* 107
4 Paramonar manumission as *tadbīr* 109

Notes 111
Works cited 159
Index 175

Preface

This book, which I have previously announced under the title 'The Roman Origins of Islamic Clientage', has its roots in a chapter of my thesis, 'The Mawālī in the Umayyad Period', London Ph.D. 1974. (Of the entire thesis it may now be said that in so far as it has not been published, it has been abrogated.) Though the roots are now exceedingly long, I should like to thank Professor B. Lewis for reading the first draft of what was in due course to become this book without reacting so negatively as to kill the idea, for all that it was undoubtedly the most chaotic piece that I have ever written. Michael Cook not only went through the same ordeal, but also read and commented on numerous subsequent drafts and suggested that I add what is now Chapter 2. I should also like to thank the Islamicists at the Hebrew University of Jerusalem for extracts from their concordance of Arabic poetry, Professor S. Moreh for help with the translation of poetry, Professor F. de Jong for help with rare publications, David Powers for making me think about bequests again, Fritz Zimmermann for comments on the first chapter, and Martin Hinds for comments on the entire final draft.

P.C.

CHAPTER 1

The state of the field

This book is concerned with the relative contributions of Roman and provincial law to the Sharīʿa, the holy law of Islam. While Roman law needs no introduction, the term 'provincial law' may puzzle the reader. It refers to the non-Roman law practised in the provinces of the Roman empire, especially the provinces formerly ruled by Greeks. In principle non-Roman legal institutions should have disappeared from the Roman world on the extension of Roman citizenship to all free inhabitants of the empire in 212; in practice they lived on and even came to influence the official law of the land. There were thus two quite different sets of legal institutions in the Roman Near East which was to fall to the Arabs, and both need to be considered in discussions of the provenance of the Sharīʿa.

This is not a new observation. It is nonetheless worth stressing it again, for in practice it has been forgotten. There is no literature on the genetic relationship between provincial and Islamic law; and though there are numerous works on the potential contribution of Roman law, their quality is mostly poor: apart from a handful of pioneer works written in the decades around the First World War, practically nothing has been added to our knowledge of the question since von Kremer wrote on it in 1875. This state of affairs reflects the intellectual isolation in which Islamic studies have come to be conducted since the First World War, and the present work is intended in the first instance as a plea for the end of this isolation: that the effect of specialist blinkers on the study of the cultural origins of Islamic law has been unfortunate should be clear from the following pages.

The first scholar to point out that a comparison of Roman and Islamic law would be of interest seems to have been Reland, a professor of Oriental languages at Utrecht who wrote in 1708.[1] Reland's perspective was however comparative rather than genetic, and it was not until the mid nineteenth century that Muslim indebtedness to Rome began to be widely suggested. The *a priori* case for Roman influence on the Sharīʿa was forcefully put by two professional lawyers, Domenico Gatteschi and Sheldon Amos, who wrote in 1865 and 1883 respectively.[2] Neither knew Arabic, but in their view the Arabs could no more have failed to be influenced by the legal systems of the people they conquered than could the barbarians in the West.[3] They pointed out that there is not much legislation in the Qur'ān,[4] that Syria was a province in which Roman law was not only practised, but also studied,[5] that converts must have brought their legal notions with them, and that such foreign notions could easily have been formulated as traditions (*ḥadīths*) from the Prophet.[6] Legal institutions, they argued, are notoriously hard to change, even for conquerors,[7] and there are in fact many parallels between Roman and Islamic law;[8] unless we assume foreign influence it is impossible to explain how Islamic law could have developed so fast.[9] Both overstated their case: Islamic law certainly is not 'Roman law in Arab dress',[10] and the Muslims did not themselves study Roman lawbooks.[11] But unlike Henry Hugues, another lawyer who wrote on the same subject between 1878 and 1880,[12] they had perceived a fundamental point: Islamic law, as Santillana later put it, cannot have been born by parthenogenesis.[13]

Meanwhile Orientalists had arrived at similar conclusions. In 1853 Enger noted both the general likelihood of Roman influence on Islamic law and specific parallels in the terminology of ownership and methods of taxation.[14] Further parallels relating to sale and hire were adduced by van den Berg in 1868,[15] and in 1875 the question was taken up for extensive discussion by von Kremer in his *Culturgeschichte*. Von Kremer referred to van den Berg and added numerous parallels of his own; he rejected the theory that the Muslims studied Roman lawbooks, but allowed for continuity of legal practice, and pointed out that several Roman institutions could have entered Islamic law indirectly through borrowing from the Jews.[16] His discussion was in fact a well drafted programme of research.

Execution of the programme, however, was not and is not easy. The Islamic tradition consistently presents Islamic law as a modified version of Arab law, virtually every legal institution being traced back to pre-Islamic Arabian practice and/or to rulings by the Arabian Prophet and his immediate successors. Even institutions rejected by Islamic law are traced back in this fashion, pre-Islamic practice being in this case presented as pagan rather than Arab, while the Prophet and his immediate successors are employed to condemn rather than to validate. It is obvious that this presentation is doctrinally inspired, but the tradition is in fact armed to the teeth against imputations of foreign influence. Practically no borrowings are acknowledged, loan-words are extremely rare; and since both patriarchal practice and Canaanite malpractice are located in the Arab past, foreign systems are hardly ever mentioned, let alone discussed, not even by way of polemics.[17] At the same time no sources survive from the formative first century of Islamic law. We are thus entirely dependent on a late tradition hostile to our designs.[18]

Moreover, the one legal system which, despite the asseverations of the lawyers, manifestly did contribute to the formation of the Sharīʿa is not

Roman, but Jewish law. The Sharīʿa and the Halakha are both all-embracing religious laws created by scholars who based themselves on scripture and oral tradition, employed similar methods of deduction and adopted the same casuistic approach: the structural similarity between Jewish and Islamic law is obvious to the naked eye,[19] and the habit of dubbing the *ʿulamāʾ* 'Muslim rabbis' is as old as Snouck Hurgronje.[20] Since the order of the subjects in the Mishna and the Muslim lawbooks is related,[21] while in a subject such as ritual purity there is virtual identity of both overall category and substantive provisions,[22] it evidently was not by parthenogenesis that the similarity arose;[23] and it does not take much knowledge of Jewish law to see its influence in the most diverse provisions of Islamic law.[24] This clearly does not make the identification of Roman elements any easier. Roman institutions transferred to so alien a setting were necessarily denatured, and what parallels there are between Roman and Islamic law tend to be either general or elusive or else specific, but isolated; either way they are hard to pin down.[25] And even when they can be pinned down, the possibility remains that they were borrowed via Jewish law.

Despite these problems, by the early twentieth century it appeared as if the problem of Roman influence on the Sharīʿa was going to be solved. In 1890 Goldziher published the second volume of his *Muhammedanische Studien*, in which he demonstrated that Ḥadīth, far from conserving the words of the Prophet, reflects the legal and doctrinal controversies of the two centuries following his death.[26] This was the first step towards a proper study of the Islamic tradition, and its implications for law, as for other subjects, were immense. Goldziher was moreover a zealous adherent of the theory of Roman influence. It must however be said that his writings on this question are uncharacteristically weak: he postulated large-scale borrowing of Roman concepts on the basis of purely external similarity, disregarded the possibility of transmissions via Jewish law, and had only the most elementary knowledge of the legal system to which he attributed so crucial a role.[27] But though his contributions were of poor quality, his authority lent prestige to the subject; and coming as they did in the wake of his work on Ḥadīth, his ideas held out the exhilarating prospect of demonstrating that Islamic civilisation did not spring from an Arabian void. It was this exhilaration which animated the researches of Becker published between 1902 and 1924,[28] Schmidt's study of *occupatio* which appeared in 1910,[29] and Heffening's monograph on laws relating to aliens which appeared in 1925.[30] It was these three scholars who for the first time tried to demonstrate, and not merely suggest, the Roman origin of specific institutions of Islamic law.[31]

At about the same time Santillana and Morand, two Orientalists active in Islamic legal reform,[32] also began to occupy themselves with the question, though not, apparently, under the influence of Goldziher.[33] Santillana, who accepted the *a priori* case for Roman influence, believed that the groundwork on Islamic law had to be done before the question could be profitably discussed;[34] he accordingly limited his contribution to the provision of Roman parallels in his various publications.[35] But Morand, in the course of a discussion of the legal nature of the Muslim *waqf*, more or less incidentally set out a crisp argument in favour of its Roman origin.[36] This was published in 1910, and together with the German researches already mentioned marked the beginning of studies in depth.

There is another and quite different reason why the early twentieth century ought to have been a turning point. In 1891 Mitteis published his *Reichsrecht und Volksrecht*,[37] a book as epoch-making in the field of late Roman law as was Goldziher's *Muhammedanische Studien* in that of early Islam. Mitteis demonstrated that the non-Roman subjects of the Roman empire in no way abandoned their native legal institutions on their acquisition of Roman citizenship in 212, and his work put the discussion of the relationship between Roman and provincial (Greek and Oriental) law on a new footing. This discussion was fed by a stream of papyrological publications, the discovery of Syriac lawbooks, and the first studies of Egyptian and ancient Near Eastern law. It continued into the 1930s, and it generated an immense amount of research on a subject of manifestly crucial importance to historians of Islamic law, viz. the nature of the law practised in the provinces conquered by the Arabs. One might accordingly have expected the Islamicists to join this second front. In fact, given the superb quality of the scholarship produced on this subject, especially by the Germans and the Italians, it is hard to see how anyone interested in the subject could fail to join in: whether one turns to books, articles or short notices, one finds prodigious learning deployed in relation to a single, overarching issue. And at first the Islamicists did indeed join in. Sachau helped to stock Mitteis' armoury,[38] Nallino himself participated in the fray,[39] and Santillana was aware that there was such a thing as provincial law.[40] But even then the Islamicists were curiously reluctant to reconsider their own views in the light of the discoveries of the classicists. Sachau, for example, had a very considerable knowledge of both Syriac and Islamic law, and he wrote on both; yet he never attempted to relate them. In so far as he was forced to consider both in his commentaries on the Nestorian lawbooks of early Islamic times, he took it for granted that whenever there was agreement between Nestorian and Islamic law, it was simply because the Nestorians were indebted to the Muslims; the idea that *both* might be equally indebted to the provincial law on which his colleague Mitteis wrote seems never to have suggested itself to him. Similarly Nallino never brought his impressive knowledge of Syriac law to bear on the question of the provenance of the Sharīʿa. And to Santillana 'provincial law' was clearly a label without much concrete content. In any case, the Islamicists did not participate in the excitement of the classicists for long: after the First World War they dropped out.

The work of Heffening and Bussi apart,[41] the post-war period was marked by a sudden loss of enthusiasm for the theory of Roman influence on the Sharīʿa. In 1925 Bergsträsser published an article arguing that it was Arab custom rather than Near Eastern law (Roman or other) which went into the Sharīʿa,[42] and in 1933 Nallino argued much the same.[43] In 1947 and 1949 Bousquet, Hassam and Wigmore all asserted the parthenogenetic origins of Islamic law,[44] while FitzGerald in 1951 classified Roman influence as 'alleged';[45] and though occasional discussion, and even occasional suggestion, of Roman influence has continued since then, it has not been to much effect.[46] There is no more striking illustration of this loss of interest than the fate of the Nessana papyri. These papyri are the literary and documentary remains of a Christian Arab settlement in a remote outpost of the Roman empire in the desert nowadays known as the Negev. Written between 500 and 700, they include a number of legal documents, one of which is bilingual in Greek and Arabic. The legal documents were discovered in 1936 and reported in the following year at a papyrologist conference where the news of their discovery created a stir.[47] They were discussed by historians of late Roman law in various publications of 1938, 1940–1, 1943, 1947, 1948, 1961, 1964 and 1967,[48] and they were lavishly edited with translations, indices and helpful comments in 1958.[49] So far not a single historian of Islamic law has as much as mentioned them.

Why was the subject dropped? It is certainly unfortunate that one of the first classicists to take an interest in Islamic law was Carusi, a believer in the essential unity of the legal systems of the 'Mediterranean Orient' who picked up a smattering of Syriac and Arabic and made propaganda for the view that Islamic law had its roots in 'Oriental Roman law'.[50] His ideas were as wild as they were woolly, and some of Griffini's more fanciful notions would appear to have been developed under his influence.[51] Having been exposed as an incompetent, not to say fraudulent scholar by Nallino in 1921,[52] his effect on the Islamicist front was largely negative.[53] Since the claims of Goldziher, the most authoritative Islamicist, were no better founded than those of Carusi, the most notorious classicist, it began to look as though there were nothing to the subject but wild speculation. All the papers subsequently written against the theory of Roman influence were devoted to refuting these two scholars; the works of Becker, Schmidt, Morand and Heffening were ignored.[54]

Yet it clearly was not Carusi's excesses that killed the subject, any more than it was Lammens' excesses that killed the critical approach to the Sīra which Goldziher's research had initiated.[55] For one thing, no paradigm shift fails to be accompanied by a proliferation of misguided claims; the fact that wild ideas were rampant in the early study of provincial law did not cause the classicists to ignore Mitteis' conclusions.[56] For another thing, the criticism levelled at the theory of Roman influence was pitched at none too high a level. Nallino's views on Roman and Islamic law (as opposed to his views on

Carusi) were presented in a conference paper which was published after his death: a short sketch without notes, it merely set out an *a priori* case against the theory.[57] Hassam's article was a piece of Muslim apologetics,[58] while the notes appended by Wigmore are unworthy of an undergraduate.[59] And though FitzGerald's criticism of Goldziher was to the point, he too perpetrated an impressive number of mistakes.[60] But above all, the withering of the discussion of Roman influence was not isolated. It could not be said that wild speculation was all there was to the question of *Jewish* influence on Islamic law. Yet here too Heffening was the only Islamicist not to lose interest after the First World War.

This loss of interest is one out of many examples of a general shift in the direction of research in Islamic studies, or indeed in the arts at large, after the First World War. All branches of the arts suffered from professionalisation, or in other words from the transfer of scholarship to universities, where standard syllabi, departmental divisions and academic career structures soon led to loss of depth and range alike. It was not just Islamic studies that went into Splendid Isolation at that time.[61] In the case of legal studies, the change was all the more drastic in that Germany and Italy, the leading countries as regards the study of Roman and provincial law, had begun to exchange Roman law for national codes about the turn of the century, thereby depriving Roman legal studies of their practical importance.[62] But for Islamicists a political factor was also at work. As the era of the colony gave way to that of the mandate and eventually to that of independence, Islamicists increasingly preferred to study Islam as an autonomous system developing internally in response to its own needs and by the use of its own resources.[63] At the same time the Russian revolution helped to redirect attention from cultural origins to socio-economic problems. In principle, of course, there is no reason why the study of Islam as a system in its own right should preclude an interest in its genetic make-up, anymore than socio-economic preoccupations should rule out an interest in the way in which cultures are formed. But in practice an interest in genetic links has long come to be regarded as somewhat old-fashioned – philological as opposed to sociological, diffusionist as opposed to structuralist. Worse still, it is now considered ethnocentric and offensive to Islam; and though Greco-Roman influences are likely to be somewhat less offensive than Jewish ones, it is only in the field of Islamic art, science and philosophy that the classical *Fortleben* is nowadays discussed without circumlocution or apology.[64] (All three fields are of course considerably more marginal to the Muslim self-definition than theology and law.) As the old-fashioned Orientalist has given way to the modern historian, Arabist or social scientist with a tender post-colonial conscience and occasionally more substantial interest in maintaining Muslim good-will, both the inclination and the ability to view the *Werden und Wesen* of the Islamic world from the point of view of the Fertile Crescent have been lost, and Islamic civilisation has come to be taught and studied with almost total disregard for the Near East in which it was born. It is hard to imagine historians of Europe confining their attention to the tradition of the barbarian invaders in more or less complete neglect of the Roman world in which they made themselves at home, and there are encouraging signs that historians of the Islamic world are now abandoning the one-sided approach. But it is still prevails in the field of law.

Nothing was to happen in our field until Schacht resumed Goldziher's work on the Islamic tradition. Schacht's *Origins of Muhammadan Jurisprudence*, which appeared in 1950, may be regarded as a belated sequel to Goldziher's *Studien*, and like the *Studien* it is a work of fundamental importance. It showed that the beginnings of Islamic law cannot be traced further back in the Islamic tradition than to about a century after the Prophet's death, and this strengthened the *a priori* case in favour of the view that foreign elements entered the Sharīʿa. Schacht was himself a zealous adherent of this view; it is his numerous writings on the subject which currently define it. But though he deserves full credit for having restored the issue to its former prominence, the restoration was in one respect too faithful: if Goldziher's writings on the subject were uncharacteristically poor, the same is true of Schacht's.

In part the weakness of Schacht's work on the cultural origins of Islamic law arises from the fact that deference to Goldziher made him repeat all Goldziher's mistakes, but more particularly it is due to the fact that he wrote at a time when Islamicists had lost contact with the Near Eastern background to Islam. His perspective was that of the purebred Arabist to whom the pre-Islamic Near East is *terra incognita*; and most of what he wrote on the subject will have to be discarded as a result. Ungrateful though it may seem (given my own debt to him), I should like to demonstrate the truth of this contention in detail.

The limits of Schacht's perspective are apparent in his very definition of the problem. Goldziher and Becker had both regarded the Arab façade of Islamic civilisation as deceptive,[65] and Becker in particular insisted that the real origins of this civilisation lay in the cultural traditions of the Fertile Crescent: it was for their value as residues of and clues to these traditions that he was interested in foreign elements, be they in law or elsewhere.[66] Since Schacht was an admirer of Goldziher, made reference to Becker's views,[67] and described the formation of Islamic law in a vein similar to theirs,[68] one might have expected his approach to be the same. In fact, however, this approach was alien to him. He had a strong sense of the nature of the evolution from the Prophet's Arabia to the scholars' Iraq: Islamic law was not born in its classical form. But he had virtually no sense that the Fertile Crescent played a role in this evolution: the transition from *antiquity* to the scholars' Iraq is almost wholly lost in his work. Though he frequently spoke of the heterogeneous origins of the Sharīʿa, his actual presentation evaded the question of what non-Arab traditions went into its making.[69] He identified the foreign elements sometimes as irregularities introduced by converts into a nascent or existing system,[70] and sometimes as residues of foreign borrowings which had been rejected when the system arrived:[71] his favourite metaphor described them as infiltrations.[72] But they were never the raw material of the system itself.[73] His work showed that the system had taken longer to develop than had so far been assumed, but not out of *what* it had developed.

The Arabist's perspective reappears in his discussion of the problem of transmission. Goldziher had no doubt that the transmission of Roman elements took place in Syria,[74] and the same conclusions emerged, with considerably more evidence, in Heffening's discussion of the laws regarding aliens, which also demonstrated that from the later Umayyad period onwards the borrowings were subject to erosion at the hands of the *ʿulamāʾ*. Since Schacht similarly regarded the 'popular and administrative practice' of the Umayyads as having furnished the *ʿulamāʾ* with their starting point,[76] one might have expected him to examine the nature of this practice in detail; and it is of course here that he might have considered the evidence which the historians of late Roman law had by now made available. But the 'popular and administrative practice' remained a somewhat nebulous concept. He did try to identify a considerable number of Umayyad regulations; but he did so with a view to tracing the evolution of Islamic jurisprudence, not in connection with his work on foreign elements in Islamic law,[77] and he never compared these regulations, or for that matter popular practice, with the legal institutions of the Near East. He cited no papyri, not even Arabic ones, being completely ignorant, it would seem, of those from Nessana; he displayed no interest in the Syriac lawbooks, and he made virtually no use of the massive secondary literature on late Roman and provincial law.[78] The only explanation for so uncharacteristic a lapse from scholarship is that he found it impossible to transcend the orientation of the Islamic tradition.

Schacht never discussed the possibility that Roman law was transmitted to Islam through Umayyad Syria. On the whole he believed all foreign elements to have been picked up in Iraq, the province in which the classical Sharīʿa was born; and the fact that supposedly Roman elements frequently looked somewhat un-Roman he attributed to the wear and tear to which they had been exposed before transmission to Islam. He frequently referred to them as 'worn coins', Pretzl's expression for ideas of classical origin which had lost their classical contours in the course of circulation in the Fertile Crescent;[79] and the bearers of such coins he proposed to find in converts with a rhetorical education.[80] This theory must be characterised as far-fetched.

Nothing was wrong with its basic ingredients. 'Worn coins' are an apt metaphor for such phenomena as Roman law transmitted by Jews or philosophical ideas transmitted by rhetors; and since rhetorical studies were extremely popular in the classical world, the chances that they acted as a channel of transmission of late antique culture are high. In fact, it has recently been demonstrated that they played a crucial role in the formation of the style of argument which the Arabs were to call *kalām*.[81] It is also true that advocates in the classical world were once trained as orators, not as jurists, with the result that forensic oratory was taught to all students of rhetoric regardless of whether they intended to go on to a legal career. But between these facts and the hypothesis which Schacht put together from them there is a considerable gulf.

First, granted that rhetorical studies are likely to have transmitted late antique culture to Islam, they are still most unlikely to have transmitted Roman *law*. They never imparted much legal knowledge. Their purpose was not to acquaint the student with the law, but rather to teach him how to argue, and this was done by presenting him with the most unlikely cases. The forensic skills of Greek and Roman students were nurtured on legal problems involving 'tyrants and pirates . . . plagues and madmen, kidnapping, rape, cruel stepmothers, disinherited sons, ticklish situations, remote questions of conscience';[82] and the laws used for their solution were typically imaginary or obsolete.[83] Students of such a course did not receive instruction in even the most elementary aspects of securities for debts, contracts or hire, or modes of acquisition – these being some of the Roman elements which they transmitted to Islam according to Schacht.[84] According to Cicero, students of rhetoric learnt little more than verbal fluency.[85] Cicero and Quintilian both argued for a closer integration of legal and rhetorical studies, Quintilian being particularly insistent that if the exercises did not imitate real pleadings, they were merely 'theatrical display, or insane ravings';[86] but both argued in vain. To this must be added that it was Latin rather than Greek rhetors who excelled at legal *controversies*. It was Latin rhetoric that Cicero and Quintilian wished to reform. And the rhetor who taught Gregory Thaumaturgos some Roman law on the ground that it was the best equipment for life whatever career he might take up was likewise a teacher of Latin.[87] But nobody in the east studied Latin unless, like Gregory, they intended to go on to legal studies proper. It was precisely as an author of 'insane ravings' that Jacob of Edessa, almost five centuries later, thought of the minor rhetor.[88]

Evidently, students of rhetoric who proceeded to a career as advocates would acquire some knowledge of the law in the course of so doing; but that is merely to say that it was advocates, not educated laymen in general, who had a smattering of legal knowledge. Whether such advocates would have been able to transmit what Schacht believed to be Roman elements in Islamic law is beside the point: by the later empire they had lost their predominance to professionals. Already by the fourth century it was legal rather than rhetorical studies which led to both advocacy and high office; those who knew only the art of eloquence were now laughed out of court, as Libanius bitterly complained.[89] When, in 460, an examination in law became an official requirement for practice in court, the role of the amateur lawyer was further reduced.[90] To be sure, rhetoric continued to be a popular subject, and future advocates would usually study it before proceeding to a study of the law.[91] But whatever legal knowledge it may have imparted in the past, there was no reason why it should impart any now.[92]

Secondly, it is not obvious that rhetoric of any kind was studied in Sasanid Iraq. If rhetoric was taught anywhere in Iraq, it was taught at Nisibis, and one could perhaps adduce some evidence that it was.[93] But even if we accept this evidence, and for good measure accept that it was also taught in the monastic schools,[94] it is clear that it can only have been taught as an exercise in literary composition, not as a training for advocacy. It is not easy to imagine forensic pleadings in the classical style being conducted in the Nestorian episcopal courts, and it was hardly on the strength of proficiency in Greek oratory that the Nestorians found jobs in the Shāhānshāh's bureaucracy. At any rate, the Nestorians would scarcely have nurtured their rhetorical skills on *Roman* law. It certainly was not on the strength of proficiency in Roman law that the Nestorians found their aforesaid jobs; and as Nallino pointed out long ago, there is no evidence that Roman law was known to the Nestorians before the arrival of the Syro-Roman lawbook in Iraq about a century after the Arab conquest.[95]

The idea that *Roman* law was transmitted by *Greek* rhetoric in the *Persian* province of Iraq is so patently implausible that it could only have been proposed by a scholar to whom the non-Islamic world was unknown territory about which anything could be said and nothing checked. That this was indeed the frame of mind in which Schacht wrote is easy enough to demonstrate.

Schacht, following Goldziher, identified the Arab maxim *al-walad li'l-firāsh* as the Islamic version of the Roman principle that *pater est quem* (*iustae*) *nuptiae demonstrant*.[96] Both phrases do indeed mean that the child belongs to the marriage bed. According to Schacht, the Roman principle passed to the Arabs because it was 'familiar to all persons trained in Greco-Roman rhetoric'.[97] But how did he know? By late antiquity the two most popular rhetorical handbooks were those of Aphthonius and Hermagoras; by Byzantine times they had come to constitute the rhetorical *cursus*.[98] Aphthonius, a late fourth-century author (and in fact a pupil of Libanius) owed his popularity to the fact that he gave not only rules, but also illustrations, and his illustration of a legal *controversia* is of direct relevance to us. It is an argument against a proposed law to the effect that the adulterer caught in the act should be killed on the spot (an obsolete Roman law); in the course of it the speaker (after referring to non-existent city laws) maintains that on the contrary the adulterer should be publicly tried and executed, among other things because 'a publicly tried and executed adulterer will make the parentage of the child better known. For no one will be uncertain as to whom the child belongs to by birth, as a descendant of a departed adulterer'.[99] Had Schacht cast a glance at the standard rhetorical handbook, he would have seen that Roman law might say, in rhetoric the child belonged to the progenitor.

The idea of rhetoric as the transmitter of Roman law was suggested to Schacht by the fact that a number of Roman (or supposedly Roman) elements are found in Jewish and Islamic law alike. The simplest explanation of this fact is of course that the Muslims borrowed the elements in question from the Jews, as von Kremer pointed out,[100] and both Goldziher and Schacht conceded that this might at least sometimes be the case.[101] Both however adhered to the somewhat implausible view that the Jews and the Muslims borrowed independently, though somehow identically, from the same Roman source. Schacht was familiar with Daube's argument that the Jews (of first-century Palestine) had borrowed something classical (viz. Hellenistic modes of reasoning) through the medium of rhetoric; and what he did was simply to recycle this argument.[102] He replaced first-century Jews of Palestine by eighth-century Muslims of Iraq, added Roman law to Hellenistic modes of reasoning, postulated widespread availability of a rhetorical education imparting knowledge of both in Iraq, and proceeded to argue that the presence of the same classical elements in Jewish and Islamic law *proved* that the Muslims had borrowed these elements through the medium of rhetoric;[103] in short, he substituted tortuous reasoning for evidence.[104] His ideas have nonetheless won widespread acceptance.

Not a single item of Goldziher's and Schacht's list of Roman elements in Islamic law has been proved, and several are demonstrably wrong. There never was such a thing as *opinio prudentium* in Roman law; the Romans knew of *interpretatio prudentium* and *responsa prudentium*, but neither has anything to do with either *ra'y* or *ijmāʿ*. *Istiṣlāḥ* (or *maṣlaḥa*) is not the Roman notion of *utilitas publica*, nor is *istiṣḥāb* identifiable with a Roman notion of presumptions.[105] There is no real parallel to adultery as an impediment to marriage in eastern canon law; there is a Jewish parallel,[106] just as there is a Jewish parallel to *al-walad li'l-firāsh*.[107] A couple of lines do not suffice to establish Roman influence on the laws regarding hire, security and theft, particularly not when theft is a subject in which there are manifest Jewish elements.[108] In general, no argument suffices until the Jewish side has been checked. Becker's *Lesefrucht* from Severus did not 'decisively prove' Morand's theory regarding the origins of *waqf*, nor did it pretend to do so.[109] Brunschvig did not 'confirm' von Kremer's suggestion regarding the *legitima aetas* in Ḥanafī law: he merely repeated it.[110] Van den Bergh did not demonstrate the Stoic origins of the *aḥkām al-khamsa*: he merely asserted them.[111] And it is sheer accident that the identification of the Hellenistic *agoranomos* with the Muslim *muḥtasib* may have something to it.[112] (The supposedly Persian loans, incidentally, are no better.)[113] Schacht's list of Roman borrowings is a cardboard citadel hastily erected for defensive action against Nallino, Bergsträsser and others, and he patrolled it faithfully enough for almost twenty years. But it deserves nothing better than to be razed.

If we raze Schacht's citadel, what are the foundations on which we start to rebuild? To this question I should like to devote the rest of the chapter.

We may begin by noting that there was no Roman law in Iraq except in so far as it had arrived in the guise of Jewish law. Admittedly, it is commonly assumed that the Nestorians of Sasanid Iraq adopted a combination of canon and Roman civil law for the regulation of their internal affairs – a view which I have previously espoused myself.[114] But as Nallino demonstrated long ago, this view is mistaken. Roman law did not spread to Nestorian Iraq except in the form of the Syro-Roman lawbook; and this lawbook, though composed in the fifth century, was not accepted by the Nestorians until early ʿAbbāsid times.[115] It must be conceded that Nallino dated both the Syriac translation of this book and its arrival in Iraq slightly too late. Thus the earliest surviving Syriac manuscript dates from the end of the seventh or the beginning of the eighth century at the latest, not from the ninth as Nallino would have it;[116] the work must in other words have existed in translation by mid-Umayyad times, which is more than he would grant. And the first attestation of the book in Nestorian literature is without doubt the passage identified by Sachau in Ishoʿbokht (who wrote about 775), not that identified by Nallino himself in Timothy (Patriarch 780–823),[117] though Timothy is indeed the first to *accept* the book as a Christian code.[118] But these objections do not affect Nallino's general argument. The only work of Roman law known to have been translated into Syriac,[119] the Syro-Roman lawbook was almost certainly translated after the Arab conquests, and very likely in response to them. Since the translators chose a work which was comprehensive, though quite impractical, the point of the translation was presumably to refute Arab accusations to the effect that Christianity had no law;[120] and it was certainly as a showpiece of Christian law that the book was to be accepted throughout eastern Christianity without ever being applied.[121] In short, the career of this work testifies to the impact of Islam on eastern Christianity, but it has no bearing on the question of the sources of Islamic law. It follows that if we succeed in identifying Roman elements in Islamic law which have no parallels on the Jewish side, the elements in question can only have been transmitted through Egypt and Syria.

Now Roman law clearly *was* to be found in Syria and Egypt, though opponents of the theory of Roman influence are apt to belittle the extent to which it was known and practised there. The evidence may be summarised as follows.

As regards the extent to which Roman law was known, it is generally accepted that when legal studies replaced rhetoric as the road to high office, legal knowledge came to be widely diffused in the eastern provinces. Law was taught at Alexandria, Caesarea, Beirut and elsewhere,[122] and numerous papyrological fragments bear witness to the fact that the works of the classical jurists, as well as Justinian's *Codex* and *Digest*, were read in the remotest corners of Egypt.[123] Parallel evidence for legal studies in Syria outside Caesarea and Beirut is lacking; but given that Syria was the official centre of legal studies, knowledge of the *Reichsrecht* can hardly have been less widespread here than it was in Egypt, where the accident of papyrological evidence enables us to see its extent. The fifth-century Syro-Roman lawbook has been taken to show that the level of legal education in Syria at large was low, but this it does not. For one thing, this book was only one out of many composed in Syria at the time. It may be a 'wretched cram-book';[124] but the fact that only the cram-book was translated into Syriac does not make it more representative than, say, the *Scholia Sinaitica*[125] of the level of legal education in Syria before the Arabs arrived. For another thing, the book actually does cram together a great deal of legal knowledge. Schulz thought that it could only be a product, directly or indirectly, of the school of Beirut and proposed to rename it 'the Berytean lawbook';[126] so if it was written by a notary, as has been conjectured,[127] we must conclude that in the fifth century even notaries were well educated.[128]

The usual argument against the possibility of a Roman legacy in Islamic law is that none of this survived the reign of Justinian. In 533 Justinian forbade the teaching of law outside Rome, Constantinople and Beirut in an effort to maintain its purity;[129] in 551 Beirut was destroyed by an earthquake, and though the law school was transferred to Sidon and later back again to Beirut, it was destroyed once more in 560, this time by fire, and there is no evidence for its existence after this date.[130] Henceforth, one is told, Constantinople was the only source of legal knowledge in the east.[131] But Constantinople could not possibly have coped with the training of all high officials, let alone advocates, in the east; and what is more, the Constantinopolitan law school seems itself to have disappeared about this time.[132] Are we then to take it that the Romans themselves lost their knowledge of Roman law? Evidently not. Since legal knowledge was an administrative necessity, alternative arrangements must have been made. In fact it would seem that the legal schools disappeared because the course was becoming impossibly long.[133] The teaching was taken over by advocates, whose approach was practical rather than intellectual, and the prohibition of legal studies outside Constantinople and Beirut had no effect on their activities. Thus Athanasius, one of the three known authors of legal works in the sixth and seventh centuries, appears to have taught in Antioch.[134] Presumably members of the provincial bureaucracies also imparted some knowledge of the *Reichsrecht* to their administrative trainees: inasmuch as the decree, edicts, mandates and rescripts of the emperors were filed together with those of the governors in the provincial offices,[135] there was at all events no lack of teaching material.

Now the Egyptian papyri do not apparently throw any light on the level of legal education after the reign of Justinian, but this is precisely what the Nessana papyri do. Nessana, a village in the Negev, was located in what from the point of view of Beirut or Antioch was the very edge of the civilised world. Yet right up to the Arab conquest its legal documents are drawn up in impeccable style by local officials who were either lawyers or notaries, at all events well educated.[136] The population of the village included a former lawyer,[137] while its literature included legal treatises on subjects such as succession and boats and water transport.[138] What, one may well ask, is the practical relevance of laws regarding boats and water transport in the middle of the *Negev*? Should we perhaps infer that some Nessanites studied law for its own sake? However this may be, the Nessana documents decisively refute the view that Roman law in seventh-century Syria was an 'esoteric mystery' familiar only to the Byzantine magistrates who were to leave on the Arab conquest.[139] The idea that Roman law in Syria was destroyed by an earthquake can thus be dismissed as no less absurd than it sounds.

The extent to which Roman law was actually practised in Syria and Egypt is of course an altogether different question. It is plain from papyrological and other evidence that the law of the Near Eastern provinces was never wholly Romanised and that numerous peregrine institutions survived under a more or less Roman veneer.[140] This is a point of fundamental importance to historians of Islamic law, and the conclusion of the present work is that provincial practice contributed far more to the Sharīʿa than did Roman law. But it would nonetheless be a mistake to preclude the possibility of Roman influence on the ground that Roman law was not really practised in the Roman Near East at all.

It has often been claimed that the provincials of the Roman Near East practised a local, or even national, law of their own which they recorded in the Syro-Roman lawbook and to which they clung in defiance of Justinian's legislation.[141] This is quite wrong. In the first place, the Syro-Roman lawbook is a book of Roman, not Syrian law, as Nallino and Selb have amply demonstrated.[142] It could have been composed anywhere in the Greek-speaking world, being 'Syrian' only in the sense that it was to pass into Syriac literature; and it was probably composed as a textbook, so that it is unlikely ever to have been applied, let alone applied in defiance of imperial law.[143] In the second place, there is nothing to suggest that the provincials *wished* to defy the law of the land. Most of them were undoubtedly quite unaware that much of what they practised was *Volksrecht* rather than *Reichsrecht*. Thus the Nessanites, who bore names such as Flavius Valens and Flavius al-Ubayy, who toiled over Greek-Latin glossaries with a view to reading Virgil in the original, and who explicitly stated that one legal transaction of theirs was to be regulated in accordance with 'the Imperial Decree',[144] surely did not know that their transactions were not in fact always conducted in accordance with the emperor's law.[145] Those who were sufficiently Romanised to tell the difference between *Reichsrecht* and *Volksrecht*, on the other hand, displayed no sign of pride in the latter. There were no attempts to record provincial deviations or otherwise present them as alternatives to Roman ways (given that the Syro-Roman lawbook is none). Roman versus provincial law, in short, was not an issue on a par with Melkite versus Monophysite Christology. There was no conscious struggle against Romanisation; it was simply that the provincials had long been familiar with non-Roman ways of doing things and that familiar ways died hard. In the third place, the provincials would scarcely have been able to defy imperial legislation even if they had wanted to do so. Roman law was the law of the land, and the Roman state was not prepared to let its subjects flout it. To be sure, it had to tolerate customary law even in Hellenised cities such as Caesarea and Ascalon,[146] while at the same time it had to grant tacit or even explicit recognition to various non-Roman institutions common in the Near East.[147] But it allowed such institutions to persist as a supplement to Roman law, not as an alternative to it, and the papyri testify to the strong impact of Justinian's legislation on provincial practice in Egypt.[148]

The fact of the matter is that provincial law should not be seen as an autonomous system competing with that of Rome; the only legal *system* in the Christian Near East was Roman law. But Roman law in the Near East was seen through alien eyes and supplemented by numerous alien institutions, and it is this alien element which is labelled provincial law. It may well be the case that Roman law was rarely practised without provincial modifications in the Near East, but it is no less important to remember the obverse of this statement, namely that provincial practice usually contained a Roman element. The precise proportion of Roman to non-Roman elements clearly varied from one institution of the law to another, as well as from place to place, and it can be hard to determine even where papyrological evidence is available. Islamic law may well prove to be the single most important corpus of information on the nature of legal practice in the Roman Near East, as Becker in effect predicted.[149] This is an exciting prospect. But in order for Becker's prediction to come true, it is important not to prejudge the question.

Turning now to the Islamic side, what was the nature of the Umayyad administrative practice which the *ʿulamāʾ*, according to Schacht, took as their starting point for the creation of Islamic law? The basic point to note here is that all legal authority, be it legislative or adjudicative, would appear to have been concentrated in the caliphs before it was usurped by the *ʿulamāʾ*.[150] The Umayyads saw themselves, and were generally seen by others, as deputies of God on earth. The title of *khalīfat Allāh*, 'deputy of God', is an unmistakable claim to supreme religious authority which leaves no room for the claims of *ʿulamāʾ*, and the Umayyads would seem to have regarded themselves as entitled above all to define and administer God's law. Thus official documents and court poetry consistently describe them as charged with the establishment and maintenance of God's *sunan*, *ḥudūd*, *farā'iḍ, ḥuqūq* and *sharā'iʿ*; and numerous references are made in both poetry and prose to the Qur'ānic passage in which God's caliph is associated with adjudication (38:25). Early Ḥadīth similarly describes (indeed invokes) them as supreme authorities in matters of law, presenting them as adjudicators whose verdicts constitute binding precedents, and as ultimate sources of legal wisdom for governors and private individuals alike. It would thus seem that law in the first century of Islam was caliphal law, and that Schacht's 'administrative practice' is a euphemism for a nascent legal system which might in due course have become the classical law of Islam: there is nothing to suggest that it was any less authoritative or any less comprehensive than that which the scholars were to create. This is a point of obvious importance here. On the one hand, the Umayyad caliphs resided in Syria, not in Iraq where the scholars were to emerge; and on the other hand, caliphs of God are more likely than scholars to have felt at liberty to borrow foreign law.[151] The *a priori* case for a Roman and/or provincial component in Umayyad law is thus very strong; and given that it was Umayyad law which the scholars took as their starting point for the creation of the classical Sharīʿa, there may in principle be residues of this component anywhere in the classical system.

How then do we identify these residues? If the decisions attributed to the Umayyads were genuine, it would be a comparatively simple task; but this they are not, or rather we do not know when they are.[152] Theophanes, for example, tells us that it was ʿUmar II who instituted the rule that a Christian cannot testify against a Muslim;[153] but though countless rules are attributed to ʿUmar II on the Muslim side, this one would not appear to be among them. The Islamic tradition, on the other hand, tells us that it was ʿUmar II who fixed the blood-money of Christians at half that of a free Muslim;[154] but it also attributes this rule to the Prophet, ʿUmar I and Muʿāwiya (the latter with modifications)[155] and conversely credits ʿUmar II with acceptance of a rival view.[156] Who then ruled what? In the absence of independent evidence one simply cannot tell.

Umayyad law thus cannot be studied directly. Classical law, on the other hand, is usually too finished a product for the identification of origins. The evidence must thus come from pre-classical law, the earliest law of the scholars, which can be reconstructed partly from early Ḥadīth and partly from a systematic comparison of Sunnī and heretical law, archaic elements being fairly common in the latter.[157] This certainly is not first-class evidence, and arguments for Roman influence can probably never be as decisive as those for Jewish origins; but it is the best we have.

It is not primarily the lack of source material which makes the enterprise a difficult one, but rather a failure of imaginative nerve. When we consider what happened in the first hundred or hundred and fifty years, the sheer weight of a late, but huge and immensely repetitive tradition blights our imagination. We find it impossible to believe that the beginnings can have been very different from the end products which we know so well, and we all too often reconstruct origins by merely pushing the classical systems back in time towards the inevitable Meccan and Medinese terminals from which, in the vision of Peter Brown, we shall one day have the pleasure of recovering them by a judicious application of the spade.[158] The transition from late antiquity to Islamic civilisation is thus reduced to a simple change of actors: exeunt the Byzantines, taking classical culture with them; enter the Arabs, bringing theirs. Sundry elements apart, one is assured, Islamic civilisation is simply Ḥijāzī culture writ large. It was this assurance which made Islamicists such as Sachau and Nallino unwilling to relate the discoveries of the classicists to their own field even before the general shift in the direction of Islamic studies,[159] and it is still hard to resist it. Yet it rests on nothing but a documentary sleight of hand, and we can call our own bluff by casting a glance at Islamic art. Art is the only branch of Islamic civilisation for which we have documentation for the first hundred years: here for once we can actually *see*, as opposed to merely hope to see, what went into the formation of a highly distinctive Islamic mode of expression. And what is it that we see? Late antique sculpture, paintings in the nude, Greek allegories inscribed with Greek captions, Byzantine mosaics that would have won the admiration of spectators in Ravenna, to mention just some of the more startling surprises.[160] Now if all this had been as wholly lost as is the evidence for other aspects of early Islamic culture, who would have dared to guess at its existence? Who would not have assumed Umayyad art to be some sort of Arabian art? Who indeed would have made the impious suggestion that the aniconic coinage, which is attested as early as fifty years after the conquests, was preceded by purely Byzantine and Sasanid coinages complete with imperial effigies, crosses and fire-altars? Certainly, the suggestion that the familiar beliefs of Islam were preceded by a comparable collection of other people's beliefs has struck most of the scholarly world as utterly incredible.

What follows is an attempt to reconstruct a legal equivalent to Muʿāwiya's Byzantine coins. The coin in question was both post-classical and provincial, but as will be seen it does not make much sense to characterise it as worn.

CHAPTER 2

A practical guide to the study of Islamic law

This chapter is intended for the non-specialist who wishes to acquire some familiarity with the nature of Islamic law before proceeding to the argument presented in this book. The specialist reader can go straight to the chapter on *walā*ʾ.

(a) Immutability

Islamic law is a divine law elaborated and transmitted by private scholars. Whatever the degree to which it had been controlled by caliphs in earlier times, law-finding had ceased to be a caliphal prerogative by late Umayyad times, and the role of the ruler in classical theory is limited to that of patronising scholars (*ʿulamāʾ*), appointing judges (*qāḍī*s), and ensuring that the law is applied. The Sharīʿa is thus work of pure scholarship. This has two consequences of major importance.

The first is that the Sharīʿa is immutable. This may be thought to be a consequence of its divine nature, and to some extent it clearly is; but divine origins are not in themselves enough to secure immutability for a legal system. Thus caliphal law was divine law, yet it changed and was acknowledged to do so. Being mouthpieces of God himself, the caliphs could lay down such law as they wished: the law was unchanging only in the sense that it was God's law however much it changed.[1] Unlike caliphs, however, scholars owe their authoritative status to their learning, not to an office or position independent of it: they are authoritative because they know what others have said. Like caliphs, they may buttress their authoritative position by claiming divine origins for their knowledge; but if they insist that what is in the books is divine, they sooner or later limit their role to that of transmitting the contents of these books. Naturally, in the formative period of a legal system, when the books are still fragmentary and/or oral records still imperfectly preserved, there will be room for the opinions of the scholars themselves. As will be seen, scholarly opinion coexists with authoritative views transmitted from the past in early Ḥadīth. But once a vast array of authoritative views has been recorded, there is little for the scholars to do, except to select, comment and write theoretical accounts of what they are doing. To this must be added that scholars enjoy some insulation from the world of practical affairs. Just as it is they who can generate an immutable system, so also it is they who can maintain it. Immutability is of course purchased at the cost of a gap between divine ideal and human practice, and scholars are apt to be as pained by this as anyone else. But being mere academics, they can afford to abide by the ideal.

Unlike the Muslim *ʿulamāʾ*, however, modern Islamicists feel that Islamic law *ought* to have changed, and they are apt to argue either that it actually did so or else that special reasons are required to explain why it did not (its failures to do so being known as 'ankylosis'). In fact neither is the case. Though the law was perhaps not quite so unchanging as it was supposed to be, it certainly did not change very much before the impact of the West. Old institutions were not dropped, however irrelevant they had become, nor were new ones included (as opposed to dealt with on an *ad hoc* basis by *fatwā*s, responsa solicited from the learned). Thus *walāʾ*, the subject of this book, had lost much, though not all, of its practical relevance by about 800; yet its legal incidents are set out in the same fashion, with the same interest, and with attention to the same points of disagreement between 800 and 1800.[2] And why should it have been otherwise? Immutability was built into the system.

In practical terms, this means that any legal work composed between 800 and 1800 may be cited as evidence of classical doctrine. There is accordingly something arbitrary about the choice of references for classical views. One might simply refer to 'any classical lawbook' or 'any lawbook of such and such school' (on the schools, see below, section b), or one might list an endless number of references to specific works. Some books are of course more authoritative than others, but even authoritative works are plentiful, and one tends to choose one's own on the basis of criteria such as accessibility, clarity of style and print, and length. My own policy has been to consult a handful of works for every school (where handfuls are available) and to cite one or two, giving preference to those which make the point most clearly, are available in translation, or happen to discuss a particular point omitted by others.

(b) Schools (*madhhabs*)

The second consequence of the fact that Islamic law is created by scholars is that it is divided into schools. It is a fact about scholars that they disagree, but that they usually disagree more with some than with others. The jurists and the schools thus emerge together, and strictly speaking there has never been a single Islamic law (unless we count caliphal law as such); rather, 'Islamic law' is an ideal type incarnate in this world in a variety of different versions.

The earliest schools were geographically defined; they were congeries of scholars who lived in the same city, often making a livelihood as merchants and shopkeepers and discussing law in their spare time.[3] Early legal schools were found in Iraq (Kufa and Basra), Arabia (Mecca, Medina, the Yemen) and Syria, but not in Egypt, North Africa, Spain, Persia or eastern Iran. Iraq was the most important centre. The schools must have existed by about a century after the *hijra* (i.e. by about 720), and they may well have existed before, but the preceding period is a blank in terms of authentic information.

By the early ninth century the old schools had developed into new ones defined, in the case of the Sunnīs, by adherence to the doctrines of a single teacher, and, in that of the heretics, by sectarian affiliation.[4] These were the classical schools, of which eight (four Sunnī and four heretical ones) have survived until today. Arranged with reference to the early centres of legal studies they were the following.

Kufa

1 The Ḥanafīs, one of the four Sunnī schools which still survive today. The founder was Abū Ḥanīfa (d. 767), a silk merchant to whom several legal and doctrinal works have been ascribed, though it is not certain that he wrote anything himself.[5] The earliest Ḥanafī works to survive are those of Abū Yūsuf (d. 798) and Shaybānī (d. 805).

2 The school of Sufyān al-Thawrī (d. 778). Sufyān was a Kufan traditionist whose school still flourished in the tenth century, though it disappeared thereafter.[6] His opinions are cited in ʿAbd al-Razzāq's *ḥadīth*-collection and also in legal works. A small collection of inheritance laws transmitted by him is extant.[7]

3 The Zaydīs, a Shīʿite sect. The earliest Zaydī work is the *Majmūʿ al-fiqh* or *Corpus Iuris* which is attributed to Zayd b. ʿAlī, the eponymous founder the sect, but which is in fact a Kufan work composed, probably, by Abū Khālid al-Wāsiṭī in the second half of the eighth century.[8] The Zaydīs were later to be subdivided into schools formed by individual teachers on a par with the Sunnīs. The two main schools are the Qāsimiyya and the Nāṣiriyya, named after Qāsim b. Ibrāhīm (d. 860) and Nāṣir al-Uṭrūsh (d. 917, imam of the Caspian Zaydīs) respectively; but the Qāsimīs are themselves subdivided into Qāsimīs proper and Hadawīs, *i.e.* followers of Hādī, the first imam of the Yemeni Zaydīs (d. 1911). Qāsim was a Medinese who stood outside the Zaydī tradition, whereas Hādī's doctrine was more Kufan and Nāṣir's wholly so.[9] In fact, the Medinese tradition introduced by Qāsim seems to have disappeared even from the school which bears his name. The Zaydī works that I have used are all Kufan in character, at least in the chapters of relevance to this book.[10]

4 The Imāmīs or Ithnā-ashʿarīs, 'Twelver-Shīʿites'. Kufa was the first centre of Shīʿism, both Zaydī, Imāmī and other, and it is thus reasonable to expect Imāmī law to be Kufan in character. The Imāmīs, however, ascribe their legal doctrines to imams who resided in Medina, and if the ascription is correct, Imāmī law ought to be Medinese. It has in fact been claimed that it is.[11] It has also been claimed that there are affinities between Imāmī and old Meccan law.[12] I cannot agree with either view, or only in a modified form, for reasons which I hope to set out in detail elsewhere: the substratum of Imāmī law is Kufan; there is indeed a Medinese layer on top of much of it, but this is a fairly late addition, as is clear from the fact that is usually borrowed from the Shāfiʿī school (below, no. 9).[13] The discussion is somewhat hampered by the fact that the extant (or at least the published) legal literature of the Imāmīs is late.[14] Nothing earlier than Kulīnī (d. 939) is available, and Kulīnī frequently seems to represent a more moderate tradition than that known from Ṭūsī (d. 1068). Even in its late form, however, Imāmī law is frequently very different from that of the other schools.[15] We shall see that, whatever the ultimate provenance of Imāmī law, these differences tend to be archaisms.

5 The Ismāʿīlīs. The Ismāʿīlīs, who emerged as a distinct sect towards the end of the ninth century, seem to have been dissident Imāmīs. Their legal system is based partly on Imāmī and partly on Zaydī law.[16] Being late, their main interest from our point of view lies in the fact that they based themselves on Imāmī law taken directly from Kufa, whereas most extant (or published) Imāmī doctrine has been filtered through Qumm, the second Shīʿite centre.[17] They thus preserve a different tradition of Imāmī law. So far, their law is known only from the works of Qāḍī Nuʿmān (d. 974).

Basra

6 The Ibāḍīs, a subsect of the Khārijites. Basra did not produce a classical Sunnī school. It was however an Ibāḍī centre until the end of the ninth century when the Basran Ibāḍīs, having already set up states in North Africa and Oman, emigrated as a body to Oman.[18] The earliest legal work to survive is the *Mudawwana* of Abū Ghānim (fl. late eighth/early ninth centuries).[19] The Ibāḍīs also have a *ḥadīth*-collection attributed to the eighth-century Rabīʿ b. Ḥabīb; but this work, which only survives in a twelfth-century recension, is undoubtedly a much later compilation.[20] The tradition which survives is that of the Wahbite Ibāḍīs. There were several other Ibāḍī subsects, of which the best known is that of the Nukkarīs,[21] but the legal traditions of these sects are wholly lost.

Syria

7 The school of Awzāʿī, a Damascene who died in 774. This school was dominant for a short while in Umayyad Spain, and it is said to have had adherents in Spain and North Africa until the tenth or eleventh century. Its last known Syrian adherent was a Damascene who died in 958.[22]

Mecca and the Yemen

Neither produced a classical school, be it Sunnī or heretical.

Medina

8 The Mālikīs. The Mālikīs, who form the second Sunnī school to survive until today, are the followers of Mālik b. Anas (d. 796), whose *Muwaṭṭa*ʾ is extant in several recensions.[23]

9 The Shāfiʿīs, the third surviving Sunnī school. Shāfiʿī (d. 822) was a native of Gaza who grew up in Medina and who founded a school which has aptly been dubbed 'dissident Mālikism'.[24] His main work, the *Umm*, is a compilation of nine treatises put together by his pupils in Egypt. Shāfiʿī's views *fī'l-jadīd*, that is the Egyptian transmission of his doctrine, frequently differ from those *fī'l-qadīm*, that is the Iraqi version, which is however far less well preserved.[25]

10 The school of Layth b. Saʿd, an Egyptian scholar who studied in Medina and who died in 791. It did not survive. His views are occasionally quoted by other lawyers, and an exchange of letters between him and Mālik is extant.[26]

Other Schools

11 The Ḥanbalīs, the fourth surviving Sunnī school. The founder, Ibn Ḥanbal (d. 855), was a Baghdādī and a traditionist rather than a lawyer. The first known Ḥanbalī lawyer was Khiraqī (d. 946).[27] Ḥanbalī law is frequently close to that of the Shāfiʿīs, that is its orientation is Medinese.

12 The Ẓāhirīs. Founded by Dāwūd b. Khalaf (d. 884) in Baghdad, this school derives its name from the fact that it wished to base Islamic law and dogma on the literal meaning (*ẓāhir*) of Qurʾān and Ḥadīth. The first surviving legal works are those of Abū ʿĀṣim al-Nabīl (d. 900),[28] and by far the most famous Ẓāhirī lawbook is the *Muḥallā* of Ibn Ḥazm (d. 1064). For purposes of tracing origins, the Ẓāhirīs (and by and large also the Ḥanbalīs) are too late to be of much interest, and I do not systematically give Ẓāhirī opinions in what follows. Ibn Ḥazm's work is nonetheless very useful, partly because he regularly cites all the

traditions and legal opinions he knows on a disputed subject, and partly because he excels at analysis of legal doctrines, particularly doctrines he dislikes.

13 Miscellaneous schools. A number of lawyers of the eighth and ninth centuries might be regarded as unsuccessful founders of schools of their own; at least they did not belong to any other.[29] Ṭabarī (d. 923), the famous exegete and historian, was also a lawyer who founded a school known as the Jarīriyya.[30] Apart from being badly documented, it is too late to be of interest.

At first sight the doctrines of all these schools are very similar, but once one has got used to the similarity, one notices important differences. The most important differences (in terms of substantive law) are not those between Sunnīs and non-Sunnīs, but rather those between the Kufan and Basran schools on the one hand and the Medinese and later schools on the other. If one compares the positions of the eight surviving schools on fundamental issues such as whether a person can bequeath more than a third of his estate, whether non-agnatic and non-Qur'ānic relatives (*dhawū'l-arḥām*) can inherit, whether there is such a thing as contractual *walā'* and whether *qasāma* is a defensive or accusatory procedure, one finds that the Ḥanafīs, the Ibāḍīs and the three Shīʿite schools regularly form one bloc, while the Mālikīs, Shāfiʿīs and Ḥanbalīs form another.[31] The first five perpetuate the legal tradition of the old Iraqi schools, and it is clear from early Ḥadīth that this tradition was frequently close to that of the old schools in Arabia and Syria. But of the last three, only the Mālikīs have a direct link with an old school, that of Medina, the others being upstarts. This suggests that whereas the surviving Iraqi schools perpetuate old law in different ways and to varying extents, the Medinese (or at least the Mālikīs) made something new of this law which ultimately won out in Sunnī law at large. In the case of the *qasāma*, this is undoubtedly so,[32] and we shall see that it is also true of *walā'*. It is thus the Iraqi schools together with early Ḥadīth which are particularly important for the reconstruction of origins.

(c) Tradition (Ḥadīth)

Most legal doctrines are validated by a tradition. There are of course some which are based on the Qur'ān and others which rest on analogy (*qiyās*), mere preference (*istiḥsān*) and other modes of reasoning; but Ḥadīth is the real stuff of Islamic law.

An individual tradition (*ḥadīth*) is a short report of what an authoritative figure of the past said or did in connection with a certain problem, each report being prefaced by a chain of transmitters guaranteeing its authenticity (*isnād*). Herewith three examples:[33]

(1) ʿAbd al-Razzāq told us on the authority of Thawrī on the authority of Mughīra that Ibrāhīm used to say, 'the Qur'ānic heir has a better right than the one without a share'.

(2) ʿAbd al-Razzāq told us on the authority of Thawrī on the authority of Aʿmash that Ibrāhīm said, 'not one of Muḥammad's Companions called a uterine brother to succession in the presence of a grandfather'.

(3) ʿAbd al-Razzāq told us on the authority of Thawrī on the authority of Manṣūr that Ibrāhīm said, 'I am told that the Prophet used to give a sixth to three kinds of grandmothers.' He (sc. Manṣūr) said: 'I said, which ones?' He said, 'the two grandmothers of the propositus' father, paternal and maternal, and the maternal grandmother of his mother'.

The early schools commonly based their doctrines on traditions reporting the views of local jurists of renown such as Ibrāhīm al-Nakhaʿī (d. about 714) in Kufa and Ḥasan al-Baṣrī in Basra (d. 728f). But they also invoked early caliphs and other Companions, again with a preference for local figures; thus Ibn Masʿūd, a Companion who had settled in Kufa, counted as a particular authority in Kufa, while Ibn ʿAbbās, who had resided in Mecca, was a favourite among the Meccans, and so on. And occasionally they would invoke the Prophet himself. The three traditions just quoted illustrate these options. All three report the views of Ibrāhīm al-Nakhaʿī, the Kufan jurist; but whereas he is cited on his own authority in the first, he himself invokes earlier authorities in the next two, the Companions in the second and the Prophet in the third. Even so, the second tradition is not quite a Companion tradition, nor the third a Prophetic one: Ibrāhīm is arguing with reference to earlier practice rather than simply transmitting an authoritative view; and he fails to supply a chain of transmitters between himself and the earlier figures, whom he could not have met. A proper Companion tradition looks as follows:[34]

(4) ʿAbd al-Razzāq told us that Thawrī told him on the authority of Aʿmash on the authority of Ibrāhīm on the authority of Masrūq that ʿAbdallāh said concerning the [succession case involving a] grandfather, a daughter and a sister, 'their shares are allotted out of four . . .'

Here Ibrāhīm is no longer an authoritative figure in his own right, but a mere link in a chain of transmitters going back to ʿAbdallāh b. Masʿūd, the favourite Companion of the Kufans. A Prophetic tradition would have reduced the Companion to a mere transmitter too, stating that he had his opinion from the Prophet. In early work such as the *Āthār* of Shaybānī (d. 805) Companion traditions are less common than traditions reporting the views of early jurists; and of Prophetic traditions there are few.[35]

It is clear, however, that Ḥadīth invoking the authority of the Prophet himself was proliferating in the second half of the eighth century – presumably in response to escalating polemics between the schools, though this phase in the development of Islamic law is still badly understood. No systematic attention was paid to them at first, but a jurisprudential theory could scarcely fail to accord decisive weight to traditions which purported to record the views of the Prophet himself. The classical jurisprudential rules were worked out by Shāfiʿī (d. 822). Shāfiʿī argued that *only* Prophetic traditions should be followed, and that such traditions should *always* be followed, provided that they were authenticated by a faultless chain of transmitters. This was not so simple as it sounds, given that Prophetic traditions sometimes contradicted the Qur'ān and sometimes each other; there were also problems on which no Prophetic traditions existed, with the result that Companion traditions retained subsidiary authority. But these complications notwithstanding, it came to be almost universally accepted that Ḥadīth as a source of law meant Ḥadīth from the Prophet; indeed, the classical meaning of Ḥadīth is Ḥadīth from the Prophet unless the contrary is indicated.[36]

It was after Shāfiʿī's rules had been accepted that the Muslims began the task of putting together all the Prophetic traditions which could be considered authentic on the basis of their *isnād*s. The result was the famous collections of Ibn Ḥanbal (d. 855), Dārimī (d. 869), Bukhārī (d. 870), Muslim (d. 875), Ibn Māja (d. 887), Abū Dāwūd (d. 889), Ṭirmidhī (d. 892) and Nasā'ī (d. 915), each of which contains thousands of traditions representing, we are told, a mere fraction of the traditions examined.[37] At the same time an impressive auxiliary literature grew up devoted to the dates, domiciles and characters of the transmitters, the purpose of this literature being to establish whether they could indeed have transmitted to and from the persons between whom they appeared in *isnād*s, and whether they were likely to have done so reliably.

The acceptance of Shāfiʿī's rules drastically changed the relationship between legal doctrine and Ḥadīth. To the lawyers of the old schools Ḥadīth meant traditions emanating from local figures who were regarded as authoritative within the school; in other words Ḥadīth was a statement of school doctrine. The fact that other schools might have different traditions ascribed to different persons was irrelevant to them, inasmuch as these persons were not included among their own authorities. Thus traditions ascribed to Ibrāhīm al-Nakhaʿī once meant little or nothing to the Basrans, while traditions ascribed to Hasan al-Baṣrī conversely meant little or nothing to the Kufans.[38] When Shaybānī collected traditions from Ibrāhīm al-Nakhaʿī and others in his *Āthār*, the result was an exposition of Ḥanafī doctrine; similarly, traditions from Zayd b. ʿAlī and ʿAlī himself add up to an exposition of Zaydī doctrine in the *Majmūʿ*. In both cases valid Ḥadīth was Ḥadīth circulating within the school, not everybody's tradition.[39] But the Prophet was everybody's authority and everybody ascribed opinions to him. Prophetic traditions accordingly reflect the most diverse points of view, and a collection of such tradition never constitutes an exposition of the doctrines of a single school. The old unity between doctrine and Ḥadīth was thus broken. Prophetic Ḥadīth was material collected all over the Islamic world in a hectic 'search for knowledge' (*ṭalab al-ʿilm*), not the wisdom of a local teacher;[40] and being of largely extraneous origin, it was something which had to be accommodated within the existing systems, not their actual foundations. It was only among the Imāmīs (and, to a less extent, the other heretics) that the old unity between Ḥadīth and doctrine survived. Since the only authoritative figures in the eyes of the Imāmīs were the imams, Prophetic tradition carried no weight unless transmitted by the imams. The

Imāmīs thus resisted the temptation to chase traditions all over the Islamic world, with the result that their Ḥadīth continued to reflect school doctrine. When Ibn Babūyah (d. 991) composed his manual of law for those 'who have no jurist at hand', he simply presented Imāmī Ḥadīth interspersed with occasional commentary;[41] similarly, Ṭūsī's collections of Imāmī traditions are manifest statements of school doctrine.[42] The auxiliary literature of the Imāmīs is accordingly also poorly developed: unlike the Sunnīs, they did not need biographical dictionaries to evaluate their own transmitters.[43]

The acceptance of Shāfiʿī's rules did not however have a major impact on legal doctrine itself. The schools which had formed their views on substantive law prior to Shāfiʿī's appearance changed neither their views nor their validating traditions to any significant degree, the intrusive traditions from the Prophet being simply accommodated within their doctrine in so far as they could not be explained away: Ḥanafī law as expounded by Abū Yūsuf and Shaybānī, two founding figures, is very much like Ḥanafī law as expounded by Sarakhsī and Marghīnānī, two medieval authors; and the Mālikīs similarly remained faithful to their founder.[44] The schools which appeared after Shāfiʿī, including that named after Shāfiʿī himself, did indeed take Prophetic tradition as their starting point, but what they made of these traditions was not very new: all are squarely within the Medinese tradition. The shift from archaic to classical law must thus have started before Shāfiʿī's appearance. Indeed, given that Prophetic Ḥadīth does not reflect any one legal orientation, how could it have been the acceptance of Shāfiʿī's rules which caused the change? It is true that in so far as there is a single trend in Prophetic Ḥadīth, it goes against the old schools rather than in support of them, and to that extent Shāfiʿī may have assisted the victory of classical law. But though this is one of the many problems on which more research is required, there can be little doubt that in terms of substantive law the crucial battles had been fought before him. This is a point of major importance in the present context, and a fairly dispiriting one. Islamic law, it would seem, evolved from embryonic beginnings to classical shapes within less than two hundred years. Very much indeed must have happened in the period from about 620 to about 820, that is in the period for which our documentation is poor. Our chances of being able to reconstruct the origins of Islamic law with any degree of certainty are accordingly somewhat limited.

If we wish to try, however, it is clear that we must base ourselves on early Ḥadīth rather than that preserved in the classical collections. Such Ḥadīth is to be found in the following works.

(1) The *Muṣannaf* of ʿAbd al-Razzāq (d. 826). A *muṣannaf* is a *ḥadīth*-collection organised by subject-matter as opposed to by transmitter (a *musnad*). ʿAbd al-Razzāq was a Yemeni from Ṣanʿāʾ, and his collection is particularly rich in Yemeni, Meccan and Basran material (the Yemenis owing much to Maʿmar b. Rāshid, a Basran who went to live in the Yemen); but he also has numerous Kufan traditions.[45]

(2) The *Muṣannaf* of Ibn Abī Shayba (d. 849). This collection, which has recently been published in full, is of particular interest for its wealth of early Iraqi Ḥadīth.[46] Ibn Abī Shayba was a Kufan who went to live in Baghdad, and though he died a generation after Shāfiʿī, his traditions are overwhelmingly non-Prophetic.

(3) The *Sunan al-kubrā* of Bayhaqī (d. 1066). Bayhaqī was a Shāfiʿī from eastern Iran reputed to be ignorant of several classical *ḥadīth*-collections.[47] On the other hand, he had extensive knowledge of early material, and his mammoth work has many early traditions, some of which have been preserved only by him.

(4) Miscellaneous lawbooks. As mentioned already, Ibn Ḥazm, the Ẓāhirī, regularly starts his discussion of disputed problems by citing every tradition which he knows on the subject; many of these can now be read in ʿAbd al-Razzāq's *Muṣannaf*, of which he made extensive use, but others are known only from him. Ibn Qudāma, the Ḥanbalī commentator on Khiraqī's *Mukhtaṣar*, also refers to many early traditions, though he usually omits most of their *isnād*s and cites them in an abbreviated form. The same is true of an author such as Sarakhsī, a Ḥanafī who frequently refers to Hanafi Companion traditions without supplying full *isnād*s and/or wording. Other authors also cite or refer to early Ḥadīth, but few with such regularity.

The information given in a tradition is rarely meaningful unless one can determine where and when it was put into circulation. Fortunately, it is often easy to decide where it comes from on the basis of the *isnād*. Thus the *isnād*s of the three traditions cited above, pp. 23f, are purely Kufan. Schematically, they may be represented as follows:

(1) Ibrāhīm [al-Nakhaʿī, K., d. A.H. 95 or 96]
|
Mughīra [b. Miqsam, K., d. A.H. 134]
|
[Sufyān] al-Thawrī [K., d. A.H. 161]
|
ʿAbd al-Razzāq [Y., d. A.H. 211]

(2) Companions
|
Ibrāhīm
|
Aʿmash [K., d. A.H. 148]
|
[Sufyān] al-Thawrī
|
ʿAbd al-Razzāq

(3) Prophet
|
Ibrāhīm
|
Manṣūr [b. al-Muʿtamir, K., A.H. d. 133]
|
[Sufyān] al-Thawrī
|
ʿAbd al-Razzāq

(In schematic representations of *isnāds* it is customary to start with the oldest figure invoked, the Muslims themselves identifying the oldest authority as the 'highest'.) The information in the square brackets can be found in any dictionary of transmitters; there are of course many transmitters by the name of Mughīra and Manṣūr, but a good dictionary, such as Ibn Ḥajar's *Tahdhīb*, will supply both the dates and whereabouts of every transmitter (in so far as they are known), and the names of persons to and from whom he transmitted, thus permitting identification of the Mughīra and Manṣūr involved. The lowest link in each case is ʿAbd al-Razzāq, the Yemeni compiler from whose work the traditions have been chosen; and what ʿAbd al-Razzāq is offering the reader is clearly traditions originating in Kufa, where they were regarded as authoritative by Sufyān. The links in the *isnād* of the Companion tradition cited at p. 24 are equally Kufan. By contrast, a tradition with the following *isnād* represents a Meccan point of view:[48]

Prophet
|
Ibn ʿAbbās [Mc., d. A.H. 68]
|
ʿAwsaja [client of Ibn ʿAbbās]
|
ʿAmr b. Dīnār [Mc., d. A.H. 126]
|
[Sufyān] b. ʿUyayna [Mc., d. A.H. 198]

Naturally, these are simple (though by no means unrepresentative) examples, and *isnāds* are not always so pure. For example, the tradition which circulated under the *isnād* just cited is also found with the following chain of authorities:[49]

Prophet
|
Ibn ʿAbbās
|
ʿAwsaja
|
ʿAmr b. Dīnār
|
Ḥammād [b. Salama, B., d. 167]

But a composite *isnād* of this type is not problematic: just as the Yemeni ʿAbd al-Razzāq transmitted Kufan traditions to the Yemenis, so the Basran Ḥammād has here transmitted a Meccan tradition to the Basrans; what we have here is a Meccan tradition abroad. It is more difficult to explain a tradition ascribed, say, to Ibrāhīm al-Nakhaʿī, but otherwise equipped with a purely Medinese *isnād*: such a tradition would almost certainly represent a Trojan horse, that is to say a Medinese attempt to win the Kufans over for a doctrine of theirs through invocation of a Kufan worthy. But there are also composite *isnād*s for which it is difficult to find any explanation at all. Even so, it cannot be said that the geographical provenance of traditions constitutes a major problem.

Determining their origin in time by contrast is extremely difficult. The rule of thumb is that Prophetic traditions are later than those ascribed to Companions, which in their turn are likely to be later than those giving the opinions of early lawyers – or in other words, the older the authority invoked, the later the tradition. Similarly, a perfect *isnād* is likely to be later than an imperfect one. After all, the better a tradition conforms to the criteria evolved in the time of Shāfiʿī, the more likely it is to date from the time in which these criteria were evolved. The rule of thumb is clearly simplistic. Thus the legal point enshrined in a Prophetic tradition may well antedate its ascription to the Prophet,[50] while conversely a Prophetic tradition may have existed in an imperfect form before acquiring its canonical details and perfect *isnād*;[51] and it does happen that a Prophetic tradition on a certain subject is earlier than one ascribed to a Companion.[52] But the rule nonetheless offers a helpful starting-point.[53]

Schacht devised a number of methods for a more precise dating of traditions. The best known of these relies on the so-called 'common link'. If one puts together the *isnāds* given for a tradition in various works, it frequently happens that one gets the following pattern:

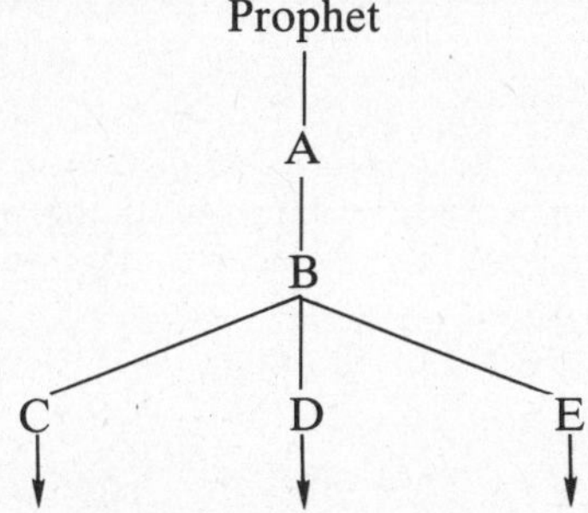

Where this pattern obtains, one might infer that the tradition was put into circulation by B, the lowest common link, or in other words the person to whom all subsequent transmitters would appear to owe it; and if this were to be so, the common link would provide us with an absolute date for the origin of the tradition involved. (That B did not owe it to A or the Prophet is taken for granted unless the contrary can be proved.) Schacht argued that the common link could be thus used.[54] But the fact that B appears as the lowest common link does not in fact guarantee that all subsequent transmitters ultimately owed the tradition to him, as has recently been demonstrated with great lucidity.[55] The method of the common link is invalidated by the phenomenon which Schacht himself called 'the spread of *isnāds*', that is the secondary creation of fictitious authorities for a particular tradition.[56] Using this method one finds that on the basis of other criteria it seems to work at times and at others not; it cannot be used as a method of dating on its own.[57]

Another method often used by Schacht is the argument from polemical silence. Where polemical authors fail to mention well-known traditions relevant to their arguments, Schacht inferred that the traditions in question did not yet exist. There are times when such an inference seems valid. Thus an author who fails to adduce a classical tradition supporting his own point of view can hardly have known the tradition in question; it may of course still have existed, but at least not with its classical fame. Polemical authors do however often ignore evidence which they dislike, sometimes asserting that no traditions contrary to their own opinion exist at all – an assertion with much the same import as the 'no doubt' of modern scholars.[58] The absence of a well known tradition accordingly carries little weight when the tradition goes against the author's views. The main shortcoming of this method, however, is that it cannot be properly used until it is too late. Given the voluminous nature of Shāfiʿī's works, the absence of a particular tradition may well be taken to show that it was still unknown in his time; but the development of Ḥadīth after Shāfiʿī is of limited importance for the evolution of substantive law, and before Shāfiʿī the literature is too scanty and above all too local in character for silences to count. The fact that Mālik fails to cite or argue against Iraqi traditions on a particular subject evidently does not mean that the Iraqi traditions did not yet exist. It is true that the lawyers of the old schools had begun to take note of each others' traditions a good deal before they were forced to adopt a common stock of Prophetic traditions and that polemics between them can occasionally be used to establish negative points; but in general other people's traditions still were not sufficiently compelling for this to be the case. Mālik's work can perhaps be used to show that certain Medinese traditions still did not exist in Medina. But before Mālik the argument from polemical silence can rarely be used at all.

In practice traditions cannot usually be dated absolutely, and even relative chronologies can be hard to obtain. The earlier the traditions involved, the more difficult it becomes. Usually one orders them on the basis of one or more of the above-mentioned methods in conjunction with the doctrinal point which they make. Thus a tradition ascribed to a Companion or early lawyer establishing a point to which no classical school subscribes can hardly fail to be early. But how early? In general one can only say that early Ḥadīth seems to date from about 700–800, that is to the period between the hypothetical emergence of the scholars and the appearance of the first legal works. A more precise dating of such material is still impossible and may very well remain so.

(d) Modern disagreement

The above account is based on the conclusions of Goldziher and Schacht, but there are still scholars who defend the authenticity of Prophetic Ḥadīth. Such scholars do not deny that many traditions were fabricated, a fact openly admitted by the traditionists themselves, but they do not believe that *all* Prophetic traditions have been falsely ascribed, and they generally accept the authenticity of traditions credited to Companions and later figures too. Theoretically, their position is not radically different from that of Schacht: after all, neither Schacht nor his followers would go so far as to deny that there *could* be authentic elements in Prophetic Ḥadīth. But they must of necessity adopt a very different methodology. For practical purposes it is impossible to prove a certain tradition authentic (with a very few exceptions), and it is often impossible to prove it inauthentic too. The allocation of the burden of proof is thus of decisive importance. Defenders of the authenticity of Ḥadīth hold that traditions should be presumed to be genuine unless the contrary can be proved, whereas followers of Schacht argue the opposite; and since the contrary usually cannot be proved, the result is a straightforward clash between those who treat Ḥadīth as essentially authentic and those who treat it as evidence for later developments.[59] This clash is an aspect of a general breakdown of consensus over the nature of the sources on the rise and early history of Islam. Islamicists are divided over the very premises on which research should be conducted – two paradigms, in Kuhn's terminology, are competing for the allegiance of practitioners in the field, and arguments based on the one are usually unpersuasive to adherents of the other.[60] My own views on the nature of the sources are to be found elsewhere.[61] Here I should like to add two examples to show why, in the field of substantive law, traditions attributed to the Prophet must indeed be presumed to be inauthentic.

The Prophet is said to have forbidden sale and gifts of *walāʾ*, that is the patronate which is the subject of this book, and all classical lawyers duly forbid such transactions without any disagreement at all.[62] One might thus infer that the Prophet actually did forbid such transactions and that the lawyers simply followed his example. In fact, however, the question was once controversial. In the Umayyad and early ʿAbbāsid periods there were lawyers who permitted sale and gifts of *walāʾ*; several eminent Companions were reputed merely to have disapproved of them; and though there were also early lawyers who prohibited them outright, they did so without reference to the Prophet's precedent.[63] There is no trace of the Prophetic tradition until about 770. Thus Ibn Jurayj (d. 767) and Maʿmar (d. 770), who both transmitted numerous traditions against sale and gifts of *walāʾ*, apparently knew none from the Prophet,[64] whereas Shuʿba (d. 777), Sufyān al-Thawrī (d. 778) and Mālik (d. 796) all knew the classical tradition from him.[65] This is a familiar situation. Time and again one finds that disagreement prevails in pre-classical law over questions which the Prophet is supposed to have settled once and for all, the discussion being conducted without reference to his precedent until a fairly belated stage.[66] It is hard to believe that authentic rulings by the Prophet were being rediscovered in the 770s, and in the case of sale and gifts of *walāʾ* the very formulation of the prohibition used by the Prophet in some traditions was current before the Prophetic precedent was known,[67] while the very Companion who allegedly transmitted the Prophetic prohibition subscribed to a different view as an authority in his own right.[68] What the lawyers attributed to the Prophet was in this case an opinion of their own; and the example is by no means an isolated one: numerous Prophetic traditions can be shown to have originated as statements made by the lawyers themselves.[69]

However many traditions are proved to be inauthentic, defenders of the authenticity of Ḥadīth will continue to argue that others might still be genuine. Let us then consider the fate of a genuine statement of the Prophet's. Practically all Islamicists accept the so-called Constitution of Medina as an essentially authentic document drawn up by the Prophet himself on his arrival in Medina. One clause in this document states that a believer should not take as his confederate (*ḥalīf*) the *mawlā* (kinsman, freedman, protégé or protector) of another believer to the exclusion of the latter;[70] and early lawyers took this to mean that a believer should not take as his client the client of another believer without the latter's permission: freedmen and converts who wished to change patrons required their patron's consent.[71] Now the various versions of the tradition in which the Prophet states this rule are authentic in the sense that they paraphrase something which the Prophet had actually said (or rather written), but is it an authentic ruling that they preserve? The meaning of the clause in the Constitution of Medina is obscure, but whatever it meant, it was a rule about confederates, not about clients changing patrons.[72] The main point to note, however, is that the lawyers changed their minds, whereupon the Prophet had to change his too. The lawyers disapproved of clients seeking new patrons and ultimately prohibited the practice altogether. Accordingly, in the classical versions of the tradition in question the Prophet categorically condemns clients who change patrons, as well as others who change kinsmen by adoption, threatening them with the distinctive curse familiar from the Constitution.[73] In this form the tradition was known to Ibn Isḥāq, who died in 767,[74] and to the caliph Mahdī, who cited it in a letter of 775–6.[75] Ibn Isḥāq has the Prophet lay down the classical rule in his famous speech delivered during the Farewell Pilgrimage towards the end of his life.[76] It thus took no more than four generations for an authentic ruling to be transformed into a spurious one endowed with a spurious setting.[77]

What these two examples demonstrate is that it was the lawyers who determined what the Prophet said, not the other way round. It is often claimed that some Ḥadīth must be authentic because the Muslims must have remembered some of what their Prophet had said, but what they remembered is beside the point: it is what they wished to remember that matters. The lawyers knew that the Prophet was on record as having permitted clients to change patrons with their patron's consent, but they also knew that what he had said was the truth; and since the truth was that no consent could be given, it was obvious to them that he must have prohibited the practice outright: the reference to consent was redundant and could be omitted.[78] What they remembered was what the Prophet meant to *them*, not what the generation before them had taken him to say, let alone what he had said or done in his own particular time and place; and it was obviously because they saw him in the light of their own preoccupations that they transformed what they remembered and remembered him as saying things which they had worked out themselves. The chances of authentic material surviving at their hands is exceedingly small. Indeed, in purely statistical terms it is minute. Bukhārī is said to have examined a total of 600,000 traditions attributed to the Prophet; he preserved some 7,000 (including repetitions), or in other words dismissed some 593,000 as inauthentic.[79] If Ibn Ḥanbal examined a similar number of traditions, he must have rejected about 570,000, his collection containing some 30,000 (against including repetitions). Of Ibn Ḥanbal's traditions 1,710 (including repetitions) are transmitted by the Companion Ibn ʿAbbās. Yet less than fifty years earlier one scholar had estimated that Ibn ʿAbbās had only heard nine traditions from the Prophet, while another thought that the correct figure might be ten.[80] If Ibn ʿAbbās had heard ten traditions from the Prophet in the years around 800, but over a thousand by about 850, how many had he heard in 700 or 632? Even if we accept that ten of Ibn ʿAbbās' traditions are authentic, how do we identify them in the pool of 1,710? We do not even know whether they are to be found in this pool, as opposed to that of 530,000 traditions dismissed on the ground that their chains of authorities were faulty. Under such circumstances it is scarcely justified to presume Ḥadīth to be authentic until the contrary has been proved. And if authentic statements by the Prophet were utterly transformed by the scholars in the course of their work, then the presumption must surely be that *no* Ḥadīth is authentic. Legal Ḥadīth must be treated as evidence for the views of the lawyers, not those of the Prophet, his Companions or the caliphs: the ascription shows us who the lawyers regarded as authoritative, not what the persons invoked believed in their own right. It is not until we reach the lawyers of the mid-Umayyad period that some of the evidence could be correctly ascribed, though one suspects that it is usually not. In sum, Schacht's conclusion that the evidence of legal Ḥadīth takes us no further back than to about a century after the hijra must be accepted as correct.

CHAPTER 3

The Islamic patronate

(a) Introductory

The institution with which this book is concerned regulated the status of freedmen and converts in early Islamic society. All societies must have a policy regarding the admission of outsiders to their ranks, and since slaves are usually recruited abroad, freedmen and other foreigners have often been governed by the same or similar rules from this point of view. Both pose the question whether they should be admitted at all. The answer to this question has sometimes been no. Thus the Athenians withheld citizenship from freedmen and other foreigners alike, assigning the status of metic, or resident alien, to both. But in societies constituted by common faith, adoption of this faith will normally result in the acquisition of membership, however partial at first.[1] Jewish law accords practically the same rights and duties to freedmen and other proselytes as it does to born Jews;[2] and Islamic law similarly grants full membership of the Muslim community to freedmen and converts, some minor disabilities apart:[3] only the *dhimmīs*, that is the non-Muslim subjects of the Muslim state, are in the position of metics. There is no reason to think that Islamic law ever circumscribed the rights of freedmen and converts in public law, though the Arab conquerors frequently treated them as second-class citizens in practice. But however this may be, this aspect of the question is not of interest to us.

Whatever the degree of membership accorded to them, newcomers in a certain society necessarily receive their rights either indirectly via an individual or group or else directly from the community itself, be it a tribe, state, religious community or other. If a newcomer is affiliated to an individual, he will automatically be affiliated to the latter's family, clan, tribe or city too: but if he affiliated to a group or directly to the community itself, the law will not normally force him into a legal relationship with an individual member of the community as well. Thus Jewish freedmen and proselytes are in principle attached to a Jewish tribe, in practice to the Jewish community at large; Jewish law accordingly severs all legal relations between the freedmen and his manumitter.[4] Similarly, the metics of Athens were placed under the direct protection of the Athenian state. They did need an individual sponsor (*prostatēs*), and freedmen had to be sponsored by their manumitter; but sponsorship did not give rise to a close or enduring legal relationship.[5] Greek law being characterised by *Privatwillkür*, Athenian (and other Greek) manumitters could, if they so wished, impose legal obligations of their own making on their freedman; but if they did not, all legal relations between manumitter and freedmen were, or came to be, severed here too.[6] The *dhimmī* of Islamic law is also placed under the direct protection of the Muslim state, and the same is true of the convert in classical law: neither owes his position to an individual. But the opposite solution is adopted for the freedman. Manumission automatically creates an enduring relationship between manumitter and freedman, and it is to this relationship (known as *walā'*) that the freedman owes his membership of Muslim society. He is admitted, in other words, as his manumitter's *mawlā*, a word usually translated as client. (It also means the opposite, viz. patron.) Now the same was once true of converts, and indeed also of unconverted hangers-on. Throughout the Umayyad period (661–750) all non-Arabs who wished to join the ranks of the conquerors had to find an Arab (or, as the Arab character of Muslim society receded, Muslim) patron, who, upon their declaration of conversion or allegiance, obtained very much the same rights and duties *vis-à-vis* them as the manumitter *vis-à-vis* his former slave.[7] (Contractual clientage survives in classical law too, but most schools reject it.) All non-Arab newcomers to Arab society, be they freeborn or freed, converted or unconverted, were thus affiliated to individual members of this society, not directly to Arab tribes, let alone directly to the Arab state; and as will be seen, the relationship in which they were placed was an unequal one: in public law freedmen and converts enjoyed the same rights and duties as other Muslims, but in private law they were dependents. It is with this distinctive feature of early Islamic law that the present work is concerned.

(b) The legal incidents of *walā'*.

i. Walā' al-ʿitq

All classical schools recognise the validity of *walā' al-ʿitq*, the tie arising upon manumission. Its main legal incidents are the following.

The manumitter

1 The manumitter acquires a title to the freedman's estate. On this point there is complete agreement in Sunnī and Shīʿī law.[8] Only the Ibāḍīs reject it, though they too probably began by accepting his title to succession.[9] In Sunnī law he inherits as the last agnate of the freedman. He will thus take the residue (if any) in competition with Qur'ānic heirs (e.g. a daughter), be excluded by a genuine agnate (e.g. a son), but

himself exclude remoter relatives (*dhawū'l-arḥām*, e.g. a sister's son).[10] The same rules apply in Qāsimī Zaydī law.[11] But the Imāmīs,[12] Ismāʿīlīs[13] and Nāṣirī Ẓaydīs[14] hold that the manumitter's title rests on *sabab* (tie, connection) rather than *nasab* (genealogical relationship), and all three schools exclude the manumitter from succession in competition with any blood relation of the freedman, however remote, though he will inherit together with a spouse.

2 The manumitter is obliged to pay blood-money on behalf of the freedman, that is to say he and his agnates form the freedman's *ʿāqila*, or blood-money group. On this point there is agreement between Sunnīs,[15] Shīʿites[16] and Ibāḍīs alike.[17] The obligation clearly applies only to the extent that the freedman has no agnates of his own, though this is not always stated (usually the freedman has none, or too few). The classical lawyers also fail to state whether the manumitter and his agnates have a corresponding right to collect blood-money in compensation for the freedman if the latter is killed, but early manumitters certainly claimed that they did.[18]

3 The manumitters may act as marriage guardian to his freedwoman or freedman's daughter. On this point, too, there is agreement in Sunnī,[19] Shīʿī[20] and Ibāḍī law.[21]

4 According to the Mālikīs, the manumitter also qualifies for the custody (*ḥaḍāna*) of the freedman's children.[22] This follows logically from the position of agnatic heir which he enjoys in Sunnī and Qāsimī law, and other schools presumably made the same inference; but they rarely make their position clear, the question being highly theoretical.[23]

The Freedman

5 The freedman does not acquire any title to his manumitter's estate. There were attempts to redress this imbalance. Thus two traditions from the Prophet call the freedman to succession if the manumitter has left no legal heirs at all.[24] This doctrine was adopted by some Imāmīs[25] and (some?) Ismāʿīlīs.[26] But most Imāmīs were against it;[27] and as for the Ismāʿīlīs, we have only the views of one jurist. Succession between manumitter and freedman is unilateral in all the other schools.[28]

6 The freedman does not qualify for membership of the manumitter's blood-money group. To this statement there are several exceptions. Manumitter and freedman pay blood-money on behalf of each other in Ibāḍī law,[29] and possibly also in that of the Ismāʿīlīs.[30] Some Mālikīs counted the freedman as a member of the manumitter's *ʿāqila* in the absence of all other candidates, including patron or patrons of the manumitter (if any), though generally the Mālikīs were against it.[31] Shāfiʿī adopted the same position in his *Umm*,[32] but his followers were against it too.[33] So were the other schools.[34]

7 The possibility that the freedman may act as marriage guardian to the manumitter's daughter is rarely considered. Mālik is said to have allowed it, though the patrons of the manumitter (if any) would take priority.[35]

8 The possibility that the freedman might be awarded custody of the manumitter's children is not often considered either. The Mālikīs permitted it, as usual in the absence of all other candidates, including patrons of the manumitter.[36]

9 No other positive rights or duties are recorded for the freedman. In practice freedmen were both expected and known to assist their manumitters, be it financially, militarily, politically or otherwise.[37] But the law did not formally oblige them to serve or honour their former masters in any way.

Other

10 The relationship between manumitter and freedman is as enduring as are kinship ties. The manumitter cannot sell, give away or otherwise alienate his rights and duties, nor is the freedman allowed to change patron.[38] The manumitter's rights and duties extend to the freedman's descendants, how low soever, as well as to his freedmen and their freedmen in perpetuity, though he will not be called upon to act as patron unless the intervening relatives or manumitters have died.[39] On his own death they pass to his descendants in perpetuity, though again they lose importance as the distance between the two parties increases.[40]

ii. Walā' al-muwālāt

Contractual *walā'* is recognised only by the Ḥanafīs, Imāmīs, Qāsimī Zaydīs and Ismā'īlīs.[41] In pre-classical law it was a tie which arose on 'conversion at the hands of another' or some other agreement or association between a Muslim and a non-Arab,[42] but none of the four schools recognises the institution in its original extent. Thus most Qāsimīs hold that mere agreement cannot give rise to *walā'*. Contractual clientage in their view arises only from conversion, and only in non-Muslim (*ḥarbī*) territory in which the convert cannot be attached to a Muslim state.[43] But according to the Ḥanafīs, Imāmīs and (implicitly) the Ismā'īlīs, it is conversion which cannot give rise to *walā'*, wherever it may take place. The client may well be a convert, and the Ḥanafīs usually envisage him as such, but his status arises from an agreement distinct from the act of conversion.[44] Indeed, no act of conversion need be involved at all. Thus the Ḥanafīs hold that the client may be an unconverted *dhimmī*,[45] or a foundling;[46] and in Imāmī and Ismā'īlī law he may also be a slave manumitted without *walā' al-'itq*, which is in fact what the Imāmīs usually assume him to be.[47] The fundamental requirement is that he should be somebody entirely devoid of blood relations and patrons within the Muslim community.[48]

The legal incidents of the tie are almost identical with those of *walā' al-ʿitq*.

The patron

1 The patron acquires a title to the client's estate. This title is not however an agnatic one. Like the manumitter in Shīʿite law, the contractual patron is excluded by any blood relation on the client's side, though he inherits together with a spouse.[49]

2 The patron assumes responsibility for the payment of blood-money on behalf of the client.[50]

3 The patron may act as marriage guardian to his client's daughter. Shaybānī disputed this on the ground that he is not an agnatic heir (marriage guardianship being vested in the agnates in the order of succession), but Abū Ḥanīfa and other Ḥanafīs allowed it.[51] The question is rarely discussed in the literature, and the position of the other schools is not clear.

4 No attention is paid to the question whether the contractual patron qualifies for the guardianship of his client's children.

The client

5 The client acquires a title to the patron's estate if the parties have stipulated that succession be mutual. The Ḥanafīs and Imāmīs allow them to do so,[52] but some Qāsimīs disagree.[53] Usually succession is assumed to be unilateral.

6 The client assumes responsibility for the payment of blood-money on behalf of the patron if the parties have stipulated that this obligation be mutual. The Imāmīs allow them to do so,[54] and the Ḥanafīs presumably regard mutual succession as the *quid pro quo* of a mutual responsibility for the payment of blood-money, though they do not explicitly say so. The obligation is usually envisaged as unilateral.

7 No attention is paid to the question whether the client may act as marriage guardian to the patron's daughter.

8 The same applies to the question of custody.

9 The contractual client is not formally obliged to serve or honour his patron.

Other

10 Unlike the servile tie, *walā' al-muwālāt* may be terminated by either party as long as the patron has not paid blood-money on the client's

> behalf. Once the patron has had occasion to pay, however, the Ḥanafīs regard the tie as no less enduring than *walāʾ al-ʿitq*; but in Imāmī law it comes to an end on the death of either party.[55] The position of the other schools is not clear. Sale and gifts of *walāʾ* are rarely discussed in connection with the contractual tie.[56]

What then was the legal nature of *walāʾ*? The classical lawyers (whatever their persuasion) invariably interpret it as a fictitious kinship tie, more precisely an agnatic one: '*walāʾ* is kinship like the kinship based on descent' (*al-walāʾ luḥma ka-luḥmat al-nasab*), as they repeat with tedious monotony;[57] the essence of *walāʾ*, as a Sunnī lawyer puts it, lies in its creation of an agnatic relationship (*ʿusūba*).[58] But this is somewhat unpersuasive. It is true that the Sunnī and Qāsimī manumitters acquire an agnatic title to his freedman's estate, and that the relationship between the two is construed along agnatic lines in other respects; but this does not hold true of the manumitter in Imāmī, Nāṣirī and Ismāʿīlī law, nor is it true of the contractual patron in any of the schools in which he survives. More importantly, the rights and duties vested in kinship ties are usually reciprocal; but though the manumitter acquires rights and duties *vis-à-vis* the freedman, the freedman acquires few or none *vis-à-vis* the manumitter; and the contractual relationship is usually also envisaged as unilateral. The position of the freedman (and, in so far as the relationship was unilateral, also that of the contractual client) was not unlike that of a child debarred from ever reaching the age of majority: othes have rights and duties *vis-à-vis* him, but he himself is passive.[59] *Walāʾ* is thus an institution which places one person in a relationship of dependence with another, as the lawyers in fact themselves concede when they distinguish between the two as 'upper' and 'lower' *mawlā*.[60] It is not for nothing that *mawlā* is usually translated as client (or patron): *walāʾ* is in fact a tie of clientage (or a patronate, depending on the angle from which it is seen). As will emerge later, this is even more apparent in pre-classical law. All non-Arab newcomers in early Islamic society thus paid for their membership of this society by acceptance of a private relationship of dependence. It is the origin of this private relationship of dependence which is the subject of this book.

(c) The question of origins

Walāʾ is generally assumed to be of Arabian origin. As is often the case with beliefs which no one has questioned, there exists no authoritative statement of the prevailing view.[61] It could, I think, be formulated as follows. There existed in pre-Islamic Arabia an institution or institutions for the incorporation of outsiders into Arab tribes. On conquering the Middle East, the Arabs proceeded, naturally enough, to use the same institutions for the incorporation of non-Arabs into the conquest society. In due course these institutions were taken up by the lawyers and given their classical legal formulation. Inevitably, the character of the institutions changed somewhat in the course of this evolution, but not so much as to call in question the basic continuity of their history

In what follows I shall challenge this belief. Pre-Islamic Arabia, I shall argue, supplied the general context for *walāʾ*: the institution manifestly served a tribal society. But it did not supply the institution itself. The crucial features of *walāʾ* derive from Roman and provincial law. The borrowed elements were reshaped to fit the new context, but not so much as to change them beyond recognition.

This contention will no doubt strike most Islamicists as implausible.[62] Since most Islamicists are familiar with *walāʾ* from the historical literature, it should be stressed that *walāʾ* as it existed in social reality was a somewhat different institution from that described in law. On the basis of the historical sources one would be inclined to conclude that freedmen and converts were affiliated directly to Arab tribes; indeed, this is what modern scholars generally do conclude: 'if a man who was not an Arab made a profession of Islam, he was attached to an Arab tribe as a "client"', as Watt in one sense quite correctly puts it.[63] The sources frequently describe non-Arab Muslims as clients of tribal groups: so-and-so was a *mawlā* of Banū ʿAdī or ʿAbd Shams, Mahra, Banū Khāzim, ʿAbd al-Qays, and so on.[64] And Abū Ḥanīfa himself allegedly stated that 'I was a peasant, then I joined this tribe of Bakr b. Wāʾil'; according to him, a convert should not just identify himself as a Muslim, but rather associate himself 'with one of these tribes'.[65] Clearly, membership of a tribe tended to be of greater significance for the client than the person through whom it was obtained. The chronicles do make it clear that clients had individual patrons and that the relationship with a patron (especially a manumitter) might be of crucial importance for the client's career.[66] But even so, patrons regularly come across as little more than sponsors who, once they had secured membership of the Muslim community for their clients, vanished from the latter's lives. In short, *walāʾ* comes across as a collective relationship of dependence. *Mawālī* were tribal protegés, or protégés of the Arabs at large (as in the global expression *al-ʿarab wa'l-mawālī*); they had streets, mosques and military regiments of their own,[67] and they suffered far more from the ethnic pride of the Arab nation than they did from the legal rights of their individual patrons,[68] indeed, no historical work indicates what legal rights and duties their patrons had at all.[69]

Now it is indisputable that *walāʾ* as described in the historical sources reflects the legacy of Arabia: in social reality the conquerors treated non-Arab Muslims much as they had treated non-Arab freedmen and other dependents in the pre-Islamic past. But if social and legal reality are at variance, the legal institution can hardly have come from Arabia too. The individual tie of the lawyers cannot descend in any straightforward way from a pre-Islamic Arab institution. It could represent some attenuation of such an institution, it could be wholly foreign, and it could be wholly new. I shall not deny that it was new. But new institutions are usually formed out of old material, and I shall argue that the material which went into the making of *walāʾ* came largely from the Roman Near East rather than Arabia.

CHAPTER 4

The case against Arabia

I shall now try to show that there was no institution similar to Islamic *walā'* in pre-Islamic Arabia; more precisely, I shall try to demonstrate that four diagnostic features of the Islamic institution were unknown to the homeland of the conquerors, these being the following:

1 The Islamic patronate is individual. It binds one person to another in a relationship of dependence. In pre-Islamic Arabia dependent relationships were formed between groups, or between individuals and groups, not between individuals. In short, in pre-Islamic Arabia such relationships were collective.

2 The Islamic patronate detaches the client from his natal group and incorporates him in that of the patron as a passive member. The Berber client is no longer a member of his Berber tribe, but nor is he a full member of an Arab one. It could be argued that it is enslavement and conversion which detach the client from his kin rather than the institution of *walā'* itself: the contractual client who remains an infidel presumably remains a member of his natal group as well.[1] But it is to the patron that the latter's group that even the free, unconverted client belongs for purposes of life in *Muslim* society, and his dependant status in this society arises from the fact that his membership of the patron's group is partial: the patron and his agnates acquire rights and duties *vis-à-vis* him, but he typically acquires none *vis-à-vis* them. Individual ties of clientage do not always affect group affiliation, and collective ones never do. Where clientage is collective, the client remains a full member of his own inferior group, as opposed to becoming a partial member of a superior one. Collective clientage creates satellite groups, not semi-members.

3 The Islamic patronate is assimilative. Having been detached from his natal group, the client sooner or later acquires full membership of the new group to which he has been assigned. A passive member *vis-à-vis* the patron and the latter's agnates, he has full rights and duties *vis-à-vis* the agnates whom he himself produces as a member of the new group, so that in the course of time he, or rather his descendants, escape dependent status. In Ḥanafī law the grandson of a client counts as an Arab from the

point of view of marriage equality;[2] and though client origins were often remembered and stigmatised far longer in practice, *walā'* did in effect turn non-Arabs into Arab tribesmen. Collective clientage, by contrast, is not necessarily assimilative, and assimilation is effected collectively if it occurs at all. Satellite groups can remain satellite groups for ever. They may shake off their dependence and gain recognition as autonomous tribes of their own, or as subdivisions of the tribe that used to protect them. But there is nothing in the tie itself to ensure that this will happen.

4 The Islamic patronate assigns to the patron the duty of paying blood-money on his client's behalf in return for a title to his estate. No such rights and duties can be assigned to patrons where clientage is collective, nor can they be documented for pre-Islamic Arabia.

(a) The status of the outsider in modern Arabia

Contrary to what the reader may expect, I shall start by reviewing the evidence for modern (or more precisely recent) Arabia. The information on Arabia in the last century before it was transformed by the inroads of modern government and oil industry provides a reasonably full and intelligible picture of the position of the outsider. This picture is not of course in itself evidence for pre-Islamic conditions; but in its light the fragmentary pre-Islamic evidence becomes more informative than when it is taken on its own. The material on which the present section is based dates from the nineteenth and early twentieth century; I shall refer to it in the anthropological present.

What status does the outsider enjoy in tribal Arabia? The answer to this question depends on whether or not the outsider is a fully accredited member of what we may call the tribal commonwealth – whether or not he is *aṣīl* or, in the terminology of South Arabia, whether or not he is a *qabīlī*.[3] The distinction between fully accredited tribesmen and others is fundamental for an understanding of Arabian ties of affiliation and dependence. We may then start by ensuring that we know what it means.

To be *aṣīl* is to have *aṣl*, origin, which is to have Arab ethnicity, personal independence and political autonomy; without these three characteristics one cannot be 'free', a term which in tribal usage has the connotation of 'noble'.[4] First, then, one must have a valid genealogy. Non-Arab ancestors do not count even if they are remembered, and African freedmen, Jews, Ṣulubbīs and other non-Arabs are not reckoned to be free.[5] Secondly, one must be a bedouin[6] or, if one is settled, one must own one's own land.[7] Landless labourers,[8] tenants,[9] blacksmiths,[10] goldsmiths, weavers, tanners, sweepers and other craftsmen and servants[11] are all excluded from tribal status because they are dependent for their livelihood on the income of others;[12] those who engage in such occupations are by definition both non-Arabs and unfree, whatever their actual descent and *status libertatis*.[13]

Thirdly, one must acknowledge no *sulṭān*, except in a purely nominal way, and one must also avoid the ignominy of having to pay other tribes for one's protection or non-molestation: those who are under the thumbs of othes are not tribesmen, but *raʿāyā*, subjects.[14] If one fulfils all these conditions, one is a member of the tribal commonwealth.[15] The members of this commonwealth marry only among themselves,[16] and they also exclude others from participation in their feuds, raids, wars and other forms of tribal politics. They do, it is true, allow slaves and freedmen to participate, but only as dependents of their masters and manumitters, not in their own right.[17] Non-tribesmen typically do not bear arms; they do not stage raids against or engage in blood-feuds with tribesmen, nor do tribesmen raid or engage in feuds with them; typically, they count as inviolable. The dividing line between fully accredited members of the tribal commonwealth and others is neither stable nor neat. Tribal groups which fall under the dominion of others are threatened with exclusion, while conversely excluded groups which muster the strength to compete in military terms are making a bid for membership, the ultimate test of membership being eligibility for marriage. But the fact that groups of intermediate status are to be found in no way deprives the dividing line of its fundamental importance.[18]

(i) Relations between tribesmen and tribesmen

Within the tribal commonwealth movements of population and changes of membership can and do take place. The fully accredited tribesman can obtain rights of residence and protection in another tribe, or he can be fully adopted into it; the same is true of tribal groups.[19] Since *walā'* was an institution for the accommodation of non-Arabs, there is no need to describe these relationships in detail. All we need to note is that essentially they are relationships of parity. No doubt newcomers can sometimes find themselves in a position of inferiority *vis-à-vis* their hosts, but they cannot be described as clients in either principle or practice.

(ii) Relations between tribesmen and non-tribesmen

Movements of population and changes of membership can presumably also take place within the non-tribal world, but this is of no concern to us. What we are interested in is the relationship between tribesmen and non-tribesmen, and this relationship is indeed one of clientage. Non-tribesmen are invariably in a position of dependence *vis-à-vis* the tribesmen, to whom they are usually obliged to make payments of various kinds. The significant point is that the relationship is collective: Ṣulubbīs, smiths, tenants, servants and so forth all form excluded *groups*. Such groups have a 'brother' (*akh*) in the protecting tribe to whom they can complain if they have been raided or otherwise maltreated and who is responsible for ensuring the return of their goods; for this service he is likely to collect a fee known as *khuwwa*, 'brotherhood'.[20] But such a brother is plainly a link between two groups, not a patron of the type we meet in Islamic law. His role is to ensure that relations between the two groups are conducted in accordance with the rules, not to attach non-tribesmen to an Arab tribe; and it is only non-tribesmen who operate on their own, such as wandering merchants and camel-traders, who are recruited individually as his clients.[21] Being a mere link between the tribal and the non-tribal worlds, he has no rights and duties *vis-à-vis* his clients other than those specified. He does not contribute to the payment of blood-money owed by them, nor does he have a title to their estates.

The status of slaves and freedmen is similar to that of other non-tribesmen, though it is closer to that of tribesmen in some respects. Practically all slaves are non-Arabs, usually Africans.[22] They are thus unfree by ascription, and it is this point which largely shapes their position. On the one hand, they can enjoy many of the same rights as the free even while they are slaves. Among the bedouin they usually do, if not always to the same extent as among Musil's Rwala. The slaves of the latter cannot be sold, being allegedly allowed even to change masters if they wish;[23] they participate in raids and keep all booty except horses; they do not require their masters' consent to marry, and they form kin group of their own, sometimes of such a size as to have their own *shaykh*s and judges; and unlike other non-tribesmen, they will exact vengeance even from the *aṣīlīn*. They may also be highly esteemed.[24] Because they are unfree by ascription there is no need to emphasise their legal status. But on the other hand, they cannot lose their ascribed unfreedom even when they cease to be slaves. They can of course be freed of their personal servitude, and such manumission formulas as we have are manumissions without conditions of further service.[25] But since manumitted slaves are not *aṣīl*, they must remain members of client groups. They may stay with the slaves of the camp, or they make take up separate nomadic existence together with other freedmen;[26] but either way they simply escape from personal servitude into collective clientage. Characteristically, they continue to be known as *ʿabīd*, slaves.[27]

In general, the literature suggests that all legal ties between freedman and former master are severed on manumission. Freedmen owe obedience to the tribe whose members have manumitted them and to whom they may pay *khuwwa* or, more commonly, military service;[28] but they owe this obedience as satellite groups, not as personal clients of their former owners. Freedmen are described as active members of their own inferior lineages, not as passive members of those of their manumitters; and manumission is not the first stage in a protracted process of assimilation whereby *ʿabīd* end up as Arab tribesmen. There are however two passages which run counter to the general tenor of the literature.

The first, by Burckhardt, refers to the status of slaves and freedmen among the bedouin. 'It is said, that if a slave has been killed, the master avenges his death as if he had been a freeman [NB, not 'freedman'] and is therefore entitled to receive the *deey* [sc. blood-money] himself; of this I am not quite certain, but an emancipated slave has all the claims of *tha'r*, or "blood-revenge", as an Arab.'[29] Nobody disputes the fact that a freedman has the same rights to vengeance as an Arab. What Burckhardt could be taken to imply, however, is that freedmen are avenged by their manumitters rather than their relatives, on a par with what he took to be the case of slaves. If so, manumitters could indeed be said to regard their freedmen as part of their own agnatic groups.[30] But Burckhardt does not actually say as much, and his tentative statement regarding slaves is contradicted by Musil, according to whom slaves (and *a fortiori* thus also freedmen) avenge themselves.[31] Burckhardt wrote almost a hundred years before Musil, with reference to more tribes than Musil, and it is not inconceivable that manumitters would claim compensation for slaves and freedmen who died without leaving any relatives of their own. But even if we assume this to be the case, the question remains whether they also regarded themselves as obliged to *pay* compensation for blood spilt *by* such persons. As regards slaves, one passage suggests that their masters may well be held responsible for their misdeeds under certain circumstances.[32] But there is no comparable statement regarding freedmen, and Jaussen implies the contrary. According to him, victims of crimes committed by freedmen will complain to the chief of the manumitter's tribe.[33] Complaints are thus lodged with the political leader under whom the freedmen have been placed, not with the manumitter; and though the political leader may well be the manumitter too (chiefs having more slaves than anyone else), it is not in this capacity that he is invoked. One might infer that manumitters are only responsible for their freedmen if the latter are under their personal protection on a par, for example, with guests. It certainly does not suggest that an agnatic relationship is involved.

The second passage, by Doughty, refers to the status of freedmen and other outsiders among the oasis-dwellers. Its wording is as follows.

> The jummaa is that natural association of households, born in affinity, that are reckoned to the same jid, or first-father, and are confederates under an elder, the head of their house, inheriting the old father's authority. In these bonds and divisions by kindreds, is the only corporate life and security in an anarchical infested country. In-coming strangers are reckoned to the alliance of their friends. Freed men are clients of the lord's household; and their children, with the children of incorporated strangers, are accounted parentage with the children of ancestry: they are 'uncle's sons' together of the same jummaa.[34]

This passage raises two questions. First, whose clients do freedmen become? 'Clients of the lord's household' could mean clients of the manumitter or clients of the elder, 'the head of their house'. If the latter, they become clients of the entire *jummaa* (*jamāʿa*?) and thus enjoy a position similar to that of the freedmen of the bedouin who, as has been seen, are placed in a relationship of dependence *vis-à-vis* the entire political community to which their manumitters belong. If the former, we must concede that the settled tribesmen of modern Arabia establish individual ties between manumitter and freedman. Had Doughty said that 'freed men are clients of *their* lord's household', he would clearly have meant the manumitter. As it is, one simply cannot tell.

Secondly, what does the clientage entail? Clearly, it meant political loyalty: political loyalty in an 'anarchical infested country' is what both this passage and its sequel are about. But does it also have genealogical effects in the sense that the client becomes a formal member of the manumitter's *jummaa*? Doughty unambiguously states that it did, at least as far as the freedman's children are concerned, with reference to the fact that these children are known as 'uncle's sons'. But it is arguable that he has misunderstood the import of this expression.

'Uncle's sons' (*banū'l-ʿamm*) is a term suggestive of metaphorical rather than fictitious kinship ties. There is a considerable difference between the two. Fictitious kinship ties disregard biological relationships whereas genuine ones are based on them, but they have precisely the same effect in at least some respects: an adopted son has the same, or similar, rights and duties as a son by birth; an adopted brother may be indistinguishable from one by birth in terms of the role assigned to him. But metaphorical kinship ties disregard *both* biological relationships *and* the precise effects ascribed to them. Thus the 'brother' of excluded groups in no way has the same rights and duties as a genuine or a fictitious one: his brotherhood is simply a loose metaphor for his protective role. Similarly a man may be called 'father' by everyone around him simply because he is old and respected. Now when tribesmen call outsiders 'uncle's sons' (sc. cousins, fellow-tribesmen), they are apt to mean, not that the outsiders in question have been adopted into their tribe, but rather that relations with them are or should be characterised by roughly the same solidarity as if they had been thus adopted. *Ben-ʿammeh*, 'uncle's sonship', for example, is the name of an alliance concluded between two tribes who desire friendly relations without wishing to merge in legal or genealogical terms.[35] 'Uncle's sons' is presumably also what the slaves and freedmen of the bedouin are supposed to be, given that they call their masters' 'uncle'.[36] And in early Islamic Basra a whole tribe of non-Arab origin was known as 'uncle's sons'. 'They settled among Banū Tamīm in Basra in the days of ʿUmar b. al-Khaṭṭāb, converted, fought with the Muslims and distinguished themselves; so people said, "although you are not Arabs, you are our brothers and our people, and you are helpers, brothers and *banū'l-ʿamm*". They came to be called this, and they became part of the general mass of Arabs.'[37] Clearly, these people were accepted as metaphorical rather than fictitious kinsmen: no *ḥilf* or other method of incorporation was used. They were simply recognised as a tribe of their own, complete with the *nisba* al-ʿAmmī.

Now if we assume that Doughty's 'uncle's sons' were similarly metaphorical kinsmen, we can harmonise his account with the literature at large: freedmen become clients of the *jummaa*, and their children are known as 'helpers, brothers and "uncle's sons" ' in the sense of close and active supporters; in principle the kin groups formed by the children of freedmen can no doubt be accepted sooner or later as subdivisions of the *jummaa* itself, but in practice their colour is likely to keep them separate. The fact that Doughty's passage *could* be read in this vein does not of course mean that it *must* so thus read. But the interpretation proposed gains some support, at least as far as the freedmen's children are concerned, from the fact that when we turn from Doughty's oases to the larger cities, the servile kin groups reappear. Thus the freedmen of nineteenth-century Mecca, far from being dispersed and absorbed into the *jummaas* of their individual manumitters, formed autonomous communities of their own headed by their own *shaykhs*, precisely as they do among the bedouin.[38] The same was probably the case in eighteenth-century Jawf,[39] and it was certainly the case in early twentieth-century Ẓufār.[40] In settled and bedouin Arabia alike relationships between manumitter and freedman would thus appear to have been characterised by convergence in terms of political allegiance, but divergence in terms of genealogical affiliation, with all that genealogical affiliation implies for the allocation of rights to blood-money, succession and so forth.

(b) The status of the outsider in pre-Islamic Arabia

On turning to pre-Islamic Arabia one's first impression is one of disheartening confusion arising from the fact that a wide variety of meanings are attached both to the term *mawlā* and to its various synonyms. Thus *mawlā* might mean a genuine agnate or fellow-tribesmen (*ibn ʿamm*), a fictitious one such as an adopted son or adopted member of the tribe (*daʿī*), or a metaphorical one such as a temporary protégé (*jār*), ally (*ḥalīf*), helper (*nāṣir*), or friend (*ṣadīq*) of any kind.[41] Everybody in pre-Islamic Arabia was a *mawlā* in some sense or other unto somebody else. However, in modern Arabia everybody is similarly a brother in some sense or other unto somebody else, brotherhood here being not just a genuine kinship tie between children of the same parents, but also a fictitious one between a tribe and its adopted member,[42] and a metaphorical one between allied friends,[43] allied tribes,[44] or, as has been seen, a tribe and its non-tribal protégés. This suggests a way out of the confusion. If we wish to enquire into the status of the brother in modern Arabia, the answer obviously depends on the type of brother we have in mind; and if we mean the protector of non-tribesmen, we evidently cannot describe his position with reference to poetry on the relationship between brothers in the sense of friends. Similarly, if we wish to enquire into the status of *mawālī* in pre-Islamic Arabia, the answer depends on the type of *mawlā* intended; and if our concern is with outsiders of non-Arab origin, it will not do to answer the question on the basis of material relating to Arabs. We thus have to sort the evidence with reference to the type of *mawlā* involved; and for this purpose it is essential to realise that the distinction between fully accredited tribesmen and others was as important in pre-Islamic Arabia as it is today.

To be an accredited tribesman in pre-Islamic Arabia was to be free, *ḥurr*, then as now with the connotation of noble.[45] In order to count as free one needed, first, an Arab genealogy. Non-Arab ancestors did not count, and members of non-Arab minority groups such as African freedmen and Jews were neither *ḥurr* nor accredited tribesmen.[46]

Secondly, one needed personal autonomy. It is not clear whether tribal status among agriculturalists depended on ownership of land, as it does today, or simply on military strength, but some agriculturalists were certainly accepted as *ḥurr* whereas others were not. Thus Banū Ḥanīfa of the Yamāma were no more excluded from tribal status than are the militant Tamīmīs who inhabit their villages today,[47] and the same is true of the tribes of Yathrib; but both were accepted *despite* their occupation. 'Go back to the Yamāma and cultivate, for you are slaves from beginning to end', a poet told Banū Ḥanīfa after the conquests.[48] 'The origin of the Imr' al-Qays is among slaves; their land is a place where the spade is wielded, not the open desert or a garrison town', as Dhū'l-Rumma put it to others.[49] Then as now there was a tendency to deny the Arab origin of cultivators: such people were mere Nabataeans.[50] And then as now they tended to be recruited from among non-Arabs as a result: many were Jews,[51] and, at least from the time of Muʿāwiya, others were *ʿabīd*.[52] As regards craftsmen and servants, blacksmiths were held in contempt;[53] descent from one was no better than descent from a slave.[54] Goldsmiths were similarly despised,[55] as were weavers;[56] and the low opinion not only of weavers, but also of tanners, sweepers and cuppers attested in Islamic law perhaps also perpetuates a pre-Islamic prejudice.[57] Being non-Arabs and unfree by ascription, such craftsmen tended to be recruited from among non-Arabs on a par with agriculturalists. Smiths and others were often slaves, usually recruited outside Arabia.[58] Goldsmiths were usually Jews,[59] as they were to remain in the Yemen until 1951.[60]

Finally, to be an accredited tribesman one needed political autonomy. Tribes were supposed to be *laqāḥ*, not ruled or dominated by others, and those who failed to live up to the ideal were mercilessly branded as 'slaves'.[61] 'The ʿUkl are slaves of the Taym, and the Taym are slaves themselves; if one tells them to leave their watering-trough [to make room for others], they leave it.'[62] The ultimate disgrace was having to pay taxes to a stronger tribe.[63]

As in the case of modern Arabia, the dividing line between tribesmen and others was neither stable nor neat. Arabs such as the unfortunate ʿUkl and other tribes reduced to dependant status were questionable members of the tribal commonwealth, while conversely non-Arabs such as the Jews occasionally rose to some sort of acceptance within it.[64] But the dividing line was nonetheless of fundamental importance.

(i) Relations between tribesmen and tribesmen

We may now proceed to sort the information on *mawālī* according to whether it relates to tribesmen or others, disposing of that relating to tribesmen first.

The *mawlā* in the sense of *ḥalīf*, ally or confederate, belongs almost exclusively in this section. *Ḥilf* (oath, compact) designated a wide variety of alliances between tribal groups or individuals ranging from short-term agreements to mutual adoption and amalgamation.[65] When the parties to a *ḥilf* were groups, they were usually autonomous tribes, though some allied groups were evidently more in the nature of satellites than others. The term could also be used of agreements with foreign states.[66] When the parties were individuals, they were usually Arab tribesmen. As will be seen, the term is occasionally used of agreements of a quite different type with members of excluded groups.[67] But it is rarely pejorative,[68] and it never has connotations of non-Arab ethnicity.

The individual *ḥalīf*/guest was usually a man who, faced with the prospect of prolonged residence among foreigners, had set up a protective relationship with a native *ḥalīf*/host without being incorporated *samawī* and *damawī*, 'by name and by blood', as the modern bedouin put it,[69] into the latter's kin. The individual *ḥilf* could perhaps amount to full incorporation by name and by blood if it was so desired;[70] it could certainly be followed by adoption.[71] But the vast majority of *ḥalīf*s known to us had retained membership of their native tribes, as is clear from their *nisbas*.[72] The *ḥalīf*s were fully accredited members of the tribal commonwealth who thanks to their accredited origins could obtain rights of residence and protection in a foreign tribe, with the option of full incorporation, very much as they can today.[73]

The *mawlā* in the sense of *jār*, protégé/protector or neighbour, on the other hand, belongs partly in this section and partly in the next. *Jiwār* is a term much more suggestive of dependence than is *ḥilf*, and the *jār* might well be a non-tribesman. The term could certainly also be one of abuse suggesting inability to defend oneself: Banū Muʿāwiya, for example, were taunted with being mere protégés (*jīrān*) unable to do anything under the protection of their patrons (*fī junūb mawālīhim*).[74] It does not suggest non-Arab ethnicity, though, and the vast majority of *jār*s were certainly Arabs. Leaving aside political underlings and recipients of temporary grants of protection (viz. the equivalents of the modern *dakhīl*), they were individual or groups who had gone to live among foreigners, be it to escape vengeance[75] or drought at home[76] or for some other reason.[77] They were thus foreign residents on a par with *ḥalīfs*.

Individual *ḥalīf*s and *jār*s of this type enjoyed very much the same status in their host tribes, though the former would appear to have been more closely integrated.[78] Both were tribesmen with a valid *nisba* and a people to whom they could in principle return,[79] and neither had been incorporated in their tribe of residence. It is because they had not been incorporated that they would go home, or be advised to do so, if hostilities broke out between their tribes of birth and tribes of residence.[80] It is also because he was an outsider that the *jār* was not supposed to be killed in retaliation for murders committed by his hosts,[81] though it is unlikely that the *ḥalīf* was similarly exempted.[82] In practice both might very well be killed in feuds, partly because the enemy did not always stop to enquire into their status,[83] and more particularly because the murder of a protected person was an outrageous act guaranteed to perpetuate a feud.[84] The fact that the host would frequently react by trying to avenge him does not mean that they had been incorporated in his kin, as is sometimes maintained.[85] It is because his personal grant of protection had been violated that the host was liable to react by a display of force. His honour had been insulted by an act which suggested, and which was no doubt calculated to suggest, weakness on his part;[86] and if the murderers were outsiders, the insult would affect the entire tribe.[87] Similarly, the fact that the host might renounce vengeance, accepting blood-money instead,[88] or simply pay blood-money to the victim's kin out of his own pocket,[89] does not mean that the protégés had been incorporated as second-class citizens. As far as the victim's kin were concerned, the host was at fault for failing to ensure that his grant of protection was respected, and he accordingly owed blood-money to them; but whether he chose to exact vengeance, or at least compensation, from the culprits was not in principle their business.[90] Given that the victim was their kinsman, not that of the host, they might well prefer vengeance where the host preferred to renounce it,[91] and they both could and did try moral blackmail.[92] But their success would depend on factors such as the identity of the murderers, the attitude of the host tribe to the prospect of hostilities, the sensitivity of the host to slurs on his reputation, and so forth, not on the position of the *jār* or *ḥalīf* in law.[93] Again, the fact that the blood-money payable for a *ḥalīf* or *jār* was half that of a fellow-tribesman does not mean that *ḥalīf*s and *jār*s were second-class citizens,[94] but rather that they were not citizens at all: the blood of outsiders is also much cheaper among the modern bedouin.[95] Similarly, when we are told that they could not grant protection against their host tribes, it simply means that they were not members of these tribes.[96] They might be permanent residents, but as long as they had not been incorporated *samawī*, 'by name', or in other words changed their *nisbas*, they remained members of their tribes of birth.[97]

Ḥalīfs and *jārs* were guests who had a claim to protection as strong as or even stronger than the host's own kinsmen.[98] They were not members of the tribe from which they received protection, but nor were they clients. Both enjoyed a position similar to that of women who have married outside their tribes of birth in modern Arabia,[99] and there was nothing in the least disreputable about it. They were free to marry women from the host tribe; indeed, it would appear to have been customary for them to do so, as it is today as well.[100] And some rose to positions of authority and eminence.[101] There must undoubtedly have been cases in which they found themselves in a disadvantageous position, but the institutions of *ḥilf* and *jiwār* did not in themselves assign them to one.

Some sources claim that the compact between two *ḥalīfs* established, or could establish, mutual succession between the two: whoever died first would leave a sixth of his estate to the other, the rest going to the heirs by blood.[102] This information is typically volunteered in explanation of Sura 4:37, which tells the believers to give their kinsmen and those with whom they have compacted the share to which they are entitled. As an explanation of the Qur'ānic passage, the information is pure guesswork: the passage is said now to be about wives, now about the 'brothers' of Medina, and now about *ḥalīfs*. The claim that *ḥalīfs* used to inherit from one another could also be false; after all, a statement attributed to ʿUmar II has it that there is no succession between *mawālī* by compact.[103] But the exegetes adduce a *ḥilf* formula which sounds extremely convincing;[104] ʿUmar's statement is clearly a reference to *walā' al-muwālāt* of Islamic law, not to the pre-Islamic *ḥilf* (that contractual clientage has no effect in law is the view of most schools, and ʿUmar II is elsewhere employed to make this very point);[105] and a story set in pre-Islamic Arabia shows us the agreement of mutual inheritance in action.[106] There is thus reason to accept the exegetical claim. Now classical Muslim scholars sometimes identify the contractual client of Islamic law with the pre-Islamic *ḥalīf*,[107] and modern scholars also tend to seek the origins of *walā'* in *ḥilf*.[108] But though *ḥilf* might establish a claim to succession, it does not in fact provide a prototype for the *walā'* of Islamic law.

In the first place, *ḥilf* only resembles contractual clientage, not *walā'* over freedmen, as the classical scholars were perfectly well aware.[109] The freedman was detached from his natal group, and his legal role in the group to which he was attached on manumission was passive; the *ḥalīf* by contrast remained a member of his natal group, and his legal role *vis-à-vis* his host was active.

In the second place, it is notable that whereas pre-Islamic *ḥalīfs* were commonly known as *mawālī*, the contractual clients of early Islamic society are never known as *ḥalīfs*. Clearly, even contractual *walā'* was something different from *ḥilf* in the eyes of those who had direct experience of both.

In the third place, contractual and servile *walā'* alike are characterised by a relationship between succession and blood-money different from that of *ḥilf*. In *ḥilf* the right to succession rests on an obligation to avenge or seek compensation for the blood of the ally if it is spilt, but in *walā'* it rests on an obligation to pay up if the client himself spills blood.[110] It is true that the *ḥalīf* assumed responsibility for the misdeeds of his ally too,[111] and that the *mawlā*/patron of early Islamic society occasionally felt morally obliged to avenge his client (though more commonly it was the clients, especially freedmen, who felt morally obliged to avenge their patrons).[112] But the assymetry is nonetheless significant. What matters to a tribesman is that his blood should not be 'wasted' (*hadar*), that is neither paid for nor avenged; and it was by way of insurance against this possibility that pre-Islamic tribesmen were willing to assign a sixth of their estates to others. But what matters to bureaucrats is that the consequences of misdeeds should be settled in accordance with the rules, not that the honour of tribesmen should be vindicated. The peculiar concatenation of a title to succession in return for responsibility for *misdeeds* is in other words likely to be of post-conquest origin. It is not attested for pre-Islamic Arabia, nor would one expect it to be.

Finally, it should be added that the lawyers never assign a fixed share of the client's estate to the patron, still less one deducted before the division of the estate among the heirs by blood. Even in pre-classical law the size of the patron's share (if any) depends on the nature of the heirs with whom he is in competition.

It is thus clear that the Arab conquerors did not simply assign the status of *ḥalīf* to the non-Arab converts and other hangers-on with whom they were confronted on the conquests. Nor is this surprising. *Ḥilf* in the sense of tribal compact was a mechanism for use *within* the tribal commonwealth, and to this commonwealth the non-Arab subjects manifestly did not belong. The non-Arab subjects of the Muslims were defeated enemies who had forgotten their genealogies,[113] and who spinelessly put up with the slavery[114] to which they were popularly seen as having been reduced by virtue of their defeat.[115] The idea that the Arabs offered their tribal *ḥilf* to men equally devoid of ancestors, autonomy and honour alike is an implausible one; and in fact the only non-Arabs to be incorporated as *ḥalīf*s were the Ḥamrā' and Asāwira, the Persian troops who deserted to the Arabs at an early stage in the course of the conquests, dictating their own spectacular terms.[116] These troops were not tribesmen, let alone Arab ones; but they were soldiers whom the Arabs could respect and whose military strength they preferred to have on their side rather than that of the Persians. Had the general run of converts been similarly able to lay down their own terms, the Muslim community might have come to consist of Arabs and *ḥalīf*s, as opposed to Arabs and *mawālī*. But where the *Asāwira* were received as a subtribe of Tamīm, complete with their own *nisba* and a say in tribal politics,[117] the vast majority of renegades were distributed among the conquerors as private dependents. This does not exclude the possibility that the mutual succession between *ḥalīfs* may somehow have been relevant to the formation of Islamic *walā'*, and I shall return to this possibility in due course.[118] But it should be clear that the contribution of *ḥilf* to the Islamic institution cannot have been very substantial or very direct.

We may now conclude this section by considering the *mawālī* of poetry.[119] They belong overwhelmingly to this section, that is to say most of them are kinsmen, *ḥalīf*s, *jār*s and other allies and friends.[120] Sometimes it is explicit that kinsmen are involved,[121] and at other times the scholiasts point out that kinsmen and/or allies and friends of various kinds are intended;[122] but even without the verdicts of the scholiasts it is clear that whoever the poets may have in mind, it is rarely someone who could be identified as a client, or for that matter a patron.[123] *Mawālī* are almost always mentioned in connection with the theme of mutual help,[124] frequently military,[125] but sometimes also material or moral.[126] The poets flatter themselves and others on having helped their *mawālī*,[127] exhort others to do the same,[128] pour abuse on those who do not,[129] complain of *mawālī* who have failed to come to their assistance,[130] or lament their absence or their loss.[131] The underlying idea is Ṭarafa's 'learn something which is not [mere] conjecture: when a man's *mawlā* is humiliated, he himself becomes weak'.[132] When *mawālī* are being abused, it is usually for being bad *mawālī* rather than for being *mawālī*;[133] even when a distinction is made between *mawālī'l-wilāda* and *mawālī'l-yamīn*, 'kinsmen by birth' and 'kinsmen by oath', it is not normally to suggest the inferiority of the latter.[134] In general, then, the *mawālī* of early poetry are not dependents.

There are striking exceptions, it is true. Yet even when *mawālī* are inferior persons, they are commonly tribesmen. Thus when Quṭāmī boasts that 'we are the reins that lead . . . everyone else is a *mawlā* and follower who allies himself (*al-mawlā al-tabī' al-muḥālif*)' he has in mind tribal groups which have been so decimated, dispersed or otherwise enfeebled that they have to attach themselves to others to survive.[135] Such groups were mere 'followers', 'tails' or 'fins',[136] mere *jār*s in the sense of political underlings, mere *mawālī* in the sense of satellite groups, indeed mere slaves in the language of abusive poetry. It is also to such groups that Nābigha al-Ja'dī refers in his famous complaint that the disunity of his people is such that they will become '*mawālī* by *ḥilf*, not *mawālī* by kinship, but rather servants who collect taxes [on behalf of their allies]'.[137] Though they had sunk to the very bottom of the tribal commonwealth, such groups can rarely be said to have been entirely excluded from it: the Bajīla had been utterly dispersed, but they had not lost their tribal status.[138] In the vast majority of cases, the *mawālī* of Arabic poetry composed before the conquests, or after the conquests in the traditional vein, are thus irrelevant to our concerns. It could of course be argued that freedmen and other non-tribesmen are included along with kinsmen and other allies in the passages concerned. If so, we would have to conclude that freedmen and other non-tribesmen were accepted as tribal peers in pre-Islamic Arabia, and this is what Tyan did conclude.[139] But this makes nonsense of our evidence. If the Arabs distinguished sharply between tribesmen and others, composed endless satires on the theme of servile descent, prided themselves on being *banū'l-ḥarā'ir*, 'sons of free women', and displayed massive contempt for freedmen even after the conquests when their religion told them not to do so, they are not very likely to have accepted freedmen and other non-tribesmen as peers within the tribal commonwealth before the conquests took place.[140] We must conclude that the bulk of references to *mawālī* in pre-Islamic and early Islamic poetry are not references to clients at all.

(ii) Relations between tribesmen and non-tribesmen

The material relating to *mawālī* in the sense of clients recruited outside the tribal commonwealth is scant in terms of both poetry and prose. As far as clients other than freedmen are concerned, however, it clearly shows that their relationship with the tribal world was one of collective dependence. The information on freedmen suggests the same, but it is less conclusive.[141]

We may start with the Jews. The Jews of northern Arabia were mostly oasis-dwellers who engaged in agriculture and craftmanship. All formed tribal groups of their own, but few were able to claim tribal autonomy. A Kalbī chief demanded 'wages' (*jaʿāla*, sc. for the service of protection) from the Jews of Fadak and duly raided them when they withheld payment.[142] Similarly the Arab tribes of Wādī'l-Qurā 'had a right to an annual tax (*ṭuʿma*) and food supplies from the Jews; they protected it (sc. Wādī'l-Qur) against the Arabs for them and warded off the tribes of Quḍāʿa from them'.[143] In both cases the Jews had thus been forced to pay the protection money which is nowadays known as *khuwwa*, and which the oasis-dwellers of northern Arabia have rarely been able to escape.[144] In both cases they became *mawālī* in the sense of political underlings, but their internal organisation was not affected by their dependent status at all.

The Jews of Yathrib, on the other hand, fell victims to enemies from within rather than outside their oasis. Reputedly lords and masters of both Yathrib and its Arab immigrants at first, they were defeated by the Arab tribes some time before the rise of Islam and reduced to client status. This did undermine their internal organisation. On their defeat, we are told, 'the Jews were weakened and lost their capacity to defend themselves; they were very afraid. So whenever a member of the Aws and the Khazraj provoked them by [doing] something which they disliked, they would no longer go to one another as they had done in the past; rather, [every] Jew would go to the protectors among whom he lived (*jīrānihi alladhīna huwa bayna aẓhurihim*) and say, "we are your protégés and clients (*jīrānukum wa-mawālīkum*)"; for every Jewish family (*qawm*) had sought refuge with a clan (*baṭn*) of the Aws or the Khazraj, seeking strength from them'.[145] Defeat thus destroyed the tribal cohesion of the Jews who, unable to take joint action against the victors, were forced to seek protection from them; and apparently it reduced them to tenants too.[146] But though they lost both their political autonomy and their land, they retained their own kinship organisation. They received their protection without being incorporated into the tribes of their protectors; and they received it as groups from groups, not as individuals from individuals.

In Yathrib we see tribesmen being reduced to clients, but in Hajar we see the reverse. Sixth-century Bahrayn was under Sasanid rule, and Hajar, its capital, was built by Persians. When the Persian emperor was informed that the workmen were unlikely to stay without women, he sent them a ship-load of prostitutes from the Sawād and Ahwāz together with a liberal supply of wine from Fars to keep them happy:

> so they intermarried and multiplied, and they constituted the majority of the population of the city of Hajar. The community spoke Arabic, and they called themselves after [the tribe of] ʿAbd al-Qays (*kānat daʿwatuhum ilā ʿAbd al-Qays*). When Islam came, they said to ʿAbd al-Qays, 'you know how many we are and how well equipped and rich we are, so incorporate us among you (*fa-adkhilūnā fīkum*) and intermarry with us'. They said, 'no, stay as you are; you are our brothers and *mawālī*'. But one ʿAbdī said, 'people of ʿAbd al-Qays, do as I say and accept them; you can't not want people like that'. Another man of the tribe said, 'have you no shame? Are you telling us that we should incorporate a people of whose origin and ancestry you are perfectly well aware?'. He said, 'if we don't, other Arabs will'. But he replied, 'in that case we don't need to feel sorry for them'. The upshot was that the community dispersed among the Arabs. Some remained with ʿAbd al-Qays and traced their ancestry to them; they did not try to stop them.[147]

Here then we have another group of non-Arab *mawālī* who stood in a relationship of collective dependence on an Arab tribe in pre-Islamic times. The fact that they were Persians of a somewhat disreputable origin was well known, for all that they spoke Arabic; and they were not members of ʿAbd al-Qays, for all that they called themselves ʿAbdīs: it was only on the rise of Islam that they applied for incorporation in ʿAbd al-Qays with all this implied in the way of intermarriage. To the extent that they called themselves ʿAbdīs without being members of the tribe, they were *daʿīs* in the sense of spurious kinsmen;[148] but since everyone knew them to be 'brothers and *mawālī*' (cf. Qur'ān, 33:5), they were not deceiving anyone. The passage well illustrates how difficult it was for tribesmen to accord tribal status to non-tribesmen. The Persian community was large, rich, desirable in every respect except for its ancestry, wanted by other Arabs now that military strength was called for, and it had long been associated with ʿAbd al-Qays. Yet the ʿAbdīs could not bring themselves to incorporate them *en bloc*. The Hajarīs acquired their tribal status at the cost of dispersing. It could be noted, though, that just as their clientage had been collective, so was their assimilation: it was clearly different *groups* which dispersed among the Arabs, just as it was a group which remained with ʿAbd al-Qays.

On the position of craftsmen and other occupational groups we are less well informed. As has been seen, some were Jews and others slaves and freedmen; but the position of those who were neither is unknown. That then leaves us with the freedmen.

We may begin by noting that the relationship between slaves and free in pre-Islamic Arabia differed from that of modern Arabia in two conspicuous respects. First, the pre-Islamic Arabs systematically took prisoners-of-war from among both the male and the female population of enemy tribes, partly to hold them to ransom and partly to enslave them.[149] Though non-Arab slaves presumably outnumbered Arab ones, it was thus a distinctive feature of pre-Islamic Arabia that part of its servile population was recruited from within the tribal commonwealth itself.[150] Secondly, the pre-Islamic Arabs, including the bedouin, cohabited with their slavegirls regardless of their colour. The children of such unions were slaves, but they could be freed and legitimated by their fathers.[151] It was thus also a distinctive feature of pre-Islamic Arabia that many members of the tribal commonwealth could be seen to have servile blood in their veins.[152] The dividing line between the tribal and the servile worlds, in short, was less neat than it is in modern Arabia, and relations between tribesmen and slaves were less relaxed as a result. There are no modern parallels to the endless imputations of servile descent to antagonists characteristic of pre-Islamic or early Islamic poetry,[153] or to the theme of slaves getting out of place.[154] What this means is, regrettably, that the modern evidence is at its least helpful where it matters most.

What happened to the slave on manumission? There is no doubt that a legal relationship *could* be formed between him and the manumitter by special agreement. Such agreements will be discussed in the next chapter. Here it suffices to say that they were in the nature of labour contracts, not contracts of clientage, and that they did not affect the freedman's affiliation unless they amounted (as was sometimes the case) to full adoption. They thus fail to answer the question of the freedman's status in tribal society.

We need not dispute that the freedman was known as his manumitter's *mawlā*; the question is what the label implied. As might be expected, the sources occasionally give us to understand that it implied very much the same in pre-Islamic Arabia as in Islamic law. But the passages in question are all legal traditions reflecting the doctrines of Muslim scholars, not the practises of pre-Islamic tribesmen, as is clear partly from the use to which Muslim scholars put them, and partly from the fact that they involve authoritative figures such as ʿUmar and the Prophet.[155] There is thus no question of accepting them as evidence on pre-Islamic conditions.

We may start by considering the significance of the expression *al-ṣamīm* (or *al-ṣarīḥ*) *wa'l-mawālī*. The *ṣamīm* are those who constitute the prime or principal part of a tribe, the *ṣarīḥ* being 'the pure'; the *ṣamīm* and the *ṣarīḥ* are thus its fully accredited members. They are the opposite of its *shiqq*, 'side', or its *shaẓā*, 'dispersed and scattered elements';[156] most commonly, they are the opposite of its *mawālī*. The expression *al-ṣamīm* (or *ṣarīḥ*) *wa'l-mawālī* is used to mean 'everybody' within a certain tribe, or 'all its fighting men', in a fashion suggesting that *ṣamīm* and were regarded as its members, as for example in the phrase 'Madhḥij . . . all their *mawālī* and *ṣamīm*'.[157] To most Islamicists it probably conjures up a distinction between citizens and second-class citizens, and this is what I wish to dispute: what the expression does refer to is a tribe and its resident protégés, be they Arabs or non-Arabs.

We may begin by noting that the 'scattered elements' or *mawālī* who are distinguished from the *ṣamīm*/*ṣarīḥ* included Arab *ḥalīf*s and *jār*s. Thus a poet informs us that everybody from a certain tribe fled on a certain occasion, *ḥilfuha wa-ṣamīmuha*.[158] Similarly, we are told that a *ḥalīf* could not grant protection against the *ṣarīḥ*, that is the members of the host tribe.[159] Of a Yathribī we are told that he was awarded the blood-money of a *ṣarīḥ* for a man variously described as his *ḥalīf*, *jār* and *mawlā*, although the blood-money for a *mawlā* was half that of a *ṣarīḥ* in law.[160] When a poet boasts that has redeemed a captive with the camels owed for a member of the *ṣamīm*, not for a *mawlā*, he is thus referring to the lower tariff applicable to *ḥalīf*s, though not necessarily to that for *ḥalīfs* alone: as will be seen, the same tariff applied to freedmen too.[161] Now it is plain that the *ḥalīf*s who are contrasted with the *ṣamīm*/*ṣarīḥ* are confederates who actually lived and fought with the confederated tribe, not allies in general. Given that such confederates could be perfectly respectable, it is not surprising that a poet could congratulate his tribe on its 'wealth of *mawālī* and *ṣamīm*'.[162] But given that such confederates could also be mere 'followers', 'tails', 'fins', 'underlings' or simply 'slaves', it is also understandable that Nābigha al-Dhubyānī could exclaim in relief, 'may it give joy to Banū Dhubyān that their land is free of every *mawlā* and *tābi*ʿ'.[163] So far, then, the *ṣamīm* and *mawālī* are Arab tribes and their Arab satellites.

But the 'scattered elements' and *mawālī* also included slaves and freedmen, as most scholars would probably agree.[164] One passage explicitly enumerates slaves among the 'followers' who are distinguished from the *ṣamīm*.[165] That freedmen also belonged there follows from a number of passages. When Ḥassān b. Thābit tells a certain Hāshimite that he is not free, not noble, not a descendant of the ancestors of Quraysh and not a member of the *ṣamīm* of Banu Hāshim, but on the contrary a *hajīn*, i.e. the offspring of a slavegirl by a free man, he is saying that descendants of slavegirls are excluded from the *ṣamīm* on a par with slaves and, by implication, anyone else of servile origin.[166] Elsewhere too the son of a black slavegirl and a free man (himself allegedly the descendant of a slavegirl) is branded as a mere 'follower' as opposed to a member of the *ṣamīm*.[167] When a pre-Islamic hero accused another of planning to expel him and his tribe and thereby to 'make us *mawālī* among the Arabs', he similarly thought of *mawālī* as non-Arabs of dependent status.[168] And when a later Muslim author speaks of *Bāhila, ʿurbuhā wa-mawālīhā*, he is presumably thinking in terms of an ancient distinction between *ṣamīm* and non-Arab clients.[169] Though none of these passages explicitly mentions freedmen, the poetic lampoons only make sense against a background in which anyone of servile and/or non-Arab origin is excluded from the ranks of the *ṣamīm*: the poets are claiming that the legitimated offspring of slavegirls ought not to be an exception. When Nābigha al-Dhubyānī congratulated his tribe on the absence of *mawālī* and followers from its lands, he may thus have had slaves and freedmen no less than Arab satellite groups in mind.

The significance of this point lies in its implication that freedmen were not incorporated in their manumitter's kin. Arab *ḥalīf*s and *jār*s were fully accredited tribesmen and thus eligible for incorporation into the *ṣamīm*; but as has been seen, the vast majority remained members of their tribes of birth. They thus remained *mawālī* in the sense of metaphorical kinsmen, that is protected persons in a tribe to which they did not belong by either birth *or* fictitious kinship ties, and it is as such that they are distinguished from the *ṣamīm*. Given that freedmen are similarly distinguished from the *ṣamīm*, they must have been *mawālī* in the same sense. This inference is confirmed by the fact that people of servile origin are commonly branded as *daʿī*s. Unlike the *ḥalīf*, the freedman did not usually have a native tribe of his own. Where the *ḥalīf* advertised his tribal status by his *nisba*, the freedman thus had the choice between going without *nisba*, thereby advertising his excluded status, or alternatively adopting that of his protectors, thereby becoming a *daʿīs* in the abusive sense of person who claims membership of a tribe to which he does not belong.[170] When poetic lampoons impute servile and/or non-Arab origin to others, they commonly describe the victims as *daʿī*s too;[171] the Hāshimite who was a mere *hajīn* in the opinion of Ḥassān b. Thābit was duly told that he was a *daʿī* for his attempt to pass himself off as a member of the *ṣamīm* of Hāshim.[172] It is thus clear that people of servile and non-Arab origin had no right to present themselves as members of the tribes which protected them, though they were liable to do so nonetheless on a par with the Persians of Hajar. In short, the only formal members of a tribe were its *ṣamīm* (those who had been born or adopted into it); all 'scattered elements' were *mawālī* in the sense of protégés regardless of whether they were Arabs or non-Arabs, slaves or freedmen, individuals or groups, permanent or temporary residents, respectable persons or otherwise.

Having established this point, we may proceed to an examination of the precise manner in which the freedman's status was regulated; the fact that slaves, freedmen, *ḥalīf*s, *jār*s and other foreign residents were all protégés does not of course mean that all enjoyed the same legal position. The two questions of interest to us are, first, who was responsible for the freedman's blood and blood spilt by him? And secondly, who had a claim to his estate?

Given that the freedman was a protected person, responsibility for his blood rested with the entire tribe if he was killed by a member of another. In principle he was presumably exempt from the feuds of his hosts, partly because he was an outsider and partly because his blood was too cheap to compensate for that of tribesmen; but in practice he was clearly at risk. 'We killed nine for Abū Lubayna, and we joined the *mawālī* to the *ṣamīm*', or in other words we killed *mawālī* too, as Labīd boasts.[173] Whether the *mawālī* were freedmen or others is impossible to tell, but then Labīd's people scarcely tried to distinguish themselves: they killed protected people in order to demonstrate the weakness of the protectors, just as others would slit the noses of the enemy's slaves in order to taunt them with inability to keep even their slaves' noses safe.[174] It follows that the protectors might well set out to avenge the freedman, but it would of course be their own honour, not that of the freedman, that they would try to vindicate. In other circumstances responsibility for the freedman's blood presumably rested with such agnates as he might have, as a story relating to the time of ʿUthmān suggests,[175] not with the manumitter. Manumitters only avenged their freedmen by way of insult to their victims, as incidents after the conquests show, the insult lying in the equation of the victim's blood with that of a slave;[176] and though post-conquest manumitters were as happy to claim blood-money for a freedman as were those of Burckhardt's Arabia,[177] there is every reason to believe that the blood of a freedman who had no agnates might simply be written off. That is certainly what a line attributed to ʿAntara suggests.[178] (As regards the value of the freedman's blood, if claimed, it was an established principle that no member of the *ṣarīḥ* could be killed in retaliation for him, a rule which may have applied to Arab protégés too.[179] If blood-money was paid, the sum owed was half that for a *ṣarīḥ*, a rule which certainly did apply to Arab protégés as well.)[180]

If the freedman himself killed or injured a tribesman, the basic principle was that compensation for the blood of a tribesman was the blood of another tribesman of equal standing: that of a *mawlā* was too cheap even if he was an Arab. Thus when a *mawlā* bit the nose of a member of the *ṣamīm*, Farazdaq found it highly meritorious that the victim and his kin 'did not want to exact vengeance from the *mawālī*; they exacted vengeance for a *ṣarīḥ* from a *ṣarīḥ*', for all that the *mawlā* in this case was an Arab tribesman.[181] It might thus be reasonable to conjecture that responsibility for the misdeeds of the freedman rested with the manumitter, but in fact the evidence suggests otherwise. Thus the avengers of the man whose nose had been bitten by a *mawlā* did not inflict retaliation upon the *mawlā*/host, but on the contrary on the natal group of the *mawlā*/guest. Given that freedmen rarely had natal groups which counted as *ṣarīḥ*, injuries inflicted by freedmen could not be similarly avenged, but even so there is no suggestion that retaliation should be inflicted upon the manumitter instead: the avengers of a tribesman killed by a *hajīn* freed reacted by killing the *hajīn* himself.[182] Nor is there any suggestion that it was the manumitter who ought to play blood-money for injuries inflicted by the freedman; on the contrary, after the conquests Ḥasan al-Baṣrī ruled that 'Arabs do not pay blood-money on behalf of *mawālī*', though this is precisely what Arab patrons were now required to do.[183] Just as it was the freedman's own agnates who were responsible for his blood unless the honour of the protecting tribe was involved, so also it was they who were responsible for his misdeeds, it would seem, no doubt with the same qualification.[184]

We are thus left with the question of who had a claim to the freedman's estate. The answer is presumably his agnates (or other relatives, in so far as other relatives had rights of succession), not the manumitter. There is no direct evidence on this point, but it is hard to see on what ground the manumitter could have made such a claim. There were no kinship ties between the two, be they real or fictitious (and the right to succession would have been reciprocal if there had been); nor was there an agreement of the type concluded by *ḥalīf*s between them. The manumitter could of course claim payment for the unilateral service of manumission and protection, and no doubt he did; but if it had been on this ground that he claimed a title to the freedman's estate, he would presumably have claimed a fixed share, not a right to succeed in the absence of certain heirs. As for the possibility that he took the estates of freedmen who died without heirs on the ground that he used to own both the freedmen and their goods, this presupposes both that slaves in pre-Islamic Arabia were devoid of proprietary rights, which is not certain,[185] and that manumitters retained ultimate ownership of the property of their freedmen, which is extremely unlikely.[186] There is every reason to assume that manumitters would take the estates of freedmen who died without heirs in their service; but this is simply to say that the estates of freedmen (and presumably anyone else) who died without heirs were open to seizure by whoever could first lay their hands on them, a principle endorsed in Jewish law.[187] In short, there is no reason to assume that the manumitter acquired a right to succession by virtue of the manumission itself.

To summarise now, freedmen could be made to serve their manumitters for a specified period, but they were not detached from their natal kin (in so far as they had any in Arabia), nor were they incorporated into those of their manumitters. Freedmen became protegés of the tribe on a par with resident aliens of Arab origin, or rather they remained such protegés, given that this is what they had been as slaves as well. No evidence suggests that manumitters acquired a right to succession, and there is positive evidence to suggest that they did not pay blood-money on their freedmen's behalf. In short, all or most legal relations between manumitter and freedmen would appear to have been severed, in so far as no stipulations of service had been made, the freedman being placed under the direct protection of the tribe and its chief. The dependant status of the freedmen may thus be described as collective. On the kinship organisation of slaves and freedmen there is admittedly little or no evidence, possibly because the evidence in general is scant, but possibly also because the servile population of Arabia was more fragmented then than in later times: fewer slaves would seem to have been homeborn then than in Musil's time; and both slaves and freedmen were more rather than less in the nature of pariahs in those days, the dividing line between the free and the servile worlds being more difficult to maintain. But the fact that the kin groups of slaves and freedmen may have been highly fragmented does not mean that their dependent status should be described as other than collective.

Collective clientage was certainly typical of relations between the tribal and the non-tribal worlds in general.[188] Then as now Arabia was characterised by a profusion of ties of dependence *between* groups, not within them, the purpose of the ties in question being to separate people of different origin and occupation, not to assimilate them. When assimilation did take place, it was accordingly achieved collectively too. Leaving aside the Persians of Hajar, who openly applied for tribal status, numerous servile groups engaged in the same occupation as their protectors would appear to have acquired such status by the mere passing of time. Thus we are told that the entire tribe of Sulaym was black.[189] Though Jāḥiẓ attributes their colour to the influence of the *ḥarra*, others might explain it with reference to the influence of African slavegirls, but it could also be the case that the Sulamīs originated as a servile group; and other tribes (or subtribes) described as black might similarly be *ʿabīd* who had gained autonomy.[190] When Farazdaq lampoons a Yemeni clan as vile slaves *inherited* by another clan, he surely has in mind freedmen who have ceased to reside with the tribe which manumitted them, but who still acknowledge its political authority, having done so for generations.[191] It is obvious that such freedmen might well gain recognition as an autonomous clan or tribe of their own in due course; and when whole tribes are taunted with being slaves by origin, the taunt presumably derives its sting from the fact that some tribes *did* have such an origin, however untrue the accusation might be in respect of those against whom it was directed.[192] By the tenth century Hamdānī soberly informs us that a certain south Arabian tribe or subtribe (of pre-Islamic origin) consisted of freedmen.[193] That the lines of exclusion and assimilation alike were collective in pre-Islamic Arabia is also what one would have guessed on the basis of the social (as opposed to legal) relationship between Arabs and non-Arabs after the conquests. It will be admitted that there is little in the evidence to suggest that the legal institution of *walāʾ* came out of pre-Islamic Arabia too.

CHAPTER 5

The case against the non-Roman Near East: *paramonē*

If the personal clientage of Islamic law did not come from Arabia, where could it have come from? A tie of this kind, i.e. one which arose automatically on manumission, attached the freedman to the manumitter's kin and granted the latter a title to the freedman's estate, was unknown to Akkadian law,[1] ancient Egypt,[2] Jewish law,[3] and, in so far as one can tell, also Sasanid Iran;[4] and though it was probably once a feature of Greek law, this had long ceased to be the case.[5] If the Islamic patronate did not come from Arabia, the only alternative source is Rome.

It is the purpose of this chapter to restate this point in more positive terms. The argument which I shall present is in essence the following. Throughout the Near East, both Roman and non-Roman, relations between manumitter and freedman were shaped overwhelmingly by the so-called *paramonē*. This institution also plays a major role in Islamic law where, as we shall see, it has been accepted in the modified form of *kitāba*, and its continuance demonstrates that Arab manumitters did indeed pay attention to the legal practices of their non-Arab subjects. It is undeniable and significant that the influence of the provincial institution on Islamic law is considerably easier to demonstrate than that of its Roman counterpart. But the absence of a patronate of the Roman or Islamic type from pre-Islamic Arabia on the one hand, and the prominence of *paramonē* throughout the Near East on the other, suggest that if the Arab conquests had not included Roman provinces, there would not have been an Islamic patronate of the type we know.

(a) *Paramonē* in the classical world

The institution of *paramonē* has its origin in the ancient Near Eastern practice of using adoption to provide for old age. When an adoption was effected with this end in view, the adoption contract would oblige the adopted son or daughter to maintain his or her adoptive parents for the duration of the latter's lives in return for a share in their estate.[6] If the adopted person was a slave, as was frequently the case, the adoption would be accompanied by a manumission qualified by the obligation to provide for the manumitter during the latter's lifetime, the usual reward in this case being full freedom on the manumitter's death rather than a share in the latter's estate.[7] Either way, the adopted person was obliged to serve under penalty of (re-)enslavement.[8]

Though the adoption clause was in due course to be omitted from the contract,[9] this institution was to enjoy a remarkable lifespan. First attested in Babylonia in the second millenium B.C., it was still there at the time of transition to Achaemenid rule.[10] Under the Achaemenids it appears in Egypt, where it is attested for the Jewish colony at Elephantine;[11] and in the fourth century B.C. it also appears in Greece, where it came to be known as *paramonē*, 'remaining by'.[12] Having gone into Greek law, it became a standard institution in the Greco-Roman Near East. Paramonar contracts with free persons are attested for Egypt in Greek papyri ranging from the third century B.C. to the seventh century A.D., as well as in Coptic papyri from the seventh and/or eighth century A.D.[13] They are also attested in the much sparser records of the Fertile Crescent, first in a Greek parchment from Dura Europos drawn up in 121 A.D.,[14] and next in a bilingual Greek and Arabic papyrus from Nessana drawn up in 687.[15] Paramonar manumissions are likewise attested for Egypt in the papyri, though considerably less amply; the examples range from the third century B.C. to 551 A.D.[16] Prior to the grant of universal citizenship in 212 A.D., the Romans acknowledged the validity of such manumussions in peregrine law, that is the law of non-Roman subjects.[17] After the universalisation of Roman law, they fought a losing battle against them,[18] and it is possible that they accepted them as Roman law in the end.[19] Manumission with *paramonē* is also attested for Nestorian Iraq.[20]

Shorn of its adoption clause, the institution had developed into a labour contract with a free party on the one hand, and a conditional manumission of the resolutive type on the other. (A conditional manumission of the resolutive type is one in which the slave is freed now on condition that he does certain things after his manumission; in a conditional manumission of the suspensive or deferred type, by contrast, he is only freed when the condition has been fulfilled.) For the free paramonar the reward of the contract lay in the advancement to him of a loan;[21] for the slave its reward was instant manumission. Either way, the diagnostic feature of the institution was the obligation of the paramonar servant to remain with the other party for the duration of the contract. Originally, this obligation was meant quite literally. The female slaves who were manumitted at Elephantine and who had to support their manumitter and the latter's son 'as a son (or daughter) supports his (or her) father' were presumably received into the manumitter's household;[22] so also were many Greek slaves;[23] and household work is frequently mentioned among the duties of the free paramonar in Egyptian contracts.[24] By Hellenistic and still more Roman times, however, the force of the expression was rather that the paramonar was obliged to do what he was told, including of course being present when required: to 'remain by' meant simply to serve.[25] But though the term had lost its original force, the obligation to remain was frequently real enough: even in Byzantine times the paramonar servant was sometimes obliged literally to remain with the other party.[26] The duration of the paramonar servant's obligations varied. The free paramonar servant might indenture himself for an unspecified period, that is until he could repay the loan; but he might also do so for limited number of years.[27] The paramonar freedman was often obliged to serve the manumitter, or another party designated by the manumitter, until the latter's death; but his period of service might also be defined in terms of a limited number of years, usually between one and ten.[28] Days lost commonly had to be paid for.[29] The manumitter might, and sometimes did, renounce his rights before expiry of the period in question,[30] and the paramonar freedman could also release himself by payment and/or by placing substitutes.[31] Failing this, he obtained full freedom on the expiry of the specified period. Whether the paramonar servant was free or freed, the dissolution of his relationship with the other party, known as *apolysis*, enabled him to 'do what he liked and go where he wished'.[32]

The legal status of the freedman manumitted with *paramonē* is a moot point. In some sense the freedom granted was undoubtedly real.[33] The freedman usually became *suis iuris* as regards his own property; he could not be sold during his period of *paramonē*, though his services could be hired out.[34] The improvement of his status is sometimes underlined by the use, in paramonar manumissions, of language normally reserved for the acquisition of full freedom.[35] Yet the manumitter retained a right to the freedman's labour, and also a right to inflict corporal punishment on him, though the beating was not supposed to be excessive.[36] The freedman's obligation to work, moreover, was undefined, the contract merely stipulating that he had to do what he was told, or the like.[37] The same is true of many contracts with free persons, and the paramonar services of free men are occasionally described as servile;[38] indeed, free persons could practically enslave themselves by means of such contracts.[39] Moreover, in addition to the *paramonē* proper, Greek manumitters could and very often did impose other conditions which ate away much of the freedom granted (and which they would appear to have invented themselves rather than inherited from the Near East). Thus the freedman might be forbidden to alienate his property, to have children or to adopt, while the manumitter installed himself or his children as heirs.[40] (Note that though such stipulations presumably originate with the right once enjoyed by Greek manumitters to the estates of freedmen who died without heirs, the title to succession is expressly stipulated, not taken for granted.) Children born under *paramonē* might be claimed as slaves,[41] and freedwomen were commonly obliged to provide one or two slave children, presumably their own.[42] Paramonar freedmen might be required to furnish their manumitters with loans,[43] or to pay them alimony, sometimes for life.[44] And as in the ancient Near East, the manumitter could stipulate that the penalty for non-fulfilment of the contract was re-enslavement.[45]

Manumission with *paramonē* has been interpreted by Samuel as a grant of full freedom subsequently circumscribed,[46] and by Koschaker as a partial manumission in which the manumitter retained such rights as he saw fit.[47] Whichever opinion one prefers, the actual position of paramonar freedmen was clearly not uniform. No doubt there were freedmen who, having become 'masters of their bodies and things',[48] could be regarded as free men merely working off a debt, but there were certainly others who were little more than slaves. A man who is obliged to stay and work for his master under penalty of re-enslavement, without the right to raise a family, or even to sell and give away his property,[49] cannot be described as free in any real sense of the word; and it is for this reason that Koschaker refused to accept paramonar manumission as a resolutive one: as he saw it, it was a grant of half-freedom.[50] The institution was an exceedingly flexible one which allowed the manumitter to define the freedman's rights with a liberty quite unknown to Roman law.[51] That, presumably, is why it was so popular.

(b) *Paramonē* in pre-Islamic Arabia

If we return now to pre-Islamic Arabia, we find that our scanty evidence on freedmen in the Ḥijāz amounts to an account of *paramonē* in its most archaic form of manumission with adoption and/or reception into the manumitter's household. The relevant information is the following.

Zayd b. Ḥāritha was an Arab who had been enslaved in an intertribal raid; he was bought by Khadīja, who subsequently gave him to the Prophet; the Prophet manumitted him by adopting him.[52] Sālim b. Maʿqil, supposedly a Persian, was the slave of an Anṣārī woman; she manumitted him without stipulations of further service (*sāʾibatan*, cf. below), but her husband adopted him.[53] Of several other slaves we are likewise told that they were adopted by their masters.[54] Ṣuhayb b. Sinān was an Arab from Mesopotamia who had been enslaved by the Byzantines and who was subsequently bought and freed by a Meccan, Ibn Judʿān; he was not adopted by Ibn Judʿān, but he stayed with his manumitter until the latter died (*aqāma maʿahu bi-Makka ilā an halaka ʿAbdallāh b. Judʿān*).[55] Ṣuhayb was thus a paramonar freedman manumitted on condition of service for the duration of the manumitter's life; this clearly suggests that the slaves who were adopted were paramonar freedmen too.

According to Ṣuhayb's descendants, however, Ṣuhayb was a free man when he arrived in Mecca, having fled from his Byzantine masters; he made a *ḥilf* with Ibn Judʿān and stayed with him until he died (*fa-ḥālafa ʿAbdallāh b. Judʿān wa-aqāma maʿahu ilā an halaka*).[56] He was thus a free party to a paramonar labour contract: the *ḥilf* was plainly an agreement to 'remain', or in other words to serve, not a tribal alliance. A Yemeni by the name of Yāsir made a *ḥilf* of the same kind with Abū Ḥudhayfa, another Meccan. Being an indentured servant, not a tribal ally, he was given a slavegirl for wife, not a Qurashī woman, with the result that his son ʿAmmār was born a slave; Abū Ḥudhayfa manumitted ʿAmmār, and both ʿAmmār and his father stayed with Abū Ḥudhayfa until he died (*wa-lam yazal Yāsir wa-ʿAmmār maʿa Abī Ḥudhayfa ilā an māta*).[57] The Meccans were thus familiar with paramonar manumissions and labour contracts alike.

That the pre-Islamic Arabs were familiar with paramonar manumission is also suggested by the practice of *tasyīb*, declaring a slave to be *sāʾiba*. In Islamic law *tasyīb* of slaves is to free them without *walāʾ*, or in other words to exempt oneself from responsibility for their blood-money and, above all, to renounce one's right to their estates.[58] In pre-Islamic Arabia, however, *tasyīb* of animals was to set them free to wander where they wished, exempting them from further service,[59] and *tasyīb* of slaves must surely once have been the same. The Muslim manumitter who pronounced his slave *sāʾiba* would in fact tell him to 'go where he wanted' or 'put himself where he wished'.[60] Declaring a slave to be *sāʾiba* must thus have been the opposite of freeing with on condition that he 'remain', that is to say it must have been an unconditional grant of freedom as opposed to a paramonar one. Being *sāʾiba* meant being free of obligations such as those of the freedman found in the service of his Anṣārī manumitter at the time of the conquest of Mecca (*kāna yakhdimuhu*), charged with the task of preparing his meals and the like.[61]

It would thus seem difficult to deny that the pre-Islamic Arabs were familiar with the institution of *paramonē*, and it may have been known not only to the settled Arabs, but also to the bedouin: the bedouin of the early Umayyad period who freed a slavegirl on condition that she remain with him (*ʿalā an takūna maʿahu*) was presumably practising the traditional law of his tribe.[62] But it should be stressed that what they knew was the institution in its ancient Near Eastern form (manumission with adoption being particularly archaic), not more sophisticated versions current in the Greco-Roman Near East. This is a point of some importance in that the more sophisticated versions are well attested in early Islamic law. The evidence relating to paramonar manumission thus confirms that the conquerors were influenced by the legal practices of their subjects.

(c) *Paramonē* in Islam: resolutive conditions

Contrary to what one might have expected, there is no reference in early Ḥadīth to the adoption of slaves, nor do we hear of free persons being adopted and/or admitted to the household with an obligation to serve. Even straightforward service for the lifetime of the manumitter, or that of a person designated by him, is surprisingly poorly attested.[63] What we do find in early Ḥadīth are all the most up-to-date methods whereby manumitters could renounce responsibility for their slaves without renouncing income.

The transmitters list these methods partly in sections on condition manumission and partly in sections on *kitāba*, a great many being listed in both. *Kitāba* is a manumission conditional upon payment of a specified sum (or service) in regular instalments over a specified period, and the condition is generally regarded as suspensive in classical law: the manumission is deferred until the condition has been fulfilled. In the early material, however, *kitāba* is still imperfectly differentiated from other forms of conditional manumission, and both are regarded now as resolutive and now as suspensive. Accordingly, I shall use material relating to both in this section, taking up the question of the origins of *kitāba* in the next.

The methods popular among the conquerors according to early Ḥadīth were the following.

i. Manumission in return for an obligation to 'remain'

'I freed this slavegirl of mine, stipulating that she was to remain with me as a slavegirl remains with her master, in all respects except for intercourse. But when I was rough with her neck, she said: "I am free" '.[64]

The anonymous Arab who presented this complaint to Ibn Mas ʿūd in Kufa had made a paramonar manumission of the most elementary kind: a slavegirl had been granted a limited form of freedom in return for staying in the household and serving very much as before. Assuming that she had been required to do so for the lifetime of the manumitter rather than a specified number of years, this is a manumission of the type attested for pre-Islamic Arabia and the pre-conquest Near East alike which tells us little about change. Ibn Masʿūd's reaction may also have been perfectly intelligible in both Arabian and Near Eastern terms; it certainly would not have surprised the Romans. The Romans (who did not practise paramonar manumission, but who did require their freedmen to do *operae*), had long agreed that 'the praetor is not prepared to put up with a man who was yesterday a slave and today is free, complaining that his master has been rude to him or mildly struck or corrected him'. And Ibn Masʿūd adopted the same stance: 'she has no right to that; take her by her neck and take her away, for you have a right to what you have stipulated'.[65] An obligation to remain is however also attested in connection with *kitāba*, that is a manumission in return for payment and/or service for a specified number of days, months or years. What happens if the manumitter stipulates that the slave thus freed (the *mukātab*) may not go away (*an lā yakhruja*)? Though Ibn Masʿūd's manumitter had a right to what he had stipulated, the answer here is generally that the *mukātab* may leave as he wishes.[66] But the very fact that the question was asked shows that some required him to stay.

ii. Manumission in return for service for a specified number of years

ʿUmar b. al-Khaṭṭāb freed every Muslim among the Arab prisoners-of war and gave the manumission immediate effect (*fa-batta ʿalayhim*). He stipulated that they should serve his successor for three years, and he made it a condition upon them that he (*sic*) should protect them as he had himself (*wa-sharaṭa ʿalayhim annahu (sic) yaṣḥabukum bi-mithli mā kuntu aṣḥabukum bihi*). Khiyār redeemed his three years of service from ʿUthmān by [placing] Abū Farwa. ʿUthmān let him go (*khallā ʿUthmān sabīl al-Khiyār*), and he left, whereupon ʿUthmān took Abū Farwa.[67]

Listed by ʿAbd al-Razzāq under the headings of *kitāba* and conditional manumission alike, this manumission was clearly of the resolutive type. ʿUmar gave it immediate effect,[68] though he still required the freedmen to serve ʿUthmān for the first three years of his reign.[69] What Khiyār obtained from ʿUthmān was thus freedom from paramonar obligations, and he obtained it by placing a substitute, a method well known from Greek law.[70] The muddled reference to ʿUthmān's duty to protect the freedmen is presumably a corrupt version of a stipulation that they should remain with him (*annakum taṣḥabūnahu*, etc).[71] But classical law is generally hostile to resolutive conditions, and ʿUmar's manumission was soon read as one of the suspensive type.[72] Yet it was plainly based on the principle that 'if anyone says to his slave "you are free on condition that you serve me for ten years", then the condition is valid',[73] or 'if they stipulate that "you shall serve us for a month after you have been manumitted", then it is valid';[74] and ʿUmar is not the only authority credited with resolutive arrangements: ʿAlī is supposed to have freed some slaves on condition that they work for five years on some property which was to be *ṣadaqa* after his death;[75] and Ibn ʿUmar freed a slave on condition that he serve him for two years.[76] Manumission in return for service for a specified period was thus an arrangement perfectly familiar to early Muslim lawyers, who generally endorsed it.

iii. Manumission in return for the payment of alimony

'A woman came to Shurayḥ and said: "I freed this slave of mine on condition that he pay me ten dirhams a month as long as I live." Shurayḥ replied: "your manumission is valid, but your condition is void" '.[77]

This stipulation, classified as an example of conditions in *kitāba*, was evidently also resolutive: the manumission had not been deferred until the woman's death, as is clear both from her wording of her problem and from the response of Shurayḥ, the legendary judge of Kufa. Shurayḥ here gives expression to the Muslim wariness of resolutive conditions, and the tradition which endorses *kitābas* in return for monthly gifts of a ram presumably envisages the condition as suspensive.[78] But what Shurayḥ condemned was a well known Greek stipulation.[79] Demanding regular payment, be it for the lifetime of the manumitter or for a specified period, was simply another way of demanding service, and the inhabitants of the pre-conquest Near East usually demanded *both* service *and* payment.[80]

iv. *Manumission in return for a share of the freedman's estate*

'Iyās b. Muʿāwiya said: "ʿAdī b. Arṭāh [governor of Basra for ʿUmar II] and Ḥasan [al-Baṣrī] asked me about the case of a man who makes a *kitāba* with a slave and stipulates that he [the manumitter] should have a share of his property when he dies. I said that it was valid, but Ḥasan said that it was without effect. So Adī wrote to ʿUmar II, who wrote back endorsing Ḥasan's view'.[81]

Though this manumission is described as a *kitāba*, the stipulation discussed is once more resolutive: if the grant of freedom had been deferred until the condition had been fulfilled, the slave would have to die in order to obtain it. It emerges from this and other traditions that early Muslim manumitters commonly reserved a right to part of the freedman's estate such as his house, or indeed to everything that he might leave,[82] precisely as Greek manumitters had done.[83] Clearly, Muslim manumitters preferred the indefeasible right to part or the whole of the freedman's estate which they could retain by a paramonar manumission to the defeasible tie which they could claim by *walāʾ*. But though Iyās is presented as having found such stipulations unobjectionable, all extant traditions unsurprisingly condemn them as an infringement of Qurʾānic inheritance law. 'What good did it do me that I made my stipulation thirty years ago?', a manumitter complained when Shurayḥ refused to uphold his claim to his *mukātab*'s house, estate, offspring (cf. below, no. vi) and *walāʾ* (cf. below, p. 86). 'God's stipulation comes before yours', was the answer, 'and God made it through his Prophet Muḥammad fifty years ago.'[84]

v. *Manumission in return for celibacy*

If he [sc. the manumitter] stipulates that he [sc. the *mukātab*] may not marry, then he may not marry, unless he gets the permission of his patron.[85]

Stipulations of celibacy are attested only in connection with manumissions identified as *kitāba*s, and they are generally endorsed, clearly on the ground that the *mukātab* is still a slave. (The word *mawlā*, translated as 'patron' above, is commonly used of the slave's master too.) But many *kitāba*s subsequently interpreted as suspensive were actually resolutive, as has been seen; and given that early Muslim manumitters were in the habit of installing themselves as heirs to their *mukatāb*s, one suspects that the requirement of celibacy originated as an attempt to safeguard the manumitter's share. This is what one could expect on the basis of the Greek evidence,[86] though Greek manumitters were in the habit of demanding childlessness rather than celibacy: it was the Romans who, with the same end in view, would forbid their freedmen to marry.[87] If the Muslim demand for celibacy originated as an attempt to safeguard inheritance rights, its formulation might be evidence of Roman contamination.

vi. Manumission in return for enslavement of the freedman's or freedwoman's children

'I asked ʿAṭāʾ: "what about the female *mukātab* whose masters stipulate that any child she bears during her period of *kitāba* is a slave?" He said: "it is valid, provided that the stipulation concerns children born within this period". "And what about the man who is granted a *kitāba* and whose master stipulates that any child he has shall be his slave?" He said: "they belong to his master".'[88]

The requirement that the children of a freedman or freedwoman should be slaves is attested only in connection with *kitāba*s, where it is accepted on the ground that the person manumitted by *kitāba* remains a slave as long as the *kitāba* lasts, that is as long as the condition imposed have not been fulfilled. But as mentioned already, *kitāba*s were frequently resolutive, that is the *mukātab* was a free person obliged in certain respects, and the manumitters who required their *mukātab*s to provide slave children did not do so on the ground that the *mukātab*s were slaves themselves. Thus the manumitter who had reserved a right to his freedman's estate *and* offspring (above, iv) evidently had not deferred his grant of manumission until the conditions specified in the *kitāba* had been fulfilled, given that the conditions could not be fulfilled until the freedman died and that Shurayḥ struck them out as opposed to declaring the freedman a slave. What early Muslim manumitters were actually doing when they stipulated that the children of their *mukātabs* be slaves was thus to free their slaves in return for the provision of others. Greek manumitters had done the same.[89]

vii. Premature apolysis

Premature *apolysis* was not a method of exploiting slaves, but rather a way of preserving one's self-esteem while doing so, that is it was an act of charity. It consisted in letting the freedman go before his paramonar obligations had been completely fulfilled, on the model of Ibn ʿUmar:

'Ibn ʿUmar freed a slave of his, stipulating that he should serve him for two years. So he [sc. the freedman] worked as his shepherd for part of a year, whereupon he came to him with his horses, either during the pilgrimage or else during the *ʿumra*. ʿAbdallāh [b. ʿUmar] said to him: "I've renounced the condition I imposed on you; you are free and owe no labour." '[90]

Such renunciations of paramonar rights are attested in Greek manumission inscriptions;[91] an Arab Muslim, presumably a conqueror, likewise saw fit to forgo twenty of the fifty solidi which he had advanced to a free party to a paramonar labour contract at Nessana in 687.[92] Classical lawyers recommend, or even require, the manumitter by *kitāba* to forgo the last instalments owed to him, as Ibn ʿUmar did both here and in another tradition;[93] they even adduce a Qur'ānic sanction for this.[94] But in fact the conquerors clearly owed the practice to the provincials of the Near East.

On the basis of early Ḥadīth one would assume paramonar manumission to have played a major role in early Muslim society: a sufficient number of such contracts must have enabled many an Arab to live a life of leisure, and the woman, presumably widow, of no. iii, was hardly the only one to depend on a paramonar freedman for her meagre income. But the inclination of the lawyers, as has been seen, was to protect the freedman, and classical law frequently conveys the impression that conditional manumissions of the resolutive type completely disappeared. In fact, they did not. Manumission in return for service for a specified period continued to be valid in Sunnī law;[95] but the Sunnīs do not pay much attention to such manumissions, and it was only the Imāmīs who preserved the pre-classical position in full. Imāmī law allows the manumitter to stipulate not only service in return for a specified period,[96] but also anything else he likes as long as it is not contrary to the book of God;[97] and it is unique in that it endorses the ancient custom of stipulating re-enslavement in the event of non-fulfilment of the contract.[98] This is one of the many respects in which Imāmī law is archaic, though the use to which it was put was sometimes startlingly new: if a man frees his slave and marries him to his daughter on condition that he is re-enslaved if he maltreats her, the condition is valid.[99] Who would have thought that paramonar manumission could be made to serve the cause of female emancipation?

(d) *Paramonē* in Islam: *kitāba*

The fact that paramonar stipulations regularly appear in manumissions implicitly or explicitly identified as *kitāba*s suggests that the institution of *kitāba* itself is simply an Islamic version of manumission with *paramonē*. The similarities between the Greek and the Islamic institutions are indeed obvious. Both are two-stage manumissions: an initial grant of limited freedom is followed by one of full freedom when certain conditions have been fulfilled. In both cases the conditions are further service and/or payment associated with a duty to remain, though other conditions could be added too. And in both cases it was customary for the manumitter to renounce some of his rights, while the penalty for non-fulfilment of the contract by the freedman was, or could be, re-enslavement.

There are of course differences between the two institutions too; but, leaving aside their different names,[100] these can all be seen as having arisen on the further evolution of the Greek institution within Islam. Thus manumission with *paramonē* almost invariably involved service, whereas *kitāba* is usually a manumission in return for payment, be it in cash or kind. This is not a hard and fast difference. On the one hand, Greek manumitters were rarely satisfied with service alone. Most slaves manumitted at Delphi, be it with or without further obligations, obtained their manumission by supplying Apollo with money with which to buy them from their masters and free them;[101] there is in fact an almost perfect parallel to *kitāba* in the case of a girl who was freed on condition that she stay with her mamumitter for six years during which she was to pay off her own purchase price in annual instalments.[102] Most slaves would *first* pay their own price and *next* work off their paramonar service obligations, but they too were usually required to make further payments during their period of *paramonē*;[103] and in the pre-conquest Near East paramonar obligations would seem regularly to have involved both service and payment.[104] On the other hand, *kitāba*s may be made in return for service alone,[105] or in return for service and payment alike.[106] But it is undeniable that the demand for payment predominates on the Muslim side. Given that manumission in return for service is well attested in early Ḥadīth, this presumably reflects a shift in the requirement of manumitters rather than institutional discontinuity: manumitters increasingly wanted the proceeds of the freedman's labour, not the labour itself.

It is probably the same shift which explains another difference, or rather two. When the *mukātab* is forbidden to leave his manumitter, the lawyers invariably take it that he has been forbidden to leave his manumitter's town or district,[107] not his house or factory as one would have expected on the basis of Greek law;[108] and unlike the Greeks, they usually hold the prohibition to be void.[109] They all assume the *mukātab* to be engaged in a craft or business of his own which he could not very well pursue without leaving the manumitter's house or place of work; the question is thus whether he should pursue it without leaving his manumitter's area of residence, and when they deny this, it is always on the ground that he needs to travel in order to pay off the *kitāba*.[110] The old obligation to remain and work in the manumitter's house was nonetheless also known to the Muslims. Thus it was in the manumitter's household that the recalcitrant freedwoman of the preceding section (no. i) had to live and work in the manner of a slavegirl; and according to Sarakhsī, stipulations of service were commonly understood to mean household work.[111] But stipulations of service are so marginal that the lawyers do not discuss the *mukātab*'s obligation to stay in this context. It should be added that inasmuch as the laywers reject the *mukātab*'s duty to remain, they fail to cite good examples of the old phrase allowing the paramonar freedman to 'go where he wished' on the completion of his contract.[112] The expression *khallā lahu al-sabīl*, 'he left his way free or open to him', used in an early tradition, nonetheless suggests that such a phrase existed.[113]

The fact that there is no *kitāba* for the lifetime of the manumitter presumably also reflects developments within Islam, for the lawyers were certainly familiar with the idea. The Sunnīs forbid manumission on condition of service for the lifetime of the manumitter;[114] Shaybānī explicitly forbids *kitāba*s on such terms;[115] and the other schools implicitly forbid it when they state that a precise time-limit expressed in terms of days, weeks, months or years is essential for the validity of the contract.[116] The reason why *paramonē* for the lifetime of the manumitter failed to survive in Islam might simply be that it involved an element of uncertainty and risk (*gharar*), something which invalidates all contracts; but if so, one would have expected more polemics against it. Alternatively, one might speculate that it was *paramonē* for the lifetime of the manumitter which became the Muslim institution of *tadbīr*, manumission deferred until the manumitter's death, and this seems a more promising hypothesis. Though the traditions preserved by ʿAbd al-Razzāq lend no obvious support to it,[117] it was certainly a paramonar manumission that a tenth-century Egyptian goldsmith known from the papyri effected, for all that he called it *tadbīr*.[118]

The crucial difference between manumission with *paramonē* and manumission by *kitāba*, however, is that the former is resolutive whereas the latter is suspensive, at least in classical Sunnī law. The Sunnīs are agreed that the *mukātab* does not become free on conclusion of the contract, but on the contrary remains a slave until the last dirham has been paid.[119] More precisely, he becomes what the Romans called a *statuliber*, that is a slave whose position is in various respects affected by a promise of future freedom. Thus he is empowered to do business: were it otherwise, he could not pay.[120] Further, he cannot be sold, or only if he consents, or only if he has not paid a single instalment yet; alternatively, the sale cannot destroy the *kitāba*.[121] And the female *mukātab* ceases to be sexually at the disposal of her master, on a par with the recalcitrant freedwoman of the preceding section.[122] But the *mukātab* is still a slave. It is for this reason that he cannot marry, alienate his property or, according to the Mālikīs, leave his master's area of residence without the latter's permission, not because he is a freedman obliged to abide by his manumitter's stipulations.[123] It is for the same reason that his children can continue to be slaves, though those born under the contract must be included in it.[124] And it is also for this reason that he is re-enslaved, or more precisely ceases to be a *statuliber*, if he fails to honour his obligations.[125] If he dies before he has completed the contract, the Shāfiʿīs and Ḥanbalīs mercilessly deem all his labour to have been in vain, though the other Sunnī schools as a rule allow the remaining instalments to be paid out of his estate.[126]

But behind the classical façade there is wild disagreement over the *mukātab*'s status. The Sunnīs who hold that he is nothing but a slave simply represent one end of the spectrum. At the opposite end of the spectrum we have the Ibāḍīs, according to whom he is freed on the very conclusion of the contract,[127] a view also found in non-Ibāḍī Ḥadīth;[128] re-enslavement of the *mukātab* is accordingly impossible in Ibāḍī law.[129] And in between we have a wide variety of opinions which failed to become school doctrine, plus Shīʿite law. Various early lawyers held that the *mukātab* becomes free when he has paid a quarter, a third, half or three quarters of the sum agreed, or when he has paid all but an insignificant amount,[130] or when he has paid his purchase price;[131] and ʿAlī reputedly held that the manumission takes effect as soon as the first instalment has been paid, though it is not completed until the entire sum has been discharged: it grows in proportion with the payments.[132] ʿAlī's position is that of the Qāsimī Zaydīs[133] (and, somewhat incongruously, also that of Ibn Ḥazm.)[134] It was adopted by the Imāmīs, Ismāʿīlīs and Nāṣirī Zaydīs too, but with a concession to the Sunnīs: if the manumitter reserves a right to re-enslave the *mukātab*, the manumission is deferred until every dirham has been paid as in Sunnī law; but if the manumitter renounces this right, the freedom takes effect at once and grows in proportion with the payments.[135]

It is clear from this disagreement that nobody knew exactly what a *mukātab* was, but what is particularly interesting about it is that it is all but identical with that of modern European scholars over the status of the paramonar freedman. At one extreme we have the Sunnīs and Bloch: the *mukātab*/paramonar freedman is nothing but a slave.[136] At the other extreme we have the Ibāḍīs and Samuel: he is a free man who cannot be re-enslaved.[137] And in between we have the Shīʿites and Koschaker. It is true that the Shīʿites agree with Samuel rather than Koschaker when they assert that the manumission takes effect on the payment of the first instalment,[138] but Samuel dissents from their view that it grows in proportion with the payments;[139] and it is Koschaker who defines the status of the paramonar freedman as a *Zwischenzustand der Halbfreiheit*[140] in agreement with Naḥwī, who calls it a *manzila bayna'l-riqq wa'l-ḥurriyya*.[141] Plainly, it is the same institution which Muslim and European scholars have found so hard to pin down.

CHAPTER 6

The case for the Roman Near East

Despite their general similarity of social organisation, the Greeks and the Romans had adopted opposite solutions to the problem of accommodating freedmen in the society into which they had been manumitted. The Greeks excluded them from citizenship, relegating them to a collective state of dependence as resident aliens; but the Romans on the contrary accepted them as citizens and subjected them to individual ties of dependence.

The dependent status of the early Roman freedman arose from his incorporation into the manumitter's household. All members of the early Roman household were subject to the paternal authority of the head of the household, the *paterfamilias*. The paternal power of the Romans was unique in that it lasted as long as the *pater* was alive, not simply until his sons come of age, as is normally the case. All his descendants were thus subject to it regardless of their age and sex, as was his wife and other members of the household such as slaves and freedmen. All were thus bound to obey them, and what is more, all were deprived of individual rights in private law. In particular, persons *in potestate* could not own, but only hold a *peculium* which automatically reverted to the *pater* on their death. There was no difference between the freedman and the *filiusfamilias* in this respect, nor did such public office as either might enjoy affect their status in private law. The only difference was that, like women, the freedman had no prospect of emancipation: on the death of the *pater*, the son would acquire his own *potestas*, becoming a *paterfamilias* himself; but the freedman would remain subject to what came to be known as the patronate; only his grandson escaped it completely. The Roman patronate is thus a form of *patria potestas*, and the patron's rights to *obsequium* (respect), *operae* (labour) and *bona* (succession) all flowed from this power. In due course the Roman jurists decided that for practical purposes the patron inherited as an agnate (*quasi haereditario iure*) and inferred that he was eligible for the guardianship of the freedman's children too. In effect they had thus created an agnatic (or quasi-agnatic) tie with unilateral effect;[1] but historically the patron took his freedman's estate because it was in the last resort his own.[2]

First attested in the Twelve Tables, the Roman patronate was still very much alive in the time of Justinian. It is true that the patronate over free persons which had coexisted with that over freedmen was now a purely social as opposed to legal institution, but then we are not concerned with this tie.[3] That over freedmen still arose automatically on manumission, granted the patron a right to respect, labour services (though these now had to be expressly imposed) and, above all, to succession; it still saddled him with the guardianship of the freedman's orphaned children, and it still passed to his own heirs on his death.[4] It was however no longer regarded as a family tie. Though numerous authors had stressed the filial aspect of the relationship between manumitter and freedman in the past,[5] the tie was now seen as simply the price exacted by the manumitter for the act of manumission on a par with the *paramonē* with which it coexisted in the Near East; indeed, to the non-Roman inhabitants of the Near East the patronate was simply a Roman version of paramonar rights.[6]

There was another institution of relevance to us in the Roman Near East, that is the Greek succession agreement. The Greek subjects of the Roman empire were in the habit of disposing of their estates not only by will, but also by contractual agreement. The agreement might take the form of a *pactum mutuum successionis*, each party stipulating that whoever predeceased the other should leave his estate to the other, but it might also be a simple contract granting one party a right to the other's estate.[7] There is little information on the circumstances in which such contracts would be made, but the point to note is this. The Roman Near East was an area in which it was customary to reward social favours with what amounted to a cheque to be encashed on the signatory's death. Everybody took it for granted that the act of manumission was rewarded with such a cheque; and though manumitters might specify their own rewards, the law automatically issued them with a cheque of this kind even if they did not. Clearly, this is the environment in which Islamic *walā'* is at home.

I shall now demonstrate that early Muslim lawyers similarly regarded *walā'* as a reward for the manumitter, or as a right reserved by him, not as a kinship tie: in terms of attitudes to the tie over freedmen, there was no discontinuity between the late Roman Near East and early Islam. Further, I shall show that the legal behaviour of the late Roman patronate coincides with that of pre-classical *walā'* in certain respects: there was actual continuity in terms of law.

(a) The pre-classical concept of *walā'*

As mentioned already, all classical Muslim lawyers hold that *walā'* should be seen as a fictitious kinship tie, specifically an agnatic one, though this interpretation is somewhat strained.[8] The strain arises from the fact that *walā'* did not originate as such a tie at all. This is clear from the fact that the patron did not generally inherit as an agnate, or indeed as a kinsman of any kind, in pre-classical law, while at the same time the patronate was treated as a piece of property which could be bought, sold, given away, renounced and inherited on a par with other things capable of ownership. In pre-classical law the patronate was a *shuʿba min al-riqq*, a residue of slavery,[9] not simply *nasab* for those who had forgotten their genealogies. What follows is detailed documentation of these points.

i. The patron was not widely regarded as an agnatic heir

ʿAbd al-Razzāq has preserved a number of traditions in which the Kufans find themselves at odds with others, apparently also Kufans, over the relative priority of the patron (defined, if at all, as the patron by manumission) and the so-called *dhawū'l-arḥām*,[10] that is female and non-agnatic relatives or, given that Islamic law does not acknowledge the concept of female agnates,[11] simply non-agnatic ones. In classical law the term is restricted to those non-agnatic heirs who have not been awarded a share in the Qur'ān, but there is no trace of this distinction in ʿAbd al-Razzāq's traditions: the issue is the relative priority of patron and non-agnatic relatives *tout court*.[12] With the exception of one, all establish that the patron is excluded from succession in the presence of a single non-agnatic relative on the freedman's side, even a half-sister's son.[13] They thus identify the patron as the last heir to be called to succession, not as an agnatic one.

The exceptional tradition argues precisely the opposite: the patron excludes any non-agnatic heir on the freedman's side, even a mother.[14] It is not clear whether the patron is here seen as an agnatic heir or rather as someone who excludes any relative on the freedman's side, agnatic or other. In favour of the latter view one might cite an Imāmī tradition in which a manumitter dies, leaving daughters, whereupon the freedman dies, leaving agnates.[15] In classical terms, this is a completely unproblematic case: the freedman's agnates exclude the manumitter's daughter in both Sunnī and Shīʿī law.[16] Yet the daughters here claim the estate, and though they do so unsuccessfully, the sheer fact that the tradition exists shows that some would have awarded it to them.[17] Now those who would award the estate of a freedman to daughters of the manumitter in competition with agnates of the freedman himself must have held that the manumitter's claim overrode that of any blood relation on the freedman's side. For such lawyers *walā'* was clearly in the nature of paramonar obligations to be honoured regardless of the presence of heirs, not an agnatic tie, and we may take it that such lawyers were to be found in Kufa too.

But though ʿAbd al-Razzāq's tradition is Kufan, it is possible that it voices the view of the Medinese. The Medinese profess always to have counted the patron as an agnatic heir.[18] They do so because succession in their view is based on agnation alone, though they obviously have to accept such non-agnatic heirs as God has appointed himself. If the patron was an heir, he was *ipso facto* an agnatic one: non-agnatic relatives did not inherit at all. If ʿAbd al-Razzāq's tradition echoes the views of the Medinese, it is thus as the last agnate that the patron excludes the freedman's mother, still not differentiated from other *dhawū'l-arḥām* as a Qur'ānic heir. But this does not mean that the patron was widely regarded as such.

It is clear that the Medinese were in the minority when they asserted that succession must be based exclusively on agnatic ties: outside Medina practically all pre-classical lawyers acknowledged non-agnatic relatives as heirs;[19] and with the exception of the Mālikīs, all the classical schools also call *dhawū'l-arḥām* to succession.[20] It follows that the Medinese must similarly have been in the minority when they cast the patron as an agnatic heir, and this is certainly also the impression one gets from references to early Ḥadīth now lost. The view that the patron is excluded by non-agnatic relatives was attested in traditions ascribed not only to Kufan authorities, but also to Basran,[21] Meccan,[22] Yemeni[23] and Syrian ones.[24] In short, it was a view once represented in every legal centre except Medina; and there were apparently even some who subscribed to it in Medina too.[25] Pre-classical law must thus be said generally to have treated the patron as a non-agnatic heir. But though the Medinese failed to oust the *dhawū'l-arḥām* from succession outside Medina, their view of the patron's status was certainly to prevail in classical law. The Ḥanafīs continued to give non-agnatic heirs priority over the contractual patron, but not over the manumitter; and all the later Sunnī schools adopted the Medinese position without a shred of hesitation, as did the Qāsimīs, though the Qāsimīs also preserved the old doctrine in respect of the contractual patron.[26] It was only the Imāmīs, Ismāʿīlīs and Nāṣirīs who retained the pre-classical doctrine in full, and it is their distinction between succession based on *nasab* and *sabab* which makes explicit what is only implicit in early non-Medinese Ḥadīth: the patron's title rested on *sabab*, a special tie or connection, not on kinship ties of any kind.[27]

ii. Walā' could be bought, sold and otherwise alienated

Sale of *walā'* is known to have been practised in the Umayyad and early ʿAbbāsid periods;[28] indeed it was practised even in Būyid times, though by now in military circles only.[29] A number of traditions explicitly declare such transactions to be valid,[30] and several early lawyers endorsed them.[31] But other traditions voice disapproval of them,[32] and still others prohibit them outright.[33] The prohibition is first ascribed to early lawyers such as Ṭāwūs, Ḥasan al-Baṣrī, ʿAṭā' and Zuhrī without further authority,[34] next to Companions such as ʿAlī, Ibn Masʿūd and Ibn ʿAbbās,[35] and finally to the Prophet himself.[36] The reason given for the prohibition is invariably that *walā'* is a kinship tie and that kinship cannot be bought, sold or given away.[37] This argument has been accepted by all the surviving schools without exception.[38] It cannot be shown that it originated with the Medinese, and it was clearly accepted in circles who resisted the Medinese agnatisation of the patron for purposes of succession, indeed even by those who denied that the patron was a kinsman at all for such purposes. There would thus seem to have been a general tendency to recast *walā'* as a fictitious, as opposed to merely metaphorical, kinship tie; and this tendency must have set in some time in the Umayyad period, given that the prohibition of sale and gifts of *walā'* was first made at a stage when the mere opinion of jurists counted as authoritative, and that it may have acquired Prophetic backing by the 770s.[39] But the starting point was clearly a situation in which *walā'* was regarded as a legitimate object of commercial transactions.[40]

iii. Walā' could be renounced

The pre-classical manumitter could renounce the patronate by declaring the freedman *sā'iba*.[41] Some lawyers held that he automatically did so unless he explicitly reserved it, but this was an uncommon view.[42] No *walā'* arose, however, if the manumitter explicitly renounced it, according to traditions citing Kufan, Meccan, Medinese and Syrian authorities alike.[43] Most classical lawyers disapprove of the practice. The Ḥanafīs, Shāfi'īs and Qạsimīs do not recognise it at all: the manumission is valid, but the renunciation is void.[44] The Ḥanbalīs and Mālikīs accept the renunciation to the point of assigning the patronate to the Muslims at large.[45] But only the Imāmīs and Ismā'īlīs endorse the pre-classical doctrine: no *walā'* arises, and the freedman may choose a patron of his own.[46]

The manumitter could also renounce the tie after it had arisen by permitting the freedman to seek another patron.[47] Freedmen who became contractual clients of men other than their manumitters are well attested in the non-legal literature.[48] But when *walā'* was identified as a kinship tie, such practices had to be forbidden. Kinship can no more be renounced than it can be sold or given away, and permitting freedmen to seek new patrons amounts to a gift of *walā'*, as several lawyers point out.[49] He who seeks *mawālī*, that is patrons and/or kinsmen, other than his own is a straightforward infidel on whom the most frightening curses are heaped in Prophetic Ḥadīth.[50] In classical law contractual clients may be recruited only from among those who have no kinsmen or patrons in Islam, in so far as they may be recruited at all.[51]

iv. Walā' could be inherited

In classical law *walā'* cannot be inherited in the strict sense of the word because one cannot inherit kinship: one can only inherit through it.[52] Succession to, or rather succession through, *walā'* is thus governed by the rule of the *kubr* (or *kabīr*), which establishes that on the death of the manumitter the rights and duties conferred by the tie pass to the nearest agnate of the manumitter regardless of who his heirs might be. If a manumitter dies leaving two sons, the two sons will share both the tie and the rest of his property, being his nearest agnates and heirs alike; they will thus share a title to the freedman's estate when he in his turn dies. But suppose now that one of the two sons dies, leaving sons of his own. If *walāʾ* were ordinary property, these children would inherit their father's share of it together with the rest of his estate; in fact, however, it passes to the surviving son of the manumitter, who thus acquires the full title to the freedman's estate.[53] Precisely the same rules applied in classical Roman law.[54]

Now Brunschvig believed the rule of the *kubr* to be an archaic survival; and since it links succession with successive generations (no member of the second generation can inherit before the first is extinct), he found an origin for it in the peculiar social structure of Strabo's Yemen.[55] But it is hard to believe that a succession rule intimately linked with a peculiar kinship organisation of such antiquity could have survived to become the classical doctrine of all the Sunnī[56] and Zaydī schools;[57] even the Imāmīs and Ismāʿīlīs tended to accept it.[58] The rule is invariably justified with reference to the same equation of *walāʾ* and *nasab* which issued in the prohibition of sale and gifts of the tie; it is thus unlikely to be any earlier than this prohibition. And it evidently cannot have gained currency before the Medinese agnatisation of the patron for purposes of succession had won general acceptance.[59] The idea behind the rule is that *walāʾ* should function as an agnatic tie, and this is precisely what it achieves: the son of the manumitter excludes the grandson from succession to the freedman's estate on the general principle of agnatic succession that the nearer in degree excludes the more remote.[60] We may take it that the rule of the *kubr* is a juristic construction made independently of both the Yemen and Rome.

This conclusion can be corroborated in two ways. First, if we turn to early Ḥadīth we find that Ibrāhīm al-Nakhaʿī declares *walāʾ* to be an inheritable piece of property when he speaks on his own authority or that of Shurayḥ, the legendary judge of Kufa who is frequently singled out as an adherent of this point of view, whereas he espouses the opposite point of view on the authority of ʿAlī, ʿUmar and, most strikingly, the Medinese Zayd b. Thābit.[61] This suggests that Ibrāhīm's name was being invoked to acclimatise a Medinese doctrine in Kufa; indeed, we are explicitly told that it was the Medinese who regarded *walāʾ* as *nasab*, or, as the variant version has it, espoused the rule of the *kubr*, whereas Shurayḥ regarded it as a source of income.[62] In other words, the rule of the *kubr* here appears as a novel doctrine foisted upon an old school.[63]

Secondly, we have the evidence of the controversy over women's *walāʾ*. If *walāʾ* is an agnatic tie, women are excluded from succession through it (there being no such thing as female agnates in Islamic law). In deference to the tradition that *walāʾ* [always and invariably] accrues to the manumitter, they are nonetheless allowed to inherit from their own freedmen and freedmen of the latter; but they cannot pass on the tie to their children, not can it pass to them from others. This is the principle.[64] Now those who refused to cast *walā'* as an agnatic tie governed by the rule of the *kubr* also refused to exclude women from succession through it;[65] unsurprisingly, the Imāmīs were among them, though they were divided over the question.[66] But what is particularly striking is that even those who accepted the principle failed to apply it consistently. Thus the Sunnīs and Zaydīs are agreed that women are excluded from succession through *walā'*, except in the case of their own freedmen;[67] on the death of a female manumitter both nonetheless award one half of the tie, that is the title to succession, to her sons, though they pass the other half, responsibility for the freedman's blood-money, to her agnates.[68] This is utterly inconsistent, as Ibn Ḥazm pointed out,[69] and there can only be one explanation for such an extraordinary defiance of logic: the sons of the female manumitter had inherited *walā'* in accordance with the normal rules for so long that depriving them of this right was felt to be impossible.

v. Walā' was a residue of ownership

Implicit in all the features of pre-classical *walā'* examined so far is the view that the tie was a residue of the master's former ownership of his slave; and this is indeed explicitly stated on some occasions.[70] 'It is as if some of the ownership ceases on manumission, but some remains', as Sarakhsī put it in elucidation of a statement attributed to Shurayḥ.[71] And it is because *walā'* was such a residue that some lawyers argued that the Muslim manumitter could inherit from a non-Muslim freedman, though he certainly could not inherit from a non-Muslim relative.[72] The residue is widely regarded as the price of manumission even in classical law: succession between manumitter and freedman is unilateral, we are told, because the manumitter has bestowed a favour on the freedman, whereas the freedman has bestowed none on the manumitter.[73] The Imāmīs go so far as to rule that the manumitter can only reserve this residue if he actually *has* bestowed a genuine favour. Thus no *walā'* arises in Imāmī law over slaves freed in expiation, in fulfilment of vows,[74] on mutilation by their masters,[75] on passing into the ownership of a close relative,[76] or on purchasing their own freedom, though in the case of slaves purchasing their own freedom, the manumitter acquires it if he expressly reserves it;[77] in general, no *walā'* arises if a slave is freed by the automatic operation of the law: for the manumitter to claim his reward, the manumission must be gratuitous.[78] This rule is evidently incompatible with the view that *walā'* is a kinship tie, and given that Imāmī deviations on the subject of *walā'* have so far proved to be an archaism, one would expect them to preserve a pre-classical doctrine here too. That this is the case is suggested by residues of the same doctrine among the Ibāḍīs; and as far as the slave who purchased his own freedom is concerned, it can actually be proved.[79]

(b) The late Roman patronate and pre-classical *walā'*

We may now turn to the similarities of detail between the late Roman and early Islamic patronates. They are the following.

i. Both conferred a title of succession in the absence of certain heirs, not a fixed share

This point differentiates the Roman and the Muslim manumitter from the pre-Islamic *ḥalīf*, who is generally (but perhaps gratuitously) said to have been entitled to a sixth in the presence of heirs.[80] As regards the specific rules, there is complete agreement between late Roman and Islamic law that the patron was entitled to the entire estate of a freedman who died leaving neither relatives nor will.[81] They differed slightly over the rules to be applied if he did leave relatives. According to the Romans, free parents, siblings or descendants on the freedman's side would exclude the patron, though other relatives would not unless the *de cujus* was a freedman's son.[82] Islamic law does not appear ever to have distinguished between freedman and freedman's son: any free relative would exclude the patron in what would seem to have been the prevailing view of pre-classical law.

The major difference between the two systems is that the Roman patron could not be excluded by will: if a freedman who left no relatives at all willed away his entire estate, the patron could still claim a *Pflichtteil*, which Justinian reduced to a third.[83] Though the Muslim attitude to wills is quite un-Roman, it is interesting to note that a pre-classical tradition on a freedman who willed away his entire estate, having no relatives of his own, duly has him leave a third of the estate to his patron.[84]

ii. Both were inherited in accordance with the normal rules of succession

By Justinian's time most of the rights vested in the Roman patronate over freedmen passed to the manumitter's heirs in accordance with the ordinary rules regarding the devolution of property.[85] On the Muslim side succession to the patronate would likewise seem to have followed the ordinary rules in pre-classical law.

iii. Both could be renounced

In classical Roman law it was impossible to renounce the patronate. The inhabitants of the Greek-speaking provinces, however, treated the patronate as a paramonar obligation which they could impose or renounce as they saw fit,[86] and Justinian in the end elevated this practice into Roman law.[87] Muslim manumitters could declare their slaves *sāʾiba*, as has been seen. In pre-Islamic Arabia *tasyib* was apparently a manumission without paramonar obligation: the freedman could go where he wanted.[88] But in Islamic law it is a manumission without patronate: the freedman could put his estate where he wanted.[89] What Muslim manumitters renounced was thus something new reminiscent of the Roman patronate. No doubt *tasyīb* continued to imply renunciation of services too;[90] but then Roman manumitters who renounced the patronate also renounced their claim to *operae*.[91] What Muslim manumitters renounced above all, was their *Pflichtteil*: slaves freed *sāʾibatan* were free to dispose of their entire estates by will, as is clear not only from the phrase that they could 'put their estates where they wanted', but also from concrete cases reported in Ḥadīth.[92] Slaves freed without *walāʾ*, in short, had *libera testamenti factio*, precisely as did slaves freed without patronate in Roman law.[93]

iv. Both failed to arise if the freedman had purchased his own freedom, including freedom from further obligations

In classical Roman law the patronate arose even over freedmen who had purchased their own freedom, but by Justinian's time it did not. The clue to this development is once more provincial practice.

According to Taubenschlag, the patronate did not arise in provincial law when the freedman had paid for his own manumission,[94] but as Harada points out, this cannot be entirely correct.[95] The provincial equivalent of the patronate was paramonar obligations, and slaves who purchased their own freedom did not necessarily escape such obligations in Greek law; on the contrary, they were usually required *first* to purchase their own freedom and *next* to work off such obligations. In the second century A.D. a Roman governor who settled a dispute between a Greek manumitter and his freedman in Egypt explicitly based himself on local Greek law when he awarded paramonar services to the manumitter for all that the freedman had paid for his own manumission; the manumitter did not deny that the freedman had purchased his own freedom: he merely denied having renounced the tie.[96] Yet, other manumitters did renounce the patronate when their freedmen paid for their freedom;[97] and though they could have done so gratuitously ,[98] two imperial constitutions unambiguously imply that those who paid for their freedom were believed to escape the patronate: this is the misconception which the two constitutions set out to correct.[99] Taubenschlag thus cannot be entirely wrong.

The solution must be that slaves who purchased *both* manumission *and* freedom from further obligations escaped the patronate. Greek manumitters who renounced the Roman tie were actually dissolving paramonar relationships, as is clear from their use of the verb *apolyein*.[100] As has been seen, they were in the habit of dissolving such relationships both gratuitously and in return for money.[101] It stands to reason that they should have continued to do both after 212, when the universalisation of Roman law caused them to call a paramonar relationship a patronate. We may thus take it that where the price of manumission had been calculated to include redemption of further services, no patronate arose in provincial law.[102]

Once more, provincial law would seem to have become Roman law. The *suis nummis emptus* of Roman law was a slave who purchased his own freedom by providing a third party with money to buy and free him.[103] In classical law the purchaser acquired the patronate; but since he had only played an instrumental role, it was of limited extent, and since the manumission had not been gratuitous, he could not impose *operae*.[104] From a provincial point of view, the *suis nummis emptus* had thus redeemed himself of further services, and he was accordingly believed to have escaped the patronate altogether.[105] Apparently, Justinian agreed; just as he endorsed gratuitous renunciation of the patronate, so also he accepted that the *suis nummis emptus* escaped it.[106]

Turning now to the Muslim side, the *mukātab* was, as has been seen, a slave who purchased his freedom from both slavery and paramonar obligations in regular instalments.[107] The *mukātab* was widely held to escape *walāʾ* in pre-classical law if the manumitter failed explicitly to reserve it for himself, or alternatively if the *mukātab* himself explicitly reserved it. The same applied to the slave freed by *qiṭāʿa*, that is on payment of a lump sum. Views to this effect are attested for Qatāda in Basra,[108] ʿAṭāʾ and ʿAmr b. Dīnār in Mecca,[109] Abū Thawr in Baghdad,[110] Makḥūl in Syria[111], and, indirectly, for Mālik's Medina.[112] Though all Sunnīs and most Zaydīs were to reject such views,[113] there were also Zaydīs who accepted them,[114] and they survived in full among the Imāmīs[115] and some Ibāḍīs.[116] Both Abū Thawr and the Imāmīs, moreover, held that if a third party takes money from a slave in order to buy and free, the slave is freed without *walāʾ*,[117] though the majority were against this too.[118] Pre-classical law thus once more coincides with that of the Roman Near East.

There is no doubt, however, that the Muslim lawyers who refused to grant the manumitter *walāʾ* on manumission in return for payment, be it by *kitāba*, *qiṭāʿa* or fictitious sale, did so in agreement with Taubenschlag rather than Harada or myself: no *walāʾ* arose for the simple reason that the slave had purchased himsef.[119] They no doubt saw it this way because they lived at a time when the payment for manumission and that for further service had all but coalesced, a process of which one can see the beginnings in the Roman sources. If Taubenschlag was not right, at least he was prophetic.

v. Imperfect fits

Naturally, several aspects of the Roman patronate fail to reappear on the Muslim side. When the Imāmīs and Ibāḍīs recommend that the manumitter provide for the freedman in need, they *could* be influenced by Roman law, but they could also be making a moral inference of their own;[120] and there is no trace of the Roman patron's right to *obsequium*, *honor*, *reverentia* and the like.[121] This is not a point of great interest in that one would not have expected otherwise. Two of Justinian's regulations, however, could have been expected to resurface on the Muslim side; yet there is only ambiguous evidence for them there.[122]

First, Justinian punished abuses such as neglect of infirm slaves and prostitution of slavegirls by freeing the slaves and depriving the former owners of their patronate; the penalty for exacting oaths of celibacy from the freedman was likewise loss of the patronate.[123] The idea of punishing abuses by a grant of freedom without *walā'* is also attested in Islamic law. Thus an Egyptian judge freed a slavegirl who had been mutilated by her mistress and awarded the *walā'* to the Muslims at large,[124] and slaves mutilated by their masters are automatically freed without *walā'* in Imāmī law.[125] The penalty for refusal to pay blood-money on behalf of freedmen was also loss of the patronate according to some.[126] But the rule that slaves mutilated by their masters must be freed is Jewish, not Roman,[127] and loss of the patronate as a punishment is not attested in a context which would clinch that the Muslims owed the idea to Justinian.[128]

Secondly, the slavegirl who had borne her master children was also freed without patronate by Justinian on her master's death.[129] This slavegirl is the Muslim *umm walad*, and Romans, Muslims and Nestorians alike all owe her, in the last resort, to Hammurabi.[130] But though the Muslims freed such slavegirls on their masters' death independently of the Romans, one would still have expected at least some of them to argue that she was exempt from *walā'*. Yet there seems to be no early Ḥadīth to this effect. In classical law the Sunnīs and the Zaydīs certainly do not exempt her,[131] and the Ibāḍīs are silent on the question. The Imāmīs clearly ought to exempt her, given that she is freed by the automatic operation of the law, not by a gratuitous act of the owner, and Āmilī insists that she does escape the tie.[132] The fact that Ṭūsī disagrees, saying that she is subject to it *bilā khilāf*, without disagreement, is of no importance,[133] for Ṭūsī's information on agreement and disagreement is worthless except as information about the Sunnīs (who are indeed completely agreed on this point).[134] and it was well known to later Imāmīs that Ṭūsī's *Mabsūṭ* abandoned the Imāmī principle that *walā'* only arises when the grant of freedom is gratuitous.[135] But ʿĀmilī's argument is based on silence, not on Ḥadīth. If the Imāmīs had always exempted the *umm walad* from *walā'*, there ought to be a positive statement to this effect, as there is in the case of the *mukātab*: the fact that none seems to exist suggests that she is exempt by simple inference from the general rule. Once more, it is thus impossible to demonstrate Muslim familiarity with Justinian's law.

Finally, it should be noted that the Muslim habit of alienating *walā'* by sale, gift and bequest is Greek, not Roman. It is true that Roman manumitters could similarly alienate the patronate over Latini Iuniani, i.e. freedmen who had been freed informally and who were thus considered to die as slaves.[136] But the status of Latin was abolished by Justinian, and the patronate over freedmen who had become Roman citizens could not be treated in this fashion. Greek manumitters were however in the habit of disposing of their paramonar rights as if they were ordinary property,[137] and it was doubtless also paramonar rights which were the object of the trade in *walā'*. At least two of the concrete cases of trade in *walā'* attested in the non-legal literature before the trade became a feature of military politics involve *mukātab*s.[138] What the purchasers acquired may thus be presumed to have been all the rights reserved by the manumitters in the *kitāba* (or, in cases not involving *mukatāb*s, conditional manumissions of other types), such as rights to labour service, regular payment, and to all or part of the freedman's estate. This is also suggested by the several versions of the classical Barīra tradition, in which the owners are willing to part with a *mukātaba* only on condition that they retain some of the rights in question.[139] In other words, *walā'* frequently seems to mean paramonar rights as opposed to simply patronate: it is not for nothing that what is generally known as manumission without *walā'* appears as manumission without further service in an Ibāḍī source.[140] The practice of trading in *walā'* thus testifies to the influence of provincial practice on that of the early Muslims, but the practice was in this case one without a Roman component.

To summarize now, it should be abundantly clear that the Arab conquerors soon came to be familiar with a cluster of provincial practices in which the predominant element was the *paramonē* of the Hellenised Near East. The cluster, however, also included a tie which the Muslims called *walā'* and which undeniably resembles the Roman patronate: both arose automatically on manumission, granted the manumitter a title to his freedman's estate, passed to the manumitter's heirs on his death, and failed to arise if the freedman had redeemed himself of both slavery and further service or if the manumitter saw fit gratuitously to renounce it. The tie in question is said to come from Arabia, yet it does not resemble institutions known from Arabia. In both positive and negative terms, the evidence thus points to the conclusion that *walā'* has its origin in the Roman Near East.

CHAPTER 7

Conclusion

(a) The history of *walāʾ*

We are now in a position to attempt an overall survey of the development of the Islamic patronate. Its history may be reconstructed along the following lines.

Once the initial phase of the conquests was over, the Arabs were confronted with the problem of defining the status of non-tribal members of their society. Among themselves, the dividing line between tribesmen and non-tribesmen had largely disappeared. Just as the Persians of Hajar were accepted as Arabs on the rise of Islam, so weavers, smiths and paramonar servants became warriors on a par with the free. The lowly origins of such persons were not necessarily forgotten, or even forgiven, but they ceased to be a bar to membership: all natives of the peninsula who participated in the conquests as adherents of the new faith were henceforth equal members of a new commonwealth distinguished from the rest of the world by Arab ethnicity, common faith and immense success. It was newcomers recruited from outside the ranks of this commonwealth who posed a problem.

During the early wars of conquest even non-Arabs from outside the peninsula had been able to benefit from this reshuffle of the tribal commonwealth; for as long as the Arabs were eager for proselytes to confirm the truth of the faith and for soldiers to swell their armies, even complete foreigners were eligible for admission as Arabs. 'You will be like us and have the same honour as one of us', as the Arabs told the Byzantine garrison at Gaza in an effort to convert it.[1] 'They converted, fought with the Muslims and distinguished themselves; so people said: "although you are not Arabs, you are our brothers and our people, and you are helpers, brothers and fellow-tribesmen" . . . and they became part of the general mass of Arabs', as we are told of the Banū'l-ʿAmm.[2] Similarly, the Asāwira and Ḥamrāʾ were accepted as *ḥalīf*s.[3] But once the early conquests were over, the reshuffle was over too. The new commonwealth had been formed, and the dividing line between tribesmen and non-tribesmen reasserted itself with all the greater force in that the former were now rulers of the world, whereas the latter were defeated enemies. It was thus at the end of the early conquests that the problem presented itself.

Converts recruited outside the new commonwealth did not qualify for tribal membership: from a tribal point of view they were pariahs. In pre-Islamic Arabia they would have been collectively placed under the protection of Arab tribes, and in social reality they did come close to forming satellite groups;[4] but a formal decision to exclude them from tribal membership would have amounted to a formal decision to close the ranks of the believers, and though the attitude of the conquerors to conversion was frequently ambivalent, they never seem to have contemplated so radical a policy. One way or the other, the pariahs thus had to be incorporated.

The solution adopted was to attach them individually to the person responsible for their presence in Arab society, that is their manumitter or whoever had sponsored their conversion or otherwise endorsed their membership. This person, their patron, became the person 'closest to them in life and death', that is he was saddled with responsibility for the payment of blood-money on their behalf and no doubt also for their good behaviour in general in return for the reward customary in the Roman Near East, a title to their estates. The vast majority of converts in the early caliphate were freedmen, and the model behind the solution would seem to have been the Roman patronate over freedmen, which was similarly an individual tie carrying with it a title to succession. But the responsibilities with which the patron was charged arose from the tribal organisation of the conquerors, and they imparted a completely new character to the old patronate: *mawlā* is one of those words which the non-Arab subjects of the Arabs never attempted to translate.[5] The Islamic institution was new also in that it applied to freedmen and free converts alike. The only difference between the two was that the free convert was in a position to vary the terms of the relationship. The free convert who consented to the position of client was in effect consenting to a contract of succession with his future patron, and this is presumably how contemporaries perceived it too.

Attached to an individual patron, the newcomer was affiliated to the tribe of the latter for administrative purposes, though he plainly was not a full member of it in either law or social fact. Indeed, the beauty of the solution lay in the fact that it kept the converts in a position of dependence all while admitting them to the Arab commonwealth. To whom then do we credit this solution? That it owed its existence to the authorities rather than popular usage seems clear from the bureaucratic concern with the client's misdeeds, the general administrative use to which the tie was put, the appearance of the patron's name next to that of the client in official documents and, above all, the failure of non-Arab converts without patrons to have their membership of Arab society officially accepted.[6] But it evidently was not during the wars of conquest that the institution was created, and there was hardly time for it during the First Civil War. The first candidate for its authorship is thus

Muʿāwiya. Muʿāwiya is also a good candidate in that he resided in Syria where, surrounded by a bureaucratic staff inherited from the Byzantines, he presumably acquired some familiarity with the law of the land. Moreover, it was Muʿāwiya who provided the Arabs with the organisation which they were to retain for almost a hundred years, until the ʿAbbāsid revolution;[7] one would expect him to have regulated the status of their non-Arab followers too. Indeed, he is the first Muslim known to have had a *mawlā'l-muwālāt*.[8] There are thus fairly good reasons for crediting the institution to him.[9]

As Arab society lost its tribal roots, the subjection of non-Arab Muslims to client status ceased to have much point and it rapidly came to be regarded as offensive; at the hands of the *ʿulamā'* the institution was to be partly reshaped and partly rejected. On the one hand, the tie was reinterpreted as one of kinship rather than dependence, and it is to this interpretation that it owes most of its classical features.[10] And on the other hand the *ʿulamā'* increasingly ruled that free converts were exempt from it, or, differently put, that they became *mawālī* in the sense of kinsmen of the Muslims at large. As has been seen the tendency to interpret *walā'* as a kinship tie is present in our earliest material: the reshaping of the institution must have been under way by the 720s at the latest. The rejection of *walā'* over free converts seems to have followed somewhat later, being first attested for lawyers who died in the 760s.[11]

Reshaped by the *ʿulamā'*, the patronate came to look more or less like a fictitious kinship tie of the type common in Arabia, and what the *ʿulamā'* achieved was in effect a third reshuffle of the tribal commonwealth: all non-Arab converts were henceforth full members of this commonwealth, not because kinship ties had ceased to matter on the universalisation of Islam, but on the contrary because Islamic law now provided them with such ties. The treatment of the institution at the hands of the scholars thus testifies to the powerful effect of the tribal after-image on the outlook of the scholars.

(b) Roman, provincial and Islamic law

If we accept that *walā'* was modelled on the Roman patronate, what have we proved? In terms of the theory of Roman influence on the Sharīʿa, clearly not very much. Examining the origins of *walā'*, we have encountered provincial practice time and again on the Muslim side, but only one Roman element which did not itself originate in such practice, that is the tie over freedmen which conferred an automatic and unilateral right to succession in the absence of certain heirs; and though we have seen that late Roman and early Muslim law regulated this tie identically in certain respects, it is plain that they did so because both were influenced by provincial practice rather than because the Muslims paid attention to the law of Rome: the patronate could be renounced in early Islamic law because the non-Roman inhabitants of the Roman Near East were in the habit of doing so, not because Justinian happened to have endorsed the practice. Substantially, it was thus provincial practice which went into the Sharīʿa in this particular case; Roman law contributed only in so far as it was part of this practice.

This is scarcely an unexpected conclusion. To speak of Roman law is to speak of a legal system. But as a legal system in the sense of an organised body of law taught, studied and consciously preserved, Roman law disappeared from the Near Eastern provinces together with the Roman state. It lived on as part of provincial practice, both bureaucratic and popular, and it was with this practice that the Arabs came into contact. The only real system which they encountered in the Near Eastern provinces was that of the Jews.

Even so, judging from this one example the proponents of the theory of Roman influence on Islamic law were not entirely wrong. Roman law did form part of provincial practice, and some of it did enter the Sharīʿa as a result. Legal historians interested in the extent to which Roman law was actually practised in the Near East and/or the extent to which Roman law lived on in other legal systems have every reason to continue their enquiry into its ramifications in the Sharīʿa. But for Islamicists concerned with the raw materials of the Sharīʿa the traditional question will undoubtedly have to be reformulated: what we need to examine is not the contribution of Roman law including its provincial variants, but on the contrary that of provincial law including such Roman elements as it may have contained.[12]

Obviously, judging from our one example the opponents of the theory of Roman influence on the Sharīʿa were not entirely wrong either. But the fact that the legal Romanisation of the Near East was incomplete does not mean that the Near East was a legal vacuum which the conquerors were bound to fill with Arabian law of their own.[13] Provincial practice is not a label for something non-existent, insignificant or unknown, but on the contrary for a well-documented set of practices shared by many or most of the inhabitants of the Near East from the Nile to the Tigris, indeed even, it would seem, by the pre-Islamic Arabs themselves to some extent. The more we belittle the contribution of Roman law, the more we make a case for that of *provincial* law, not for that of Arabia.

Provincial law is best attested for Greco-Roman Egypt thanks to the accident of papyrological preservation; but it is clear from scattered evidence that the Near East formed a legal unit in Hellenistic times,[14] and it would seem still to have formed such a unit on the eve of the conquests. No doubt legal practice varied considerably from place to place: that of the Nestorians, according to Ishoʿbokht, varied not only from country to country, but also from district to district or even town to town.[15] But like Greek law in the past, it added up to *ein grosses Ganzen*.[16] Thus manumission with *paramonē* was a single institution common in Egypt, Syria and Iraq alike, however many variations it may have exhibited in detail. Similarly, the concubine freed on her master's death on account of her children must have been known throughout the Near East,[17] as must earnest-money (*arrha*, *arrabon*), another Near Eastern institution which influenced Justinian's law.[18] Provincial law thus amounted to a legal *koinē* – a way of regulating things, usually of Greek or ancient Near Eastern origin, which was known to and understood throughout the provinces which were to form the heartlands of Islam. As has been seen, manumission with *paramonē* was known to the pre-Islamic Arabs too, as was the paramonar service contract. Whether the same applies to earnest-money and the above-mentioned concubine, as the Islamic tradition asserts, remains to be proved, given that it asserts the same about every institution known to early Muslim lawyers.[19] But now that we are familiar with the Near Eastern background, we can see that the *ḥalīf* who arranged for mutual succession between himself and his ally was in fact concluding a succession pact of the type common in the provinces;[20] and when the Prophet paired off Anṣārīs and Muhājirūn as brothers in Medina, he was undoubtedly practising the Near Eastern *adoptio in fratrem*, a special form of the succession pact whereby two men would adopt each others as brothers and institute both common property and mutual succession.[21] To some extent law in Arabia would thus appear to have been Near Eastern law, or an archaic version thereof, not simply tribal law unique to the peninsula. Now given the familiarity of the Arabs with the legal *koinē* on the one hand, and the prevalence of this *koinē* in the future heartlands of Islam, it is tempting to speculate that it was this *koinē* which came to form the substratum of the Sharīʿa: if the Sharīʿa is provincial law recast with Jewish concepts at its backbone and numerous Jewish (and other foreign) elements in its substantive provisions, it would not be surprising that it fails to resemble any known legal system. I should like to reinforce this conjecture with two further examples.

The first concerns wills. Testamentary succession has played a subordinate role in most societies unaffected by the legal tradition of Rome.[22] In some societies it has been completely unknown, as it was to the Athenians before Solon or the Germanic tribes before their encounter with the Roman world;[23] in others, testators have been allowed only minimal freedom to interfere with the normal rules for the devolution of property;[24] and still others have allowed testators to dispose of certain types of property only, other types (notably land) being reserved for the testator's kin.[25] It is likely that testamentary succession was restricted in pre-Islamic Arabia too, though this cannot be proved. Restrictions on the capacity to bequeath were certainly a distinctive feature of Greek law. Thus a Greek could not dispose of his property by will unless he was childless, or he could only dispose of a small fraction, or only with the consent of his heirs (depending on the area involved). The underlying notion was that a man's heirs had a proprietary right in the family's property even while he himself was alive; and for this reason the consent of the heirs was also required for the alienation of family property by sale and manumission.[26] Similar notions have prevailed in many parts of the world,[27] including the ancient Near East, where they are attested for Babylonian and Egyptian law;[28] apparently they prevailed in Zoroastrian law too.[29] Greek and Near Eastern law thus fused effortlessly on this point. In the provinces which fell under Roman rule the practice of seeking the consent of the heirs to alienation of family property by sale and manumission is not securely attested after Diocletian: a sixth-century example relating to manumission has been adduced, but disputed.[30] Even so, there is nothing to suggest that the *libera testamenti factio* of Roman law was widely adopted in the Near East: in practice testators felt bound not to harm the interests of their children, and disinheritance of children is unheard of, at least in Egypt.[31] The traditional attitude to wills also survived in Nestorian Iraq where Ishoʿbokht (quite wrongly) explains the limits placed by Augustus on testamentary manumission in Roman law with reference to the rights of the heirs to the family property.[32] Restrictions on the right to bequeath were thus part of the legal *koinē* of the pre-Islamic Near East.

Islamic law also places limits on testamentary dispositions: neither bequests nor gifts in death sickness may exceed one third of the estate. According to the Imāmīs, this rule has its origin in the customary law of Medina: a man who died in Medina some time before the Prophet's arrival there willed away a third of his estate, and this became *sunna*, normative practice.[33] According to the Sunnīs, however, it was instituted by the Prophet himself: the Prophet ruled that a man who leaves only a daughter, or indeed no heirs at all, may bequeath no more than a third of his estate.[34] This tradition has been accepted as authentic by Coulson[35] and Powers,[36] both on the ground that the Prophet may be assumed himself to have regulated a problem which may be assumed to have been posed by the inheritance laws of the Qur'ān (though they disagree about the nature of this problem).[37] Scholars with a taste for harmonisation might argue that the Prophet instituted the rule under the influence of Medinese customary law. But Schacht believed it to be of Umayyad origin: given that the estates of those who died without heirs fell to the Treasury, it was in the interest of the caliphs to place restrictions on testamentary dispositions and thus increase its share.[38] All these explanations are somewhat unconvincing.[39]

First, it is clear that the Prophet himself cannot have instituted the rule, be it under the influence of the customary law of Medina or otherwise. If we consider all extant traditions and doctrines on the subject of testamentary restrictions, we find that four basic positions are attested.

i. There are no restrictions

This position is best attested in Imāmī Ḥadīth. Several versions of a tradition ascribed to Abū ʿAbdallāh, i.e. Jaʿfar al-Ṣādiq, the sixth imam, contend that 'a man has the best right to his own property as long as there is any life in him; if he bequeaths all of it, that is permitted to him'.[40] This argument was not accepted even by the Imāmīs themselves.[41] A less radical version of it was to the effect that a man could at least bequeath all of his property to the imams.[42] This too was rejected by the Imāmīs,[43] but it would seem to have been taken over by the Ismāʿīlīs: a general in Fāṭimid Egypt left everything to the caliph, disinheriting his own sons.[44] There are also residues of this view on the Sunnī side. Thus a tradition attributed to ʿUmar II argues that a man may dispose of his entire estate if he bequeaths it to charity: it is only if he wishes to favour one heir over another that he can dispose of no more than a third.[45] But Sufyān al-Thawrī, the eminent Kufan lawyer and traditionist, apparently thought that the restriction did not even apply in the latter case: having lost his son, he bequeathed everything to his sister and the latter's son, thereby disinheriting his own brother.[46]

ii. There are severe restrictions

Some traditions argue that bequests limited to a fourth or a fifth of the estate are better than bequests limited to a third.[47] Most are clearly familiar with the classical restriction, and many classical works similarly recommend bequests below the legal limit.[48] But one such tradition invokes a Qur'ānic peg for bequests to the size of one fifth of the estate, arguing that this is God's own view in apparent ignorance of God's view as transmitted by the Prophet.[49] And another cautiously endorses bequests of up to a third of the estate, provided that the testator has few heirs, as if the legality of bequests so large were still in doubt.[50]

iii. There are no restrictions if there are no legal heirs

This was reputedly the view of Shurayḥ, Ibn Masʿūd, Masrūq and Abū Ḥanīfa in Kufa,[51] ʿAbīda in Basra,[52] and Isḥāq b. Rāhūyah in Baghdad;[53] in short, it was the view of all the pre-classical Iraqis.[54] It is also the view of all the classical schools which emerged from Iraq, that is the Ḥanafīs,[55] Zaydīs,[56] Imāmīs[57] and Ibāḍīs.[58]

iv. There are restrictions even in the absence of heirs

The Medinese and the upstart schools all hold that bequests are limited to a third of the estate regardless of the presence of heirs. This was the view of Mālik, Shāfiʿī, Ibn Ḥanbal (according to some), the Syrian Awzāʿī and others.[59] It survived as classical Mālikī and Shāfiʿī law too,[60] and though the Ḥanbalīs were divided (transmissions from Ibn Ḥanbal being contradictory),[61] the Ẓāhirīs also endorsed the Medinese position.[62]

Now if it was remembered that the Prophet had limited bequests to a third of the estate regardless of whether the testator left heirs designated by the law or not, how do we explain this disagreement? Why is it that not a single Iraqi seemed to remember what he had decreed? Even if we assume that the Prophet had only placed limits on bequests in the presence of heirs, it is odd that some lawyers should have been more liberal and others more severe, and odd too that the Iraqis who agreed with him should have failed to invoke his views. *Pace* Coulson and Powers, then, the limitation of bequests to a third hardly goes back to the Prophet himself. The tradition in which he formulates this rule is certainly also anything but a pristine source.[63]

Secondly, it is clear that Schacht's explanation of the rule must be rejected. The Iraqis, or in other words the first scholars to emerge, only place limits on bequests when legal heirs are present: testators without relatives are free to will away everything they possess. The Treasury thus did not stand to gain from the rule in its original form, and it cannot have been the interests of the Treasury which led to its formulation.[64]

Thirdly, it is clear that the rule should be seen in the context of provincial practice. It was obviously the interests of the heirs, not those of the Treasury, which it was designed to protect.[65] In fact, the Iraqis explicitly argued that this was its rationale (*ʿilla*);[66] and they implicitly made the same point when they compared the heir with the *shafīʿ*, the person endowed with rights of pre-emption:[67] just as the *shafīʿ* has a latent right to lands and buildings adjoining his own even while his neighbour owns them, so the heir has a latent right to his relative's property even while the latter is alive. This is the very point underlying the Greek and Near Eastern regulation of bequests.[68] Moreover, a pre-classical tradition on the limitation of bequests and gifts in death sickness to a third illustrates this limitation with reference to the manumission of slaves. In the context of Islamic law this seems a curiously indirect way of doing so, but it makes perfect sense in the context of law intended to protect the rights of the heirs to patrimonial property: land and slaves were *the* assets of the household.[69] Finally, with the exception of the Ẓāhirīs, all the classical schools, not just the Iraqi ones, allow the testator to dispose of more than a third of the estate *if the heirs consent to it*.[70] The Sharīʿa thus preserves the ancient *Beispruchsrecht* of the heirs in the law of bequests.

In sum, the evidence suggests that the Muslim restriction on testamentary dispositions originates in provincial law. Indeed, would it not be odd if developments internal to the Muslim community had simply happened to issue in much the same rules regarding bequests as those which had prevailed throughout the Near East for over a thousand years? As mentioned already, similar rules may have applied in Arabia too; yet, *pace* the Imāmīs, it was not simply Arabian law which became that of Islam. What the sources suggest is *first* a stage of total disagreement on exposure to the diverse customs of the Near East, Roman and non-Roman, and *next* a stage in which the predominant customs of this area become the generally accepted rules of Islamic law. As in the case of *walāʾ* and *paramonē*, the familiarity of the pre-Islamic Arabs with the Near Eastern *koinē* may have assisted its victory in Islam; but in none of these examples was it simply Arabian law which went into the Sharīʾa.

The second example concerns divorce. In 689 a Christian Arab girl by the name of Nonna divorced her husband at Nessana by relinquishing all rights to her dowry and other marital property.[71] In formal terms her divorce was compatible with Roman law, though there are different views about the way in which this compatibility is to be achieved.[72] But in substance it was evidently a non-Roman procedure. Had Nonna or her mother (who assisted her at the proceedings) been familiar with the imperial rules, Nonna would simply have sent her husband a *libellus repudii* without undertaking to pay so heavy a price for her freedom.[73] What she practised was provincial law. Almost five hundred years later, in 1114, a Jewish girl by the name of Jawhara similarly divorced her husband in Egypt at the cost of relinquishing all property to which she was entitled under her marriage contract, be it dowry, gifts or delayed payment.[74] And by the time of Jawhara's divorce it had long been possible for Muslim women similarly to divorce their husbands at the cost of renouncing their dowries or comparable financial sacrifices in their husbands' favour. In Islamic law the procedure is known as *khulʿ*.[75] That Christian, Jewish and Muslim women alike obtained their divorce by the same procedure is plain; but given that Islamic law scarcely existed in 689, the Christian woman can scarcely have acted under its influence: on the contrary, Nonna is more likely to have influenced the Muslims than the other way round. In fact, the procedure can be traced very far back on the Jewish side. Most Jewish attestations are late, it is true, and moreover mostly written in Arabic.[76] But the procedure has its roots in the rule concerning what the rabbis, being men, called the 'recalcitrant wife': if a woman could not bear living with her husband, she could institute divorce proceedings and, if the court accepted her claim, obtain a divorce in return for renouncing her claim to the cash settlement promised by her husband in the marriage contract. This rule, alluded to in the Palestinian Talmud, accepted in Babylonia in 650–1, and discussed in other sources too, is related to stipulations in marriage contracts attested for the Jews of Elephantine in the fourth century B.C.[77] And these stipulations in their turn are derived from an ancient Near Eastern procedure of divorce initiated by the wife.[78] Now the compartmentalization of scholarship is such that while historians of late Roman and Jewish law both know about the Islamic *khulʿ*, Roman scholars do not know about the Jewish procedure, Jewish scholars do not know about the Nessana procedure, and Islamicists do not know about either. But what we have here is clearly another institution which, first attested in the ancient Near East, survived in provincial practice from Iraq to Palestine, and presumably Egypt too, passing from there into the Sharīʿa.

The provincial *koinē* thus contributed to the Islamic law of marriage, succession and slavery alike, and in all three cases the provincial institutions came through with an extraordinary recognisability.[19] Indeed, if these cases are anything to go by the transition from provincial to Islamic law was the result of four fairly simple developments.

First, unlike the Greeks, the Muslims applied systematic thought to substantive law, with the result that the fluid notions underlying provincial practice were replaced by hard and fast legal categories of the familiar dichotomous kind. Koschaker thought it a pity that most scholars working on *paramonē* had been trained on Roman law: their concepts were too rigid; like the Romans, they thought of a man as either slave or free.[80] And no doubt Koschaker was right. But it was not just Roman legal thought which was alien to the Greeks, but legal thought altogether, and legal thought usually *is* dichotomous: a man is either slave or free, guilty or innocent, liable or not, not something in between. As Daube observes, justice everywhere seems to contain an element averse to finer differentiation;[81] and Muslim concepts are certainly no less rigid than those of the Romans. The status of the paramonar freedman might not worry the Greeks,[82] but to the Muslims, as to modern scholars, he had to be either slave or free: manumission cannot be partial, as even those who accepted proportional manumission insisted.[83]

Secondly, detailed legal regulations in a protective vein replaced the *Privatwillkür* of the Greeks. Allāh was suspicious of legal relations created by private individuals, partly because law was His domain, He being the one and only truth and power in the universe, and more particularly because contractual freedom was conducive to inequality and exploitation. Paramonar manumission may be described as an extreme example of freedom of contract in that the freedom to define the terms is entirely on the manumitter's side, and what the Muslim lawyers removed was precisely this freedom: it is the law, not the manumitter, which decides whether the *mukatāb* is a slave or a free man, whether he may travel or not, whether his children are to be included in or excluded from the contract, whether he may be re-enslaved on his failure to pay, and so forth.[84] In the same vein they struck out all elements of risk and uncertainty liable to result in unearned advantage to one party at the expense of the other from contracts of sale and took a dim view of private stipulations in general. What is so striking about Imāmī law from this point of view is that it allows one party to define the legal position of another, in the law of manumission, with a latitude quite unknown to Islamic law at large.

Thirdly, the lawyers lost direct contact with provincial law within a century and a half of the conquests. As mentioned already, they are in general quite innocent of the idea that the Sharīʿa might have its roots in legal practice other than that of Arabia, and the gradual onset of collective amnesia is well illustrated in the law of bequests; for whereas the pre-classical tradition illustrating the restriction of bequests to a third of the estate with reference to manumission is formulated in terms familiar from provincial law, the classical tradition is not: in response to Iraqi claims that the restriction was intended to protect the rights of the heirs, Ibn Ḥazm quite correctly points out that there is nothing in the Prophetic tradition to suggest that this is the case.[85] The Medinese and later schools who apply the restriction regardless of the presence or otherwise of legal heirs testify to a new development: accepted rules, generally believed to be Prophetic, are now systematically applied and extended without concern for their original point.

Finally, the law of the Near East was given a tribal imprint. 'One effect of that mixture of refined Roman law with primitive barbarian usage . . . was to revive many features of archaic jurisprudence which had died out of the Roman world, so that the decomposition [of kinship ties] which had seemed to be over commenced again and is to some extent still proceeding', as Maine put it with reference to the effect on the barbarian invasions of Europe on legal development.[86] Much the same is true of the Near East. The tribal organisation of the Arabs on the one hand, and the collective amnesia whereby the Prophet's Medina came to be revered as the true home of the Sharīʿa on the other, meant that the Arabs gave an archaic stamp to the law which they received. Thus the patronate, long dissociated from agnatic ties on the Roman side, became an agnatic institution once again, while agnatic succession, similarly long defunct by Justinian's side, was restored to almost pristine purity in Sunnī Islam. Once more, the Imāmīs are strikingly different.[87]

On the basis of the material reviewed in this book the genetic make-up Islamic law might thus be hypothetically summarised as follows. The tribal legacy of the invaders in conjunction with Jewish concepts provided the Muslims above all with the capacity to reshape, though Jewish law certainly and tribal law possibly contributed raw material too. What they reshaped was essentially provincial practice. This practice contained elements of Roman law in Syria and Egypt, just as it contained elements of Sasanid law in Iraq; and Roman law certainly, and Sasanid law probably, entered the Sharīʿa as a result.[88] But substantially it was of ancient Near Eastern and Greek origin, or in other words it was the indigenous law of the Near East as it had developed after Alexander. The Muslims sifted and systematised this law in the name of God, imprinting it with their own image in the process.

Evidently, the four examples of *walāʾ*, *kitāba*, limitation of bequests and *khulʿ* do not suffice to prove that the Sharīʿa should be thus explained: the outcome of this book is a working hypothesis, not a hypothesis vindicated. But it will be admitted that there is good reason to suspect that the clue to *la mystère de la formation et des origines du fiqh* is to be found in provincial law.

APPENDIX 1

The slavegirl's twins

What happens if a man promises his slavegirl freedom on condition that her first child is a boy, whereupon she has twins, one boy and one girl? This curious question was discussed by Roman and Muslim lawyers alike. Ulpian held that the boy is presumed to have been born first, irrespective of fact, so that the mother is freed and the daughter born free (Buckland, *Slavery*, p. 487, citing *Digest*, 34, 5, 10, 1). But this solution was too simple for the Muslims.

'When someone says to his slavegirl, "if the first child you bear is a boy, then you are free", and she bears a boy and a girl without it being known who was born first, then half of the mother and half of the girl are freed while the son remains a slave. This is because both of the two [females] are [wholly] freed in one circumstance, namely when the son is born first – the mother in accordance with the condition and the girl by following her mother, who is free by the time she is born. And both remain [wholly] slaves in another circumstance, namely when the girl is born first – the condition having failed. So [when the order is not known], both are half freed and must work off the other half' (Marghīnānī, *Hidāya*, part ii, p. 62, with a discussion of rules to be followed if the order is disputed)

Thus far the Ḥanafīs. The Ibāḍīs found the question of interest too:

'I asked Abū'l-Mu'arrij and Ibn ʿAbd al-ʿAzīz about the man who says to his slavegirl, "if you bear a boy, you are free", whereupon she bears a boy and a girl. Ibn ʿAbd al-ʿAzīz said that if the boy is born before the girl, the boy remains a slave but both she [sc. the mother] and the girl are free, [the latter] because she was born after she [sc. the mother] was freed. But if the girl is born before the boy, both the girl and the boy remain slaves and only she [sc. the mother] is freed' (Abū Ghānim, *Mudawwana*, vol. II, p. 173).

In fact, the question would seem to have been popular with all the early lawyers of Iraq, for other versions of it are attested for the Zaydīs, Imāmīs and Ismāʿīlīs, as well as for Sufyān al-Thawrī. What happens if the master promises his slavegirl that the first child she bears (as opposed to she herself) will be free if it is a boy, whereupon she has two boys, or three? Or if the boy is still-born? Or if she bears a hermaphrodite? Or if he promises his slave (as opposed to the slavegirl) freedom on condition that the slavegirl married to him has a son, and the slavegirl freedom if she has a daughter, whereupon she fails to have twins, or fails to have them in the order specified? There seems to be no end to the variations possible (Naḥwī, *Tadhkhira*, fols. 216bff; Hādī, *Muntakhab*, fol. 86a; Ṭūsī, *Nihāya*, p. 544; Nuʿmān, *Daʿāʾim*, vol. ii, no. 1162, cf. 1157; Thawrī in ʿAbd al-Razzāq, *Muṣannaf*, vol. IX, nos. 16792–3; cf. also the variations in Abū Ghānims *Mudawwana*, vol. II, p. 172). The Medinese considered the case of the still-born boy too (Saḥnūn, *Mudawwana*, vol. VII, p. 55), but neither they nor the later schools seem to have found the issue as absorbing as did the Iraqis.

What does one do with a parallel between Roman and Islamic law of this kind? Did the Muslims owe the original question to Ulpian? It might be argued that this is unlikely because casuistry is more at home in Jewish and Islamic than in Roman law. But on the one hand, the Roman lawyers were not above casuistry: there are conditional manumissions involving triplets in the *Digest* too (cf. Duff, *Freedmen*, pp. 50f). And on the other hand, I have not come across a comparable discussion on the Jewish side (which is not, it must be emphasised, much of a guarantee that it cannot be found there). Of course the question is one that the Muslim lawyers might have thought up themselves, but the coincidence is nonetheless extraordinary.

APPENDIX 2

Goldziher on Roman and Islamic law

Goldziher regarded Roman law as 'one of the chief sources of Islamite jurisprudence' ('Principles', p. 296). He first stated this in his article published by the Hungarian Academy of Sciences in 1884 ('Jogtudomány'); he returned to it in his *Muhammedanische Studien*, published in 1889–90 (cf. vol. I, p. 188n, vol. II, pp. 75f), and he reaffirmed it in his review of Savvas Pacha in *Byzantinische Zeitschrift* 1893. FitzGerald wrongly lists Savvas as an adherent of the theory of Roman influence on Islamic law. Savvas *used* to adhere to this theory, as he himself explains ('L'erreur, en effet, est si facile!'); but his book was based on his new realization that in fact it is exclusively derived from the word of God and the conduct of the Prophet (Savvas Pacha, *Études sur la théorie du droit musulman*, vol. I, Paris 1892, pp. xviff, xxi). When Goldziher insisted on Roman influence in his review, debiting Savvas' *naiveté* to his Oriental origins, Savvas wrote a vehement reply, affirming his position on the origins of the Sharīʿa and pointing out that whereas he himself [a Greek Christian] was an Aryan, Goldziher [a Hungarian Jew] was a Turanian whose aggressiveness arose from the fact that he still had some drops of Mongol blood in his veins! (Savvas Pacha, *Le droit musulman expliqué*, Paris 1896, p. 26). (The quotation which FitzGerald, 'Alleged Debt', p. 90, gives from the second edition of Savvas' *Études*, vol. I (Paris 1902) is made up of two separate passages from pp. xxi and 52, neither of which affirms Roman influence.) Undeterred, Goldziher proceeded to reaffirm his views in his 'Die Religion des Islams' in P. Hinneberg (ed.), *Die Kultur der Gegenwart*, vol. I, part iii, Berlin and Leipzig 1906, p. 102; in his 'Principles', published in 1907 (and, *pace* FitzGerald, not a translation of his Hungarian work); in his review of Schmidt in *Deutsche Literaturzeitung* 1911; and, finally, in his article 'Fiḳh' published in the *Encyclopaedia of Islam*[1] in 1913 or later. FitzGerald is thus quite wrong when he asserts that Goldziher did not attach much importance to his views on Roman influence, that he repented of them in his later and 'more fully considered work', and that his research was 'directed to emphasising the essentially Arab character of Islamic civilisation' (compare the quotation from Goldziher given below, in note 64 of Chapter 1); and the assurance that 'there is no reason to doubt the clear and unanimous tradition' does not testify to a very profound understanding of Goldziher's work on Ḥadīth (FitzGerald, 'Alleged Debt', pp. 82f, 92f, 98).

Goldziher's concrete assertions were the following.

1. Fiqh

Fiqh, he said, may be identified as *rerum divinarum atque humanarum notitia* ('Jogtudomány', pp. 19f; 'Fiḳh', p. 101). Apparently he had this idea from Hugues (to whom he refers in 'Jogtudomány', p. 8, and again in *Muhammedanische Studien*, vol. II, p. 75n). It is not clear whether he intended it as a helpful comparison or as 'une application de droit romain' (Hugues, 'Les origines', p. 171); but he certainly claimed that *fiqh* and *faqīh* are loan translations of *(juris)prudentia* and *(juris)prudens* ('Jogtudomány', p. 19; 'Principles', p. 296), sometimes adding that the Jews of Palestine had similarly called their scholars *hakhamim* under the influence of Roman law ('Religion', p. 102; 'Fiḳh', p. 102).

There are three objections to this suggestion. First, Goldziher consistently exploits a structural similarity between the concepts of early Roman and Islamic law to postulate a genetic relationship between the two without regard for the fact that it was with late Roman law that the Arabs came into contact. The *prudentes* of Rome disappeared some four centuries before the conquests (see for example B. Nicholas, *An Introduction to Roman Law*, Oxford 1962, p. 30; this point was rightly made by FitzGerald, 'Alleged Debt', pp. 96f). Secondly, here as elsewhere he fails to consider the Greek (not to mention Syriac) forms in which Roman legal concepts will have been current in the Near East (another valid point made by FitzGerald, 'Alleged Debt', p. 94). Even at Beirut, where Goldziher believed the teachers of the Muslims to have been educated ('Principles', p. 297), the teaching was done in Greek from the late fourth or early fifth century onwards, though the textbooks were in Latin (Marrou, *Education*, p. 291). Thirdly, parallels between Jewish and Islamic law are unlikely to have arisen through independent borrowing by Jews and Muslims from Roman law. Unlike the Roman *prudentes*, the Jewish *hakhamim* were well represented in the Near East at the time of the Arab conquests, and there is no doubt that Jewish law contributed to the Sharīʿa. If a genetic relationship is postulated, the presumption must thus be that, whatever the relationship between Roman and Jewish law, the parallels in Islamic law arose through Muslim borrowing from the Jews (cf. above, Chapter 1, p. 11).

2. Fatwā

Hugues equated *fatwās* with *responsa prudentium* ('Les Origines', p. 171), and Goldziher followed suit ('Jogtudomány', p. 19). The same three objections apply. Given that the equation is absent from Goldziher's later work, he probably abandoned it himself.

3. Raʾy

'Just as Roman legal practice gave great weight to the *opinio prudentium* in legal deduction, so the Islamite *prudentes* assumed the prerogative of an authoritative subjective *opinio*; for *raʾj*, as it is called in Arabic, is a literal translation of the Latin term' ('Principles', p. 297; cf. 'Jogtudomány', p. 11; *Muhammedanische Studien*, vol. II, p. 76; 'Religion', p. 102; 'Fiḳh', p. 101).

As pointed out before, there is no such expression as *opinio prudentium* in Roman law (Crone and Cook, *Hagarism*, p. 151). *Responsa prudentium* were verdicts on legal questions submitted to the jurists, on a par with *fatwā*s, while *interpretatio prudentium* was the whole phenomenon of scholarly thinking about the law, on a par with *fiqh* (cf. Nicholas, *Introduction*, pp. 28ff). Goldziher is of course right that the Romans spoke about the opinions of the jurists (cf. Gaius 1, 7: 'Responsa prudentium sunt sententiae et opiniones eorum, quibus permissum est jura condere'), and that these opinions mattered greatly in early Roman law. But the usual objections apply: by the time of the Arab conquests Roman law had long ceased to be a jurists' law; the Arabs did not translate directly from Latin; and Muslim *ra'y* is more closely related to Judaic *daʿat* and *sevara* than it is to the opinions of the jurists known to Gaius (Crone and Cook, *Hagarism*, pp. 37f).

Schacht contributed to the confusion over this issue by equating Goldziher's coinage with *ijmāʿ* rather than with *ra'y*: 'the concept of the *opinio prudentium* of Roman law seems to have provided the model for the highly organised concept of the 'consensus of the scholars' as formulated by the ancient schools in Islamic law' (*Introduction*, p. 20; cf. 'Foreign Elements', p. 134). But just as there was no concept known as *opinio prudentium* in Roman law, so also there was no notion of scholarly consensus. Hadrian is said to have ruled that if juristic opinion was unanimous, it had the force of law (Nicholas, *Introduction*, p. 32, with reference to the continuation of the passage in Gaius just cited: 'quorum omnium si in unum sententiae concurrunt, id quod ita sentiunt, legis vicem obtinet; si vero dissentiunt, judici licet quam velit sententiam sequi'); but Hadrian was imposing imperial decision procedures on the jurists, not sanctioning a principle evolved by themselves (Crone and Cook, *Hagarism*, p. 151). Once again, the Islamic notion is more likely to originate in Jewish law (*ibid.*, p. 180[11]; FitzGerald, 'Alleged Debt', p. 97).

Goldziher paraphrased *ijmāʿ* both as *consensus doctorum ecclesiae*, viz. The consensus of the scholars, and as *consensus ecclesiae*, viz. the general usage of the community, and adduced a quotation from Severus on the force of custom in illustration of the latter ('Jogtudomány', p. 18; cf. *Muhammedanische Studien*, vol. II, p. 76; 'Fiḳh', pp. 101f). At the hands of Schacht, this quotation became an illustration of the correspondence between *ijmāʿ* and *opinio prudentium* ('Foreign Elements', p. 134). No such acrobatics are required to establish a correspondence between the Jewish and early Islamic attitudes to custom (Crone and Cook, *Hagarism*, pp. 37f).

4. Written and Unwritten Law

Goldziher frequently asserted that the Jewish and Muslim distinction between written and unwritten law both reflect the Roman distinction between *leges scriptae* and *leges non scriptae* ('Jogtudomány', pp. 10f; 'Principles', p. 297 (where 'half a century' is a slip for 'half a millenium'); 'Religion', p. 102). But if the Jews borrowed it from anyone, they borrowed it from the Greeks, to whom the Romans likewise owed it (cf. Schulz, *History*, pp. 71ff; Daube, 'Rabbinic Methods', p. 248); and it is the Jewish, not the Roman distinction which recurs in Islam: the unwritten law of the Romans was a literal, not an epistemological category, and it meant customary law, not the tradition of the jurists (Crone and Cook, *Hagarism*, p. 151; cf. also FitzGerald, 'Alleged Debt', p. 95).

5. Maṣlaḥa

No principle, according to Goldziher, 'more strikingly demonstrates the profound influence of Roman law on the development of legal opinion in Islam' than *maṣlaḥa* or *istiṣlāḥ*: 'here we recognize the Roman standard of the *utilitas publica*, which gives the interpreter of the law the right . . . to wrest a plain and unambiguous law into something quite different, in the interests of public weal' ('Principles', p. 297).

Goldziher apparently had in mind Papinian's invocation of *utilitas publica* in justification of the praetor's right to supplement and correct the *jus civile* (*Digest*, I, I, 7; cf. Goldziher's formulation in his 'Das Prinzip des *Istiṣḥāb* in der muhammedanischen Gesetzwissenschaft', *Wiener Zeitschrift für die Kunde des Morgen-*

landes 1887, p. 183n; and in 'Fiḳh', p. 103). What the praetor did, however, was not to twist the meaning of unambiguous laws in the interest of public welfare, but rather to supplement, qualify and in the long run undermine a body of traditional law by edictal legislation; and to this activity there is no parallel in Islam. Moreover, the expression is usually employed in a different sense, that is in justification of the interests of the state when these conflict with the rights of individuals: what the Romans called *utilitas publica*, the Muslims less euphemistically called *jawr al-sulṭān* or *ḍarūra*, 'the tyranny of the authorities' or 'necessity' (cf. A. Steinwenter, 'Utilitas publica – utilitas singulorum' in *Festschrift P. Koschaker*, Weimar 1939, vol. I, esp. pp. 93ff).

Goldziher's *maṣlaḥa* has more in common with the phrase *utilitatis causa receptum* which is precisely an expression for departure from strict legal reasoning for the sake of an equitable result (cf. J. A. Ankum, ' "Utilitatis Causa Receptum". On the Pragmatic Methods of the Roman Lawyers', *Symbolae Iuridicae et Historicae Martino David Dedicata*, Leiden 1968, vol. I). But the Roman expression lacks the overtones of charity which the Muslim *maṣlaḥa* share with the rabbinic *mippene tiqqun ha-ʿolam* or *mippene tiqqanah* of so-and-so (M. Jastrow, *Dictionary of the Targumim, the Talmud Babli and Yerushalmi, and the Midrashic Literature*, London 1895–1903, vol. II, pp. 1666, 1693). Goldziher was of course perfectly aware of this parallel (cf. 'Das Prinzip', p. 183n; 'Fiḳh', p. 103). So was FitzGerald, who rightly pointed out that it was closer than the Roman one ('Alleged Debt', p. 97; the claim that *utilitas publica* was never an avowed principle in the development of Roman law is not however entirely correct). Schacht tentatively opted for a Roman derivation in *Origins*, p. 100; but he wisely changed his mind (*Introduction*, p. 21).

6. Istiṣḥāb

According to Goldziher, the type of presumption exemplified by *istiṣḥāb* is 'bekanntlich . . . im römischen Recht von grosser Wichtigkeit' ('Das Prinzip', p. 231). In fact, however, presumptions played very little role in classical Roman law, and though they had become common by Justinian's time (under the name of *praesumptiones*, *prolēpseis*), they were simply circumstances in which no proof was required, not rules regarding the allocation of the burden of proof (Buckland, *Text-Book*, p. 436n; D. Simon, *Untersuchungen zum Justinianischen Zivilprozess*, Munich 1969, pp. 175ff, esp. 195, 201). Presumptions are however of central importance in both Islamic and Jewish law, and the particular type which the Muslims called *istiṣḥāb* were known to the Jews as *ḥazaqa* (Jastrow, *Dictionary*, vol. I, pp. 445f). Once more, Goldziher was perfectly aware of this fact (cf. 'Das Prinzip', p. 185). And once more Schacht began by supporting Goldziher, only to opt for a Jewish derivation in the end (*Origins*, p. 100; *Introduction*, p. 21).

7. ʿIlla

Goldziher identified the Islamic *ʿilla* as the Roman *ratio legis* ('Religion', p. 102; 'Principles', p. 297; 'Fiḳh', p. 101). This could be correct, to the best of my knowledge; but whether it actually is depends on the missing Greek and Syriac links.

8. Substantive law

Goldziher rarely ventured into substantive law. He did however assert that the maxim *al-walad lī'l-firāsh* is of Roman origin, as has been seen, though this is unlikely to be correct (above, Chapter 1, pp. 10f). He also found a Roman origin for the fact that the oath principally devolves unto the defendant in Islamic law (*Muhammedanische Studien*, vol. II, p. 75). But this is also more likely to be of Jewish, or Pentateuchal, origin (Crone, 'Jāhilī and Jewish Law').

Goldziher was a Jew with an intimate knowledge of Jewish law, who could have made an effortless case for the theory that Jewish law contributed heavily to the Sharīʿa; yet time and again he opted for the view that it was 'a bygone stage of Roman legal history' which made the contribution (cf. FitzGerald, 'Alleged Debt', pp. 97f). Behind so extraordinary a choice there must have been personal rather than scholarly factors, and one may speculate that they had to do with his standing in European society: whereas a preoccupation with Jewish influence on Islamic law simply confirmed him as a Jew, a preoccupation with *Roman* influence on this law made him an exponent of one of the most prestigious aspects of European civilisation. Be this as it may, it would be unwise for even the most ardent admirer of Goldziher to practise *taqlīd* of his views on this subject.

APPENDIX 3

The muhtasib

The first scholar to suggest that the *muḥtasib* perpetuates a Greco-Roman official seems to have been Gaudefroy-Demombynes. In 1939 he declared himself convinced that the ʿAbbāsid *muḥtasib* was an Islamised version of the Roman aedile (M. Gaudefroy-Demombynes, 'Sur les origines de la justice musulmane', *Mélanges syriens offerts à René Dussaud*, Paris 1939, vol. II, p. 828), and in 1947 he reaffirmed his conviction in a review of E. Tyan, this time adding the terms *agoranomos* and *ṣāḥib al-sūq* (*id.*, 'Un magistrat musulman: le mohtasib', *Le Journal des Savants* 1947, pp. 36f. On the relationship between the Roman aedile and the Greek *agoranomos*, see B. R. Foster, 'Agoranomos and Muḥtasib', *Journal of the Economic and Social History of the Orient* 1970). It was similarly in a review of E. Tyan that Schacht first identified the ʿAbbāsid *muḥtasib* as an Islamised version of the Byzantine *agoranomos*, an idea which he was to repeat several times thereafter without reference to Gaudefroy-Demombynes (Schacht in *Orientalia* 1948, p. 518; *id.*, 'The Law', p. 75; *id.*, 'Droit byzantin', p. 207; *id.*, *Introduction*, p. 25. He was familiar with Gaudefroy-Demombynes' article of 1939, cf. *Introduction*, p. 224, but possibly not that of 1947, unearthed by Foster, 'Agoranomos and Muḥtasib', p. 128n).

Schacht observed that the Greek and early Islamic market inspectors had similar functions and similar names, the first name attested for the Muslim official being *ṣāḥib/ʿāmil al-sūq*, which looks like a translation of *agoranomos* and which survived in Spain long after the title of *muḥtasib* had ousted it in the East. He did not however cite any literature on the Greek market inspector, and he was not apparently perturbed by the fact that the last inscriptional record of the *agoranomos* dates from about three centuries before the Arab conquest (cf. *Encyclopaedia of Islam*², *s.v.* 'ḥisba'; included in the bibliography of Schacht's *Introduction*, p. 231). That it ought to have perturbed him is clear from Foster's systematic review of the evidence which concludes that there was probably no genetic link between the two institutions: since all cities in antiquity must have had market inspectors, the argument for continuity must rest primarily on terminology; and though the term *agoranomos* was still in use in Justinian's time, it had been replaced by other terms in Syria (Foster, *op. cit.*, esp. pp. 134, 139, 143). This might seem to settle the question, but in fact it does not.

Among the various Greek officials charged with the duty of market inspection in antiquity there was a *logistēs*. The terms *logistēs* and *agoranomos* were used interchangeably by the Jews, who sometimes transliterated them and sometimes translated them as *ḥashban* and *baʿl ha-suq* (S. Liebermann, 'Roman Legal Institutions in Early Rabbinics and in the Acta Martyrum', *Jewish Quarterly Review* 1944–5, p. 37n). *Ḥashban* and *muḥtasib* are related terms, both meaning something like 'calculator' on a par with *logistēs* (*ibid.*, p. 52). As Sperber has pointed out, this means that not only *muḥtasib*, but also *ṣāḥib al-sūq* are likely to be derived from the Greek terms (D. Sperber, 'On the Term *Ḥeshbon*', *Tarbiz* 1969–70, pp. 96f (in Hebrew with English summary); cf. id., 'On the Office of the Agoranomos in Roman Palestine, *Zeitschrift der Deutschen Morgenländischen Gesellschaft* 1977). Sperber is undoubtedly right. Whereas *ṣāḥib al-sūq* is an obvious name for a market inspector, it is odd that its synonym should be *muḥtasib*. Schacht claimed that the second term was of Qur'ānic inspiration and testified to the Islamisation of the Hellenistic institution ('Droit byzantin', p. 207). But he did not state what Qur'ānic verse he had in mind; and as Cahen and Talbi point out, 'there seems to exist no text which states explicitly either the reasons for the choice of this term or how the meanings mentioned above have arisen from the idea of 'calculation' or 'sufficiency' which is expressed by the root' ('Ḥisba', pp. 485f). The only possible explanation for this odd choice of root is that the term *muḥtasib* is a loan translation; and if this term is a loan translation, the same is presumably true of its synonym.

It should thus be clear that the term *muḥtasib* must be as early as that of *ṣāḥib al-sūq*: the two terms merely happen to be attested at slightly different times in the extant literature. But it is not obvious that the Arabs translated directly from Greek, as Sperber seems to assume. They did not usually do so; and if Foster is right that the term *agoranomos* had disappeared from the pre-conquest provinces, they cannot have done so. Now if they borrowed their terminology from a Semitic-speaking population, the only population from which they could have borrowed it would appear to be the Jews. There is admittedly a *rabb shūq* = *agoranomos* in a third-century bilingual Palmyrene inscription (Sperber, 'On the Office of the Agoranomos', p. 231n); but there are no Syriac translations of *agoranomos* and *logistēs* in Payne-Smith's *Thesaurus*. The Syriac-speaking Christians simply transliterated the Greek terms; and the Arabs scarcely had the philological competence to translate *logista* as *muḥtasib*. Payne-Smith's *Thesaurus* is an old dictionary, and it is not impossible that Syriac translations of the Greek terms may turn up. But until they do so, it must be concluded that the *ṣāḥib al-sūq*/*muḥtasib* is a late antique official taken over by the Arabs under a Jewish terminology. In other words, the *muḥtasib* tells us more about the relationship between the Arab conquerors and Judaism than it does about that between Greek, Roman and Islamic law.

APPENDIX 4

Paramonar manumission as *tadbīr*

Manumission documents are poorly represented in the Islamic no less than in the Greek papyri (cf. above, Chapter 5, note 16). Only three Arabic manumission documents have turned up so far, and only two of these are complete (cf. A. Grohmann, 'Arabische Papyri aus den staatlichen Museen zu Berlin', *Der Islam* 1935, p. 28; the claim that P. Cair. B. E tarīkh no. 1900 is a *kitāba* is not correct). None of them dates from the formative period of Islamic law, but P. Berlin 13,002 (A.D. 916), published by Grohmann, *ibid.*, pp. 19ff, is nonetheless of considerable interest. The crucial lines are reproduced as follows in Grohmann's publication (p. 19):

4 innī aʿtaqtuka ʿan dursatī bi-khidmatī mā ʿishtu
5 fa-idhā muttu mā ḥa[yyān] Mubārak ḥurr li-wajh Allāh wa'l-dār al-ākhira, lā sabīl ʿalayka illā sabīl
6 al-walā', fa-inna walā'aka lī wa-liman varithuhu ʿannī. . .

If we follow Grohmann (pp. 24f), this means:

4 If have freed you from my discipline in my service as long as I live.
5 If I die while [you are al]ive, [you] Mubārak shall be free for the sake of God and the hereafter. Nobody shall have any claims on you except by way of
6 *walā'*; for your *walā'* belongs to me and whoever inherits it from me. . .

In fact, however, neither the transliteration nor the translation can be entirely right. First, some emendation is required for *ʿan dursatī* in line 4. There is no such expression as *ʿitq ʿan dursa*, but there is an expression *ʿitq ʿan dubur*; and given that the manumitter explicitly characterises the manumission as a *tadbīr* and the slave as a *mudabbar* (lines 6, 8), we must clearly read *ʿan duburī*, 'after my death'. (The plates supplied by Grohmann are illegible.) Secondly, the *bi-khidmatī* of line 4 cannot mean 'in my service', as opposed to 'in return for service to me'. What the manumitter (an Egyptian goldsmith) states is thus:

4 I have freed you after my death in return for service as long as I live.
5 If I die while [you are al]ive, [you] Mubārak shall be free. . .

The translation offered by B. Lewis (tr.), *Islam from the Prophet Mumammad to the Capture of Constantinople*, New York 1974, vol. II, p. 236, is similar (though it simply omits *ʿan dursatī/duburī*): 'I manumit you so that you remain in my service as long as I live; but if I die and you, Mubārak, still live, then you are free for the sake of God. . .'

What sort of manumission then was this? It seems nonsensical for a manumitter to reserve a right to service from a slave who is not to be manumitted before his own death. This suggests that the manumission took place here and now (as inferred by M. San Nicolò, review of Grohmann, *Zeitschrift der Savigny-Stiftung für Rechtsgeschichte* 1935, p. 460, on the basis of Grohmann's translation; Grohmann's own comments can be discounted). Yet the manumitter explictly deferred the manumission until his own death (given the emendation of *ʿan dursatī* to *ʿan durburī*). There is thus no doubt that he did reserve service from a slave who had not yet been freed. Now precisely such a reservation is attested in a will (possibly two) drawn up in Egypt over a millennium earlier. Dion of Heraclea, who wrote his will in the third century B.C., provided for the manumission of two slaves after his death with the words, 'Melainis and Ammonius, her son begotten by me . . . I set free if they remain (*parameinōsin*) with me as long as I live . . . and let them be free . . . and let no one lay hands on them' (P. Petrie III, 2; cf. Kreller, *Erbrechtliche Untersuchungen*, pp. 352f). This was clearly a paramonar manumission: the slaves were freed in return for staying with the manumitter until he died. But whereas paramonar manumission was normally resolutive, here it was deferred: Dion actually freed his slaves on condition that they *had* stayed with him until his death. Manumission in return for service for the lifetime of the manumitter is thus attested in a suspensive form over a thousand years before the Arabs conquered the Near East. This suggests that though *tadbīr* seems to be suspensive even in early Ḥadīth, it may well originate in the same institution as *kitāba*. The fact that the Egyptian goldsmith imposed a paramonar condition all while deferring the manumission until his death certainly lends some support to this hypothesis.

The papyrus is of interest in two other respects. First, the goldsmith (or the notary who drafted his document) found it necessary explicitly to stipulate *walāʾ* over the freedman, which the female manumitter of P. Cair. 1900 (A.D. 1003) did not. This suggests that renunciation of *walāʾ* was still practised in tenth-century Egypt (cf. above, Chapter 6, p. 81). Secondly, he evidently regarded *walāʾ* as something which could be inherited (cf. line 6), not as a kinship tie through which one could inherit (cf. Chapter 6, pp. 81f). The papyrus thus corroborates the conclusion that *walāʾ* was regarded as a residue of ownership, not as an agnatic tie.

Notes

1. The state of the field

1 H. Reland, *Dissertationes Miscellaneae*, trajecti ad Rhenum 1706–8, vol. iii, pp. 3f.
2 D. Gatteschi, *Manuale di diritto pubblico e privato ottomano*, Alexandria 1865; S. Amos, *The History and Principles of the Civil Law of Rome*, London 1883.
3 Gatteschi, *Manuale*, p. lxxiii, with the transmission of Greek philosophy to the Arabs as a supporting example. This example was also used by Amos, *Civil Law*, p. 409.
4 Gatteschi, *Manuale*, p. lxxvi; Amos, *Civil Law*, p. 408.
5 Gatteschi, *Manuale*, pp. lxxiiiff; Amos, *Civil Law*, p. 407.
6 Gatteschi, *Manuale*, pp. lxxiif, lxxvii.
7 Amos, *Civil Law*, p. 406, with British India as illustration.
8 Amos, *Civil Law*, pp. 412ff; Gatteschi, *Manuale*, p. lxxvi (he also provided references to Roman parallels in the text).
9 Gatteschi, *Manuale*, pp. lxxiii, lxxvi.
10 Amos, *Civil Law*, pp. 405, 414.
11 Gatteschi, *Manuale*, p. lxxiv.
12 H. Hugues, 'La justice française et le droit musulman en Algérie', *La France Judiciaire* 1878–9; *id.*, 'Les origines du droit musulman', *ibid.* 1879–80. Hugues, a French lawyer workir ι Algeria, refers to an anonymous pamphlet entitled *Une question de droit mixte* as his source of inspiration, and it would appear to have been the anonymous author rather than Hugues himself who formulated the statement that basically Islamic law is 'du droit romain à peine alteré' for which he has become notorious in Orientalist literature ('Justice française', p. 336). Neither article is worth reading.
13 D. Santillana, review of M. Fathy in *Rivista degli Studi Orientali* 1916–18, p. 766.
14 M. Enger (ed.), *Maverdii constitutiones politicae*, Bonn 1853, pp. xiv, 14f, 22ff. Enger's suggestions as regards taxation were followed up by M. van Berchem, *La propriété territoriale et l'impôt foncier sous les premiers califes*, Geneva 1886, similarly on the basis of Māwardī.
15 L. W. C. van den Berg, *De contractu "do ut des" iure mohammedano*, Leiden and Batavia 1868, pp. 17f and *passim*.
16 A. von Kremer, *Culturgeschichte des Orients under den Chalifen*. Vienna 1875–7, vol. 1, Ch. 9, especially pp. 532ff.
17 For a rare example, see the passage frequently adduced by Schacht on whether the caliph is allowed to change an old non-Arab *sunna* (Balādhurī, *Kitāb futūḥ al-buldān*, ed. M. J. de Goeje, Leiden 1866, p. 448; J. Schacht, 'The Law' in G. E. von Grunebaum (ed.), *Unity and Variety in Muslim Civilization*, Chicago 1955, p. 70; *id.*, 'Foreign Elements in Ancient Islamic Law', *Mémoires de l'Académie Internationale de Droit Comparé* 1955, p. 129; *id.*, 'Pre-Islamic Background and Early Development of Jurisprudence' in M. Khadduri and H. J. Liebesny (eds.), *Law in the Middle East*, vol. 1, Washington 1955, pp. 35f; *id.*, *An Introduction to Islamic Law*, Oxford 1964, pp. 19f). First adduced by Goldziher, the *sunna* in question is completely nondescript, and the frequency with which Schacht cited the passage suggests that not even he had never come across another (I. Goldziher, 'A muhammedán jogtudomány eredetéröl', *A Magyar Tudományos Akadémia*, Értehezéseh

a nyelv-és széptudományok köréből kötet, XI, (Budapest) 1884, pp. 7f; cf. J. Schacht, *The Origins of Muhammadan Jurisprudence*, Oxford 1950, p. vii; it is also cited by C. Snouck Hurgronje, *Verspreide Geschriften*, vol. II, Bonn and Leipzig 1923, pp. 72f).

18 Given that the foreign origin of Islamic philosophy is openly admitted, the parallel with philosophy adduced by Gatteschi, Amos and later also by Goldziher is somewhat unfortunate (cf. above, note 3; I. Goldziher, 'The Principles of Law in Islam' in H. S. Willians (ed.), *The Historians' History of the World*, London 1907, vol. VIII, p. 296). But this does not mean that it is gratuitous to asume a 'conspiracy of silence' regarding the origins of Islamic law, as FitzGerald inferred (S. V. FitzGerald, 'The Alleged Debt of Islamic to Roman Law', *The Law Quarterly Review* 1951, pp. 86n, 101). The undisguised Greek nature of Islamic philosophy is the *quid pro quo* of its marginal status.

19 Cf. G.-H. Bousquet, 'Le mystère de la formation et des origines du fiqh', *Revue Algérienne, Tunisienne et Marocaine de Législation et de Jurisprudence* 1947, pp. 75ff, a forceful account of the feeling of *déjà-vu* which the innocent Islamicist experiences on leafing through the Talmud.

20 C. Snouck Hurgronje, *Selected Works*, ed. G.-H. Bousquet and J. Schacht, Leiden 1957, p. 249; cf. P. Crone and M. Cook, *Hagarism, The Making of the Islamic World*, Cambridge 1977, *passim*.

21 Cf. W. Heffening, 'Zum Aufbau der islamischen Rechtswerke' in W. Heffening and W. Kirfel (eds.), *Studien zur Geschichte und Kultur des nahen und fernen Ostens – Paul Kahle zum 60. Geburtstag*, Leiden 1935.

22. Cf. A. J. Wensinck, 'Die Entstehung der muslimischen Reinheitsgesetzgebung', *Der Islam* 1914.

23 Though this is precisely what Bousquet argues in the expectation, apparently, that children ought to be exact replicas of their fathers ('Le mystère', pp. 78f).

24 Cf. p. 11 and the notes thereto (adultery as an impediment to marriage, *al-walad li'l-firāsh*, theft and *al-aḥkām al-khamsa*); appendix 2 (reason, custom, written and unwritten law, *maṣlaḥa*, *istiṣḥāb*); P. Crone, 'Jāhilī and Jewish Law: the *Qasāma*', *Jerusalem Studies in Arabic and Islam* 1984 (the collective oath in criminal procedure); M. A. Cook, 'Magian Cheese: an Archaic Problem in Islamic Law', *Bulletin of the School of Oriental and African Studies* 1984, pp. 462ff (dietary law). The influence of *both* Roman *and* Jewish law needs further investigation, as pointed out by K. Dilger, 'Orientalistik und Rechtswissenschaft', *Deutscher Orientalistentag 1975* (= *Zeitschrift der Deutschen Morgenländischen Gesellschaft* 1977, supplement no. 3), p. xxxii.

25 Thus there is a certain overall familiarity between Roman and Muslim guardianship (cf. A. d'Emilia, 'Roman and Muslim Law', *East and West* 1953, p. 6), and at the level of detail we have the Roman *legitima aetas* reappearing among the Ḥanafīs (von Kremer, *Culturgeschichte*, vol. I, p. 517; R. Brunschvig, 'Considérations sociologiques sur le droit musulman ancien', *Studia Islamica* 1955, p. 64). Even so, it is impossible to recognize a Muslim structure here. And what is one to make of the joint interest displayed by Roman and Muslim jurists in the conundrum posed by the slavegirl's twins? (cf. Appendix 1).

26 I. Goldziher, *Muhammedanische Studien*, Halle 1889–90, vol. II, Chs. 1–8.

27 Cf. Appendix 2.

28 C. H. Becker, *Beiträge zur Geschichte Agyptens under dem Islam*, Strassburg 1902–3; *id.*, *Islamstudien*, Leipzig 1924–36, vol. I (which includes all his earlier works of relevance and which is dedicated, inter alios, to Goldziher). For Goldziher's review of the *Beiträge*, see *Deutsche Literaturzeitung* 1902–3.

29 F. F. Schmidt, 'Die Occupatio im islamischen Recht', *Der Islam* 1910 (also published in book form in Strassburg in the same year). For his indebtedness to Goldziher, Becker and von Kremer, see p. 300 and the note thereto; for Goldziher's approving comments, see his review in *Deutsche Literaturzeitung* 1911, and his 'Fikh' in the *Encyclopaedia of Islam*,[1] Leiden 1913–38, p. 102.

30 W. Heffening, *Das Islamische Fremdenrecht*, Hannover 1925. Goldziher and Becker, especially the latter, are acknowledged at p. 3.

31 A fourth attempt was made in Germany by J. Hatschek, *Der Musta'min*, Berlin and Leipzig 1919. Like Schmidt, Hatschek was a lawyer by training; but where Schmidt was interested in the relationship between classical and Islamic culture ('Die Occupatio', p. 300), Hatschek was inspired by contemporary politics (*Der Musta'min*, p. 4), and the result

was unsatisfactory (cf. the review by Heffening in *Der Islam* 1923, and by R. Hartmann, who had less reason to be harsh than Heffening, in *Orientalistische Literaturzeitung* 1923).

32 Cf. Schacht, *Introduction*, pp. 98, 108.

33 Santillana nowhere seems to discuss Goldziher's views, while Morand in his article on *waqf* cites him only for a non-legal work (M. Morand, *Études de droit musulman algérien*, Alger 1910, p. 255n; he had however read Gatteschi, cf. pp. 243ff).

34 D. Santillana, *Code civil et commercial Tunisien, avant-projet discuté et adopté*, Tunis 1899, pp. xiif; id., review of M. Fathy in *Rivista degli Studi Orientali* 1916–18, p. 766; *id.*, 'Il libro di diritto di Zayd b. ʿAlī e il sistema zaydita' (review of E. Griffini), *ibid.* 1919–20, pp. 773, 775; I. Guidi and D. Santillana (trs.), *Il "Muḫtasar" o sommario del diritto malechita*, Milan 1919, vol. I, pp. xiif.

35 In addition to the works cited in the previous note, see his *Istituzioni di diritto musulmano malichita*, Rome 1926–38.

36 Morand, *Etudes*, Ch. 4. Note that a strong case can also be made for its Iranian origins (E. Perikhanian, 'Iranian Society and Law' in E. Yarshater (ed.), *The Cambridge History of Iran*, vol. III, part ii, Cambridge 1983, pp. 665f).

37 L. Mitteis, *Reichsrecht und Volksrecht in den östlichen Provinzen des römischen Kaiserreichs*, Leipzig 1891.

38 Partly by publishing the Syriac lawbooks (cf. K. G. Bruns and E. Sachau (eds. and trs.), *Syrisch-römisches Rechtsbuch*, Leipzig 1880; E. Sachau (ed. and tr.), *Syrische Rechtsbücher*, Berlin 1907–14), and partly by keeping Mitteis informed of his discoveries (L. Mitteis, *Über drei neue Handschriften des syrisch-römischen Rechtsbuchs* (reprinted from the *Abhandlungen der Königlichen Preussischen Akademie der Wissenschaften*), Berlin 1905, p. 3).

39 Nallino, who held a chair in Islamic history and institutions at Rome, was a fully-fledged historian of both Syriac and Islamic law and the only Islamicist to have contributed (decisively at that) to the debate on the Syro-Roman lawbook. His contributions have been assembled in his collected works (C. A. Nallino, *Raccolta di scritti editi e inediti*, vol. iv, Rome 1942).

40 Cf. his review of Fathy, *Rivista degli Studi Orientali* 1916–18, p. 766.

41 Cf. above, note 30; E. Bussi, *Richerche intorno alle relazioni fra retratto bizantino e musulmano*, Milan 1933.

42 G. Bergsträsser, 'Anflänge und Charakter des juristischen Denkens im Islam', *Der Islam* 1925.

43 Nallino, 'Considerazioni sui rapporti fra diritto romano e diritto musulmano' in his *Raccolta*, vol. IV.

44 Bousquet, 'Le mystère'; A. Hassam, 'Le droit musulman et le droit romain', *Archives d'Histoire du Droit Oriental* 1949, with observations by J. Wigmore appended.

45 FitzGerald, 'Alleged Debt'.

46 C. Chehata, *Essai d'une théorie générale de l'obligation en droit musulman Hanéfite*, Paris 1969, p. 49, notes that the controversy over Roman origins have yielded no result, and though his own works are frequently comparative, they are not concerned with origins. The same is true of the publications of d'Emilia. M. Daoualibi, *La jurisprudence dans le droit islamique*, Paris 1941, pp. 135ff, argues against Goldziher, Santillana and others in *a priori* terms, while M. Ḥamīdullāh, *Muslim Conduct of State*,[2] Hyderabad 1945, p. 36, accepts a limited measure of foreign influence, both without advancing the discussion. (Ḥamīdullāh's 'Influence of Roman Law on Muslim Law', *Journal of the Hyderabad Academy* 1943, was not available to me.) The *a priori* case for Roman influence was fully accepted by E. Schram-Nielsen, *Studier over Erstatningslæren i Islamisk Ret*, Copenhagen 1945, p. 29, and parallels between Roman and Islamic law in the field of liability and compensation are frequently noted in his work; but all are in the nature of suggestions rather than demonstrations. The same is true of A. Fattal, *Le statut légal des non-musulmans en pays d'Islam*, Beirut 1958, p. 75.

47 C. J. Kraemer, 'The Colt Papyri from Palestine', *Actes du Ve congrès international de papyrologie, Oxford 30 août–3 Septembre 1937*, Brussels 1938; P. Koschaker, 'Bericht über den 5. internationalen Papyrologenkongress in Oxford', *Zeitschrift der Savigny-Stiftung für Rechtsgeschichte* 1938, p. 448.

48 C. J. Kraemer and N. Lewis, 'A Divorce Agreement from Southern Palestine', *Transac-*

tions and Proceedings of the American Philological Association 1938; U. Wilcken, 'Urkunden-Referat', *Archiv für Papyrusforschung* 1941, pp. 179f; R. Taubenschlag, 'The Legislation of Justinian in the Light of the Papyri' in his *Opera Minora*, Warsaw 1959, vol. II, p. 73 and the note thereto; A. Steinwenter, 'Eine Ehescheidung aus dem Jahre 689', *Zeitschrift der Savigny-Stiftung für Rechtsgeschichte* 1943; A. Christophilopoulos, 'Zu Nessana Inv. Nr. 14', *ibid.* 1947; A. Merklein, *Das Ehescheidungsrecht nach den Papyri der byzantinischen Zeit*, Erlangen–Nürnberg 1967, pp. 43f, 51f (all on P. Nessana III, 57); M. Schwabe, 'Writ of Manumission among Papyri in Auja al-Hafir in Southern Palestine', *Magnes Anniversary Book*, Jerusalem 1938 (in Hebrew); J. Falenciak, 'Note on P. Colt Inv. Nr. 13,306 – Release from *Paramonē*', *Journal of Juristic Papyrology* 1948; W. L. Westermann, 'The Paramone as General Service Contract', *ibid.*; B. Adams, *Paramoné und verwandte Texte*, Berlin 1964, p. 52 (all on P. Nessana III, 56). H. J. Wolff, 'Der byzantinische Urkundenstil Ägyptens im Lichte der Funde von Nessana und Dura', *Revue Internationale des Droits de l'Antiquité* 1961.

49 C. J. Kraemer, Jr. (ed. and tr.), *Excavations at Nessana*, vol. III (*Non-literary Papyri*), Princeton 1958.

50 For a bibliography of his works (many of which are now difficult to get hold of), see C. A. Nallino, 'A proposito di alcuni studi sui diritti orientali', in his *Raccolta*, vol. IV, pp. 98f; or E. Volterra, *Diritto romano e diritti orientali*, Bologna 1937, pp. 60ff.

51 Cf. E. Griffini (ed.), "*Corpus Iuris*" *di Zayd Ibn ʿAlī*, Milan 1919, introduction. Griffini tried to define Zayd's position in the legal history of the 'Mediterranean Orient' (p. clxxxiv); he equated *codex*, *novella*, *authenticum* and *iura* with *kitāb*, *ḥadīth*, *ṣaḥīḥ* and *fiqh* (p. cxcii), and he believed that Roman-Hellenistic anthologies of imperial law would turn out to be the common model behind the legal writings of all the confessional communities of the Near East (p. clxxxviii; but cf. the caution expressed at p. viii). Carusi responded by asserting that Griffini had stolen all his ideas (E. Carusi, *Diritto e filologia*, Bologna 1925, pp. 105f, 336ff). Though Carusi overestimated his own importance (cf. Nallino's review of Carusi in *L'Oriente Moderno* 1925, pp. 165f; and note that it is Santillana rather than Carusi who is singled out as a source of inspiration by Griffini in *Corpus Iuris*, pp. vif), Griffini's sense of the ultimate unity underlying all the legal systems of the 'Mediterranean Orient' must no doubt be credited (or debited) to him. Griffini had in fact considered collaborating with Carusi before Nallino exposed the latter as a fraud (cf. Nallino, *loc. cit.*).

52 C. A. Nallino, 'Gli studi di E. Carusi sui diritti orientali', *Rivista degli Studi Orientali* 1921–3, reprinted in an abbreviated form in his *Raccolta*, vol. IV, under the title given above, note 50.

53 Volterra generously thought that he could be credited with having drawn attention to a number of important problems, even though his hypotheses were largely wrong (*Diritto romano e diritti orientali*, p. 65). But he did not draw attention to much that had not been seen already. His idea of the ultimate unity behind all the legal systems of the 'Mediterranean Orient' goes back to D. H. Müller, *Die Gesetze Hammurabis und ihr Verhältnis zur mosaischen Gesetzgebung, sowie zu den XII Tafeln*, Vienna 1903 (cf. Volterra, *op. cit.*, p. 51; Nallino, 'Gli Studi', p. 104). The view that Roman legal historians should study all the legal systems of antiquity had been formally launched by Wenger in his inaugural lecture of 1904 (L. Wenger, *Römische und antike Rechtsgeschichte*, Graz 1905, pp. 26f). And it was in Germany, not in Italy (where Carusi published his first article in 1913) that historians of Roman law first displayed an interest in Islam. For better or worse, though, he does appear to have been a source of inspiration not only to Griffini (above, note 51), but also to Bussi (cf. *Retratto*, p. 46n, where his publications are listed together with Nallino's, without indication of their incompatibility).

54 Nallino did note that Islamicists had done research on 'punti specialissimi', but the only specific assertions which he tried to refute were that the Muslims were dependent on Roman legal science, and that they read Roman lawbooks in translation (= Goldziher, Carusi and others) (Nallino, 'Considerazioni', pp. 86, 92f). Hassam's article is similarly directed against Carusi, Goldziher and Santillana, in that order, Santillana receiving partial absolution on grounds of his supposed *tawba* in his later works (Hassam, 'Le droit musulman', pp. 301n, 306, 311n, 317n; Nallino is cited and relied on in several places). Wigmore also singled out Goldziher and Carusi in his appended observations (ibid., pp.

317, 319, with an anonymous reference to Bussi at p. 320). FitzGerald only argued against Goldziher, but still felt obliged to dispose of the misconception that Shāfiʿī and Awzāʿī had studied Roman law at Beirut ('Alleged Debt', pp. 89, 93ff). The misconception does indeed deserve the exclamation mark which FitzGerald gives it, but forty years after Becker and Schmidt had identified the foreign elements in Islamic law as *residues*, there were better things to discuss.

55 Cf. P. Crone, *Slaves on Horses, the Evolution of the Islamic Polity*, Cambridge 1980, note 82.

56 Cf. Volterra, *Diritto romano e diritti orientali*, pp. 40ff. Not all of the fanciful claims advanced on this front were inspired by Mitteis' work, a great many having been advanced before it appeared; but though he himself condemned them, his work stimulated the growth of hazardous theories (cf. Mitteis, *Reichsrecht und Volksrecht*, p. 13; id., 'Antike Rechtsgeschichte und romanistisches Rechtsstudium', *Mitteilungen des Wiener Vereins der Freunde des humanistischen Gymnasiums* 1917, pp. 4, 14).

57 For a critique, see Schacht, 'Foreign Elements', pp. 130ff.

58 It argued against Roman influence on the ground that it would deprive the Sharīʿa of its originality (Hassam, 'Le droit musulman', p. 301).

59 Wigmore thought that Mālik was called Ibn Mālik, a mistake which, incredibly, he had picked up from Hassam ('Le droit musulman', pp. 310, 318, 320f; correctly at p. 320). He also believed that Abū Ḥanīfa worked at Damascus (*ibid.*, p. 320), that 'two or three' of the Syriac lawbooks published by Sachau were translations from Greek, that Griffini's list of non-Muslim legal works was a list of works translated into Arabic (*ibid.*, pp. 320f), and more besides.

60 Cf. appendix 2. Schacht's comment on FitzGerald's article was not entirely fair (J. Schacht, 'Droit byzantin et droit musulman', *Academia Nazionale dei Lincei, Fondazione Allesandro Volta, Ati dei convegni*, no. 12, Rome 1957, p. 204n).

61 Classics did too, cf. S. C. Humphreys, *Anthropology and the Greeks*, London 1983, p. 17.

62 Cf. P. Crone, 'Weber, Islamic Law and the Rise of Capitalism', paper presented at the Conference on Weber and Islam, Bad Homburg 1983, to appear (in German) in W. Schluchter (ed.), *Max Webers Studie über den Islam* (forthcoming).

63 This preference grew in proportion with the appearance of Muslim names among the contributors to the subject. It was not difficult for Goldziher to confront a lone and slightly ridiculous Savvas Pacha, not a Muslim, but a Greek who in the traditional style of Christians under Muslim rule was more pro-Islamic than the Muslims (cf. appendix 2). But by 1949 sheer politeness made it akward not to find oneself, like Wigmore, 'entirely in accord with the conclusions of Sir Abdel-Rahman Hassam'.

64 Few, of course, wish to suffer the dire punishment meted out to von Grunebaum by E. W. Said, *Orientalism*, London 1978, pp. 304f.

65 According to Goldziher, *fiqh* was no more a product of the 'Arab genius' than grammar or *kalām*; 'the stubborn antagonism of Islam to the rest of the world, its inflexible protest against the influence of foreign elements, is an illusion which historical study of the movement must dissipate if it is to rise to a scientific comprehension of this great historic phenomenon' (*Muhammedanische Studien*, vol. II, p. 76; 'Principles', p. 298). Becker dismissed the 'Märchen von der "arabischen Kultur"'; arguing that 'vom mehr als einem arabischen *Einschlag* kann in der islamischen Zivilisation nicht die Rede sein' (*Islamstudien*, vol. I, pp. 15f).

66 'Die Araber haben sich einfach einer bereits vorgefundenen einheitlichem Zivilization angepasst'; 'es wird eine Zeit kommen, in der man rückwärtsschauend aus der islamischen Tradition heraus den späten Hellenismus wird verstehen lernen' (Becker, *Islamstudien*, vol. I, pp. 16, 201). Compare Schmidt, 'Occupatio', p. 300.

67 Schacht, 'Foreign Elements', p. 127n.

68 Thus he frequently spoke of the 'far-reaching reception of the most varied elements' in the first stages of legal evolution, the 'widespread adoption of legal and administrative institutions of the conquered territories', and the assimilation of these institutions until their foreign origin became 'well-nigh unrecognizable' (Schacht, 'The Law', p. 65; *id.*, 'pre-Islamic Background', p. 35; *id.*, 'Foreign Elements', p. 128; *id.*, *Introduction*, p. 19).

69 Cf. Schacht, 'The Law', pp. 66f, where it is Arabian inheritance law, Meccan commercial law, Arabian ideas of penal law as well as the pre-Islamic *ḥakam* which are shown to have

gone into Islamic law with 'Koranic and Islamic' modifications and some Jewish influence.

70 The clearest statement to this effect is Schacht, 'Droit byzantin', especially p. 202, where the methodology is set out: foreign elements are to be recognised by their irregularity, be it historical, systematic, sociological or other. (Note also his curious view that 'whether these influences amount to little or much is irrelevant; the important fact is that they did happen', 'Foreign Elements', p. 140.)

71 See for example Schacht, 'The Law', p. 65.

72 This is a word he used in connection with theology, grammar and law alike (Schacht, 'The Law', p. 71; *id.*, 'Droit byzantin', p. 201; *id.*, 'Pre-Islamic Background', p. 36; *id.*, 'Remarques sur la transmission de la pensée grecque aux arabes', *Histoire de la Médicine* 1952, pp. 11, 15, cf. p. 17).

73 When he says that the raw material of Islamic law is to a large extent non-Islamic, he means that most of it is non-Qur'ānic (cf. Schacht, 'Pre-Islamic Background', p. 28; id., 'The Law', p. 65). His favourite metaphor for the creation of the system itself is condensation: a basic attitude came to form a solid core, whereupon foreign elements were rejected or transformed (cf. especially 'The Law', p. 65). But to say that Islamic law was born by condensation of a fundamental attitude is not very different from saying that it was born by virgin birth.

74 Cf. Goldziher, 'Principles', p. 297; id., 'Fiḳh', p. 102; *id.*, review of Savvas Pacha in *Byzantinische Zeitschrift* 1893, p. 321.

75 Heffening, *Fremdenrecht*, Ch. 3.

76 Schacht, *Origins*, pp. 190ff; id., 'The Law', pp. 70, 72; *id.*, *Introduction*, p. 29.

77 Schacht, *Origins*, pp. 190ff.

78 Cf. his 'Droit byzantin', p. 198; though he stressed the importance of provincial practice elsewhere (Schacht, 'Pre-Islamic Background', p. 35; id., 'Foreign Elements', p. 128), Roman law to him meant Roman law as found in the standard textbooks. In 1927 he proposed continuity between Babylonian and Islamic contracts on the basis of an article by San Nicolò (J. Schacht, 'Vom babylonischen zum islamischen Recht', *Orientalistische Literaturzeitung* 1927). Substantiation of this idea would have required work on provincial law too, but he simply repeated the idea almost forty years later (*Introduction*, p. 22).

79 Schacht, 'Remarques', p. 15; id., 'Foreign Elements', p. 137; cf. O. Pretzl, 'Die frühislamische Atomenlehre', *Der Islam* 1931, p. 122 (Schacht nowhere credits the expression to Pretzl; I owe the reference to Dr F. W. Zimmermann).

80 Schacht, *Origins*, pp. 99f; id., *Introduction*, p. 20; *id.*, 'The Law', p. 71; id., 'Remarques', p. 14; id., 'Droit byzantin', p. 201; id. 'Foreign Elements', pp. 133f (where Iraq is explicitly singled out at the locus of transmission).

81 F. W. Zimmermann, '*Kalām* and the Greeks', paper read at the tenth congress of the Union Européenne des Arabisants et Islamisants, Edinburgh 1980.

82 H. I. Marrou, *A History of Education in Antiquity*, London 1956, p. 286, with nice examples from Seneca at p. 287; cf. pp. 202 for the corresponding Greek subjects and an example from Hermagoras.

83 D. L. Clark, *Rhetoric in Greco-Roman Education*, New York 1957, p. 233. Cf. also M. L. Clarke, *Higher Education in the Ancient World*, London 1971, pp. 28ff, for a brief, but illuminating account of rhetorical studies.

84 Schacht, 'Droit byzantin', pp. 210ff.

85 Clarke, *Higher Education*, p. 43.

86 Clark, *Rhetoric*, p. 215, citing Quintilian, *Institutio Oratio*, ed. and tr. H. E. Butler, London 1921–2, ii, x, 8. Quintilian died about A.D. 100.

87 F. Schulz, *History of Roman Legal Science*, Oxford 1946, p. 268. It was with an Egyptian institution (*nomos tōn Aigyptiōn*), not a Roman one, that the second-century Greek rhetor of CPR 18 displayed some familiarity (R. Taubenschlag, 'The Legal Profession in Greco-Roman Egypt' in his *Opera Minora*, vol. II, p. 164).

88 R. Schröter (ed. and tr.), 'Erster Brief Jakobs von Edessa an Johannes den Styliten', *Zeitschrift der Deutschen Morgenländischen Gesellschaft* 1870, p. 269 = 274. The stylite had asked Jacob to examine some homilies attributed to Jacob of Sarug; they turned out to be Gnostic treatises on heavenly powers and much other nonsense which Jacob contemptuously dismissed as the work of a 'minor rhetor' (*melilona*).

89 Schulz, *History*, pp. 268ff; Mitteis, *Reichsrecht*, pp. 192ff.

90 Schulz, *History*, p. 270. He retained some minor roles, but from the sixth century onwards even lower judges had to be professional jurists (A. Claus, *Ho Skholastikos*, Cologne 1965, pp. 88f, 98, 100f).

91 As did for example Agathias (A. Cameron, *Agathias*, Oxford 1970, appendix B). For numerous other examples, see A. Steinwenter, 'Rhetorik und römischer Zivilprocess', *Zeitschrift der Savigny-Stiftung für Rechtsgeschichte* 1947, pp. 111ff (I owe my knowledge of this article to Dr. F. W. Zimmermann).

92 Yet Schacht not only wrote that the profession of advocate was quite distinct from that of jurists properly speaking in the *last* centuries of the classical world, but also did so with reference to the very pages by Schulz devoted to showing that 'by the fourth century things had changed in the eastern Empire: advocates were really lawyers' (Schacht, 'Droit Byzantin', p. 201; Schulz, *History*, pp. 268ff).

93 Cf. A. Vööbus, *History of the School of Nisibis* (= CSCO, subsidia, vol. XXVI), Louvain 1965, pp. 99ff. But Vööbus conjectures that the *mehageyane* attached to this school were teachers of the ABC rather than of rhetoric.

94 As suggested by H. Daiber, *Aetius Arabus, die Vorsokratiker in arabischer Überlieferung*, Wiesbaden 1980, pp. 68ff, on the ground that the Nestorian translators appear to have been familiar with the style of Greek rhetoric. Daiber seeks support from Schacht at p. 71.

95 C. A. Nallino, 'Sul libro siro-romano e sul presunto diritto siriaco' in his *Raccolta*, vol. IV, pp. 553ff.

96 Goldziher, *Muhammedanische Studien*, vol. I, p. 188n; Schacht, 'Foreign Elements', p. 135; id., 'Droit byzantin', pp. 208f; id., 'Remarques', p. 13; id., 'The Law', p. 71; id. *Origins*, pp. 181f; id., *Introduction*, p. 21.

97 'Foreign Elements', p. 135.

98 G. L. Kustas, *Studies in Byzantine Rhetoric*, Thessalonica 1973, p. 22.

99 H. Rabe (ed.), *Aphthonii Progymnasmata* (*Rhetores Graeci*, vol. x), Leipzig 1926, xiv = R. Nadeau (tr.), 'The Progymnasmata of Aphthonius', *Speech Monographs* (Ann Arbor, Michigan) 1952, pp. 283ff.

100 Von Kremer, *Culturgeschichte*, vol. I, pp. 534f.

101 Goldziher, 'Fiḳh', p. 102; Schacht, 'Droit byzantin', p. 202; id., *Introduction*, p. 21.

102 D. Daube, 'Rabbinic Methods of Interpretation and Hellenistic Rhetoric', *Hebrew Union College Annual* 1949, cited together with other articles by Daube in Schacht, *Origins*, p. 99; id., 'Foreign Elements', p. 133; id., 'Droit byzantin', p. 202; id., 'Remarques', p. 15. He knew Daube personally (cf. *Origins*, pp. vif).

103 Thus in all his publications on the subject except *Origins*, where the argument is still tentative.

104 Note the way in which he disposes of the problem that Iraq was not a country of Roman law: 'at the period in question it was deeply imbued with the spirit of Hellenistic civilisation and at the same time contained the great centres of Talmudic learning. These are all the data we need to account for the existence of concepts and maxims of Roman jurisprudence in early Islamic legal science, and the regular occurrence of Talmudic parallels.' But if the Muslims took over the concepts and maxims in question from the Jews who, as Schacht goes on to explain, had previously borrowed them through the medium of rhetoric, they can hardly at the same time have borrowed them independently through the medium of rhetoric. Conversely, if the Muslims borrowed them independently through the medium of rhetoric, the existence of Talmudic learning in Iraq is irrelevant. Schacht solves the problem by having it both ways ('Foreign Elements', p. 133). By 1964 even Sasanid law had come to receive Roman elements through the dual channel of Hellenistic rhetoric and Talmudic law, and we are now informed that concepts and maxims originating in Roman, Byzantine, Talmudic, rabbinic, Sasanid and Canon law all entered Islam 'in this way' (Schacht, *Introduction*, pp. 20f). One must grant him that he could make much of a little information.

105 Cf. appendix 2.

106 M. A. Cook, 'Monotheist Sages' (forthcoming).

107 *Babylonian Talmud*, *Soṭah*, fols. 27b, 37a.

108 Cf. Schacht, 'Foreign Elements', pp. 135ff; id., 'Droit byzantin', pp. 212f. According to the rabbis, the finder of lost property worth more than one *peruṭa* or more must announce his find; the thief of property worth one *peruṭa* or more must be punished; and one *peruṭa* is

also the minimal sum for which a woman can be engaged according to Hillel (B. S. Jackson, *Theft in Early Jewish Law*, Oxford 1972, pp. 126ff). The Jewish rule of the *peruṭa* is the Muslim rule of the *niṣāb*. In Ḥanafīlaw the *niṣāb* is ten dirhams. Thus the finder of lost property worth ten dirhams or more must announce his find for a year (Marghīnānī, *al-Hidāya*, Cairo n.d., part ii, p. 175); the thief of property worth ten dirhams or more must have his hand cut off (Schacht, *Introduction*, pp. 38, 180); and ten dirhams are also the minimal sum for which a woman can be married (*ibid.*, p. 167). Schacht asserts that 'the minimum value of stolen goods provided the starting point for fixing, by a crude analogy, the minimum amount of the nuptial gift (*mahr*)' (*ibid.*, p. 38) in ignorance of the fact that the crude analogy had been made already by the rabbis; and the element in the Islamic law of theft which he believed to be of Roman origin, viz. the idea that the thief to whom the Qur'ānic punishment does not apply should be responsible for twice the value of the object stolen, can be found in *Exodus* 22:4, 7, 9. It is thus hard to agree that 'the Roman law of *furtum* offers itself instantly as the most likely source' ('Foreign Elements', p. 136).

109 C. H. Becker, 'Zur Entstehung der Waqfinstitution', *der Islam* 1911; cf. Schacht, 'Droit byzantin', p. 214. The article by Köprülü cited by Schacht, *ibid.*, adds nothing to Morand (F. Köprülü, 'L' institution de vakouf', *Vakıflar Dergisi* 1942).

110 Schacht, 'Droit byzantin', p. 203n; cf. above, note 25.

111 So at least in his published work (S. van den Bergh, *Averroes' Tahafut al-tahafut*, London 1954, vol. I, p. xi, vol. II, pp. 117f). The lecture to which Schacht refers was not published ('Foreign Elements', p. 134n). The Jewish parallel would again seem to be considerably closer (cf. R. Brunschvig, 'Herméneutique normative dans le Judaïsme et dans l'Islam', *Atti della Accademia Nazionale dei Lincei* (Rendiconti, vol. xxx, Rome) 1975, p. 237).

112 Cf. Appendix 3.

113 Thus Schacht held that Ibn al-Muqaffaʿ's plea for a codification of Islamic law was 'obviously' influenced by the Persian administrative tradition (*Origins*, p. 95); having read Goitein, he added that he disagreed ('Foreign Elements', p. 140 and the note thereto). Since Goitein pointed out that there is no evidence at all for codification of Sasanid law (S. D. Goitein, 'A Turning Point in the History of the Muslim State', *Islamic Culture* 1949, p. 128), it is not clear how he *could* disagree. He tried to have it both ways: whether Ibn al-Muqaffaʿ owed the idea to the Sasanids or not, his plea illustrates the transmission of foreign culture to Islam ('Remarques', p. 18). But in the last resort he found it easier to forget about Goitein, reaffirming his original view (*Introduction*, pp. 21f). He also held that the Muslim clerk of court was 'obviously' derived from the Sasanid equivalent (cf. his review of Tyan in *Orientalia* 1948, p. 519; 'Pre-Islamic Background', p. 38; *Introduction*, p. 21). But it is hard to believe that Byzantine, Nestorian and Jewish courts had no clerks, and the fact that only the Sasanid clerk is mentioned in the secretarial literature merely proves that the secretaries took a greater interest in Sasanid than in Christian or Jewish statecraft.

114 Crone and Cook, *Hagarism*, p. 98. The claim that there is no trace of Muslim influence on Ishoʿbokht's code is also a rash one (*ibid.*, p. 151; cf. R. Taubenschlag, 'Syrische Rechtsbücher' in his *Opera Minora*, vol. I, pp. 561ff); but Taubenschlag's *fatwā*s on the cultural origin of legal rules were arbitrary (similarly Nallino, 'Sul libro siro-romano', p. 555), and it can still be said that no Muslim influence has been proved.

115 Nallino, 'Sul libro siro-romano', pp. 553ff.

116 The manuscript in question is British Library, Add. 14528. It was Nallino who discovered that this manuscript consists of two halves accidentally bound together, and that Wright's sixth-century dating is based on the first half. The lawbook comes in the second half, preceded by a lectionary written by the same scribe. Cheered by this immensely deflationary discovery, Nallino dated the second half to the eighth or ninth centuries, but his dating was hardly unbiased. It has been challenged by W. Baars and P. A. H. de Boer, 'Ein neugefundenes Fragment des syrisch-römischen Rechtsbuches', *Symbolae Iuridicae et Historicae Martino David Dedicata*, Leiden 1968, vol. II, p. 45n, on the ground that the lectionary preceding it has the old *capitulare lectionum* which had disappeared by the late seventh or early eighth centuries; and in the opinion of Dr S. P. Brock, who kindly checked the manuscript for me, this feature only confirms 'what is already palaeographically patent' (letter of 18 June 1980).

117 Cf. Sachau, *Syrische Rechtsbücher*, vol. III, p. 176 = 177, with comments at p. 334; Nallino, 'Sul libro siro-romano', pp. 555n, 557, 560. Sachau identified Ishoʿbokht's passage as a

reference to *Lex Fufia Caninia*, a law which is indeed to be found in the Syro-Roman lawbook. Nallino disputed this on the ground that this law was concerned with testamentary manumission, which Ishoʿbokht does not make clear, and that Ishoʿbokht's passage does not reflect Roman ideas, but rather provincial ones concerning limitations on the right to dispose of family property. Both points are correct, but neither invalidates Sachau's point. Ishoʿbokht speaks of limitations on the right to manumit in Roman law; Roman law knew of no such limitations except for *Lex Fufia Caninia*, and the fact that this law only placed limits on testamentary manumission is a point which might easily have been lost in transmission. The fact that Ishoʿbokht attributes a Greek (or Iranian, cf. below, Ch. 7) rationale to it merely proves that he evaluated the law in the light of local ideas. Nallino's objections fail to account for the fact that Ishoʿbokht referred to a law actually written 'in the laws of the Romans'. The only place in which he can have seen such a law, or on the basis of which he can have heard of it, is the Syro-Roman lawbook (*Lex Fufia Caninia* was abolished by Justinian, some two centuries before he wrote).

118 To Ishoʿbokht the law familiar from the Syro-Roman lawbook was part of 'the laws of the Romans', as opposed to those of 'our land' (cf. the preceding note); but to Timothy the laws of this book were 'imperial laws which were issued in accordance with the sacred synods of the fathers' and an example of 'the pure laws of Christianity' (Nallino, 'Sul libro siro-romano', p. 558; as Nallino points out, though, Timothy clearly did not regard this example of pure Christian law as the law actually to be practised by the Nestorians: his own canons differ from those of the Syro-Roman lawbook, and he never invokes it here).

119 Since Nallino wrote, Selb has discovered further 'laws of the Christian kings' in a Syriac manuscript in the Vatican. Though most of the manuscript is given over to the Syro-Roman lawbook, these 'laws' do not belong to it, not do they come from any known work of Byzantine law. Their origin is still unknown (W. Selb, 'Sententiae syriacae', *Zeitschrift der Savigny-Stiftung für Rechtsgeschichte* 1968).

120 Cf. P. Crone, 'Islam, Judeo-Christianity and Byzantine Iconoclasm', *Jerusalem Studies in Arabic and Islam* 1980, p. 71, where this point should have been made.

121 Cf. Nallino, 'Sul libro siro-romano', pp. 564ff. Nallino himself believed the book to have been translated because the Christians needed a code of law when the Arabs placed them under their own administration: as it happened, the translators picked on a work of little practical use, being attracted by the fact that it was presented as the work of the Christian emperors (*ibid.*, pp. 561ff). But the Nestorians had always been a minority under alien rule, and the Arab conquest hardly made much difference to the way in which they were administered. Moreover, if they were looking for a practical guide, why did they keep the Syro-Roman lawbook even when they found that it was none? Indeed, why did it spread even to Armenians and Copts? The attribution of its laws to the Christian emperors is unlikely to have been found in the Greek original, and Nallino himself had a strong sense that the Christians were looking for something which could be presented as Christian law comparable to that of the Muslims and Jews. The fortunes of the lawbook are thus inexplicable except in terms of the desire for a book of *fiqh al-naṣrāniyya*.

121 Schulz, *History*, p. 273.

123 E. Seidl, *Rechtsgeschichte Ägyptens als römischer Provinz*, Sankt Augustin 1973, pp. 49ff.

124 FitzGerald, 'Alleged Debt', p. 86. Selb also concluded that it reflects a low level of legal thinking, in so far as one can tell from the translation in which it survives (W. Selb, *Zur Bedeutung des syrisch-römischen Rechtsbuches*, Munich 1964, p. 262).

125 Cf. Schulz, *History*, pp. 325ff.

126 Schulz, *History*, p. 324.

127 Selb, *Zur Bedeutung*, p. 262.

128 They were certainly to become well educated in later times: in the Macedonian period they were required to know the forty titles of the *Procheiron* and the sixty books of the *Basilica* by heart, and to have a good general education too (P. Lemerle, *Le premier humanisme byzantin*, Paris 1971, pp. 261f).

129 Schulz, *History*, p. 273.

130 P. Collinet, *Histoire de l'école de droit de Beyrouth*, Paris 1925, pp. 54ff.

131 FitzGerald, 'Alleged Debt', p. 89; the same is implied by Nallino, 'Considerazioni', p. 93; cf. also Daoulabi, *Jurisprudence*, p. 141f.

132 H. J. Scheltema, *L'enseignement de droit des antecesseurs*, Leiden 1970, esp. pp. 62f.

133 Scheltema, *Enseignement*, p. 49.
134 Scheltema, *Enseignement*, pp. 61f.
135 Schulz, *History*, p. 154. Private practitioners may also have had collections of this kind of material.
136 Kraemer, *Nessana*, vol. III, p. 158.
137 That is Sergius (d. 610), later a monk (Kraemer, *Nessana*, vol. III, p. 28).
138 P. Nessana II, 11, 12, in L. Casson and E. L. Hettich (eds. and trs.), *Excavations at Nessana*, vol. II, Princeton 1950, pp. 160f. The treatise on succession could be read as one on guardianship.
139 Cf. FitzGerald, 'Alleged Debt', p. 86; Nallino, 'Considerazioni', p. 93. Note that contrary to what Nallino believed, the administration of justice in Syria had not devolved unto ignorant churchmen before the Arabs arrived; it was only after the conquests that the local administration passed into the hands of the Church, and only then that the scribes began to lose their Greek (cf. Kraemer, *Nessana*, vol. III, p. 158).
140 The literature on this subject is immense. For a classical work, see R. Taubenschlag, *The Law of Greco-Roman Egypt in the Light of the Papyri*,[2] Warsaw 1955, based largely on the various articles assembled in his *Opera Minora*; for a more recent statement, see Seidl, *Rechtsgeschichte Ägyptens*; cf. also H. J. Wolff, 'Zur Romanisierung des Vertragrechts der Papyri', *Zeitschrift der Savigny-Stiftung für Rechtsgeschichte* 1956; id., 'Das Vulgarrechtsproblem und die Papyri', *ibid.* 1974.
141 Cf. Bruns in Bruns and Sachau, *Syrisch-römisches Rechtsbuch*, p. 332; A. A. Vasiliev, *History of the Byzantine Empire*, Madison and Milwaukee 1964 (first published 1928), vol. I, p. 89; FitzGerald, 'Alleged Debt', p. 86 (for all that he believed himself to have adopted Nallino's conclusions); and Kraemer, *Nessana*, vol. III, pp. 18f (for all that he notes the effect of Justinian's legislation in the Nessana documents).
142 Nallino, 'Sul libro siro-romano'; Selb, *Zur Bedeutung*. Taubenschlag dismissed Nallino's conclusions with a priceless argument: if the book contained Roman law, all law in Syria must have been as Roman as in Rome itself; since we know from the papyri that this is unlikely to be the case, it must reflect provincial practice! (R. Taubenschlag, 'Il diritto provinciale nel libro siro-romano' in his *Opera Minora*, vol. I, p. 291n; cf. p. 312, where Carusi finds himself in complete agreement).
143 Cf. Nallino, 'Sul libro siro-romano', pp. 544f.
144 Cf. P. Nessana II, 1–2; P. Nessana III, 18.
145 As in P. Nessana III, 56–7. That the provincials in general believed themselves to be practising Roman law is also pointed out by Wolff, 'Vulgarrechtsproblem', p. 63.
146 H. J. Scheltema, 'The Nomoi of Iulianus of Ascalon', *Symbolae ad Jus et Historiam Antiquitatis Pertinentes Julio Christiano van Oven Dedicatae*, Leiden 1946, p. 356.
147 For the Roman policy of tacit recognition, see Wolff, 'Romanisierung', p. 10n; explicit recognition took the form of imperial constitutions legislating on behalf of particular provinces (cf. Volterra, *Diritto romano e diritti orientali*, pp. 281ff).
148 Cf. A. Steinwenter, 'Was beweisen die Papyri für die praktische Geltung des justinianischen Gesetzgebungswerkes?' *Aegyptus* 1952, p. 136; R. Taubenschlag, 'Geschichte der Rezeption des römischen Privatrechts in Ägypten' in his *Opera Minora*, vol. I, p. 280; cf. the English and slightly updated version of the relevant part, 'The Legislation of Justinian in the Light of the Papyri', *ibid.*, vol. II,
149 Cf. above, note 66.
150 What follows is based on P. Crone and M. Hinds, *God's Caliph, Religious Authority in the First Centuries of Islam*, Cambridge 1986, esp. Ch. 4.
151 Cf. Crone and Cook, *Hagarism*, pp. 132ff.
152 Cf. Crone, 'Jāhilī and Jewish Law', pp. 187f.
153 Theophanes, *Chronographia*, ed. C. de Boor, Leipzig 1883–5, A. M. 6210.
154 ʿAbd al-Razzāq b. Hammām al-Ṣanʿānī, *al-Muṣannaf*, ed. Ḥ.-R. al-Aʿẓamī, Beirut 1970–2, vol. x, nos. 18,478, cf. no. 18,487. This is *not* confirmed by non-Muslim historians, as Schacht maintains (*Origins*, p. 205, where the rule regarding the blood-money of Christians has been mixed up with that regarding testimony).
155 ʿAbd al-Razzāq, *Muṣannaf*, vol. x, nos. 18,475–6, 18,491; Schacht, *Origins*, p. 206.
156 ʿAbd al-Razzāq, *Muṣannaf*, vol. x, no. 18,482.
157 Cf. below, Chapter 2.

158 P. Brown, 'Understanding Islam', *The New York Review of Books*, 22 February 1979, p. 33.
159 Cf. Nallino, 'Considerazioni', p. 88, where it is argued that since there must have been a highly developed law in the commercial Ḥijāz, we may assume that it was the customary law of the Ḥijāz which went into the Sharīʿa.
160 R. Ettinghausen, *Arab Painting*, Cleveland 1962, pp. 20ff. And note that not a single feature of the Umayyad summer palaces has been traced to Mecca or for that matter anywhere else in the Ḥijāz (O. Grabar, *The Formation of Islamic Art*, New Haven and London 1973, pp. 78f).

2. A practical guide to the study of Islamic law

1 Cf. Crone and Hinds, *God's Caliph*, p. 52.
2 Similarly, 'the treatment of partnership and *commenda* in Islamic legal treatises remained essentially the same from the time of Shaybānī to that of the Ottoman *Majallah*' (A. L. Udovitch, *Partnership and Profit in Medieval Islam*, Princeton 1970, p. 14).
3 Schacht, *Origins*, pp. 6ff; id., *Introduction*, pp. 28f; H. J. Cohen, 'The Economic Background and Secular Occupation of Muslim Jurisprudents and Traditionalists in the Classical Period of Islam', *Journal of the Economic and Social History of the Orient* 1970.
4 Schacht, *Origins*, p. 10.
5 Cf. *Encyclopaedia of Islam*,[2] s.v.
6 H.-P. Raddatz, *Die Stellung und Bedeutung des Sufyān aṯ-Ṯaurī (gest. 778)*, Bonn 1967, pp. 107ff.
7 H.-P. Raddatz, 'Frühislamisches Erbrecht, nach dem Kitāb al-farāʾiḍ des Sufyān aṯ-Ṯaurī. Edition und Kommentar', *Die Welt des Islams* 1971.
8 Cf. R. Strothmann, 'Das Problem der literarischen Persönlichkeit Zaid b. ʿAlī', *Der Islam* 1923, pp. 18ff; similarly W. Madelung, *Der Imam al-Qāsim ibn Ibrāhīm und die Glaubenslehre der Zaiditen*, Berlin 1965, pp. 54f. For a full survey of the literature, see F. Sezgin, *Geschichte des arabischen Schrifttums*, vol. 1, Leiden 1967, pp. 552ff (where the ascription to Zayd is defended).
9 Madelung, *Qāsim*, pp. 137, 160, 168; cf. also id., 'Shiʿi Attitudes towards Women as Reflected in Fiqh' in A. L. al-Sayyid-Marsot (ed.), *Society and the Sexes in Medieval Islam*, Malibu 1979, pp. 76f.
10 Though for a possible exception, see below, chapter 7, note 11.
11 Madelung, 'Shiʿi Attitudes', pp. 70f, 76n.
12 I. K. A. Howard, '*Mutʿa* Marriage Reconsidered in the Context of the Formal Procedures for Islamic Marriage', *Journal of Semitic Studies* 1975, p. 82.
13 Cf. the example of *qasāma* (Crone, 'Jāhilī and Jewish law').
14 But Schacht's claim that the legal literature of the Imāmīs only started about 900 is undoubtedly wrong (*Origins*, p. 262; cf. Madelung, 'Shiʿi Attitudes', p. 71n).
15 The differences between Imāmī law and that of the other schools are frequently minimised in the secondary literature, but they are rightly stressed by N. J. Coulson, *A History of Islamic Law*, Edinburgh 1964, pp. 105ff.
16 W. Madelung, 'The Sources of Ismāʿīlī Law', *Journal of Near Eastern Studies* 1976.
17 Madelung, 'Sources', p. 3.
18 *Encyclopaedia of Islam*[2], *s.v.* 'Ibāḍiyya', col. 651a.
19 *Encyclopaedia of Islam*[2], *s.v.* 'Abū Ghānim'.
20 J. C. Wilkinson, 'Ibāḍī Ḥadīth: an Essay on Normalization', *Der Islam* 1985.
21 *Encyclopaedia of Islam*[2], *s.v.* 'Ibāḍiyya', cols. 659f.
22 *Encyclopaedia of Islam*[2], *s.v.* 'Awzāʿī'; Sezgin, *Geschichte* vol. 1, pp. 516f; cf. also Ṣ. al-Maḥmaṣānī, *al-Awzāʿī*, Beirut 1978.
23 Sezgin, *Geschichte*, vol. 1, pp. 457ff.
24 R. Brunschvig, 'Polémiques médiévales autour du rite de Mālik', *al-Andalus* 1950, p. 379.
25 Cf. H. Halm, *Die Ausbreitung der šāfiʿitischen Rechtsschule von den Anfängen bis zum 8./14. Jahrhundert*, Wiesbaden 1974, p. 18.
26 Brunschvig, 'Polémiques', pp. 379ff.
27 *Encyclopaedia of Islam*[2], *s.v.* 'Khiraḳī'.
28 Sezgin, *Geschichte*, vol. 1, p. 522.

29 Thus Zufar b. Hudhayl (d. 775), a dissident Ḥanafī (cf. Sezgin, *Geschichte*, vol. I, p. 419, where he is a straightforward Ḥanafī), Isḥāq b. Rāhuyah (d. 853), claimed by Shāfiʿīs and Ḥanbalīs alike (Halm, *Ausbreitung*, pp. 42f), or Abū Thawr (d. 854), a Baghdādī said to have ended up as a Shāfiʿī (Sezgin, *ibid.*, p. 491).
30 Sezgin, *Geschichte*, vol. I, pp. 323ff.
31 Crone, 'Jāhilī and Jewish Law' (*qasāma*); below, Chapter 3, p. 38 (contractual clientage); below Chapter 7, p. 95 (bequests). This is a point I hope to demonstrate in greater detail in connection with the origins of Imāmī law.
32 Crone, 'Jāhilī and Jewish Law'.
33 ʿAbd al-Razzāq, *Muṣannaf*, vol. x, nos. 19,127, 19,077, 19,079.
34 *Ibid.*, no. 19,072.
35 Schacht, *Origins*, p. 33.
36 This is the evolution reconstructed by Schacht in his *Origins*.
37 A. Guillaume, *The Traditions of Islam, An Introduction to the Study of the Hadith Literature*, Oxford 1924, pp. 23ff.
38 Cf. G. H. A. Juynboll, *Muslim Tradition*, Cambridge 1983, p. 39.
39 It is clear that this had to some extent ceased to hold true for Shaybānī. As Juynboll notes, contacts between the old schools seem to have been established between about 720 and 750 (*Muslim Tradition*, p. 39); and Sufyān al-Thawrī, Abū Ḥanīfa, Abū Yūsuf as well as Shaybānī himself all displayed an interest in Medinese Ḥadīth (Raddatz, *Stellung und Bedeutung*, p. 13; Schacht, *Origins*, pp. 33f). But Shaybānī's attempt to refute the Medinese nonetheless took the form of a collection of Iraqi Hadīth too (cf. his *Kitāb al-ḥujja ʿalā ahl al-Madīna*, ed. A.-W. al-Afghānī, Hyderabad 1965–71).
40 On the beginning of *ṭalab al-ʿilm*, see now Juynboll, *Muslim Tradition*, pp. 66ff.
41 Ibn Bābūyah, *Man lā yaḥḍuruhu al-faqīh*, ed. H. M. al-Khursān, Tehran 1390.
42 Ṭūsī, *Tahdhīb al-aḥkām*, ed. H. M. al-Khursān, Tehran 1390; id., *Kitāb al-istibṣār*, ed. H. M. al-Khursān, Tehran 1390.
43 Cf. Kashshī, *al-Rijāl*, ed. A. al-Ḥusaynī, Najaf n.d., an unimpressive work by Sunnī standards. The Imāmīs never produced an Ibn Ḥajar.
44 Cf. Schacht, *Introduction*, p. 59.
45 Publication details are given above, Chapter I, note 154.
46 Ibn Abī Shayba, *al-Kitāb al-muṣannaf fī'l-adādīth wa'l-āthār*, ed. M. A. al-Nadwī, Bombay 1979–83. I only gained access to a copy after the completion of the present work and have thus been unable to make systematic use of it here.
47 Bayhaqī, *Kitāb al-sunan al-kubrā*, Hyderabad 1344–55; cf. *Encyclopaedia of Islam*², *s.v.* 'Bayhaḳī, Abū Bakr'.
48 Ibn Ḥanbal, *al-Musnad*, Cairo 1313, vol. I, p. 221; Ṭirmidhī, *al-Ṣaḥīḥ*, Cairo 1931–4, vol. VIII, p. 256; ʿAbd al-Razzāq, *Muṣannaf*, vol. IX, no. 16,192 (cf. 16,191, where Sufyān is replaced by Ibn Jurayj, another Meccan authority): Bayhaqī, *Sunan*, vol. VI, p. 242[13f]. (The tradition concerns succession between freedman and manumitter.)
49 Bayhaqī, *Sunan*, vol. VI, p. 242[10].
50 This is very often the case. For an example, see below, pp. 31f.
51 This too is commonly the case. For an example, see Crone, 'Jāhilī and Jewish Law', p. 195.
52 This cannot often be shown to be the case, but an example figured in G. R. Hawting, 'The Dispute in Muslim Law about the Rights of a Divorced Woman during her "Waiting Period"', paper presented at the Colloquium on Qur'ān and Ḥadīth, Cambridge 1985: the Medinese tradition of Fāṭima bint Qays from the Prophet concerning *nafaqa* and *suknā* is clearly earlier than the Iraqi tradition ascribed to ʿUmar which seeks to refute it.
53 Recent work on apocalyptic Ḥadīth casts doubt on the validity of the rule: apocalyptic traditions ascribed to Companions and others do not seem to be any older than those ascribed to the Prophet, which may be very old indeed (L. I. Conrad, 'Portents of the Hour: Ḥadīth and History in the First Century A.H.', paper presented at the Colloquium on Qurʾān and Hadīth, Cambridge 1985; M. A. Cook, 'Eschatology, History and the Dating of Traditions', paper presented at the Third International Colloquium on 'From Jāhiliyya to Islam', Jerusalem 1985, to appear in *Jerusalem Studies in Arabic and Islam*). But it is clear that the choice of authorities on eschatological subjects was governed by different rules from that on law, so that conclusions based on one type of material cannot simply be transferred to the other (as Conrad himself points out). Schacht's rule of thumb

rests on the assumption that the concept of *sunna* was subject to an evolution culminating in acceptance of the Prophet as the one and only source thereof. If this assumption is correct, the rule of thumb *must* be roughly right. But eschatology was not subject to this evolution: here the Prophet seems to have been invoked long before he had come to be invoked by the lawyers, while at the same time *ahl al-kitāb* and local worthies continued to be invoked long after the lawyers had ceased to make use of them. The rule of thumb thus cannot be expected to apply to such traditions.

54 Schacht, *Origins*, pp. 171ff. For an enthusiastic recommendation of the method, see Juynboll, *Muslim Tradition*, pp. 206ff.

55 M. Cook, *Early Muslim Dogma*, Cambridge 1981, pp. 107ff.

56 Cook, *Dogma*, pp. 109ff; Schacht, *Origins*, pp. 166ff.

57 The common link theory has also done badly in tests on apocalyptic material (cf. the references given above, note 53; and unlike the rule of thumb discussed there, it ought to apply equally well to all types of Ḥadīth).

58 Cf. Crone, 'Jāhilī and Jewish Law', pp. 196f, with reference to Mālik; Abū Zurʿa, a Damascene scholar who died in 893, similarly claimed not to know of a single scholar who rejected the classical tradition on *walāʾ al-islām*, for all that most scholars had rejected it by then (Ibn Ḥajar, *Tahdhīb al-tahdhīb*, Hyderabad 1325–7, vol. VI, p. 47).

59 Cf. the clash between Schacht and Coulson, who regarded Schacht's theory as irrefutable in its broad essentials, but who still held that 'an alleged ruling of the Prophet should be tentatively accepted as such unless some reason can be adduced as to why it should be regarded as fictitious' (*History*, pp. 64f). Schacht's response was bad-tempered (cf. his review, 'Modernism and Traditionalism in a History of Islamic Law', *Middle Eastern Studies* 1965, pp. 392ff), but his sense that a refusal to shift the burden of proof would nullify his own work was quite right; for Coulson held that though the vast majority of traditions attributed to the Prophet were apocryphal in a formal sense, this simply meant that they could not be taken at face value: substantively, they might still represent approximations to decisions by the Prophet, and they should be treated as such unless there were reasons to do otherwise (*History*, pp. 65, 69f). In short, Ḥadīth should be treated as basically genuine in practice. (Coulson envisaged a situation in which the Prophet's decisions were passed on *bi'l-maʿnā*, not *bi'l-lafẓ*, that is to say oral tradition preserved their general meaning, not the precise wording. When stringent criteria of authenticity were evolved, *isnād*s were fabricated and the wording evolved by later generations attributed to the Prophet himself. *Pace* Schacht, the hypothesis is perfectly reasonable; it just happens not to fit the facts, as will be seen in a moment.)

60 Cf. T. S. Kuhn, *The Structure of Scientific Revolutions*², Chicago 1970.

61 P. Crone, *Slaves on Horses, The Evolution of the Islamic Polity*, Cambridge 1980, Ch. 1; id., *Meccan Trade and the Rise of Islam*, Princeton 1987, Ch. 9.

62 See the references given below, Chapter 6, note 38.

63 Cf. below, Chapter 6. Note in particular the tradition in ʿAbd al-Razzāq, *Muṣannaf*, vol. IX, no. 16,151: Ibn Jurayj asks ʿAṭāʾ whether gifts of *walāʾ* are allowed; ʿAṭāʾ denies it twice. Since Ibn Jurayj has previously heard him say that gifts of *walāʾ* are unobjectionable, he presses him to elaborate: why do you prohibit gifts of *walāʾ*, he asks, when you allow clients to change patrons, something which amounts to the same? ʿAṭāʾ replies by citing a Prophetic tradition which condemns changes of patron without permission and which thus implies that if permission is obtained, the practice is allowed. ʿAṭāʾ apparently did not know of a Prophetic tradition prohibiting gifts of *walāʾ*: he prohibited it for reasons of his own and would clearly have prohibited changes of patrons too if it had not been for this tradition from the Prophet.

64 ʿAbd al-Razzāq cites five traditions from Ibn Jurayj and four from Maʿmar against the practice (*Muṣannaf*, vol. IX, nos. 16,139, 16,143–4, 16,146–8, 16,150–1). This clearly suggests that both collected traditions against it and would have included traditions from the Prophet if they had known of any. (Differently put, here the argument from polemical silence seems to work.)

65 ʿAbd al-Razzāq, *Muṣannaf*, vol. IX, no. 16,138; Raddatz, 'Erbrecht', p. 41; Shāfiʿī, *Kitāb al-umm*, Būlāq 1321–6, vol. vii, p. 208; Bukhārī, *Le recueil des traditions mahométanes*, ed. L. Krehl and T. W. Juynboll, Leiden 1862–1908, vol. IV, p. 289. Cf. Schacht, *Origins*, p. 173, where the classical tradition is dated to the generation before Mālik on the basis of the

lowest common link (ʿAbdallāh b. Dīnār). There are in fact other *isnāds* overlooked by Schacht, but all can be regarded as later (cf. Abū Ḥanīfa (attrib.), *al-Musnad*, ed. Ṣ. al-Ṣaqqā, Aleppo 1962, no. 305; Ibn Qudāma, *al-Mughnī*, ed. Ṭ. M. al-Zaynī, A. ʿA. al-Fāyid and ʿA. A. ʿAṭā', Cairo 1968-70, vol. VI, p. 409; Bayhaqī, *Sunan*, vol. VI, p. 240[18]).

66 This is the major reason why Coulson's theory must be rejected (cf. above, note 59). Coulson assumes that the Prophet made rulings which were remembered and followed by the lawyers, though *isnāds* were still absent and the precise wording lost. But in fact the early lawyers frequently seem to have been unaware that the Prophet had said anything on the subject at all. Coulson does not see the importance of Schacht's point that the early schools operated with authorities other than the Prophet. As long as other authorities sufficed, there was no need to remember rulings by the Prophet; when such rulings became necessary, everybody had long forgotten what, if anything, he had said on the questions involved.

67 Cf. ʿAbd al-Razzāq, *Muṣannaf*, vol. IX, no. 16,147 (*al-walā' nasab lā yubāʿu wa-lā yūhab*, attributed to Ḥasan al-Baṣrī), no. 16,149 (*al-walā' luḥma ka'l-nasab lā yubāʿu wa-lā yūhab*, attributed to Ibn al-Musayyab); Bayhaqī, *Sunan*, vol. VI, p. 240[18] (*al-walā' luḥma ka-luḥmat al-nasab lā yubāʿu wa-lā yūhab*, attributed to Ḥasan al-Baṣrī from the Prophet); Sarakhsī, *al-Mabsūt*, Cairo 1324–31, vol. VIII, p. 97 (the same, attributed to Ibn ʿUmar from the Prophet – the classical *isnād*).

68 Cf. ʿAbd al-Razzāq, *Muṣannaf*, vol. IX, no. 16,150, where Ibn ʿUmar strongly disapproves of sale and gifts of *walā'* in apparent ignorance of the fact that the Prophet had totally prohibited such transactions; no. 16,138, where he transmits the Prophetic prohibition.

69 Cf. most recently Juynboll, *Muslim Tradition*, pp. 15f.

70 *Lā yuḥālifu mu'min mawlā mu'min dūnahu* (Ibn Hishām, *Das Leben Muhammed's nach Muhammed Ibn Ishâk*, ed. F. Wüstenfeld, Göttingen 1858–60, p. 342 = *The Life of Muhammad*, tr. A. Guillaume, Oxford 1955, p. 232, (where the translation is 'a believer shall not take as an ally the freedman of another Muslim against him').

71 *Kataba al-nabī ʿalā kulli baṭn ʿuqūlahu thumma kataba annahu la yuḥillu [li-muslim] an yatawālā mawlā rajul muslim bi-ghayri idhnihi. Qāla: ukhbirtu annahu laʿana fī saḥīfatihi man faʿala dhālika* (Jābir in ʿAbd al-Razzāq, *Muṣannaf*, vol. IX, no. 16,154; cf. no. 16,153: *man tawālā [mawlā] rajul muslim bi-ghayri idhnihi aw āwā muḥdithan fa-ʿalayhi ghaḍab Allāh lā yaqbalu Allāh minhu ṣarfan wa-lā ʿadlan*. Both are summaries of the Constitution. Similarly nos. 16,156, 16,309; Ibn Ḥanbal, *Musnad*, vol. III, p. 349. Compare above, note 63, on ʿAṭā'.

72 For a discussion of the original meaning, see below, Chapter 4, note 141.

73 *Man tawālā ghayra mawālīhi fa-ʿalayhi laʿnat Allāh wa'l-malā'ika wa'l-nās ajmaʿīn lā yaqbalu Allāh minhu ṣarfan wa-lā ʿadlan* (ʿAbd al-Razzāq, *Muṣannaf*, vol. IX, no. 16,305). *Laʿana Allāh man iddaʿā ilā ghayri abīhi aw tawallā ilā ghayri mawālīhi* (*ibid.*, no. 16,307; similarly nos. 16,306, 16,308). Or more simply: *man tawallā ghayra mawālīhi fa-huwa kāfir* (ibid., no. 16,304). Numerous versions of the categorical prohibition of *muwālāt* are cited in Ibn Ḥanbal, *Musnad*, vol. I, pp. 309, 317f, 328; and all *ḥadīth*-collections cite some.

74 Ibn Hishām, *Leben*, p. 970.

75 Ṭabarī, *Ta'rīkh al-rusul wa'l-mulūk*, ed. M. J. de Goeje and others, Leiden 1879–1901, ser. iii, p. 480.

76 Similarly ʿAbd al-Razzāq, *Muṣannaf*, vol. IX, nos. 16,306–8, but here the Prophet gives the speech at Minā, not at ʿArafa as in Ibn Isḥāq, though the *isnād* is the same. Note the proliferation of details designed to corroborate the historicity of the incident. In ʿAbd al-Razzāq, no. 16,307, the speech is transmitted by Shahr b. Ḥawshab from somebody who heard the Prophet gives it, sitting so close to him that his she-camel dropped spittle on his thigh. In no. 16,306 this person is identified as ʿAmr b. Khārija who adds more information on the Prophet's she-camel. And in Ibn Isḥāq we are told how ʿAmr came to be there at the time.

77 But in Muslim b. Ḥajjāj, *al-Jāmiʿ al-ṣaḥīḥ*, Constantinople 1329–33, vol. IV, p. 217, the spurious clause has been written back into the Constitution.

78 According to Ibn al-Athīr, *al-Nihāya fī-gharīb al-ḥadīth*, ed. Ṭ. A. al-Zāwī and M. M. al-Ṭannāḥī, Cairo 1963–5, vol. V, pp. 227f, even the traditions which retain the reference to the need for permission should be understood to imply unqualified prohibition. And note how Mālik happily counters the Prophet's own words with other words ascribed to him:

'even if a man permits his freedman to become *mawlā* of whoever he wishes, this is not allowed because the Prophet said "*walā'* belongs to the manumitter" ' (Mālik, *Muwaṭṭa'*, Cairo n.d., vol. II, p. 143). This example also runs counter to Coulson's theory (cf. above, note 52): having preserved the Constitution of Medina, the Muslims had preserved the precise wording used by the Prophet himself; yet they both changed his wording and lost the general meaning of the rule which he had enunciated.

79 Guillaume, *Traditions of Islam*, p. 28.

80 Juynboll, *Muslim Tradition*, pp. 29f; cf. *ibid.* pp. 27, 29, on the proliferation of traditions transmitted by ʿUmar and Ibn Masʿūd.

3. The Islamic patronate

1 There are exceptions. Conversion to Zoroastrianism will not today make the convert a member of the Zoroastrian community; one 'cannot convert to Zoroastrianism', as this point is popularly put (J. R. Hinnells, *Zoroastrianism and the Parsis*, London 1981, pp. 49ff).

2 B. J. Bamberger, *Proselytism in the Talmudic Period*[2], New York 1968; cf. also *Encyclopaedeia Judaica*, Jerusalem 1971–2, *s.v.* 'slavery'.

3 *Encyclopaedia of Islam*[2], *s.v. 'mawlā'*.

4 Cf. B. Cohen, *Jewish and Roman Law*, New York 1966, vol. I, pp. 146ff.

5 Though it may well have done so at an early stage (A. R. W. Harrison, *The Law of Athens*, Oxford 1968, pp. 189ff).

6 Again there is evidence that this was once different (Harrison, *Law of Athens*, p. 148). For the obligations which Athenian and other Greek manumitters could impose on their freedmen, see below, Chapter 5.

7 This point is denied by J. Juda, *Die sozialen und wirtschaftlichen Aspekte der Mawālī in frühislamischer Zeit* (Inaugural-Dissertation), Tübingen 1983, p. 87, according to whom converts did not necessarily become clients. Naturally the inner act of seeing the light did not in itself have any social effects, and naturally a great many professed to have seen the light without having acquired sponsors. But every convert nonetheless had to become a client if he wanted the authorities to acknowledge his transfer to the Muslim community. To have a patron was to have an entrance visa to this community, to lack one was to be an illegal immigrant, and a great deal of Umayyad history is taken up with the problem posed by such immigrants (typically they were repatriated, sc. sent back to their villages). In the eyes of the authorities, a convert who had failed to acquire a patron (be it by conversion at the hands of another or otherwise) did not count as a Muslim at all.

8 Cf. Sarakhsī, *Mabsūṭ*, vol. VIII, pp. 81ff; Qudūrī, *Le statut personnel en droit musulman hanéfite*, ed. and tr. G.-H. Bousquet and L. Bercher, [Tunis 1952], p. 263 (Ḥanafī); Khalīl, *Sommario*, vol. II, pp. 789f; Saḥnūn, *al-Mudawwana al-kubrā*, Cairo 1323–4, vol. VIII, pp. 85ff (Mālikī); Shirbīnī, *Mughnī'l-muḥtāj*, [Cairo 1308], vol. IV, pp. 465f; Shīrāzī, *Kitāb al-tanbīh*, tr. G.-H. Bousquet, Alger n.d. [1949–52], part ii, pp. 113f (Shāfiʿī); Ibn Qudāma, *Mughnī*, vol. VI, nos. 4932ff (Ḥanbalī); Ibn Ḥazm, *al-Muḥallā*, ed. M. M. al-Dimashqī, Cairo 1347–52, vol. IX, p. 300, no. 1736 and *passim* (Ẓāhirī; Brunschvig mistakenly lists the Ẓāhirīs as dissenters in the *Encyclopaedia of Islam*[2], *s.v.* "ʿAbd' – perhaps he meant the Ibāḍīs); Ibn al-Murtaḍā, *al-Baḥr al-zakhkhār*, Cairo and Baghdad 1947–9, vol. VI, pp. 358ff; Siyāghī, *Kitāb al-rawḍ al-naḍīr*, completed by ʿAbbās b. Aḥmad al-Ḥasanī, Cairo 1347–9, vol. V, pp. 71ff; Hawsamī, *Kitāb sharḥ al-Ibāna*, MS Ambrosiana D. 224, fols. 122aff (Qāsimī and Naṣirī Zaydī); Ṭūsī, *al-Nihāya*, Beirut 1970, pp. 669f; Ḥillī, *Sharāʾiʿ al-islām*, ed. ʿA.-Ḥ. M. ʿAlī, Najaf 1969, vol. IV, pp. 35ff (Imāmī); Nuʿmān b. Muḥammad, *Daʿāʾim al-islām*, ed. A. ʿA. A. Fayḍī, Cairo 1960–63, vol. II, no. 1385; *id.*, *Kitab al-iqtiṣār*, ed. M. W. Mīrzā, Damascus 1957, p. 136 (Ismāʿīlī).

9 Basyānī (or Basyūnī, Basyāwī, Basīwī or Basyawī), *Kitāb mukhtaṣar al-Basyawī*, ed. ʿA.-Q. ʿAṭāʾ and M. ʿA. al-Zarqa, printed for the Ministry of the National Heritage, Sultanate of Oman, n.p., n.d., pp. 149, 157; Aṭfayyish, *Sharḥ al-Nīl wa-shifāʾ al-ʿalīl*, vol. VIII, Cairo 1343, pp. 392ff; E. Sachau, 'Muhammedanisches Erbrecht nach der Lehre der Ibaditischen Araber von Zanzibar und Ostafrika', *Sitzungsberichte der Königlichen Preussischen Akademie der Wissenschaften zu Berlin* 1894, p. 181. The eighth-century Abū Nūḥ Ṣāliḥ al-Dahhān is however said to have accepted the manumitter's status as heir (Aṭfayyish,

Sharḥ, vol. VIII, p. 394; cf. Shammākhī, *Kitāb al-siyar*, Cairo n.d. [1301], p. 88); and other Ibāḍīs apparently also accepted the contractual patron as heir (Aṭfayyish, *Sharḥ*, vol. VIII, p. 111). Moreover, the Ibāḍīs at large hold that there is no *walā'* over *mukātabs* (cf. below, chapter 6, p. 86). As will be seen, this is an archaic doctrine which makes little sense if *walā'* confers no privileges. It would thus seem that the Ibāḍīs at large once accepted the manumitter's status of heir.

10 Cf. the references given above, note 8, or J.-D. Luciani, *Traité des successions musulmanes*, Paris 1890, pp. 58ff (Shāfiʿī, with some use of Mālikī texts).

11 Ibn al-Murtaḍā, *Baḥr*, vol. VI, pp. 358f.

12 Ṭūsī, *Nihāya*, pp. 669, cf. 623.

13 Nuʿmān, *Iqtiṣār*, p. 136 (without explicit mention of *nasab* and *sabab*).

14 Hawsamī, fols. 98a, 101a–b (that Nāṣir's inheritance laws are identical with those of the Imāmīs is also pointed out by Madelung, 'Shiʿi Attitudes', pp. 77f).

15 See for example Marghīnānī, *Hidāya*, part iii, pp. 271, 272; Khalīl, *Sommario*, vol. II, p. 688f; Shirbīnī, *Mughnī*, vol. IV, p. 88; Ibn Qudāma, *Mughnī*, vol. VIII, no. 6830. But the Ẓāhirīs disagreed (Ibn Ḥazm, *al-Muḥallā*, vol. XI, pp. 58ff).

16 Siyāghī, *Rawḍ*, vol. IV, p. 261; Hawsamī, *Ibāna* (D. 224) fol. 125a; Ṭūsī, *Nihāya*, p. 547; Nuʿmān, *Daʿā'im*, vol. II, no. 1197.

17 Aṭfayyish, *Sharḥ*, vol. VIII, pp. 110f.

18 Cf. Kindī, *The Governors and Judges of Egypt*, ed. R. Guest, Leiden and London 1912, pp. 333f, where a mid-Umayyad judge observes that manumitters were prone to claim this right.

19 Marghīnānī, *Hidāya*, part I, p. 200; Khalīl, *Sommario*, vol. II, p. 6; Shirbīnī, *Mughnī*, vol. 3, p. 143; Ibn Qudāma, *Mughnī*, vol. VII, no. 5095.

20 Ḥillī, *Sharā'iʿ*, vol. II, p. 276; Naḥwī, *al-Tadhkira al-fākhira fī fiqh al-ʿitra al-ṭāhira*, MS British Library, Or. 3809, fols. 88a–b; Mu'ayyad, *al-Tajrīd*, MS Ambrosiana, G. 7, fol. 32a; Hawsamī, *Sharḥ al-ibāna*, part II, MS Ambrosiana, E. 262, fol. 157b; Nuʿmān does not explicitly mention the patron among the marriage guardians in either of his two works, but if he had disagreed with the other Shīʿites, he could be expected to have said so.

21 Abū Isḥāq, *Kitāb mā lā yasaʿu jahluhu*, MS British Library, Or. 3744, fol. 89a.

22 Khalīl, *Sommario*, vol. II, p. 169.

23 The Ḥanafīs and Qāsimīs only award custody to agnates within the prohibited degrees (Y. Linant de Bellefonds, *Traité de droit musulman comparé*, Paris and the Hague 1965– , vol. III, p. 160; Naḥwī, *Tadhkira*, fol. 129b); in these two schools he is thus excluded (cf. Marghinānī, *Hidāya*, part II, p. 38).

24 Cf. the references given above, chapter 2, notes 48–9; ʿAbd al-Razzāq, *Muṣannaf*, vol. IX, nos. 16,193–5.

25 Ibn Babūyah, *Man lā yaḥḍuruhu*, vol. IV, p. 224 (no. 151); ʿĀmilī, *Miftāḥ al-karāma fī sharḥ qawā'id al-ʿallāma*, vol. VI), Cairo 1326, p. 199.

26 Nuʿmān, *Iqtiṣār*, p. 136.

27 Ḥillī in ʿĀmilī, *Miftāḥ*, vol. VI, p. 199; Ḥillī, *Sharā'iʿ* vol. IV, p. 37. (According to Ṭūsī, all agree that the freedman is excluded from succession, except for Shurayḥ and Ṭāwūs (Ṭūsī, *al-Mabsūṭ fī fiqh al-imāmiyya*, ed. M. T. al-Kashfī, Tehran 1387, vol. IV, p. 95. Ṭūsī thus did not know that some Imāmīs disagreed too: here as elsewhere, he is better informed about disagreement within the Sunnī than the Imāmī camp.)

28 For the Mālikīs, see Saḥnūn, *Mudawwana*, vol. VIII, p. 93; ʿAbd al-Wahhāb al-Baghdādī, *al-Ishrāf ʿalā masā'il al-khilāf*, Tunis n.d., vol. II, p. 302. For the Ḥanafīs, see Sarakhsī, *Mabsūṭ*, vol. XXX, p. 38, 45. For the Shāfiʿīs, see Luciani, *Successions*, p. 73, or E. Sachau, *Muhammedanisches Recht nach schafiitischer Lehre*, Stuttgart and Berlin 1897, pp. 186, 772; unilateral succession is *qawl ʿāmmat ahl al-ʿilm*, as Ibn Qudāma notes, including that of the Ḥanbalīs (*Mughnī*, vol. VI, no. 4974). As for the freedman's right to inherit, *qalla man yaqūlu fīhi*, as Aṭfayyish observes for all that the question has no bearing on Ibāḍī doctrine (*Sharḥ*, vol. VIII, p. 395); similarly Ibn al-Murtaḍā, *Baḥr*, vol. IV, p. 231; Hawsamī, *Ibāna* (D. 224), fol. 123b.

29 Muṣʿabī in Aṭfayyish, *Sharḥ*, vol. VIII, p. 111.

30 Nuʿmān, *Iqtiṣār*, p. 139, defines the *ʿāqila* as the heirs with certain exceptions. As has been seen, the heirs include the freedman, and the freedman is not mentioned among the exceptions.

31 Khalīl, *Sommario*, vol. II, p. 688f; Ibn Qudāma, *Mughnī*, vol. VIII, no. 6831.
32 Shāfiʿī, *Umm*, vol. VI, p. 102.
33 Shīrāzī, *Tanbīh*, part iv, p. 30; Shirbīnī, *Mughnī* vol. IV, pp. 88f; Sachau, *Recht*, p. 772.
34 The Ḥanafīs and Zaydīs make this clear by their failure to mention the freedman in definitions of the *ʿāqila*; Ḥillī, *Sharāʾiʿ*, vol. IV, p. 288, and Ṭūsī, *Mabsūṭ*, vol. VII, p. 179, explicitly exclude him; so also does Ibn Qudāma, *Mughnī*, vol. VIII, no. 6831, adding that Abū Ḥanīfa and the Mālikīs do not include him either. (The translation by H. Laoust, *Le précis de droit d'Ibn Qudāma*, Beirut 1950, p. 251, should be corrected accordingly: the *mawālī* who are included are patrons, not freedmen.)
35 Ibn Rushd, *Bidāyat al-mujtahid*, ed. M. S. Muḥaysin and Sh. M. Ismāʿīl, Cairo 1970–4, vol. II, p. 15; Khalīl describes the question as controversial (*Sommario*, vol. II, p. 6).
36 Khalīl, *Sommario*, vol. II, p. 169.
37 *Encyclopaedia of Islam*[2], *s.v.* 'mawlā'.
38 Cf. below, Chapter 6.
39 Khalīl, *Sommario*, vol. II, p. 788; Ibn Qudāma, *Précis*, pp. 156f. Other works take this point for granted.
40 For the rules of its devolution, see below, Chapter 6.
41 Practically no information is available on its legal incidents in Ismāʿīlī law.
42 For the classical tradition on *walāʾ* arising on conversion (*man aslama ʿalā yadayhi fa-huwa mawlāhu*), see ʿAbd al-Razzāq, *Muṣannaf*, vol. IX, no. 16,271, and any collection of Prophetic traditions, usually in the section on *farāʾiḍ*. For other forms of contractual clientage, see Crone, *Slaves on Horses*, p. 49.
43 Ibn al-Murtaḍā, *Baḥr*, vol. IV, pp. 227f; Naḥwī, *Tadhkira*, fol. 224a; Muʾayyad, *Tajrīd*, fol. 91a. Some Qāsimīs state that the tie arises if a *ḥarbī* converts *and* makes an agreement with the persons at whose hands he has converted, suggesting that it is the agreement which gives rise to it (Hawsamī, *Kitāb al-ifāda*, MS British Library, Or. 4031, fol. 36a; Hawsamī, *Ibāna* (D. 224), fol. 122a). The phraseology is that used by the Ḥanafīs, but Ibn al-Murtaḍā explicitly states that it arises on conversion; so does Ṣanʿānī in Siyāghī, *Rawḍ*, vol. V, p. 76; and Naḥwī specifies that it arises even if no agreement is made (*Tadhkira*, *loc. cit.*).
44 Sarakhsī, *Mabsūṭ*, vol. VIII, pp. 91f, where this point is explained at length. Other Ḥanafī authors simply point out that the tie arises if somebody converts at the hands of another *and* make an agreement with him (e.g. Marghīnānī, *Hidāya*, part III, p. 274; Qudūrī, *Statut*, p. 267). Ṭūsī makes the same point as Sarakhsī in his *Kitāb al-khilāf*, [Tehran] n.d., vol. III, pp. 368f; cf. also id., *Tahdhīb*, vol. IX, nos. 1414–15; ʿĀmilī, *Miftāḥ*, vol. VI, pp. 9, 197f, 204.
45 Sarakhsī, *Mabsūṭ*, vol. VII, p. 96; N. B. E. Baillie, *A Digest of Moohummudan Law*[2], London 1875–87, vol. I, p. 390.
46 Sarakhsī, *Mabsūṭ*, vol. VIII, p. 113.
47 Ṭūsī, *Nihāya*, p. 548; cf. *id.*, *Tahdhīb*, vol. IX, nos. 1406–11, 1415; Ḥillī, *Sharāʾiʿ*, vol. IV, p. 40; Ḥillī in ʿĀmilī, *Miftāḥ*, vol. VI, p. 204; Nuʿmān, *Iqtiṣār*, p. 128.
48 Sarakhsī, *Mabsūṭ*, vol. VIII, p. 96; Ḥillī, *Sharāʾiʿ* vol. IV, p. 40; Ḥillī in ʿĀmilī, *Miftāḥ*, vol. VI, p. 204; Baillie, *Digest*, vol. I, p. 390; vol. II, p. 360.
49 Sarakhsī, *Mabsūṭ*, vol. XXX, p. 45; Ḥillī, *Sharāʾiʿ*, vol. IV, p. 40; Ibn al-Murtaḍā, *Baḥr*, vol. V, p. 358. This is simply another way of saying that for the tie to be effective, the client must be somebody entirely devoid of relatives.
50 Qudūrī, *Statut*, p. 267; Ḥillī, *Sharāʾiʿ*, vol. IV, pp. 39f (I have no explicit Qāsimī or Ismāʿīlī statement on this point). It is for this reason that the Imāmīs usually call the tie *walāʾ taḍammun al-jarīra* rather than *walāʾ al-muwalāt*.
51 Sarakhsī, *Mabsūṭ*, vol. IV, pp. 222f; Hawsamī, *Ibāna* (E. 262), fols. 158a–b.
52 Sarakhsī, *Mabsūṭ*, vol. XXX, p. 45; Ṭūsī, *Mabsūṭ*, vol. VII, p. 181; *id.*, *Khilāf*, vol. III, p. 145 (where the rights and duties vested in the tie are even defined as mutual); ʿĀmilī, *Miftāḥ*, vol. VI, pp. 204f; Baillie, *Digest*, vol. I, p. 390; vol. II, p. 361.
53 Hawsamī, *Ifāda*, fols. 36a–b; but Yaḥyā b. Ḥamza allowed it (Ibn al-Murtaḍā, *Baḥr*, vol. IV, p. 227).
54 Ṭūsī, *Khilāf*, vol. III, p. 145; Baillie, *Digest*, vol. II, p. 361.
55 Sarakhsī, *Mabsūṭ*, vol. VIII, p. 97; cf. Shaybānī, *Kitāb al-makhārij fiʾl-ḥiyal*, ed. J. Schacht, Leipzig 1930, pp. 60f; Baillie, *Digest*, vol. II, pp. 361f. If the patron dies first, his heirs do not inherit the tie (Ḥillī in ʿĀmilī, *Miftāḥ*, vol. VI, p. 204). If the client dies, he leaves no

heirs over which it could be exercised: whereas the Ḥanafīs rule that children born after the conclusion of the contract are included in it, the Imāmīs apparently deem that the birth of children invalidates it (Sarakhsī, *Mabsūṭ*, vol. VIII, p. 93; Shaybānī, *Ḥiyal*, p. 61; Baillie, *Digest*, vol. I, p. 390; vol. II, p. 360).

56 For an example, see Shaybānī, *Kitāb al-aṣl*, ed. A.-W. al-Afghānī, Hyderabad 1966– , vol. IV(1), pp. 201f.

57 Sarakhsī, *Mabsūt*, vol. VIII, pp. 82f; Saḥnūn, *Mudawwana*, vol. VIII, p. 79; Shirbīnī, *Mughnī*, vol. IV, pp. 88, 465; Ibn Qudāma, *Mughnī*, vol. VI, p. 409; Basyānī, *Mukhtaṣar*, p. 239; Ṭūsī, *Mabsūṭ*, vol. IV, p. 93; Ibn al-Murtaḍā, *Baḥr*, vol. IV, pp. 226, 229; Hawsamī, *Ibāna* (D. 224), fol. 124b; cf. also above, Chapter 2, note 60. The list could be greatly extended. Note that the maxim is accepted even by the Ibāḍīs, who reject the patron's right to succession, and by the Imāmīs and Nāṣirīs, who hold that he inherits by *sabab* as opposed to *nasab*.

58 Kharashī, *Sharḥ ʿalā'l-mukhtasar*, Cairo 1307–8, vol. V, p. 404. Others speak of *taʿṣīb*, 'agnatisation' (see for example Qudūrī, *Statut*, p. 265).

59 He is in fact frequently compared with a child: the manumitter has given life to him as a father gives life to his son (Sarakhsī, *Mabsūṭ*, vol. XXX, pp. 38f; Marghīnānī, *Hidāya*, part III, p. 271; Shāfiʿī, *Umm*, vol. V, p. 56; Khalīl, *Mukhtaṣar*, vol. II, p. 786[351]; ʿĀmilī, *Miftāḥ*, vol. VI, pp. 197f; Aṭfayyish, *Sharḥ*, vol. VIII, p. 395).

60 See for example Saḥnūn, *Mudawwana*, vol. VIII, p. 93. Though common, the distinction is not common enough for the modern reader: given that *mawlā* means both patron and client, and that *mʿtq* means both manumitter and freedman, the lawbooks are not always models of clarity.

61 Goldziher's *Muhammedanische Studien*, vol. I, Ch. 3 comes close to being such a statement; but it is concerned with attitudes to *mawālī* rather than the institution of *walā'*.

62 Though it would not have struck von Kremer as such; von Kremer came close to arguing much the same himself (*Culturgeschichte*, vol. I, pp. 525ff, 547).

63 W. M. Watt, *Islam and the Integration of Society*, London 1961, p. 108; similarly B. Lewis, *The Arabs in History*[4], London 1966, p. 58.

64 See for example Ṭabarī, *Ta'rīkh*, ser. ii, pp. 681, 1518, 1550, 1771.

65 Wakīʿ, *Akhbār al-quḍāh*, ed. ʿA.-ʿA. M. al-Marāghī, Cairo 1947–50, vol. II, p. 167; Ṭaḥāwī, *Mushkil al-āthār*, Hyderabad 1333, vol. IV, p. 54.

66 *Encyclopaedia of Islam*[2], *s.v.* 'mawlā'. but note that it was only towards the end of the Umayyad period that ties between patron and client began to play a conspicuous role in Muslim politics (Crone, *Slaves on Horses*, pp. 53ff).

67 Goldziher, *Muhammedanische Studien*, vol. I, p. 120; Ṭabarī, *Ta'rīkh*, ser. ii, p. 681.

68 This comes across very forcefully in Goldziher's account (*Muhammedanische Studien*, vol. I, Ch. 3), in which patrons scarcely figure at all.

69 If historical works were all that survived, daring scholars might postulate that the patron had a right to succession on the basis of Balādhurī's remark that the sons of the caliph Mahdī inherited an *iqṭāʿ* from a client of Mahdī's (Balādhurī, *Futūḥ* p. 148). But they would not be able to go further than that.

4. The case against Arabia

1 It seems unlikely that Sarjūn b. Manṣūr, the Christian *mawlā'l-muwālāt* of Muʿāwiya and grandfather of John of Damascus, was regarded as a Qurashī (see the references in Crone, *Slaves*, note 358).

2 Sarakhsī, *Mabsūṭ*, vol. V, p. 24.

3 For attestations of the term *aṣīl* or *aṣīlī*, see for example C. M. Doughty, *Travels in Arabia Deserta*, London 1936 (first published 1888), vol. I, p. 326; vol. II, p. 146; Naʿūm Bak Shuqayr, *Ta'rīkh Sīnā*, Cairo n.d. [preface dated 1916], pp. 406f; A. Musil, *The Manners and Customs of the Rwala Bedouins*, New York 1928, p. 136; H. R. P. Dickson, *The Arab of the Desert*, London 1949, p. 111. For the use of the term *qabīlī* (or *qubaylī*) in the same sense, see H. Freiherr von Maltzan, *Reise nach Südarabien*, Braunschweig 1873, p. 216; J. Chelhod, 'Le droit intertribal dans les hauts plateaux du Yémen', *al-Bahit, Festschrift Joseph Henninger*, Bonn 1976, p. 50 and *passim*.

4 Cf. Musil, *Rwala*, p. 282.

5 Cf. Musil, *Rwala*, p. 278; A. Jaussen, *Coutumes des arabes au pays de Moab*, Paris 1908, pp. 125f; E. Marx, *Bedouins of the Negev*, Manchester 1967, p. 67 (freedmen); von Maltzan, *Reise*, p. 186; R. A. B. Hamilton, 'The Social Organization of the Tribes of the Aden Protectorate', *Journal of the Royal Central Asian Society* 1942, pp. 246ff (freedmen and other Africans, Jews); J. Henninger, 'Pariastämme in Arabien', *Sankt Gabrieler Studien, Festschrift des Missionshauses Sankt Gabriel*, Vienna and Mödling 1939, pp. 502ff, 527ff (Ṣulubbīs, other ethnic minorities); T. al-Hilali, 'Die Kasten in Arabien', *Die Welt des Islams* 1940, pp. 108f (Qawāwila, *i.e.* gypsy-like pariahs).

6 Musil, *Rwala*, pp. 44f; Dickson, *Arab of the Desert*, pp. 108ff.

7 As do the tribesmen of the Yemen and Oman, and the Tamīmī peasants of Najd. Note the rule, cited by Hamilton, 'The Aden Protectorate', p. 245, that loss of one's land means permanent demotion from tribal status.

8 Such as the Banū Khaḍīr of Najd (*Encyclopaedia of Islam*^{2}, *s.v.* (based exclusively on Philby); *A Handbook of Arabia* n.p. 1916–17, vol. I, pp. 75, 363, 607; Hilali, 'Die Kasten', pp. 105ff); the Bayādīr of Oman (J. C. Wilkinson, 'Bayāsirah and Bayādīr', *Arabian Studies*, vol. I, Cambridge 1974, pp. 80ff); and various members of landless classes in south Arabia (Hamilton, 'The Aden Protectorate', pp. 244f; W. H. Ingrams, *A Report on the Social, Economic and Political Conditions of the Hadhramaut*, London 1937, p. 44).

9 Such as the *ʿabīd* cultivators, i.e. ex-slaves, of Doughty's Ḥijāz and Philby's Najd (Doughty, *Travels*, vol. II, pp. 133f; H. St. J. B. Philby, *The Heart of Arabia*, London 1922, vol. I, pp. 171, 180; vol. II, pp. 12f, 92, 94).

10 Doughty, *Travels*, vol. I, pp. 324, 326 and *passim*; Musil, *Rwala*, p. 281; Hilali, 'Die Kasten', p. 105; J. L. Burckhardt, *Notes on the Bedouins and Wahábys*, published by the Association for Promoting the Discovery of the Interior of Africa, London 1830, p. 37.

11 Von Maltzan, *Reise*, pp. 182ff; Hamilton, 'The Aden Protectorate', pp. 244f; Ingrams, *Hadhramaut*, pp. 43f; D. Ingrams, *A Survey of Social and Economic Conditions in the Aden Protectorate*, Eritrea 1949, p. 51; Wilkinson, 'Bayāsirah and Bayādīr', pp. 76ff; cf. also Doughty, *Travels*, vol. I, p. 662; vol. II, pp. 20, 429, on craftsmen and butchers in Ḥāʾil and Najd.

12 Professional poets, singers and dancers in south Arabia are thus also excluded from tribal ranks (von Maltzan, *Reise*, pp. 187f, 190; Hamilton, 'The Aden Protectorate', pp. 245f; Ingrams, *Aden Protectorate*, p. 51; compare T. Ashkenazi, *Tribus semi-nomades de la Palestine du Nord*, Paris 1938, p. 98, where the professional singer is a slave).

13 The tribesmen regard them as freedmen, *mawālī*, white slaves, sons of slave-mothers, descendants of prisoners-of-war, of Ethiopians or of Ḥaḍramīs, and so on, even if they are physically indistinguishable from the local population (Hilali, 'Die Kasten', p. 106; Wilkinson, "Bayāsirah and Bayādīr', pp. 76f; Ingrams, *Hadhramaut*, p. 44; von Maltzan, *Reise*, p. 189).

14 Von Maltzan, *Reise*, pp. 192, 216; Musil, *Rwala*, pp. 60, 136. The shepherd tribes, who are always under the thumb of the camel-breeders, are thus not accepted as *aṣīl* (Musil, *Rwala*, pp. 44f; cf. Burckhardt, *Notes*, p. 13).

15 There are apparent exceptions. Thus the Ḥutaym and Sharārāt, who do not on the face of it differ from other bedouin, are branded as pariahs (for a survey of the literature, see Henninger, 'Pariastämme', pp. 515ff). But though it would go too far to demonstrate this here, their exclusion is not in fact anomalous.

16 On this point there is total agreement in the literature.

17 Musil, *Rwala*, p. 277; Jaussen, *Coutumes*, p. 126 (the *ʿabīd* who had begun to stage raids in their own right in Jaussen's time were clearly exceptional, cf. *Coutumes*, p. 125).

18 In addition to the references given already, see Ingrams, *Hadhramaut*, pp. 43f; Ingrams, *Aden Protectorate*, pp. 50ff; Hamilton, 'The Aden Protectorate', pp. 245ff; Henning, 'Pariastämme', p. 506, 527, 529; B. Thomas, *Arabia Felix*, London 1932, p. 32; A. Musil, *Arabia Petraea*, Vienna 1907–8, vol. III, pp. 224ff.

19 Cf. Chelhod, 'Droit Intertribal', pp. 68ff; Jaussen, *Coutumes*, pp. 115f, 164, 218ff; Musil, *Rwala*, pp. 267f; *id.*, *Arabia Petraea*, vol. III, pp. 25f.

20 Cf. Burckhardt, *Notes*, pp. 109f; Doughty, *Travels*, vol. I, p. 406; Musil, *Rwala*, pp. 60, 281; Jaussen, *Coutumes*, pp. 162ff; for the Yemeni version of *khuwwa*, see Chelhod, 'Droit intertribal', pp. 67f.

21 Musil, *Arabia Petraea*, vol. III, pp. 226f.

22 Though some bedouin had slaves stolen as children from Egyptian and North African tribes until quite recently (Musil, *Arabia Petraea*, vol. III, p. 224).
23 Musil, *Rwala*, p. 276; contrast Jaussen, *Coutumes*, p. 125.
24 Musil, *Rwala*, pp. 276ff, 629; *id.*, *Arabia Petraea*, vol. III, p. 225; cf. also J. Henninger, 'Die Familie bei den heutigen Beduinen Arabiens und seiner Randgebiete', *Internationales Archiv für Ethnographie*, vol. 42, 1943, pp. 136ff, where full references to the earlier literature are given.
25 Musil, *Arabia Petraea*, vol. III, p. 225.
26 Jaussen, *Coutumes*, p. 125; Burckhardt, *Notes*, p. 103.
27 Jaussen, *Coutumes*, p. 125; Marx, *Negev*, p. 67.
28 Jaussen only mentions military service, and Burckhardt explicitly adds that freedmen do not pay *khuwwa* now (*Notes*, p. 103), implying that they had done so in the past.
29 Burckhardt, *Notes*, p. 88.
30 In the case of slaves the blood-money could be construed as compensation for loss of property.
31 Musil, *Rwala*, pp. 277f.
32 Cf. ʿĀrif al-ʿĀrif, *Kitāb al-qaḍāʾ bayna'l-badw*, Jerusalem 1933, p. 112 = L. Haefeli (tr.), *Die Beduinen von Beerseba*, Luzern 1938, p. 79, where it is the master of a slave or servant who must pay compensation if the slave or servant steals and slaughters a sheep, provided that it has been slaughtered in the master's tent. The principle would seem to be that the master is responsible if the slave or servant acts in his capacity of protégé of the latter, but not otherwise.
33 Jaussen, *Coutumes*, p. 126.
34 Doughty, *Travels*, vol. I, p. 527.
35 They keep their separate names and genealogies; the blood of such an *ibn al-ʿamm* continues to be as cheap as that of a foreigner, and various other rules obtaining between unrelated tribes continue to apply (Musil, *Rwala*, p. 47; Jaussen, *Coutumes*, pp. 149ff).
36 Musil, *Rwala*, p. 277.
37 Abū'l-Faraj al-Iṣbahānī, *Kitāb al-aghānī*, Cairo 1927–72, vol. III, p. 257.
38 C. Snouck Hurgronje, *Mekka in the Latter Part of the 19th Century*, Leiden and London 1931, p. 11.
39 G. A. Wallin, *Travels in Arabia (1845 and 1848)*, Cambridge 1979, p. 143 (where the families of negro origin are concentrated in one quarter).
40 Thomas, *Arabia Felix*, p. 31.
41 Cf. Ibn Manẓūr, *Lisān al-ʿarab*, Bulāq 1307, *s.v. wly*.
42 Chelhod, 'Droit intertribal', p. 69.
43 A. Blunt, *Bedouin of the Euphrates*, London 1879, vol. II, pp. 327f.
44 Shuqayr, *Sīnā*, p. 406.
45 Cf. Ḥassān b. Thābit, *Dīwān*, ed. H. Hirschfeld, Leiden and London 1910, nos. 227:3; 228:1 (addressed to the same person): *lasta bi-ḥurr. . .lasta min al-maʿshar al-akramīn*. See also C. J. Lyall (ed. and tr.), *The Mufaḍḍalīyāt*, Oxford 1918–21, no. 43:1 and the note thereto; Ṭarafa, *Dīwān*, ed. and tr. M. Seligsohn, Paris 1901, no. 18:8; Labīd, *Dīwan*, ed. I. ʿAbbās, Kuwait 1962, no. 18:7; Ṭabarī, *Ta'rīkh*, ser. ii, p. 415; Goldziher, *Muhammedanische Studien*, vol. I, p. 122, on the free and the sons of free mothers.
46 On slaves, freedmen and descendants of slavegirls, see Goldziher, *Muhammedanische Studien*, vol. I, pp. 121ff; there is no comparable evidence on Jews, but note their tendency to slide into despised occupations and client status.
47 Cf. *Encyclopaedia of Islam*[2], *s.v.* 'Ḥanīfa b. Ludjaym'; J. Wellhausen, *Die religiöspolitischen Oppositionsparteien im alten Islam*, Berlin 1901, p. 29; compare Philby, *Heart*, vol. II, p. 277.
48 Ṭabarī, *Ta'rīkh*, ser. ii, pp. 155f.
49 Dhū'l-Rumma, *Dīwān*, ed. C. H. H. Macartney, Cambridge 1919, no. 29:48.
50 Dhū'l-Rumma, *Dīwān*, no. 53:30f; J. Wellhausen, 'Medina vor dem Islam' in his *Skizzen und Vorarbeiten*, vol. IV, Berlin 1889, p. 17.
51 As in the oases of Khaybar, Fadak and Yathrib, as well as in Wādī'l-Qurā.
52 Wellhausen, *Oppositionsparteien*, p. 30: Khaḍārim was a large property of Muʿāwiya's in the Yamāma which was cultivated by 4,000 slaves. Cf. above, n. 9.
53 Several attestations are given in M. Freiherr von Oppenheim, *Die Beduinen*, vol. IV, part i, ed. W. Caskel, Wiesbaden 1967, pp. 104f. For the story that Abū Lahab enslaved a

Makhzūmī and made him work as his blacksmith as a result of gambling debt, see F. Rosenthal, *Gambling in Islam*, Leiden 1975, pp. 71ff, with numerous references.

54 Cf. Hassān b. Thābit's lampoons on the theme 'your father was a smith', 'their fathers are slaves *and* smiths', 'you are the slave of a smith' or simply 'you are an *ʿabd hajīn*' (Hassan b. Thabit, *Dīwān*, nos. 48:3; 59:2; 127:1; 181:3; and *passim*). Compare Ibn Hishām, *Leben*, p. 753; Mubarrad, *al-Kāmil*, ed. W. Wright, Leipzig 1867–92, p. 274.

55 Cf. M. J. Kister, 'On the Wife of the Goldsmith from Fadak and her Progeny', *Le Muséon* 1979, p. 323; O. Rescher (tr.), 'Die Qaçîden des ʿAmr b. Kulthûm' in his *Orientalistische Miszellen*, vol. II, Constantinople 1926, p. 102, no. 5:5. (Caskel's objections, in Oppenheim, *Beduinen*, vol. IV, p. 105, are beside the point: the fact that the woman in question is elsewhere mentioned in flattering terms does not dispose of the fact that her descent from a goldsmith is here a cause for satire.)

56 Thus a satire of Salmā, the daughter of a goldsmith who married Nuʿmān of Ḥīra, has it that she had no hope of marrying even a smith or a weaver in Khawarnaq (Rescher, 'Die Qaçîden', no. 7:2; cf. the preceding note). Muhallab and Ibn al-Ashʿath were both denigrated as former weavers (Yāqūt, *Muʿjam al-buldān*, ed. F. Wüstenfeld, Leipzig 1866–73, vol. II, p. 387; Farazdaq, *Dīwān*, ed. and tr. R. Boucher, Paris 1870, pp. 208^{9}, $211^{11} = 625^{14}$, 633^{6}).

57 Cf. R. Brunschvig, 'Métiers vils en Islam', *Studia Islamica* 1962. It is the same professions which are despised in modern south Arabia. See also I. Goldziher, 'Die Handwerke bei den Arabern', *Globus* 1894.

58 One account of the origin of the Ḥaḍramī family in Mecca has it that its ancestor was a Persian craftsman enslaved in a raid (Ibn Ḥabīb, *Kitāb al-munammaq*, ed. Kh. A. Fāriq, Hyderabad 1964, pp. 320f). In the same vein we are told that Balʿām was a Christian *aʿjamī* who worked as a smith in Mecca (Ibn Ḥajar, *al-Iṣāba fī tamyīz al-ṣaḥāba*, Cairo 1323–5, vol. I, no. 738); Khabbāb b. al-Araṭṭ, the smith who became a Companion of the Prophet, was an Arab slave, later freedman (Ibn Saʿd, *Ṭabaqāt*, vol. III, p. 164; Ibn Ḥajar, *op. cit.*, vol. II, no. 2206); the occasional carpenter in Medina would also be a slave (Wellhausen, 'Medina vor dem Islam', p. 6n); Azraq, the father of the eponymous leader of the Azāriqa, was a Byzantine slave working as a smith (Balādhurī, *Futūḥ*, p. 56). Note also that Muhallab was taunted with being both a weaver *and* a non-Arab (Yāqūt, *Buldān*, vol. II, p. 387).

59 Wellhausen, 'Medina vor dem Islam', p. 14; Kister, 'On the Wife of the Goldsmith'.

60 Cf. A. Shivtiel, W. Lockwood and R. B. Serjeant, 'The Jews of Ṣanʿā'' in R. B. Serjeant and R. Lewcock (eds.), *Ṣanʿāʾ, an Arabian Islamic City*, London 1983, pp. 391, 394, 397n, 424.

61 Cf. Farazdaq, *Dīwān*, pp. $81^{3} = 212^{1}$ (where Banū Ziyād are branded as slaves inherited by Banū'l-Ḥusayn), $141^{11f} = 403^{12-16}$ (where Bāhilīs are branded as slaves who cannot protect the honour of their spouses), $191 = 577^{7}$ and the note thereto (where others are *ʿabīd al-ʿaṣā*, an expression used, according to Thaʿālibī, *Thimār al-qulūb*, ed. M. A.-F. Ibrāhīm, Cairo 1965, no. 1045, of every *dhalīl* and *tābiʿ*).

62 Ṭirimmāḥ, no. 8:35 in F. Krenkow (ed. and tr.), *The Poems of Ṭufail Ibn Auf al-Ghanawī and aṭ-Ṭirimmāḥ Ibn Ḥakīm al-Ṭāʾyī*, London 1927; cf. Marzubānī, *al-Muwashshaḥ*, Cairo 1343, p. 99 ('do you slander a tribe . . . without whom you would be protégés (*mawālī*) like the ʿUkl?').

63 M. Nallino, 'An-Nābiġah al-Ǵaʿdī e le sue poesie', *Rivista degli Studi Orientali* 1934, p. 426; ʿĀmir in C. Lyall (ed. and tr.), *The Dīwāns of ʿAbīd Ibn al-Abraṣ, of Asad, and ʿĀmir Ibn aṭ-Ṭufail, of ʿĀmir Ibn Ṣaʿṣaʿa*, Cambridge 1913, no. 9:2; cf. also Ṭirimmāḥ, no. 47: 54.

64 As they did in Yathrib before they were reduced to client status.

65 Cf. Goldziher, *Muhammedanische Studien*, vol. I, pp. 63ff; W. Robertson Smith, *Kinship and Marriage in Early Arabia*[2], London 1903, pp. 53ff; J. Wellhausen, *Reste arabischen Heidentums*, Berlin 1887, p. 128; J. Pedersen, *Der Eid bei den Semiten*, Strassburg 1914, pp. 21ff; E. Tyan, *Institutions du droit publique musulman*, vol. I, Paris 1954, pp. 36ff; Juda, *Aspekte*, pp. 2ff.

66 Cf. Ibn Saʿd, *Ṭabaqāt*, vol. I, p. 78, where it is used of the agreement which Hāshim is reputed to have made with Byzantium.

67 Cf. below, Chapter 5, pp. 67f.

68 It is used in a pejorative sense of satellite groups by Dhū'l-Rumma, *Dīwān*, no. 87:59, cf. the scholiast's comment thereto; Nābigha al-Jaʿdī, *Dīwān*, ed. and tr. M. Nallino, Rome 1953, no. 12:41; Juda, *Aspekte*, pp. 14f.

69 Jaussen, *Coutumes*, p. 115; Musil, *Arabia Petraea*, vol. III, p. 26.

70 Cf. Ṭabarī, *Tafsīr*, ed. M. M. Shākir and A. M. Shākir, Cairo 1954– , vol. VIII, p. 280; Robertson Smith, *Kinship*, pp. 53f. (Prophetic statements to the effect that the *ḥalīf* is a member of his host's tribe are not of course evidence that the *ḥalīf* could be fully incorporated, such statements being of purely Islamic inspiration, cf. below, n. 72).

71 Thus Miqdād b. ʿAmr, a Quḍāʿī *ḥalīf* in Mecca, was adopted by his host (Ibn Saʿd, *Ṭabaqāt*, vol. III, p. 161), as were ʿĀmir b. Rabīʿa, an Asadī *ḥalīf* (*ibid.*, p. 386), and others (Juda, *Aspekte*, pp. 17f). The tradition is of course keen to supply concrete examples of people who were adopted before the supposed Qurʾānic prohibition of the practice, but this does not explain why it is *ḥalīf*s (and, as will be seen in Chapter 5, slaves) who are chosen as examples. The pattern may thus be assumed to have been historical.

72 Thus the very man of whom the Prophet is supposed to have said 'he is ours by *ḥilf*' (in illustration of the dictum that *mawlāʾl-qawm minhum wa-ḥalīf al-qawm minhum*) was known as ʿUkkāsha b. Miḥṣan *al-Asadī* (Ibn Hishām, *Leben*, p. 453). Other examples are Akhnas b. b. Sharīk al-Thaqafī (*ibid.*, p. 438), Walīd b. ʿAbdallāh al-Yarbūʿī (Ṭabarī, *Taʾrīkh*, ser. i, p. 1277), ʿUtba b. Ghazwān al-Sulamī (*ibid.*, p. 1277), and Abū Marthad al-Ghanawī (Khalīfa b. Khayyāṭ, *Kitāb al-Ṭabaqāt*, ed. A. Ḍ. al-ʿUmarī, Baghdad 1967, p. 8), all of whom were *ḥalīf*s of various Qurashīs.

73 Compare Musil, *Arabia Petraea*, vol. III, p. 26; Chelhod, 'Droit intertribal', p. 69.

74 Ṭabarī, *Taʾrīkh*, ser. i, p. 2003.

75 Tyan, *Droit publique*, p. 62. Compare C. R. Raswan, *The Black Tents of Arabia*, London 1935, p. 33: the hero of this book was a Shammarī whose family had lived among the Ruwāla for sixteen years because of a blood-feud.

76 Thus for example J. Wellhausen (ed. and tr.), 'Letzter Teil der Lieder der Hudhailiten' in his *Skizzen und Vorarbeiten*, vol. I, Berlin 1884, no. 220 (introduction to the poem); compare Juda, *Aspekte*, p. 19; Jaussen, *Coutumes*, pp. 164, 218.

77 The reasons are not usually given, presumably because the phenomenon was very common. It is also very common today (Jaussen, *Coutumes*, p. 216).

78 The terms *ḥalīf* and *jār* are frequently used synonymously (every *ḥalīf* being a *jār* in the general sense of protégé of the tribe), but occasionally we hear of people who were *jīrān* of one tribal group all while being *ḥalīf*s of members of another (*Aghānī*, vol. II, p. 242; Ibn Ḥabīb, *Munammaq*, pp. 125f). Such people were residents of the tribe in which they were *jīrān*, but it was their *ḥalīf*s who formed their blood-money and vengeance group (as is clear from Ibn Ḥabīb); and the fact that *ḥalīf*s were jointly responsible for each other's blood also meant that *ḥalīf*s were, or could be, more closely linked with their host tribe than ordinary *jīrān* (cf. below, n. 82).

79 In practice there might be nobody to return to, the entire people living as *jīrān* of others, as did for example the Ghanī (Krenkow, *Poems*, p. xix) and most of Bajīla (*Encyclopaedia of Islam*^{2}, *s.v.* 'Badjīla').

80 J. G. L. Kosegarten (ed.), *The Hudsailian Poems*, London 1854, p. 120; O. Procksch, *Über die Blutrache bei den vorislamischen Arabern*, Leipzig 1899, pp. 34f (*jīrān*); Wellhausen, 'Lieder', no. 195 (*ḥalīf*s).

81 Cf. Tyan, *Droit publique*, pp. 60f: when ʿIjlīs killed a *jār* of Māzinīs in revenge for an ʿIjlī, they were blamed for having avenged themselves on a foreigner. Compare Musil, *Arabia Petraea*, vol. III, p. 26; Chelhod, 'Droit intertribal', p. 69).

82 *Ḥalīf*s had mutual responsibility for each other's blood, or they could have such responsibility (cf. the formulas in Ṭabarī, *Tafsīr*, vol. VIII, pp. 275f). If the *ḥalīf*/guest could avenge his host, he could presumably also be killed in retaliation for murders committed by him.

83 Cf. Ibn Hishām, *Leben*, p. 543, where Qurashī raiders kill an Anṣārī and a *ḥalīf* of his working in the fields in an outlying district of Medina, clearly without paying too much attention to the identity of their victims. (According to Wāqidī, *Kitāb al-maghāzī*, ed. M. Jones, London 1966, vol. I, p. 181, the victims were an Anṣārī and his *ajīr*, hireling.) Compare Ibn Ḥabīb, *Munammaq*, p. 139, where raiders kill two Muḥāribīs and a *jār* of theirs.

84 Cf. E. L. Peters, 'Some Structural Aspects of the Feud among the Camel-herding Bedouin of Cyrenaica', *Africa* 1967, p. 269: 'it is never a matter of simple homicide, but of killing a man at the entrance to his tent, between the centre poles of his tent, of taking the life of a minor, or an elder too old to carry arms and so on'. The victims to avenge not only the

injury, but also the breach of the tabu. It was such a breach that the Liḥyān perpetrated when they picked on a Khuzāʿī *jār* of Abū Jundab's, took his property and killed his *wife* while Abū Jundab was lying *ill*; Abū Jundab was so outraged that he performed the sacred ceremonies at Mecca before setting out to avenge the dead (Wellhausen, 'Lieder', no. 198, an expanded version of Kosegarten, *Hudsailian Poems*, no. 32).

85 W. Reinert, *Das Recht in der altarabischen Poesie* (Inaugural-Dissertation), Cologne 1963, p. 17; cf. also Proksch, *Blutrache*, pp. 34f.

86 A point well seen by Wellhausen ('Medina vor dem Islam' p. 28).

87 When Ṣakhrīs killed a Muzanī *jār* of Abū'l-Muthallam, the latter accordingly reacted by inciting his entire tribe to vengeance (Kosegarten, *Hudsailian Poems*, no. 3).

88 As did Mālik b. al-ʿAjlān in Yathrib (*Aghānī*, vol. III, pp. 19f, 40f), and a Hudhalī (Kosegarten, *Hudsailian Poems*, no. 121). Both would have preferred retaliation.

89 As several *ḥalīf*-hosts preferred (or were obliged?) to do when the culprits were fellow-tribesmen (cf. the following note).

90 When ʿAmr b. al-Ḥaḍramī was killed by a Muslim, his Qurashī *ḥalīf*/host acknowledged that he was obliged to pay compensation for the blood and property of his *ḥalīf*/guest; but this was all he proposed to do: he did not wish to fight the Muslims because many of them were Qurashīs (ibn Hishām, *Leben*, p. 441). When Ḥārith b. ʿAwf invited an Anṣārī to act as religious instructor among his people, offering himself as *jār*/protector, his people killed the Anṣārī, whereupon Ḥārith paid the *diya* for breach of protection: clearly he too was neither inclined nor obliged to seek vengeance or compensation from fellow-tribesmen (*Aghānī*, vol. IV, p. 155). When a Muslim killed two ʿĀmirīs with whom the Prophet had an agreement of *jiwār*, the Prophet said, 'you have killed two men whose blood-money I have to pay', making it clear that (given that he did not wish to extradite fellow-Muslims) blood-money was all he owed in law; the Jewish Naḍīr, who also had a *ḥilf* with ʿĀmir, were obliged to contribute to the blood-money too (ibn Hishām, *Leben*, pp. 650, 652, cf. p. 392). When Abū Uzayhir, an Azdī *ḥalīf* of Abū Sufyān's, was murdered by fellow-Qurashīs, the latter also sent blood-money to the kinsmen of his protégé (Ibn Ḥabīb, *Munammaq*, p. 241). And when ʿĀmir b. Ṭufayl undertook to give Aʿshā *jiwar* against 'mankind, *jinn* and death' and the latter asked him how he proposed to give him *jiwār* against death, ʿĀmir replied, 'if you die in my *jiwār*, I will send your *diya* to your people' (*Aghānī*, vol. IX, pp. 120f). Compare C. Rathjens, 'Tâghût gegen scherî'a', *Jahrbuch des Lindenmuseums* 1951, pp. 181f (if you acquire a *rafīq* in modern south Arabia and he gets killed, you must avenge him; if you do not, you are responsible for the payment of blood-money).

91 The ideal *jār*/protector from their point of view was Muʿādh b. Jaʿda, who unwittingly acquired a *jār*/protégé while he was away at the water; a man attached his cloak to his tent-poles in his absence, only to be mortally wounded before he had returned. On discovering what had happened, Muʿādh pursued the culprit, caught him and handed him over to the victim's kin for retaliation (*Aghānī*, vol. III, pp. 59ff).

92 When ʿĀmir b. al-Ḥaḍramī, the brother of ʿAmr, heard that ʿUtba b. Rabīʿa was going to fob him off with blood-money instead of vengeance, he 'poured dust on his head and cried "O ʿAmr", thereby disgracing ʿUtba, for the latter was his *ḥalīf* among Quraysh' (Wāqidī, *Maghāzī*, vol. I, pp. 64f; cf. Ibn Hishām, *Leben*, vol. I, p. 442; above, note 92). When Huraym b. Mirdās was killed in the *jiwār* of ʿĀmir al-Khuzāʿī, ʿAbbās b. Mirdās composed poetry which induced the *jār* to vow not to wash until he had avenged the victim (*Aghānī*, vol. XIV, pp. 311f). Cf. also Reinert, *Recht*, note 153.

93 Cf. Kosegarten, *Hudsailian Poems*, no. 121, where Salma b. Muqʿad is induced by his people to accept blood-money in lieu of retaliation for the family of his slain *jāra*. ʿUtba b. Rabīʿa, on the other hand, was induced by his people (and above all Abū Jahl) to go to war, the result being the battle of Badr (cf. the preceding note).

94 *Aghānī*, vol. III, pp. 19, 40 (both referring to a Medinese dispute); cf. Tyan, *Droit publique*, pp. 29f.

95 Seven camels as against fifty camels for a fellow-tribesman, and that even when two tribes have bestowed kinship rights on each other (Musil, *Rwala*, p. 47).

96 Ṭabarī, *Ta'rīkh*, ser. i, p. 1203; Reinert, *Recht*, note 155.

97 Compare Musil, *Rwala*, p. 46: a Sirḥānī who had stayed with the Ruwāla for thirty years, intermarried with them and participated in their military ventures, was still a Sirḥānī for all legal purposes.

98 Cf. Reinert, *Recht*, note 157; S. Fraenkl, 'Das Schutzrecht der Araber' in C. Bezold (ed.), *Orientalische Studien T. Nöldeke*, vol. I, Giessen 1906, pp. 297ff.

99 Such a woman remains a member of her natal tribe. If she injures or kills another, the *diya* is payable by her own agnates, not those of her husband, and it is also her agnates who receive the *diya* if she herself is killed (M. J. L. Hardy, *Blood Feuds and the Payment of Blood Money in the Middle East*, Beirut 1963, p. 94). She is exempt from the feud because she is a woman rather than because she is a foreigner. Nonetheless, in the Yemen such a woman will go home on the outbreak of hostilities between her tribes of birth and residence, as would *jīrān* and *ḥalīf*s (Chelhod, 'Droit intertribal', p. 61). As a woman her blood-price is however four times higher than that for men whether she is foreign or not, i.e. she is treated as a privileged person (compare Raswan, *Black Tents*, p. 27, on the guest), whereas *ḥalīf*s and *jīrān* were treated as ordinary outsiders.

100 Abū Tammām, *Hamasae carminae cum Tebrisii scholiis*, ed. G. Freytag, Bonn 1828, p. 449; Ibn Saʿd, *Ṭabaqāt*, vol. VIII, pp. 14f; Juda, *Aspekte*, p. 6; compare Musil, *Arabia Petraea*, vol. III, p. 26; *id.*, *Rwala*, p. 46.

101 Cf. Ibn Hishām, *Leben*, p. 438; other examples are given by Juda, *Aspekte*, pp. 16f.

102 Ṭabarī, *Tafsīr*, vol. VIII, pp. 273ff. Several versions mention mutual inheritance with specification of a sixth (thus also Juda, *Aspekte*, p. 13).

103 Ibn ʿAbd Rabbih, *Kitāb al-ʿiqd al-farīd*, ed. A. Amīn and others, Cairo 1940–65, vol. IV, p. 436; cf. Goldziher, *Muhammedanische Studien*, vol. I, p. 106.

104 *Damī damuka wa-hadamī hadamuka wa-tarithunī wa-arithuka wa-taṭlubu bī wa-aṭlubu bika* (Ṭabarī, *Tafsīr*, vol. VIII, pp. 275f). Compare the formulas without reference to mutual inheritance cited in Pedersen, *Eid*, p. 27n (*damī damuka wa-hadamī hadamuka*, and variants), and the modern formula cited by Shuqayr, *Sīnā*, p. 406 (*damī yasuddu ʿan damika wa-mālī yasuddu ʿan mālika. . .*). The exegetes could of course simply had added the words concerning succession to a genuine *ḥilf* formula, but this seems unlikely.

105 Saḥnūn, *al-Mudawwana al-kubrā*, Cairo 1323, part viii, p. 73.

106 *Aghānī*, vol. x, p. 28 (on the *ḥilf* between Durayd b. al-Ṣima and Muʿāwiya b. ʿAmr).

107 Cf. Marghīnānī, *Hidāya*, part iii, p. 271; Bayḍāwī, *Anwār al-tanzīl wa-asrār al-taʾwīl*, Istanbul n.d., vol. I, p. 273 (ad 4:37); Hawsamī, *Sharḥ al-ibāna*, Ambrosiana, D. 224, fols. 122a–b.

108 C. A. Nallino, 'Intorno al divieto romano imperiale dell'affratellamento e ad alcuni paralleli arabi' in his *Raccolta*, vol. IV, pp. 624f; cf. also Goldziher, *Muhammedanische Studien*, vol. I, pp. 104ff, where one is apt to gain the same impression, though at the crucial point Goldziher says the opposite; Juda, *Aspekte*, p. 75.

109 They never adduce *ḥilf* in explanation of servile *walāʾ*. Goldziher correctly notes that the pre-Islamic freedman did *not* become a client by oath (*Muhammedanische Studien*, vol. I, p. 106).

110 That the patron's right to succession is the *quid pro quo* of his responsibility for the payment of blood-money on the client's behalf is explicit, for example, in ʿAbd al-Razzāq, *Muṣannaf*, vol. IX, no. 16,176; cf. also no. 16,220 in which responsibility for the payment of blood-money actually constitutes *muwālāt*.

111 Thus Quraysh were held responsible when a *ḥalīf* of theirs murdered the leader of a Ḥīran caravan, an act which embroiled them in tribal war (cf. E. Landau-Tasseron, ' "The Sinful Wars": Religious, Social and Historical Aspects of *Ḥurūb al-Fijār*', *Jerusalem Studies in Arabic and Islam* 1986). For several other examples of *ḥalīfs*/hosts paying blood-money on behalf of their allies, see Juda, *Aspekte*, p. 12.

112 *Encyclopaedia of Islam*^{2}, *s.v.* 'mawlā'.

113 Thus ʿUmar II in Kindī, *Governors*, p. 334; similarly Ṭabarī, *Tafsīr*, vol. VIII, p. 271 (ad 4:37).

114 Cf. Ḥassān b. Thābit, *Dīwān*, no. 189:8 (the Ḥimāsī is someone who cannot defend himself, like the Nabatean who patiently endures when one enslaves him).

115 'O men, do you not see how Persia has been ruined and its inhabitants humiliated? They have become slaves who pasture your sheep, as if their kingdom was a dream' (Nābigha al-Jaʿdī, *Dīwān*, no. 8:12–13). Compare Ibn Hishām, *Leben*, p. 829 ('Our swords have left you a slave', addressed to Quraysh on the conquest of Mecca).

116 Ṭabarī, *Taʾrīkh*, ser. i, pp. 2562ff; Balādhurī, *Futūḥ*, pp. 280, 373.

117 The *nisba* was Uswārī (Ṭabarī, *Taʾrīkh*, ser. ii, p. 579). The Asāwira participated in the feuds of Basra in the second civil war (*ibid.*, pp. 452, 454, 465).

118 Cf. below, p. 93.

119 I am indebted to the Poetry Concordance of the Hebrew University of Jerusalem for references to *mawālī* and *ʿabīd* in early poetry.

120 According to A. Goto, 'An Aspect of Arab Society of the Early Seventh Century' *Orient* (Tokyo) 1976, p. 76, it is clear from reliable sources that *mawlā* only meant 'freedman' in pre-Islamic Arabia, not 'free men of other kins' (sc. *ḥalīf*s). But though he is right that the word is almost invariably used in the sense of 'freedman' in accounts of the Prophet's life, this is not true of either poetry or the Qur'ān.

121 Thus the much-cited *mahlan banī ʿamminā, mahlan mawālīnā*, addressed to the Umayyads (*Ḥamāsa*, p. 110); similarly *Aghānī*, vol. IX, p. 12, where Kuthayyir ʿAzza, who wished his tribe to be affiliated to Kināna, tells his fellow-tribesmen to honour Kināna because they are their *mawālī*, i.e. relatives; for other examples, see Goldziher, *Muhammedanische Studien*, vol. I, p. 105. *Mawlā* also means kinsman in Qur. 4:37; 19:5; 44:41, as the commentators are agreed (see for example Ṭabarī, *Tafsīr*, vol. VIII, pp. 269ff).

122 *Al-mawlā hāhunā ibn al-ʿamm* is a standard comment (see for example Ṭarafa, *Dīwān*, ad nos. 1:77, 4:13; ʿAlqama b. ʿAbāda, *Dīwān*, ed. M. Ben Cheneb, Algiers 1925, ad 8:1). Cf. also *Ḥamāsa*, pp. 104, 327, 446, 519, 629; Ibn Muqbil, *Dīwān*, ed. ʿA. Ḥasan, Damascus 1962, pp. 80n, 103n, 154n; *Aghānī*, vol. XI, p. 228n.

123 The fact that connotations of authority are almost entirely absent from the poetic use of the term *mawlā* was exploited to the full by Bāqillānī, *Kitāb al-tamhīd*, ed. M. M. al-Khuḍayrī and M. A.-H. Abū Rīdah, Cairo 1947, pp. 169ff. An examination of Arabic poetry, he argued, shows that the term *mawlā* was used to mean *ibn al-ʿamm, ḥalīf, jār, nāṣir, muḥibb*, and so on, but not 'lord'; the Prophet's saying *man kuntu mawlāhu fa-ʿAlī mawlāhu* therefore cannot be taken to mean that the Prophet designated ʿAlī as his successor.

124 Cf. Labīd, *Dīwān*, ed. and tr. C. Brockelmann, Leiden 1891, no. 27:21 ('those who are nearer to me in *walā*', and their help is close'); Wellhausen, 'Lieder', no. 192:2 ('your *mawlā*, a trustworthy and helpful man'); *Lisān*, vol. X, p. 237[4] ('a *mawlā* we agreed to help'). Compare the Qur'ān, 8:41, 22:78; 44:41.

125 A man's sword is like a *mawlā* whose help is reliable (*Ḥamāsa*, p. 216), just as an *ibn ʿamm* is like his arms (*Aghanī*, vol. XIII, p. 202[13]). When the *mawlā* turns against you, the *gawm* will surprise you (*Lisān*, vol. XI, p. 69[17]); but the Ashjaʿ are a *mawlā fī'l-ḥurūb wa-nāṣir* to Dhubyān (Marzubānī, *Muwashshaḥ*, p. 100), whereas he for whom Hawāzin are a *mawlā* will be oppressed (ʿAbbās b. Mirdās, *Dīwān*, ed. Y. al-Jubūrī, Baghdad 1968, no. 75:1). And when the *mawlā* who is *ḍaʿīf al-naṣr* sees ʿAmr b. Qamī'a coming, he starts winning against the adversary (C. Lyall (ed. and tr.), *The Poems of ʿAmr Son of Qamī'a*, Cambridge 1919, no. 8:1f).

126 'I rescue my *mawlā* from calamity when he has slipped like a stumbling camel, and I give him my help, my love and my property, even when he gives me hatred', an Asadī boasts (*Ḥamāsa*, p. 518; also attributed to Ṭarafa, cf. his *Dīwān*, appendix, no. 4:7). ʿUrwa b. al-Ward was patient with *mawālī* begging until the pastures became green (T. Nöldeke (ed. and tr.), *Die Gedichte des ʿUrwa Ibn Alward* (= *Abhandlungen des königlichen Gesellschaft der Wissenschaften zu Göttingen*, vol. XI), Göttingen 1863, no. 2:13).

127 'I do not abandon my *mawlā* when he first stumbles' (Kosegarten, *Hudsailian Poems*, no. 101:6; similarly Ḥātim Ṭayyi', *Dīwān*, ed. and tr. F. Schulthess, Leipzig 1897, no. 37:13). 'We defend the *mawlā*' (*Ḥamāsa*, p. 726). 'When the *mawlā* feared oppression, he called on you and nobody but you for help' (*Aghānī*, vol. XI, p. 230[6]). 'I keep my *jār* by not visiting his wife, and I do not seek to do evil to my *mawlā*' (*Lisān*, vol. X, p. 108[8]). A poet boasts of not slandering and not depriving his *mawlā* (*Lisān*, vol. V, p. 294[5]). Ibn Muqbil similarly boats that he did not curse, slander or harm his *mawlā*, but gave him more than he needed and protected him when he was wronged (*Dīwān*, pp. 80. 274). Ḥātim Ṭayyi' boasted of his willingness to defend the *mawlā* who was wronged (*Dīwān*, no. 37:14). Others pride themselves on suppressing their anger and hatred *vis-à-vis* the *mawlā*, even when the latter cannot help (*Ḥamāsa*, pp. 500, 519), or of neither slandering nor abandoning him even though the *mawlā* might abandon him (Ḥātim Ṭayyi', *Dīwān*, no. 42:30; cf. no. 46:9). And so on; the theme is so commonplace that example could be piled on example.

128 Don't betray the *mawlā* and don't deprive him of your help, for he is your brother and you don't know when you'll be asking him (*Ḥamāsa*, p. 514; cf. Qur'ān, 33:5). And don't

blame the *mawālī*, for their closest ancestor is also yours (I. Goldziher, 'Der Dîwân des Ǵarwal b. Aus Al-Ḥuṭej'a', *Zeitschrift der Deutschen morgenländischen Gesellschaft* 1892, p. 212 (no. 8:21f)).

129 'If you were strong and endowed with zeal, you would defend your *mawlā* while the night is dark' (Zabīdī, *Taj al-ʿarūs*, Būlāq 1306–7, vol. x, p. 389[16]). But those who assist the *mawlā* when he comes in financial distress have all gone (Mu'arrij al-Sadūsī, *Kitāb ḥadhf min nasab Quraysh*, ed. Ṣ. al-Munajjid, Cairo 1960, p. 47; for the indebted *mawlā*, see also *Hamāsa*, p. 495; *Aghānī*, vol. XIII, p. 94[15]). Somebody withheld his gifts and delayed his help to his *mawlā* (*Tāj*, vol. x, p. 70[31]). Another let his closest *mawlā* go hungry (*Lisān*, vol. VI, p. 31[7]).

130 'Our two *mawālī* were slow in coming, and when they were asked for help, they gave it to others' (Mu'arrij, *Ḥadhf*, p. 15); 'I saw the *mawālī* who betrayed me in the calamities of time' (*Tāj*, vol. x, p. 426[11]); 'how many a *mawlā* disobeyed me' (*Lisān*, vol. VIII, p. 241[16]); and so on.

131 'I followed them and lost the *mawālī*' (Goldziher, 'Ḥuṭej'a', p. 515 (27:7)); 'the valley of Rikā' has become empty of *mawālī* (Ibn Muqbil, *Dīwān*, no. p. 132; for the fate of those who are far from their *mawālī*, see *Aghānī*, vol. XIII, p. 71; *Līsān*, vol. XVI, p. 74[22]). For *mawālī* shunned by their *mawālī*, see *Lisān*, vol. III, p. 427[7]; *Tāj*, vol. v, p. 371[4]; Nābigha al-Jaʿdī, *Dīwān*, no. 1:1.

132 Ṭarafa, *Dīwān*, no. 4:13; cited in *Ḥamāsa*, p. 632.

133 'May God reward our *mawlā* Ghanī with blame, the worst *mawālī* of ʿĀmir as regards firmness' (Marzubānī, *Muwashshaḥ*, p. 99). For people whose eyes were painted with the kohl of ignominy and who were shortnecked and bad *mawālī*, see *Tāj*, vol. x, p. 391, 5 up; for envious and hateful *mawālī* who are like a pain in the belly, or like an ant-hill, and who only slander their *mawālī*, see *Lisān*, vol. IX, p. 69[20]; *Ḥamāsa*, p. 515; Jāḥiẓ, *Kitāb al-ḥayawān*, ed. ʿA-S. Hārūn, Cairo 1937–47, vol. IV, p. 32.

134 Lyall, *Mufaḍḍaliyāt*, no. 12:3 (cf. W. Caskel, 'Ein Missverständniss in den Mufaḍḍalīyāt', *Oriens* 1954, p. 292); *Ḥamāsa*, p. 187; Ibn Hishām, *Leben*, p. 467.

135 Quṭāmī, *Dīwān*, ed. J. Barth, Leiden 1905, no. 6:26; compare Dhū'l-Rumma, *Dīwān*, no. 87:59 and the gloss thereto (*mawālī* in the sense of *atbāʿ*, *ḥulafā'*).

136 Cf. Goldziher, *Muhammedanische Studien*, vol. I, pp. 105f.

137 Nābigha al-Jaʿdī, *Dīwān*, no. 12:41.

138 *Encyclopaedia of Islam*[2], *s.v.* 'Badjīla'.

139 Tyan, *Droit publique*, p. 26.

140 Cf. Goldziher, *Muhammedanische Studien*, vol. I, pp. 121f.

141 Our one surviving document, the Constitution of Medina, throws no light on the question, though it uses the word *mawlā* twice in connection with the believers and three times in connection with the Jews. As regards the former, we are told that a believer shall not make a *ḥilf* with the *mawlā* of another believer against/ to the exclusion of/without the permission of the latter. *Mawlā* could mean freedman here, as the lawyers assumed it to do (cf. above, Chapter 2, p. 32), but it seems unlikely. The section continues that all believers shall be united against a troublemaker, even if he is a son of theirs, that a believer shall not be killed for an unbeliever, and that all can grant protection of behalf of the community at large because all believers are *mawālī* of each other to the exclusion of outsiders, that is they are each other's kinsmen, guardians and trustees (*awliyā'*). The overall message is thus that the believers must be united against the world at large, and one would accordingly expect the first clause to ban internally divisive *ḥilf* in general, not merely divisive or unauthorized *ḥilf* with freedmen. If so, the clause states that a believer may not set kinsman against kinsman by allying with one against the other (and this clause could have formed the starting point for the Prophetic dictum that there is no *ḥilf* in Islam). As regards the passages referring to Jews, they state that the Jews, both they themselves and their *mawālī* (or, in one instance, *biṭāna*), have such and such a position. The term might means or includes freedmen here, but it is odd that only the Jews seem to have them. Why are we not similarly told that *mawālī* of Arab clans enjoy the same position as the clans themselves? However this may be, the distinction between Jews of certain clans and their *mawālī* is perfectly compatible with the proposition that clientage was collective (Ibn Hishām, *Leben*, pp. 341ff).

142 Kister, 'On the Wife of the Goldsmith', p. 321.

143 Yāqūt, *Buldān*, vol. IV, p. 81; Bakrī, *Kitāb al-muʿjam mā istaʿjam*, ed. F. Wüstenfeld, Göttingen and Paris 1876–7, vol. I, p. 30.

144 The Jews of Wādī'l-Qurā were still paying protection money in the days of Bakrī (*Muʿjam*, vol. I, p. 31). In Hamdānī's time the inhabitants of Taymā' were deemed to be *mawālī* (Hamdānī, *Ṣifat Jazīrat al-ʿarab*, ed. D. H. Müller, Leiden 1884–91, vol. I, p. 131): in Doughty's time they paid their (*khuwwa* to B. Sakhr (*Travels*, vol. I, p. 331). The inhabitants of Khaybar also *khuwwa* in the nineteenth century (C. Huber, *Voyage dans l'Arabie centrale* (*Extrait du Bulletin de la Société de Géographie 1884–5*), Paris 1885, pp. 121, 129), as did villagers and cultivators in general according to Wallin (*Travels*, pp. 122, 133).

145 *Aghānī*, vol. XXII, p. 115; cf. Wellhausen, 'Medina vor dem Islam', pp. 7ff.

146 Wellhausen, 'Medina vor dem Islam', p. 10.

147 Ṭabarī, *Ta'rīkh*, ser. i, pp. 985f.

148 On this term, see below, note 170.

149 G. Jacob, *Altarabisches Beduinenleben*[2], Berlin 1897, pp. 137f; I. Lichtenstädter, *Women in the Aiyâm al-ʿarab*, London 1935, pp. 29ff; Tyan, *Droit publique*, vol. I, pp. 32, 48 (but Tyan's claim that only women and children were enslaved, adult males being merely held to ransom is incorrect, cf. for example Kosegarten, *Hudsailian Poems*, nos. 46, 58; Wellhausen, 'Lieder', nos. 153, 231; Juda, *Aspekte*, p. 22). Modern tribesmen do not take prisoners (though men may be held to ransom for their mares according to Lady Blunt), and women are never touched (Burckhardt, *Notes*, p. 81; Chelhod, 'Droit intertribal', p. 61 and the note thereto; Dickson, *Arab of the Desert*, p. 124; Blunt, *Bedouin Tribes of the Euphrates*, vol. II, pp. 239f).

150 And a fairly substantial part too. Thus Sumayfaʿ b. Nākūr al-Kalāʿī had 4000 Arab slave families descending from prisoners of war (*qinn min al-ʿarab mamālīk asarahum fī'l-jāhiliyya*). Asked by ʿUmar to sell them, he ended up by freeing them all *li'llāh* (A. A. Bevan (ed.), *The Nakā'iḍ of Jarīr and al-Farazdak*, Leiden 1905–12, vol. I, p. 46, ad no. 27:15).

151 Cf. *Aghānī*, vol. VIII, p. 237, on ʿAntara.

152 The modern bedouin do not cohabit with black slavegirls (Jaussen, *Coutumes*, pp. 61f; Musil, *Arabia Petraea*, vol. III, p. 225), though the townsmen have no comparable inhibitions.

153 Cf. Goldziher, *Muhammedanische Studien*, vol. I, pp. 121f.

154 'They raised a slave and abased the free', as someone reputedly commented on ʿAntara's meteoric rise to prominence (ʿAntara, *Dīwān*, tr. A. Wormhoudt, William Penn College 1974, introduction to no. 92). 'No black shall be in command of us' (Ḥātim Ṭayyi', *Dīwān*, no. 51:6). The leaders of ʿAbs were once their slaves, today they are their women (*Hamāsa*, p. 672); Taym are ruled by slaves (*Aghānī*, vol. VIII, p. 298[2–3]); and among the Imr' al-Qays slaves and free are equal (Dhū'l-Rumma, *Dīwān*, no. 23:22).

155 See for example Ibn Saʿd, *Ṭabaqāt*, vol. III, p. 86.

156 Cf. E. W. Lane, *An Arabic-English Lexicon*, London 1863–93, s.v. 'ṣamīm'.

157 Yāqūt, *Buldān*, vol. III, p. 520; similarly *Aghānī*, vol. XVI, p. 334[2] (*qawmī . . . ṣarīḥahā wa'l-ākharina al-mawāliyā*); *Lisān*, *s.v.* 'ṣamīm' (*Tamīm min shaẓā wa-ṣamīm*). The context is military in all these examples, as is usually the case elsewhere too, cf. Qays b. al-Khaṭīm, *Dīwān*, ed. and tr. T. Kowalski, Leipzig 1914, no. 14:13 (*aslamnā al-mawālī wa-fāraqanā al-ṣarīḥ*); ʿAbbās b. Mirdās, *Dīwān*, no. 35:1 (*fa-hum qatalū al-mawālī wa'l-ṣamīmā*).

158 Ibn Hishām, *Leben*, p. 528.

159 Ṭabarī, *Ta'rīkh*, ser. I, p. 1203.

160 *Aghānī*, vol. III, p. 26 (where Mālik b. al-ʿAjlān is awarded the *diya* of a *ṣarīḥ* for his *ḥalīf* (line 3) or *jār* (line 9); *ibid.*, p. 40 (where we are told that the *diya* of a *mawlā* (glossed as *ḥalīf*) was half that of a *ṣarīḥ*, in connection with the same story).

161 Ibn Hishām, *Leben*, p. 463.

162 Marzubānī, *Muwashshaḥ*, p. 82.

163 Nābigha al-Dhubyānī, *Dīwān*, ed. and tr. H. Derenbourg, Paris 1869, no. 13:1; compare Goldziher, *Muhammedanische Studien*, vol. I, p. 106.

164 Cf. ʿAbbās b. Mirdās, *Dīwān*, no. 35:1, where the editor glosses the *mawālī* distinguished from *ṣamīm* as *atbāʿ* and *ʿabīd* for all that the poem itself provides no clue to their identity.

165 Mubarrad, *Kāmil*, pp. 536, 683.

166 Ḥassān b. Thābit, *Dīwān*, nos. 226–9, cf. below, note 172.
167 ʿĀmir b. Ṭufayl, *Dīwān*, no. 35.
168 *Aghānī*, vol. XI, p. 136.
169 Ṭabarī, *Taʾrīkh*, ser. iii, p. 305.
170 A *daʿī* was anyone whose name defined him as a member of a group other than that into which he had been born, and the term was abusive only if the name had been improperly assumed. The adopted son was a *daʿī* (cf. Ibn Saʿd, *Ṭabaqāt*, vol. III, p. 43), and so was the person who had been incorporated into a foreign tribe 'by name and by blood', cf. Tabarī *Taʾrīkh*, ser. i, p. 3345, where an old man asked by ʿAlī about his tribal affiliation replies that 'as for the *aṣl*, it is in Salāmān of Ṭayyiʾ, and as for the *jiwār* and *daʿwa*, they are with Sālim b. Manṣūr', i.e. though a Salāmānī by birth, he both lived with and was known as a member of Sālim b. Manṣūr. This man was a fully-fledged tribesman and thus eligible for adoption into foreign tribes; but non-tribesmen were necessarily *daʿīs* in the abusive sense: 'you son of an Iṣṭakhrī woman! What have you got to do with the *ashrāf*? You are just an inhabitant of Qaṭar and a *daʿī* of Asad, among whom you have neither *qarīb* nor *nasab*' (Muṣʿab b. al-Zubayr in Ṭabarī, *Taʾrīkh*, ser. ii, p. 802).
171 *ʿAbd daʿī min Thamūd aṣluhu* (Ṭabarī, *Taʾrīkh*, ser. ii, p. 917; cf. Balādhurī, *Ansāb al-ashrāf*, vol. v, ed. S. D. F. Goitein, Jerusalem 1936, p. 267); Farazdaq, *Dīwān*, p. 192^{3-6} = 581 (as a son of a Nubian you are not entitled to call yourself a Murrī); Dhū'l-Rumma, *Dīwān*, no. 27:38f (you are a slave, and your father was a *sāqiṭa* (viz. a non-Arab trader in Arabia, cf. Crone, *Meccan Trade*, Ch. 6, note 31) as well as a *daʿī*; note the characteristic equation here of non-Arab origin and servile status).
172 Ḥassān, *Dīwān*, no. 226:6f. (In this poem the victim's father is called a slave (line 4), though the victim himself is branded as a *hajīn*. Either *hajīn* meant any person of servile background, not merely the offspring of a slavegirl and a free man as the lexicographers say, or else Ḥassān's abuse was somewhat indiscriminate.)
173 Labīd, *Dīwān* (Brockelmann), 48:3; cf. Reinert, *Recht*, note 190.
174 Cf. Akhṭal, *Shiʿr*, ed. F.-D. Qabāwa, Aleppo [1970]–71, p. 83 (no. 6:25).
175 In the days of ʿUthmān a son of a slavegirl by a free Arab (who had apparently acknowledged him) killed a tribesman accidentally, whereupon the fellow-tribesmen of the victim killed the culprit intentionally. The freedman's brother complained to Marwān, governor of Medina in the days of Muʿāwiya, and Marwān awarded him fifty camels or, as Farazdaq put it, the *diya* of a *hajīn* (not that of a *slave*, as the scholiast asserts). But the fact that this freedman was a *hajīn* rather than an ordinary ex-slave makes this story inconclusive (Farazdaq, *Dīwān*, pp. 195ff = 593ff).
176 *Encyclopaedia of Islam*², *s.v.* 'mawlā'.
177 Cf. above, Chapter 3, note 18.
178 ʿAntara proclaims his love for Banū ʿAbs, *wa-law hadarū damī*, 'even if they were to seek neither vengeance nor compensation for my blood' (ʿA.-M. ʿA.-R. Shalabī (ed.), *Sharḥ dīwān ʿAntara b. Shaddād*, Cairo n.d., p. 84 = ʿAntara, *Dīwān*, tr. Wormhoudt no. 80:10). Apparently ʿAntara is here envisaged as a slave (he goes on to speak of *maḥabbat al-ʿabd*); but since he is envisaged as a slave in all his poetry, his famous manumission notwithstanding, it was apparently assumed that a freedman basically *was* a slave. The implication is that the blood of a slave *or* freedman might well be written off.
179 *Aghānī*, vol. III, p. 41 (*innaʾl-ṣarīḥ lā yuqtalu biʾl-mawlā*); cf. the post-conquest version of this rule in Balādhurī, *Ansāb al-ashrāf*, vol. IV a, ed. M. Schloessinger and M. J. Kister, Jerusalem 1971, p. 220 (*lā aqtulu ʿarabiyyan bi-nabaṭī*). The pre-Islamic rule is given in connection with the Sumayr feud in Yathrib, of which there are two accounts in the *Aghānī*. Both version state that the feud started when a member of Aws killed a *mawlā* of a Khazrajī, and the version in which the rule is cited envisaged the *mawlā* as a non-tribesman (he has no *nisba*, indeed no name, and is known as a *mawlā* throughout, the gloss at p. 40 being intrusive; there were even versions in which he became a slave, cf. Qays b. al-Khaṭīm, *Dīwān*, pp. 45, 90 = 84, 88; Wellhausen, 'Medina vor dem Islam', p. 38). Whether the rule applied to Arab protégés too is not clear. The *mawlā* is an Arab in the other version given in the *Aghānī* (vol. III, pp. 18ff: he has a *nisba* and is identified as a *ḥalīf* or *jār*); but here the reason why there is no retaliation is that the protector does not have sufficient proof against the killer (cf. p. 19: *innahu laysa laka an taqtula Sumayran bi-ghayri bayyina*). This suggests that the killer would indeed have been

killed if proof had been forthcoming, for all that he was a member of the *ṣarīḥ* and his victim not.

180 Cf. the references given above, notes 94, 175; Juda, *Aspekte*, pp. 27f.

181 Farazdaq, *Dīwān*, pp. 232f = 699.

182 Cf. above, note 175.

183 Ibn Ḥazm, *Muḥallā*, vol. XI, p. 59; Balādhurī in Juda, *Aspekte*, p. 187; compare the refusals to pay blood-money on behalf of freedmen (or rather *statuliberi* and freedmen) in Kindī, *Govenors*, pp. 333f, 335f; ʿAbd al-Razzāq, *Muṣannaf*, vol. IX, no. 17,852, 17,855. The problem was also familiar to Mālik, cf. Ibn Ḥazm, *ibid.*, p. 47.

184 If it had been a freedman rather than a *ḥalīf* of Quraysh who had murdered the leader of the Hiran caravan, Quraysh would presumably have been held responsible too in their capacity of protecting tribe (cf. above, note 111).

185 According to Taubenschlag, *Law*, pp. 65ff, slaves had proprietary capacity in most legal systems of the Near East and the Mediterranean in antiquity, the Roman slave being exceptional in that he did not; but the literature at large does not agree with him (see for example Mendelsohn, *Slavery*, pp. 66ff; or, more recently, M. Dandamayev, 'The Economic and Legal Character of the Slave's Peculium in the Neo-Babylonian and Achaemenid Periods' in D. O. Edzard (ed.), *Gesellschaftsklassen im alten Zweistromland und in den angrenzenden Gebieten*, Munich 1972, pp. 37f). Slaves do however have proprietary capacity in modern Arabia (cf. Musil, *Rwala*, pp. 276f).

186 It is the Roman concept of *patria potestas* which explains not only why the Roman slave could not own, but also why the manumitter once retained ultimate ownership of his property even after he had been freed (cf. below, Chapter 6). There was no comparable concept in Arabia; indeed, the Romans may have been right when they asserted that there was no comparable concept of paternal power outside Rome.

187 Cf. below, Chapter 5, note 3.

188 Similarly A. F. L. Beeston, 'Kingship in Ancient South Arabia', *Journal of the Economic and Social History of the Orient* 1972, p. 266: Sabaean clientage, like the parallel North Arabian *mawlā* institution, was essentially a group relationship, though it was sometimes expressed in terms of relations with the head of the superior group.

189 Jāḥiẓ, *Tria Opuscula*, ed. G. van Vloten, Leiden 1903, pp. 81f; paraphrased by Thaʿālabī, *Thimār*, no. 175; translated by C. Pellat, *The Life and Works of Jāḥiẓ*, London 1969, p. 196.

190 Thus a subtribe of Muḥārib was also black (*Aghānī*, vol. XXII, p. 31).

191 Farazdaq, *Dīwān*, p. 81^{3} = 212^{1-3}.

192 Farazdaq, *Dīwān*, p. 171^{4} = 151^{20}, on Qays; cf. p. $150^{4,8}$ = 437^{7}, 438^{4}, where all Qays are slaves and the ancestors of B. Sālim b. Numayr are *mawālī* (mistranslated as 'slaves'); at p. 141^{11-13} = 403^{13-19}, Bāhila are also slaves paying slaves' tribute to Taghlib, but here the stress is on weakness rather than disreputable descent (to Farazdaq, of course, the two were synonymous).

193 Hamdānī, *al-Iklīl*, book x, ed. M.-D. al-Khaṭīb, n.p., n.d. (preface dated Cairo 1368), p. 9 (the *baṭn* of Alnān are numerous *wa-hum qawm ʿitāq ʿibād*).

5. The case against the non-Roman Near East: paramoné

1 One looks in vain for anything resembling the Islamic patronate in I. Mendelsohn, *Slavery in the Ancient Near East*, New York 1949. That something in the nature of *walāʾ* existed in Akkadian law has been suggested by W. von Soden, 'Muškēnum und die Mawālī des frühen Islam', *Zeitschrift für Assyriologie* 1964, p. 140, where the *muškenum* is tentatively identified as a freedman of the tribe or its chief on a par with the *mawlā* of early Islam. But the analogy proposed is in fact between the *muškēnum* and the freedman of the modern bedouin: von Soden, who derived his information on *mawālī* from Goldziher, did not realise that the *mawālī* of early Islam were bound to their individual manumitters in the manner of the freedmen of Rome.

2 Domestic slavery was not very common in ancient Egypt, and according to a famous papyrus (P. Oxy. IV, 706, A.D. 117), Egyptian law knew nothing about *tēs* [. . . .] *ēs exousias tōn apeleutherōsantōn*. The lacuna has been variously filled (*patrōnikēs*? *paramonēs*?), and the papyrus variously interpreted; but it does seem to rule out the existence of a patronate in Egypt (cf. K. Harada, 'Der Verzicht auf den Patronate und das

Gesetz Justinians in C. 6, 4, 3', *Zeitschrift der Savigny-Stiftung für Rechtsgeschichte* 1938, pp. 138ff; Taubenschlag, *Law of Greco-Roman Egypt*, p. 7; Seidl, *Rechtsgeschichte Ägyptens*, p. 133).

3 *Encyclopaedia Judaica*, *s.v.* 'slavery'; cf. also Cohen, *Jewish and Roman Law*, vol. I, p. 150: the estate of the freedman who dies without heirs belongs to whoever first seizes it.

4 There is not to my knowledge any mention of such a tie in the extant Zoroastrian literature, for all that this literature includes a lawbook which devotes considerable attention to slavery (S. J. Bulsara (tr.), *The Laws of the Ancient Persians*, Bombay 1937; this translation is admittedly notoriously unreliable – the new translation by M. Macuch, *Das Sasanidische Rechtsbuch 'Māktakdān I Hazār Dātistān'*, *Teil II*, Wiesbaden 1981, does not, unfortunately, cover this subject). Isho'bokht explicitly rejects *reshanutha* over freedmen (Sachau, *Syrische Rechtsbücher*, vol. III, pp. 176f = 179); whether this *reshanutha* is to be identified as the Roman or, less plausibly, the Islamic patronate is uncertain. But Isho'bokht was a Persian who became metropolitan of Persis and whose work was originally written in Persian; his rejection of the patronate is thus not unlikely to reflect the legal tradition of Persia.

5 Cf. above, Chapter 3, note 6.

6 Mendelsohn, *Slavery*, pp. 19ff.

7 *Ibid.*, pp. 78ff.

8 *Ibid.*, pp. 20f, 81; cf. also p. 83 for a case of re-enslavement from the time of Nabonidus.

9 It is omitted already in a number of Babylonian documents (Mendelsohn, *Slavery*, p. 81), but three cases of manumission with adoption are known from Greece (A. Babakos, 'Adoption von Freigelassenen im alt-griechischen Recht' in *Syntaleia Vicenzo Arangio-Ruiz*, Naples 1964, vol. I. Babakos thinks that the purpose of the adoption was protection of the freedman and refers to Babylonian law as a parallel (p. 516 and the note thereto); but the Babylonians adopted their freedmen to claim their labour, not to protect them, and the same was presumably true of the Greeks: one of the inscriptions explicitly states that the freedwoman was to work as a daughter for her adoptive parents. The evolution of the institution is well presented in C. Bradford Welles, 'Manumission and Adoption', *Revue Internationale des Droits de l'Antiquité* 1949 (= *Mélanges Fernand de Visscher*, vol. II), though the actual example of manumission with adoption which is adduced there seems to be false (cf. A. Babakos, 'Zur angeblichen Freilassung mit anschiessender Adoption in Kalymna', *Zeitschrift der Savigny-Stiftung für Rechtsgeschichte* 1963).

10 Mendelsohn, *Slavery*, pp. 78, 83; Welles, 'Manumission and Adoption', pp. 517f.

11 E. G. Kraeling (ed.), *The Brooklyn Museum Aramaic Papyri*, New Haven 1953, no. 5; cf. J. J. Rabinowitz, 'Brooklyn 5 and Manumission with Paramone in Greece' in his *Jewish Law, its Influence on the Development of Legal Institutions*, New York 1956; O. Rubensohn (ed.), *Elephantine-Papyri*, Berlin 1907, nos. 3–4, with the comments of J. Partsch, review of A. Calderini, in *Archiv für Papyrusforschung* 1913, p. 469; cf. also U. Wilcken, 'Papyrus-Urkunden', *ibid.*, p. 209.

12 The earliest attestation is literary (cf. W. L. Westermann, 'Two Studies in Athenian Manumission', *Journal of Near Eastern Studies* 1946, on the wills of the philosophers). But the bulk of the evidence from Greece is epigraphic, and most of it comes from Delphi, where about a quarter of some 1,200 manumission inscriptions are manumissions with *paramonē*. They range from the second century B.C. to the first century A.D. (There is a good sample and discussion of these inscriptions in R. Dareste, B. Houssoulier and T. Reinach (eds. and trs.), *Recueil des inscriptions juridiques grecques*, ser. ii, Paris 1898; the classic study is A. Calderini, *La manomissione e la condizione dei liberti in Grecia*, Milan 1908.) The universalisation of Roman law notwithstanding, such manumissions continued to be practised in the third century A.D. (cf. A. Cameron, 'Inscriptions relating to Sacral Manumission and Confession', *Harvard Theological Review* 1939, on attestations from Edessa in Macedonia).

13 Cf. the lists in Westermann, 'The Paramone as General Service Contract', pp. 37ff; Adams, *Paramoné*, pp. 10ff. For paramonar contracts published since then, see O. Montevecchi, *La papirologia*, Turin 1973, p. 223, to which P. Köln II, 102 may now be added.

14 M. I. Rostovtzeff and C. B. Welles (eds. and trs.), *A Parchment Contract of Loan from Dura Europos on the Euphrates* (= *Yale Classical Studies*, vol. II), New Haven 1931. A

debtor by the name of Barlaas here undertakes to stay with the lender, Phraates, until the time of repayment of the loan, performing the services of a slave for him and not absenting himself by day or night without Phraates' permission.

15 P. Nessana III, 56. Aswad b. ʿAdī, presumably one of the conquerors, here releases the son of a Christian monk from the obligation to stay with him [and work for him] on receipt of part of the loan which he had advanced to the monk, gratuitously renouncing the rest. For a discussion of this papyrus, see the references given above, Chapter 1, note 48.

16 Paramonar manumission clauses are attested in three wills, P. Petrie I, 16 (237 B.C.); P. Petrie III, 2 (third century B.C.; cf. appendix 4); and PSI XII, 1263 (second century A.D.). Paramonar freedmen are also attested in P. Oxy. III, 494 (A.D. 156); P. Oxy. IV, 706 A.D. 117; cf. above, note 2; below, Chapter 6, p. 85), and P. Oxy. XIX, 2238 (A.D. 551). This is a fairly meagre harvest, though not if one considers that manumission documents are under-represented in the papyri (cf. Montevecchi, *Papirologia*, p. 201; add now P. Köln III, 157 (A.D. 589)).

17 P. F. Girard, *Textes de droit romain*[6], ed. F. Senn, Paris 1937, p. 507; cf. A. M. Honoré, 'The "Fragmentum Dositheanum" ', *Revue Internationale des Droits de l'Antiquité* 1965.

18 Mitteis, *Reichsrecht und Volksrecht*, pp. 391ff; R. Taubenschlag, 'Das römische Privatrecht zur Zeit Diokletians' in his *Opera Minora*, vol. I, p. 110; *id.*, 'Le droit local dans les Digesta et Responsa de Cervidius Scaevola', *ibid.*, p. 506.

19 Conditional manumissions of the resolutive type (cf. above, p. 65) are accepted in the Syro-Roman lawbook (Bruns and Sachau, *Syrisch-römisches Rechtsbuch*, P §30; Sachau, *Syrische Rechtsbücher*, vol. I, R.II, §35; cf. J. Partsch, review of Sachau, *Zeitschrift der Savigny-Stiftung für Rechtsgeschichte* 1907, p. 428, on the paramonar nature of such manumissions). Mitteis conjectured that it records a change in late Roman law (*Reichsrecht und Volksrecht*, pp. 545f), and what the lawbook reproduces here may well be an imperial constitution (cf. Selb, *Zur Bedeutung*, pp. 246ff). I cannot however see that there is any evidence other than the lawbook itself for the acceptance of such manumissions in late Roman law, although Selb's discussion of this paragraph implies as much (*ibid.*, p. 194 and the note thereto).

20 Ḥenan-Ishoʿ, who lost office in 693, deals with a case in which the heirs of a manumitter have tried to re-enslave a freedman who has failed to render services and payments owed (Sachau, *Syrische Rechtsbücher*, vol. II, p. 12 = 13; cf. J. Partsch, 'Neue Rechtsquellen der nestorianischen Kirche', *Zeitschrift der Savigny-Stiftung für Rechtsgeschichte* 1909, pp. 365f); Ḥenan-Ishoʿ upheld the manumission and prohibited all attempts to impose further services and payments on the freedman. Elsewhere, the re-enslavement of freedmen is condemned in emphatic terms (J. B. Chabot (ed. and tr.), *Synodicon Orientale ou Recueil de Synodes Nestoriens* (= *Notices et extraits des manuscripts de la Bibliothèque Nationale*, vol. XXXVII), Paris 1902, p. 144 = 406 (synod of A.D. 585); similarly Ishoʿbokht in Sachau, *Syrische Rechtsbücher*, vol. III, p. 176 = 177).

21 Historically, this presumably represents advance payment of the inheritance to which the adopted son was once entitled. Westermann is certainly persuasive when he argues that the paramonar contract is distinct from agreements in which labour is employed to repay interest on or the principal of loans ('The Paramone as a general Service Contract', p. 25). But the nature of the Hellenistic institution is controversial, cf. Adams, *Paramoné* (who denies its Oriental origins); J. Hengstl, *Private Arbeitsverhältnisse freier Personen in den hellenistischen Papyri bis Diokletian*, Bonn 1972 (who distinguishes between two types of *paramonē* with free persons); and the literature cited in B. Kramer and D. Hagedorn, *Kölner Papyri*, vol. II, Opladen 1978, ad no. 102 (in which a woman who has received an advance of two solidi promises to stay with and obey the orders of the lender; when she wants to dissolve the contract, she must return the solidi).

22 Kraeling, *Brooklyn Museum Aramaic Papyri*, no. $5^{11,12}$; cf. Rabinowitz, 'Brooklyn 5', pp. 26f.

23 P. Koschaker, *Über einige griechische Rechtsurkunden aus den östlichen Randgebieten des Hellenismus* (= *Abhandlungen der philosophisch-historischen Klasse der Sächsischen Akademie der Wissenschaften*, vol. XLII), Leipzig 1931, p. 25.

24 Adams, *Paramoné*, pp. 54ff.

25 Adams, *Paramoné*, pp. 53, 113; Westermann, 'The Paramone as General Service Contract', p. 26; cf. also R. Payne Smith, *Thesaurus Syriacus*, Oxford 1879–1901, vol. II,

col. 3267 (Rabbinowitz took this to be the meaning of *paramenein* from the start, cf. 'Brooklyn 5', p. 28.)

26 Adams, *Paramoné*, pp. 49ff.

27 For examples, see above, notes 14–15, 20; Westermann, 'The Paramone as General Service Contract', p. 27; Adams, *Paramoné*, pp. 44f.

28 Calderini, *Manomissione*, pp. 277ff.

29 Koschaker, *Rechtsurkunden*, p. 26, note 4.

30 Koschaker, *Rechtsurkunden*, p. 36, note 5. The paramonar employer might similarly renounce part of the sum owed to him, as did Aswad b. ʿAdī at Nessana (above, note 15).

31 Koschaker, *Rechtsurkunden*, pp. 36f and the notes thereto; A. E. Samuel, 'The Role of Paramone Clauses in Ancient Documents', *Journal of Juristic Papyrology* 1965, pp. 260, 261ff.

32 Numerous examples are given in Koschaker, *Rechtsurkunden*, p. 25, note 4. For the term *apolysis*, see *ibid.*, p. 36. Compare also P. Nessana III, 56.

33 That much one may grant Samuel, 'Role', though the argument otherwise seems overstated.

34 Dareste, Hausoullier and Reinach, *Recueil*, p. 275.

35 Koschaker, *Rechtsurkunden*, p. 40; Samuel, 'Role', pp. 271ff.

36 Dareste, Hausoullier and Reinach, *Recueil*, p. 275; Calderini, *Manomissione*, p. 296.

37 Koschaker, *Rechtsurkunden*, p. 27.

38 Thus for example in the Dura fragment (Rostovtzeff and Welles, *Parchment Contract*, p. 6[8]), and in a sixth-century papyrus (Adams, *Paramoné*, p. 56).

39 Adams, *Paramoné*, pp. 44f, where a woman of Ptolemaic Egypt agrees to *paramonē* for 99 years.

40 Koschaker, *Rechtsurkunden*, p. 32; Calderini, *Manomissione*, p. 290; Samuel, 'Role', pp. 279f; cf. Dareste, Hausoullier and Reinach, *Recueil*, p. 286, where Libanos, a slave of Arab race, is manumitted on condition that he has no children, under penalty of re-enslavement.

41 Koschaker, *Rechtsurkunden*, p. 48. This point is all but suppressed by Samuel in the interest of his contention that 'the obligation of paramone . . . is an obligation appropriate to a free man' ('Role', p. 283). One Delphic inscription states that children born under the contract may be sold in case of necessity; another forbids a freedwoman to raise children of her own, all while obliging her to provide her manumitter with two; a third explicitly states that children born under the contract are to be slaves; and a Chaeronean inscription states the same. Samuel refuses to see any enslavement in the first two, ignores the third and treats the fourth as an exception (*ibid.*, pp. 281, 291). It is hard to avoid Koschaker's conclusion that the status of the children depended on what the manumitter saw fit to stipulate.

42 Koschaker, *Rechtsurkunden*, p. 35; Samuel, 'Role', pp. 262f.

43 Koschaker, *Rechtsurkunden*, p. 33; Calderini, *Manomissione*, pp. 288ff.

44 Koschaker, *Rechtsurkunden*, p. 34. Compare the manumission documents from the reign of Nabonidus and Cyrus in which freedmen are obliged to provide their manumitters with food, oil and clothing (Mendelsohn, *Slavery*, p. 83). In Greece such stipulations are attested for manumissions with and without *paramonē* alike (Koschaker, *loc. cit.*; cf. also Taubenschlag, *Law*, p. 101).

45 Koschaker, *Rechtsurkunden*, pp. 30f; Calderini, *Manomissione*, p. 295; Samuel, 'Role', p. 275; cf. above, notes 20, 40. Some manumitters explicitly renounced this right.

46 Samuel, 'Role', pp. 283f, 295, 306. Cf. also Westermann, 'The Paramone as General Service Contract', p. 12.

47 Koschaker, *Rechtsurkunden*, pp. 40ff. Cf. also M. I. Finley, 'The Servile Statuses of Ancient Greece', *Revue Internationale des Droits de l'Antiquité* 1960, pp. 178ff.

48 Cf. Calderini, *Manomissione*, p. 291.

49 Cf. *ibid.*, p. 290.

50 Koschaker, *Rechtsurkunden*, pp. 46ff.

51 Cf. Mitteis, *Reichsrecht und Volksrecht*, pp. 387ff, and especially p. 391, on the 'unbegrenzte Privatwillkür in den griechischen Freilassungen'. It was this *Privatwillkür* which made the paramonar manumission of the Greeks so different from that of Babylonia. There can be little doubt that paramonar manumission *originated* as a grant of

full freedom subsequently circumscribed (after all, even the freeborn person could be enslaved in Babylonia if he failed to abide by the adoption agreement). But the complete arbitrariness with which Greek manumitters would grant or withhold rights from their freedmen changed its character: to argue that even the *Greek* institution is such a grant is difficult (unless legal freedom in Greece meant no more than a capacity to own, cf. Samuel, 'Role', p. 295). It was also this arbitrariness which differentiated paramonar manumission from paramonar agreements with free persons in the Hellenistic world (cf. Adams, *Paramoné*, pp. 42ff, where this is wrongly taken to mean that the two institutions originated separately).

52 Ibn Saʿd, *Ṭabaqāt*, vol. III, pp. 40–2; Balādhurī, *Ansāb al-ashrāf*, vol. I, ed. M. Ḥamīdullāh, Cairo 1959, pp. 466f.

53 Ibn Saʿd, *Ṭabaqāt*, vol. III, p. 86; Ṭabarī, *Taʾrīkh*, appendix, ser. iii, p. 2544. Sālim looks curiously like an early shot at Salmān al-Fārisī: both were Persians, both nonetheless bore Semitic names formed from the root *slm*; both were freedmen, and both were adopted, Sālim literally and Salmān by the phrase *anta minnā ahl bayt* (Ibn Saʿd, *Ṭabaqāt*, vol. IV, p. 83 – presumably the nearest one could get to adoption after God had banned it).

54 Juda, *Aspekte*, p. 27; M. J. Kister, 'On Strangers and Allies in Mecca', paper presented at the Third International Colloquium on 'From Jāhiliyya to Islam', forthcoming in *Jerusalem Studies in Arabic and Islam*.

55 Ibn Saʿd, *Ṭabaqāt*, vol. III, p. 226.

56 *Ibid.*

57 *Ibid.*, p. 246.

58 Cf. below, Chapter 6, p. 81.

59 This is the practice condemned in the Qurʾān (5:102), cf. the commentaries to this verse; cf. also Lane, *Lexicon*, *s.v.* 'sāʾiba'.

60 Ṭūsī, *Tahdhīb*, vol. VIII, nos. 909, 929, cf. also 927–8 (*an yadaʿa nafsahu ḥaythu shāʾa; idhhab ḥaythu shiʾta*). The formulae add that the manumitter has no right to the freedman's estate and no responsibility for his misdeeds, as if these rights and duties were affected by the freedman's whereabouts.

61 Ṭabarī, *Taʾrīkh*, ser. i, p. 1640.

62 *Aghānī*, vol. XXII, p. 39.

63 Umm Salama freed Safīna on condition that he serve the Prophet as long as the latter lived (Ibn Ḥazm, *Muḥallā*, vol. IX, p. 185). More commonly the condition is service as long as he himself lived (see for example Abū Dāwūd, *Ṣaḥīḥ sunan al-muṣṭafā*, Cairo 1348, vol. II, p. 161; the editor of Ibn Ḥazm has emended the beginning (though not the end) of Ibn Ḥazm's tradition to bring it into conformity with the classical version. But manumission on condition of service for the lifetime of the manumitter or a person designated by him seems to have merged with, or to have been rendered redundant by, the institution of *tadbīr* (cf. appendix 5).

64 Ibn Ḥazm, *Muḥallā*, vol. IX, p. 186. The text has *fa-lammā* GHLẒT RQBTHʾ *qālat*. The editor presumably read *fa-lammā ghaluẓat raqabatuhā qālat*, 'when her body became gross, she said', but it is clear that pregnancy is not the issue: whatever happened, the manumitter had acted in accordance with the stipulations, as Ibn Masʿūd proceeded to declare. One could read *fa-lammā ghaluẓat raqabtuhā fa-qālat* 'when she acted coarsely, I put a rope around her neck, whereupon she said', but the second *fa* is not in the text, and the fact that Ibn Masʿūd goes on to speak about her *raqaba* suggests that *raqaba* is also a noun rather than a verb here. I have read *fa-lammā ghallaẓtu raqabatahā qālat*, 'when I acted rudely in respect of her neck (or body) [sc. when I disciplined her], she said'. The lexicographers do not, it is true, give any support for this meaning of *ghallaẓa*, but then they give no support for *aghlaẓa* in that sense either, and *aghlaẓa* nonetheless means precisely that in the tradition cited below, note 99.

65 J. A. Crook, *Law and Life of Rome*, London 1967, p. 51, citing *Digest*, 47, 10, 7, 2.

66 ʿAbd al-Razzāq, *Muṣannaf*, vol. VIII, nos. 15,600–1, 15,603, 15,623; cf. below, notes 109–10.

67 ʿAbd al-Razzāq, *Muṣannaf*, vol. VIII, no. 15,612; for variants, see nos. 15,613, 15,619 and (vol. IX) 16,779–81, 16,783.

68 Cf. *fa-batta ʿitqahum* in no. 16,781.

69 The absence of reference to service during ʿUmar's own lifetime implies that the

manumission was testamentary, as is in fact explicitly stated in no. 15,613. Paramonar manumissions were frequently testamentary too, cf. above, notes 12, 16, 20.

70 Above, note 31.

71 All variants emend the inconsistency to make it a condition on ʿUthmān, but it recurs in a different form in no. 15,613, once more suggesting that originally it was a condition on the freedmen.

72 Only nos. 15,612 and 16,781 refer to the immediate effect of the manumission; Khiyār is explicitly described as a slave by Zuhrī in no. 16,783; and Ibn Rushd refers to the tradition with the comment that 'there is no disagreement on the point that if a slave is freed by his master on condition that he serve him for some years, his manumission is not completed until he has served for those years (*Bidāya*, vol. II, p. 420).

73 ʿAbd al-Razzāq, *Muṣannaf*, vol. VIII, nos. 15,621–2; vol. IX, nos. 16,787, 16,789; Wakīʿ, *Quḍāh*, vol. III, p. 115.

74 ʿAbd al-Razzāq, *Muṣannaf*, vol. VIII, no. 15,602.

75 ʿAbd al-Razzāq, *Muṣannaf*, vol. VIII, no. 15,616; vol. IX, nos. 16,784–5.

76 ʿAbd al-Razzāq, *Muṣannaf*, vol. VIII, no. 15,615; vol. IX, no. 16,782.

77 ʿAbd al-Razzāq, *Muṣannaf*, vol. VIII, no. 15,611.

78 *Ibid.*, no. 15,608.

79 Cf. Partsch, review of A. Calderini, in *Archiv für Papyrusforschung* 1913, p. 469, on *tropheia*. (Taubenschlag's interpretation of BGU 567 as an example of *Roman* law is scarcely acceptable, cf. his *Law of Greco-Roman Egypt*, p. 101; id., 'Geschichte der Rezeption des römischen Privatrechts in Ägypten', in his *Opera Minora*, vol. I, p. 206; *id.*, 'Das Sklavenrecht im Rechte der Papyri', *ibid.*, vol. II, pp. 255f.)

80 *Douleia kai apophora* (cf. P. Oxy. III, 494, in which a husband bequeaths such rights to his wife). The freedman saved by Ḥenan-Ishoʿ from re-enslavement had also been obliged to render both services and payments (cf. above, note 20).

81 ʿAbd al-Razzāq, *Muṣannaf*, vol. VIII, no. 15,610; Wakīʿ, *Quḍāh*, vol. I, p. 327.

82 ʿAbd al-Razzāq, *Muṣannaf*, vol. VIII, nos. 15,596–9; Ṭūsī, *Tahdhīb*, vol. VIII, no. 983.

83 Above, note 40.

84 ʿAbd al-Razzāq, *Muṣannaf*, vol. VIII, no. 15,599; similarly Ṭūsī, *Tahdhīb*, vol. VIII, no. 983; Ibn Qudāma, *Mughnī*, vol. X, no. 8851.

85 ʿAbd al-Razzāq, *Muṣannaf*, vol. VIII, no. 15,601; cf. nos. 15,603, 15,623.

86 Above, p. 66.

87 P. Bonfante, *Corso di diritto romano*, vol. I, Rome 1925, p. 180; A. M. Duff, *Freedmen in the Early Roman Empire*², Cambridge 1958, p. 46.

88 ʿAbd al-Razzāq, *Muṣannaf*, vol. VIII, no. 15,605; cf. 15,599, 15,606–7.

89 Above, notes 41–2.

90 ʿAbd al-Razzāq, *Muṣannaf*, vol. VIII, no. 15,615; vol. IX, no. 16,782 (I have adopted the editor's reading of *bḥylh* as *bi-khaylihi*). Note that though Ibn ʿUmar has manumitted the slave, he declares him free (*anta ḥurr*) on releasing him from labour; compare Mitteis, *Reichsrecht und Volksrecht*, p. 387, on the Delphic manumission inscriptions: the typical formula of paramonar manumission is 'the slave shall be free, but he shall stay for so-and-so long with his master . . . when that period is over the slave shall be free'.

91 Above, p. 66.

92 P. Nessana III, no. 56, line 2 of the Arabic version (*fa-qad ṣaddaqa ʿalayhi bi-ʿishrīna dīnār*), line 9 of the Greek (*ekharisato*). Kraemer interprets this to mean that twenty of the fifty solidi were given as wages for the work done by the boy during the life of the contract (Kraemer, *Nessana*, vol. III, p. 156). But the boy had clearly been indentured for an indefinite period, viz. until the loan was repaid (compare above, notes 14, 21). It follows that he was not working off the loan, and wages are hardly given as charity. His wages presumably consisted of food and clothing as in P. Dura 10 (cf. above, note 14). The twenty solidi must have been remitted gratuitously, as the wording indicates.

93 Saḥnūn, *Mudawwana*, part vii, p. 82 (Ibn ʿUmar freed a slave by *kitāba* in return for 35,000 dirhams, but released him when he had paid 30,000).

94 24:33; cf. Ibn Rushd, *Bidāya*, vol. II, pp. 409f. The verse is in fact unlikely to refer to manumission, cf. below, note 100.

95 'They agree on the permissibility of stipulating that the freedman serve for a specified

period before or after the manumission [has taken effect], (Ibn Rushd, *Bidāya*, vol. II, p. 407). Only the Ẓāhirīs disagreed (Ibn Ḥazm, *Muḥallā*, vol. IX, p. 185).

96 Ibn Bābūyah, *Man lā yaḥḍuruhu*, vol. III, nos. 235, 262; Ṭūsī, *Tahdhīb*, vol. VIII, nos. 797, 857 (five years or any number); Ṭūsī, *Nihāya*, p. 542 (a year or two); cf. also Ḥillī, *Nukat al-nihāya* in *al-Jawāmiʿ al-fiqhiyya*, unpaginated lithograph, Tehran 1276, fol. 332b of the copy in the British Library.

97 Ṭūsī, *Nihāya*, pp. 542, 551; similarly the Ismāʿīlīs (Nuʿmān, *Iqtiṣār*, p. 127).

98 Ṭūsī, *Nihāya*, p. 542; Ḥillī, *Sharāʾiʿ*, vol. III, p. 108 (according to whom, some disagree).

99 Ṭūsī, *Tahdhīb*, vol. VIII, no. 795; cf. no. 796 and Ibn Babūyah, *Man lā yaḥḍhuruhu*, vol. III, nos. 233–4. The text has *in huwa aghlaẓahā*, which clearly means 'if he acts roughly towards her', or in other words 'if he maltreats her', not 'if he finds her coarse', as one might infer on the basis of the lexicographers (according to whom the text ought to have said *in huwa aghlaẓa* (or *ghallaẓa*) *lahā al-kalām* or *al-fiʿl* or the like in order to mean what I have taken it to mean). The freedman is evidently not going to be re-enslaved for finding fault with his wife, as opposed to having acted faultily towards her: the variant versions say that if he is manumitted and married off to the daughter on condition that he pay a hefty fine if he takes a second wife or a concubine, then that condition is valid too. Like *ghallaẓa* in note 64, *aghlaẓa* must mean 'act rudely towards' here.

100 The term *kitāba* is completely non-descript. It suggests a contract, or simply a document (*kitāb*, a term used synonymously with it on occasion, cf. Ibn Saʿd, *Ṭabaqāt*, vol. V, pp. 85, 86; and to write a *kitāb* for a slave presumably meant no more, originally, than to write him a manumission document of any kind. The institution is supposed to be attested in the Qurʾān (24:33), but this is scarcely the case. Sura 24:1–35 is concerned with sexual morality (after verse 35 it suddenly changes both subject and character). It covers subjects such as *zinā*, *qadhf*, *liʿān* and female modesty, not manumission. Verse 32 enjoins the believers to marry off those without spouses, including righteous slaves and slavegirls; God will provide [money for the dower] if they are poor, but (verse 33) those who do not have the means to marry must be chaste until God provides for them. Verse 33 continues: 'and those whom your right hands possess who want a *kitāb*, write a *kitāb* for them (*fa-kātibūhum*) if you know of some good in them; and give them of the wealth of God that He has given you. And constrain not your slavegirls to prostitution. . .' Clearly, *kitāb* is here a marriage document (cf. Hebrew *ketubah*), not a manumission agreement; marriage is what the entire passage is about, and verse 33 simply paraphrases verse 32: marry off those slaves and slavegirls of yours who are righteous/in whom you know some good; if they are poor, God will provide for them/you should provide for them out of the wealth that God has given you; if they do not have the means to marry, they must be chaste/not constrained to prostitution. Masters are paying money to their slaves here, not the other way round. (The lawyers took this to mean that masters must renounce the last instalments or that all Muslims must contribute to the instalments out of the alms-taxes, cf. above, note 94.) Exegetes and lawyers alike were unfamiliar with the Qurʾānic use of the word *kitāb*, it would seem.

101 Samuel, 'Role', p. 258.

102 Koschaker, *Rechtsurkunden*, p. 35; Samuel, 'Role', pp. 260f, both with reference to H. Collitz (ed.), *Sammlung der griechischen Dialektinschriften*, Göttingen 1884–1915, vol. II, no. 1867 (for another parallel, see no. 1749).

103 Koschaker, *Rechtsurkunden*, pp. 33ff; Samuel, 'Role', pp. 258ff.

104 Cf. above, note 80.

105 Shaybānī, *Aṣl*, vol. III, pp. 415f (service for a month on behalf of the manumitter or a person designated by him); Saḥnūn, *Mudawwana*, vol. VII, p. 85 (service for a month); Ibn Qudāma, *Mughnī*, vol. X, no. 8725 (service in general). This is rejected by Ibn Ḥazm (*Muḥallā*, vol. IX, p. 241).

106 Sarakhsī, *Mabsūṭ*, vol. VII, p. 211; Mālik, *Muwaṭṭaʾ*, part ii, p. 155; Ibn Qudāma, *Mughnī*, vol. X, no. 8725; Nawawī, *Minhāj al-ṭālibīn*, ed. L. W. C. van den Berg, Batavia 1882–4, vol. III, p. 479.

107 Cf. Shaybānī, *Aṣl*, vol. III, p. 411 (his *miṣr*); Sarakhsī, *Mabsūṭ* vol. VII, p. 209 (Kufa, for example); Mālik, *Muwaṭṭaʾ*, part ii, p. 155 (the manumitter's *arḍ*); Abū Ghānim, *al-Mudawwana al-kubrā*, ed. M. Aṭfayyish, Beirut 1974, vol. II, p. 178 (his *balad*).

108 I do not know of any classical texts which define the paramonar freedman's duty to remain, but of the free paramonar servant it is said that he must stay with/not absent himself from

his master by day, or by day and by night, or that he may not go away from his house by day or by night without his knowledge, or that he must stay in the inn or factory in which he is to work (Adams, *Paramoné*, pp. 49ff; cf. above, note 14).

109 Of the classical lawyers only the Imāmīs endorse it: 'the *mukātab* is bound by every condition which has been imposed on him; if a man were to free a slave by *kitāba* and stipulate that he may not go away (*an lā yabraḥa*) without his permission until he has paid off his *mukātaba*, then it would not be lawful for him to go away without his permission' (Ibn Bābūyah, *al-Muqniʿ*, in *al-Jawāmiʿ al-fiqhiyya*, unpaginated lithograph, Tehran 1276, fol. 19b of the copy in the British Library). But there were also pre-classical lawyers who held that the *mukātab* was only allowed to travel if nothing to the contrary had been stipulated (Ibn Rushd, *Bidāya*, vol. II, p. 418; Ibn Qudāma, *Mughnī*, vol. X, nos. 8743–4; Sarakhsī, *Mabsūṭ*, vol. VII, p. 210). All the classical Sunnī schools, however, reject such stipulations, the Mālikīs on the ground that the *mukātab* may not leave without his master's permission anyway and the others on the ground that he may leave as he likes (Ibn Rushd, *loc. cit.*; Ibn Qudāma, *Mughnī*, vol. X, no. 8744). The Ibāḍīs and the Zaydīs also favour the view that he may leave as he likes (Abū Ghānim, *Mudawwana*, vol. II, p. 178; Hawsamī, *Kitāb al-kāfī*, MS Ambrosiana, H. 137, fol. 128a; Ibn al-Murtaḍā, *Baḥr*, vol. IV, p. 216).

110 Ibn Rushd, *Bidāya*, vol. II, p. 418; Shaybānī, *Aṣl*, vol. III, p. 411; Sarakhsī, *Mabsūṭ*, vol. VIII, p. 2 (where trade is explicitly mentioned); Abū Ghānim, *Mudawwana*, vol. II, p. 178 (he should be allowed to go and seek *faḍl Allāh*); ʿAbd al-Razzāq, *Muṣannaf*, vol. VIII, no. 15,623 (similarly, adding *al-khurūj min al-ṭalab*).

111 Sarakhsī, *Mabsūṭ*, vol. VII, p. 148.

112 Those who reject stipulations obliging the *mukātab* to remain say that he can go where he wants (*kharaja in shāʾa, al-khurūj ilā ḥaythu shāʾa, al-tijāra ḥaythu shāʾa*); but it is hard to see what else they could have said (cf. ʿAbd al-Razzāq, *Muṣannaf*, vol. VIII, no. 15,601; Sarakhsī, *Mabsūṭ*, vol. VII, pp. 209f; vol. VIII, p. 2).

113 Cf. no. vii of the previous section. The Greek part of P. Nessana III, 56 states that the Christian monk (and/or his son) has authority to go where he wishes and that Aswad has no authority over him, but the Arabic version is illegible at this point.

114 Ibn Ḥazm, *Muḥallā*, vol. IX, p. 185.

115 Shaybānī, *Aṣl*, vol. III, p. 422.

116 The time limit (*ajal*) is one of the pillars of the contract (Ibn Rushd, *Bidāya*, vol. II, p. 408); it is not valid except *bi-thaman maʿlūm ilā ajal maʿlūm* (Shāfiʿī, *Umm*, vol. VII, p. 373; cf. also Sarakhsī, *Mabsūṭ*, vol. VII, p. 146). If the manumitter has omitted a precise time limit, it must be fixed for him (Saḥnūn, *Mudawwana*, part vii, p. 84).

117 There seems to be no disagreement in these traditions that *tadbīr* is a manumission deferred until the manumitter's death, as opposed to one with immediate effect in return for continued service.

118 Cf. appendix 4.

119 Cf. Ibn Rushd, *Bidāya*, vol. II, p. 413.

120 Cf. Ibn Qudāma, *Mughnī*, vol. X, no. 8755, where this point is made with great clarity.

121 Cf. Ibn Rushd, *Bidāya*, vol. II, p. 419. (The opinion recorded for Shāfiʿī there is presumably *fī'l-qadīm* (cf. above, Chapter 2, note 25), at least it conflicts with that recorded for him *fī'l-jadīd* by Nawawī, *Minhāj*, vol. III, p. 486).

122 Thus the *jumhūr*, as Ibn Rushd points out, though there were some who disagreed (*Bidāya*, vol. II, p. 418).

123 Ibn Rushd, *Bidāya*, vol. II, pp. 417f; cf. above, note 109.

124 Ibn Rushd, *Bidāya*, vol. II, p. 417. The practice of claiming future children as slaves is explicitly rejected by Shaybānī, *Aṣl*, vol. III, p. 422; *id.*, *al-Jāmiʿ al-kabīr*, ed. A.-W. al-Afghānī, Cairo 1356, p. 304.

125 Ibn Rushd, *Bidāya*, vol. II, pp. 413f. All the lawyers customarily speak of 're-enslavement' (*al-radd fī'l-riqq* and the like) for all that the slave has not in fact been freed.

126 Cf. the surveys in Ibn Rushd, *Bidāya*, vol. II, pp. 415f; Ibn Ḥazm, *Muḥallā*, vol. IX, p. 238.

127 Abū Ghānim, *Mudawwana*, vol. II, pp. 178f (*al-amr ʿindanā. . .annahu ḥurr ḥīna waqaʿat ʿalayhi al-kitāba*); Shammākhī, *Kitāb al-īḍāh*, Beirut 1971, vol. IV, pp. 571, 573. (But some early Ibāḍīs apparently subscribed to the doctrine of proportional manumission, cf. J. van Ess, *Das Kitāb al-Nakṯ des Naẓẓām und seine Rezeption im Kitāb al-Futyā des Ǧāḥiẓ*, Göttingen 1972, p. 61.)

128 A tradition credited Ibn ʿAbbās with this opinion (Sarakhsī, *Mabsūṭ*, vol. VII, p. 206; Ibn Ḥazm, *Muḥallā*, vol. IX, p. 229; Hawsamī, *Sharḥ al-ibāna*, MS Ambrosiana, D. 225, fol. 240a). This tradition was not however known to the early Ibāḍīs, cf. Abū Ghānim, *Mudawwana*, vol. II, pp. 178f, where Abū'l-Mu'arrij admits that the non-Ibāḍīs hold a different view for which they can adduce Companion traditions, whereas his own authorities are 'our *fuqahā*'' and the Qur'ān (9:60, subjected to strained exegesis). The possibility that there might be Prophetic traditions on the subject is not considered at all, though the Sunnīs were later to adduce the Barīra tradition as proof that the *mukātab* was a slave (thus for example Zurqānī, *Sharḥ ʿalā Muwaṭṭa' al-imām Mālik*, n.p. 1936, vol. IV, p. 102; for the tradition in question, see below, Chapter 6, note 139).

129 Abū Ghānim, *Mudawwana*, vol. II, p. 178: the *mukātab* who fails to pay cannot be re-enslaved because he is free and simply a debtor. (Ibn Qudāma came close to arguing the same: the *mukātab* can travel because he has control of himself; he merely owes his master money and thus resembles the free debtor (*Mughnī*, vol. X, no. 8743).)

130 For a rich collection of such opinions, see Ibn Ḥazm, *Muḥallā*, vol. IX, pp. 228ff. Good samples are also given in Ibn Rushd, *Bidāya*, vol. II, pp. 413f; Zurqānī, *Sharḥ*, vol. IV, p. 102; ʿAbd al-Razzāq, *Muṣannaf*, vol. VIII, nos. 15,718, 15,721, 15,736–8; Sharīf al-Murtaḍā, *al-Intiṣār*, Najaf 1971, pp. 174f.

131 This view is attributed now to Ibn Masʿūd and now to others (while conversely Ibn Masʿūd is also said to have espoused different views).

132 Ibn Ḥazm, *Muḥallā*, vol. IX, p. 230; ʿAbd al-Razzāq, *Muṣannaf*, vol. VIII, no. 15,741; cf. also the references given above, where the doctrine of proportional manumission is sometimes ascribed to others.

133 Ibn al-Murtaḍā, *Baḥr*, vol. IV, pp. 219ff; Siyāghī, *Rawḍ*, vol. V, pp. 95ff; Mu'ayyad, *Tajrīd*, fols. 89b–90b. The Qāsimīs stress that a slave freed proportionally remains a slave until the last dirham has been paid, as in Sunnī law; but unlike the Sunnī *mukātab* he gradually ceases to be one: he inherits, bequeaths, pays blood-money and qualifies for *ḥadd*-punishment in accordance with the proportion paid.

134 Ibn Ḥazm, *Muḥallā*, vol. IX, pp. 227ff. The founder of the Ẓāhirī school by contrast subscribed to the Sunnī view (*ibid.*, p. 229).

135 Al-Sharīf al-Murtaḍā, *Intiṣār*, p. 173; Ṭūsī, *Nihāya*, pp. 549f; id., *Khilāf*, vol. III, pp. 376ff; id., *Tahdhīb*, vol. VIII, no. 968; Nuʿmān, *Daʿā'im*, vol. II, no. 1178; Hawsamī, *Ibāna* (D. 225), fols. 236a, 239b. A *kitāba* with a clause of re-enslavement is termed *mashrūṭa* as opposed to *muṭlaqa* (but there were also some Imāmīs who held that once the *mukātab* had paid the first instalment he could not be enslaved even if the manumitter had reserved this right, cf. the traditions in Ibn Bābūyah, *Man lā yaḥḍuruhu*, p. 354; Ṭūsī, *Tahdhīb*, vol. VIII, no. 973). The distinction is old, though the terminology may not be, cf. Shaybānī, *Aṣl*, vol. III, p. 411 (the *mukātab* is re-enslaved on failure to pay regardless of whether the manumitter has reserved this right or not).

136 M. Bloch, *Die Freilassungsbedingungen der delphischen Freilassungsinschriften*, Strassburg 1914, discussed by Samuel, 'Role', pp. 223f; more recent scholars have also come close to this view, cf. A. M. Babakos, 'Le droit de famille appliqué à l'île de Calymnos au Ier siècle après J.C.', *Revue Internationale de Droits de l'Antiquité* 1964, p. 84; H. Rädle, *Untersuchungen zum griechischen Freilassungswesen*, Munich 1969, pp. 141f.

137 Cf. Samuel, 'Role', p. 275 (what is normally called re-enslavement was in fact an annulment of the whole act, not re-enslavement of a free man).

138 Samuel, 'Role', p. 269.

139 Samuel, 'Role', p. 269.

140 Koschaker, *Rechtsurkunden*, p. 41, cf. pp. 43ff.

141 Naḥwī, *Tadhkira*, fol. 223a.

6. The case for the Roman Near East

1 But this tie was not known as *servilis cognatio*, as von Kremer would have it (*Culturgeschichte*, vol. I, p. 526). *Servilis cognatio* was not a fictitious kinship tie between manumitter and freedman, but on the contrary the genuine kinship ties between slaves which had no legal force at all until Justinian and only a very limited one thereafter. *Vocabularium Iurisprudentiae Romanae*, Berlin 1903–83, *s.v.*; M. Kaser, *Das römische Privatrecht*[2], Munich 1971–5, vol. II, pp. 126ff.

2 On the origin and history of the Roman patronate, see G. Wissowa (ed.), *Pauly's Realencyclopädie der classischen Altertumswissenschaft*[2], Stuttgart 1893– , *s.v.* 'clientes' (and the corrections thereto in E. Badian, *Foreign Clientelae*, Oxford 1958, introduction); J. Lambert, *Les operae liberti*, Paris 1934; M. Kaser, 'Die Geschichte der Patronatsgewalt über Freigelassene', *Zeitschrift der Savigny-Stiftung für Rechtsgeschichte* 1938.

3 Cf. Pauly-Wissowa, *Realencyclopädie*, *s.v.* 'clientes'; F. de Zulueta, 'De Patrociniis Vicorum' in P. Vinogradoff (ed.), *Oxford Studies in Social and Legal History*, vol. I, Oxford 1909; J. H. W. G. Liebeschuetz, *Antioch: City and Imperial Administration in the Later Roman Empire*, Oxford 1972, pp. 192ff.

4 Cf. the survey in Kaser, *Privatrecht*, vol. II, pp. 137ff.

5 Cf. Duff, *Freedmen*, Ch. 3.

6 Cf. below, section b; Kaser, *Privatrecht*, vol. II, pp. 137f.

7 R. Taubenschlag, 'Das römische Privatrecht zur Zeit Diokletians' in his *Opera Minora*, vol. I, pp. 155f.

8 Cf. above, Chapter 3, p. 40.

9 Cf. below, note 70.

10 ʿAbd al-Razzāq, *Muṣannaf*, vol. IX, nos. 16,196–8, 16,203–6, 16,212.

11 *ʿAṣaba* are males. Females are occasionally treated as agnates for purposes of succession, but they are never agnates in their own right.

12 I hope to return to this fairly startling point elsewhere.

13 The general principle is stated in no. 16,203.

14 No. 16,206. The text is corrupt, but there can be no doubt as to the meaning.

15 Ṭūsī, *Tahdhīb*, vol. VIII, no. 923. Ṭūsī's version is cited in illustration of the tenet that women cannot inherit *walāʾ* (cf. below); but this cannot be what the tradition was originally about, for the doctrine concerning women's *walāʾ* states that since women are not agnates, the tie must pass to agnatic relatives *of the manumitter*. The tradition is however so unclassical that it would not have survived if it had not been misread.

16 In Sunnī and Qāsimī law the patronate would have passed to the manumitter's agnates, not to his daughters, and the patron, whatever his identity, is always excluded by genuine agnates on the freedman's side; in other Shīʿite law the patron is excluded by *any* blood relation of the freedman's (cf. above, chapter 2).

17 The reader who thinks of Ḥadīth as an Islamic version of *All England Law Reports* may find this claim unintelligible: why should there not have been a case in which daughters claimed the estate against all odds? But Ḥadīth never reports real cases: it only reports fictitious ones illustrative of contentious points.

18 No Medinese traditions exclude the patron in the presence of non-agnatic heirs, though one Medinese authority is credited with this view (Ibn Qudāma, *Mughnī*, vol. VI, no. 4830, on ʿUbaydallāh b. ʿAbdallāh b. ʿUtba); and Medinese authorities are consistently linked with the doctrine that non-agnatic relatives do not inherit at all (see for example ʿAbd al-Razzāq, *Muṣannaf*, vol. IX, nos. 16,207–9; vol. X, nos. 19,109ff).

19 Cf. Sarakhsī, *Mabsūṭ*, vol. XXX, pp. 2f; Aṭfayyish, *Sharḥ*, vol. VIII, p. 411.

20 N. J. Coulson, *Succession in the Muslim Family*, Cambridge 1971, Chs. 7–8 (Sunnī and Imāmī); Ibn al-Murtaḍā, *Baḥr*, vol. V, p. 352; Hawsamī, *Ibāna* (D. 224), fol. 98a; Aṭfayyish, *Sharḥ*, vol. VIII, pp. 411ff.

21 Ibn Qudāma, *Mughnī*, vol. VI, no. 4830; Aṭfayyish, *Sharḥ*, vol. VIII, p. 394 (ʿAbīda, Jābir b. Zayd; Jābir is also cited for this view along with Muḥammad al-Bāqir in Baillie, *Digest*, vol. II, p. 346).

22 Aṭfayyish, *Sharḥ*, vol. VIII, p. 394 (Ṭāwūs).

23 Aṭfayyish, *Sharḥ*, vol. VIII, p. 394 (Ibn ʿAbbās, Mujāhid).

24 Aṭfayyish, *Sharḥ*, vol. VIII, p. 394 (Muʿādh b. Jabal, Abū'l-Dardāʾ); Ibn Qudāma, *Mughnī*, vol. VI, no. 4830 (ʿUmar II, frequently an authority for the Medinese, but here in the company of his Mesopotamian associate, Maymūn b. Mihrān).

25 Cf. above, note 18.

26 Above, Chapter 3, pp. 36f, 39.

27 Cf. above, Chapter 3, pp. 37, 39. The doctrine that succession is based on either *nasab* or *sabab* is common to the Imāmīs, Nāṣirīs and Qāsimīs alike (cf. Ṭūsī, *Nihāya*, p. 623; Hawsamī, *Ibāna* (D. 224), fol. 98a; Hawsamī, *Ifāda*, fol. 36a). The Qāsimīs do not always use it in their presentation of the laws of succession, but they commonly distinguish between agnates by *nasab* and agnates by *sabab*, viz. patrons (thus for example Siyāghī,

Rawḍ, vol. IV, p. 261; Naḥwī, *Tadhkira*, fol. 88a). This suggests that the distinction is old, and it is in fact attested for the ninth century (cf. Jāḥiẓ, *Rasāʾil*, ed. H. al-Sandūbī, Cairo 1933, p. 77, where the Hāshimites state that the Marwānids had no right to the caliphate by either *nasab* or *sabab*, except for the fact that they were Qurashīs).

28 One account of how Sāʾib Khāthir became a *mawlā* of ʿAbdallāh b. Jaʿfar has it that the latter bought his *walāʾ* (*Aghānī*, vol. VIII, p. 321). Similarly, one acount of how the poet Nuṣayb, a former *mukātab*, became a client of ʿAbd al-ʿAzīz b. Marwān has it that the latter bought his *walāʾ* (*ibid.*, vol. I, p. 324; Ibn Khallikān, *Wafāyāt al-aʿyān*, ed. I. ʿAbbās, Beirut 1968–72, vol. VI, p. 89, no. 308). Sālim b. Abīʾl-Jaʿd, a *mawlā* of Ghaṭafān who died in the reign of ʿUmar II, was allowed by three men, presumably his patrons, to sell the *walāʾ* over one of his own *mawālī* to ʿAmr b. Ḥurayth for 10,000 (dirhams) (Ibn Saʿd, *Ṭabaqāt*, vol. VI, p. 291). The mother of the caliph Mahdī bought the *walāʾ* of Abū Maʿshar, the scholar who was a former *mukātab* (Ibn Qutayba, *al-Maʿāṛif*, ed. M. I. ʿA. al-Ṣāwī, Beirut 1970, p. 220; cf. Schacht, *Origins*, p. 173). For further details, see Juda, *Aspekte*, pp. 156f.

29 R. Mottahedeh, *Loyalty and Leadership in an Early Islamic Society*, Princeton 1980, p. 86. The claim (*ibid.*, p. 85) that the patronate was inheritable and transferable according to the lawbooks is not correct.

30 Ibn Abī Shayba, *Muṣannaf*, vol. XI, nos. 11,663–70; Aṭfayyish, *Nīl*, vol. VIII, p. 395; Ibn Qudāma, *Mughnī*, vol. VI, no. 4936; Shāfiʿī, *Umm*, vol. IV, p. 57; Sarakhsī, *Mabsūt*, vol. VIII, pp. 97f; Wakīʿ, *Quḍāh*, vol. I, p. 300.

31 ʿAṭāʾ is said to have begun by accepting the validity of gifts of *walāʾ*, though he changed his mind (ʿAbd al-Razzāq, *Muṣannaf*, vol. IX, no. 16,151). Hishām b. Hubayra, a *qāḍī* of the mid-Umayyad period, also endorsed them, though only on condition of special rules regarding the devolution of the tie on the death of the recipient (Ibn Abī Shayba, *Muṣannaf*, vol. XI, no. 11,667; Wakīʿ, *Quḍāh*, vol. I, p. 300). Mālik is said to have accepted them with reference to the tradition on Maymūna's gift of *walāʾ* to Ibn ʿAbbās (Hawsamī, *Ibāna*, D. 224, fols. 124b–125a; cf. Ibn al-Murtaḍā, *Baḥr*, vol. IV, p. 229). For the lawyers who accepted the validity of such transactions in the time of Shāfiʿī, with reference to the same tradition, see Shāfiʿī, *Umm*, vol. IV, p. 57. The fact that Ibn Abi Shayba's chapter *fī bayʿ al-walāʾ wa-hibatihi: man karihahu* is followed by another on *man rakhkhaṣa fī hibat al-walāʾ* suggests that the question remained controversial for at least another generation (*Muṣannaf*, vol. XI, nos. 11,654–70).

32 ʿAbd al-Razzāq, *Muṣannaf*, vol. IX, nos. 16,143–4, 16,150 (Jābir, Ibn ʿAbbās, Ibn ʿUmar). Ibn Abī Shayba has none of these traditions though his chapter against gifts and sale of *walāʾ* is entitled 'those who disapprove of it' (cf. the preceding note).

33 ʿAbd al-Razzāq, *Muṣannaf*, vol. IX, nos. 16,138 (Prophet), 16,139–40 (ʿAlī), 16,142 (Ibn Masʿūd, possibly voicing disapproval only), 16,145–9 (Ibn ʿAbbās, Ṭāwūs, Ḥasan, Zuhrī, Ibn al-Musayyab), 16,151 (ʿAṭāʾ). Most of these traditions, including the Prophetic one, are also cited by Ibn Abī Shayba, who adds others from Ibrāhīm al-Nakhaʿī, Ibn Sīrīn, Shaʿbī and ʿUmar (*Muṣannaf*, vol. XI, nos. 11,654–62).

34 Cf. the preceding note, and Saḥnūn, *Mudawwana*, vol. VIII, p. 79 (Makḥūl and Rabīʿa b. Abī Abd al-Raḥmān agreed).

35 In addition to the examples above, note 33, see Raddatz, 'Erbrecht', p. 41; Saḥnūn, *Mudawwana*, vol. VIII, p. 79.

36 In addition to the example above, note 33, see Raddatz, 'Erbrecht', p. 41; Ṭirmidhī, *Ṣaḥīḥ*, vol. VIII, p. 284; Bukhārī, *Recueil*, vol. II, p. 121, and other classical collections.

37 *Al-walāʾ nasab. . .al-walāʾ luḥma kaʾl-nasab. . .a-yubīʿu aḥadukum nasabahu?* (ʿAbd al-Razzāq, *Muṣannaf*, vol. IX, nos. 16,142, 16,147, 16,149).

38 Sarakhsī, *Mabsūṭ*, vol. VIII, pp. 97f; Saḥnūn, *Mudawwana*, vol. VIII, p. 78f; Shāfiʿī, *Umm*, vol. IV, pp. 52, 57; vol. VII, p. 208; Ibn Qudāma, *Mughnī*, vol. VI, no. 4936; Ḥillī, *Sharāʾiʿ*, vol. IV, p. 37; Naḥwī, *Tadhkira*, fol. 224a; Hawsamī, *Ibāna* (D. 224), fol. 124b; Nuʿmān, *Iqtiṣār*, p. 128; Aṭfayyish, *Sharḥ*, vol. VIII, p. 395. Complete agreement among the lawyers, Sunnī, Shīʿite and Ibāḍī, clearly does not necessarily mean that the question had never been controversial.

39 Cf. above, Chapter 2, p. 32.

40 Cf. Aṭfayyish, *Sharḥ*, vol. VIII, p. 395, where sale of *walāʾ* is identified as a Jāhilī practice forbidden by the *sharʿ*, clearly correct if Jāhilī is taken to mean pre-*sharʿī* rather than pre-Islamic Arabian.

41 Cf. above, Chapter 5, p. 68.

42 Sarakhsī, *Mabsūṭ*, vol. vii, p. 61: some people say that no *walāʾ* arises unless it was expressly stipulated. Like most opinions discussed in the lawbooks, this view presumably goes back to the first centuries of Islam, but I have not come across it elsewhere.

43 Thus Ibn Masʿūd, ʿAṭāʾ, Zuhrī, Sulaymān b. Mūsā (a Damascene *mawlā* who died about A.H. 119), and ʿUmar I, ʿUmar II are all said to have allowed the slave freed *sāʾibatan* to choose a patron of his own, sometimes adding that if he did not chose any and left no heirs of his own, his estate would pass to the manumitter despite the renunciation, or to the Muslims at large, i.e. the Treasury (ʿAbd al-Razzāq, *Muṣannaf*, vol. ix, nos. 16,226–8, 16,230–1, 16,236; Ibn Qudāma, *Mughnī*, vol. vi, no. 4938; Mālik, *Muwaṭṭaʾ*, part ii, p. 145; cf. Zurqānī, *Sharḥ*, vol. iv, p. 100).

44 Marghīnānī, *Hidāya*, part iii, p. 271; Qudūrī, *Statut*, p. 263; Shāfiʿī, *Umm*, vol. iv, p. 53; Shirbīnī, *Mughnī* vol. iv, p. 465; Ibn al-Murtaḍā, *Baḥr*, vol. iv, p. 229. This view is attributed to Ibn Masʿūd, Shaʿbī and others in ʿAbd al-Razzāq, *Muṣannaf*, vol. ix, nos. 16,222–6, 16,232, 16,237. Some traditions state that if the manumitter refuses the estate, the authorities should spend it on the purchase and manumission of slaves.

45 Mālik, *Muwaṭṭaʾ*, part ii, p. 145; Khalīl, *Sommario*, vol. ii, pp. 787f; Ibn Qudāma, *Mughnī*, vol. vi, no. 4938. This view is ascribed to Zuhrī in ʿAbd al-Razzāq, *Muṣannaf*, vol. ix, nos. 16,228, 16,235.

46 Ṭūsī, *Nihāya*, p. 547; *id.*, *Tahdhīb*, vol. viii, nos. 909, 927–30; vol. ix, nos. 1406–11, 1415; Ibn Bābūyah, *Muqniʿ*, fol. 19b; cf. Kulīnī, *Kāfī*, vol. vi, pp. 197f; Nuʿmān, *Daʿāʾim*, vol. ii, no. 1201; id., *Iqtiṣār*, p. 128. I have not found any Nāṣirī or Ibāḍī statements on this point.

47 This was allowed with reference to the clause in the Constitution of Medina discussed already (cf. above, Chapter 2, p. 32).

48 Ḥayyān al-Nabaṭī was a *mawlā*/freedman of Maṣqala b. Hubayra al-Shaybānī (Ṭabarī, *Taʾrīkh*, ser. ii, pp. 1204, 1330); he acquired a new patron in Muqātil b. Sulaymān al-Qurashī (Narshakhī, *Description de Boukhara*, ed. C. Schefer, Paris 1892, pp. 56f = *id.*, *The History of Bukhara*, tr. R. N. Frye, Cambridge Mass. 1954, p. 58). A Persian *mawlā* changed his *walāʾ* on taking military service with B. Fahm (R. Guest, 'Relations between Persia and Egypt under Islam up to the Fâtimid Period' in *A Volume of Oriental Studies Presented to E. G. Browne*, Cambridge 1922, p. 165). Of some freedmen we are told that they 'stuck to' (*lazima*) or 'attached themselves to' (*inqaṭaʿa ilā*) others, thereby becoming clients of the latter (Ibn Saʿd, *Ṭabaqāt*, vol. v, pp. 295, 304, 307). These and other examples relate to the Umayyad period, but there is also one relating to that of the ʿAbbāsids: Isḥāq b. Ibrāhīm al-Mawṣilī, whose family were contractual clients of B. Naḍla of Tamīm, became a client of (*tawallā*) Khāzim b. Khuzayma, also of Tamīm, in the time of Maʾmūn (*Aghānī*, vol. v, p. 278, cf. p. 154).

49 Thus Mālik, *Muwaṭṭaʾ*, part ii, p. 143, where *muwālāt* is forbidden on this ground; similarly Ibn Jurayj in ʿAbd al-Razzāq, *Muṣannaf*, vol. ix, no. 16,151.

50 Cf. the references given above, Chapter 2, note 73.

51 Cf. above, Chapter 3, pp. 38f.

52 See for example Sarakhsī, *Mabsūṭ*, vol. viii, p. 83; Shirbīnī, vol. iv, p. 465, Ibn Qudāma, *Mughnī*, vol. vi, nos. 4931, 4937; Naḥwī, *Tadhkira*, fol. 224a; Luciani, *Successions*, p. 68.

53 Cf. R. Brunschvig, 'Un système peu connu de succession agnatique dans le droit musulman', *Revue de Droit Français et Etranger* 1950, pp. 26f. The rule is also illustrated in ʿAbd al-Razzāq, *Muṣannaf*, vol. ix, nos. 16,238ff.

54 'Again, in the inheritance of a citizen freedman a patron shuts out the son of a second patron, and the son of a patron the grandson of a second patron' (Gaius, *Institutes*, ed. and tr. F. de Zulueta, Oxford 1946–53, iii, 60; cf. Lambert, *Operae liberti*, pp. 254f; but note that Sufyān al-Thawrī did not think the rule applied between one patron and another patron's son, according to ʿAbd al-Razzāq, *Muṣannaf*, vol. ix, no. 16,252). In classical Roman as in classical Muslim law the patronate was governed by rules different from that of the *hereditas* (cf. Kaser, *Privatrecht*, vol. i, p. 674).

55 Brunschvig, 'Système', p. 31.

56 Sarakhsī, *Mabsūṭ*, vol. viii, p. 83; Saḥnūn, *Mudawwana*, vol. viii, p. 85; Shāfiʿī, *Umm*, vol. iv, p. 53; Ibn Qudāma, *Mughnī*, vol. vi, no. 4971 (with the remark that this is the *qawl akthar ahl al-ʿilm*).

57 Ibn al-Murtaḍā, *Baḥr*, vol. iv, pp. 229f; Hawsamī, *Ibāna* (D. 224), fol. 126a.

58 Neither could make up their minds, cf. ʿĀmilī, *Miftāḥ*, vol. vi, pp. 199ff; Nuʿmān, *Daʿāʾim*, vol. ii, nos. 1196, 1202, 1205; id., *Iqtiṣār*, p. 128. As usual, Ṭūsī's *ijmāʿ* is the *ijmāʿ* of the Sunnīs (*Khilāf*, vol. ii, pp. 285f).

59 Brunschvig was perfectly aware that the rule of the *kubr* rested on the interpretation of *walāʾ* as *nasab*, but he regarded this interpretation as archaic on general evolutionary grounds (cf. 'Succession', pp. 32f; Goldziher also assumed the maxim *al-walāʾ luḥma ka-luḥmat al-nasab* to be of pre-Islamic origin, cf. *Muhammedanische Studien*, vol. i, p. 107). Schacht, who realised that this interpretation was not archaic nonetheless regarded Brunschvig's theory to have been positively proved (*Origins*, p. 173; *Introduction*, p. 40).

60 A point made with great clarity by Sarakhsī, *Mabsūṭ*, vol. viii, p. 83.

61 ʿAbd al-Razzāq, *Muṣannaf*, vol. ix, no. 16,251, contrast 16,238–9; Sarakhsī, *Mabsūṭ*, vol. xxx, p. 39; Ibn Qudāma, *Mughnī*, vol. vi, nos. 4937, 4971; Baghdādī, *Ishrāf*, vol. ii, pp. 306f; Wakīʿ, *Quḍāh*, vol. ii, p. 291; Ibn al-Murtaḍā, *Baḥr*, vol. iv, p. 230; Ibn Abī Shayba, *Muṣannaf*, vol. xi, nos. 11,606–7.

62 Cf. Juda, *Aspekte*, p. 157, citing Ibn ʿAsākir and Fasawī; compare Ibn Abī Shayba, *Muṣannaf*, vol. xi, no. 11,613.

63 ʿAṭāʾ nonetheless presents it as a general custom for which he can name no authority (*adraknā al-nās ʿalayhi*, ʿAbd al-Razzāq, *Muṣannaf*, vol. ix, no. 16,243).

64 Cf. Ibn Rushd, *Bidāya*, vol. ii, p. 397.

65 Sarakhsī, *Mabsūṭ*, vol. viii, p. 83; ʿAbd al-Razzāq, *Muṣannaf*, vol. ix, no. 16,251; cf. no. 19,002.

66 Cf. Ibn Bābūyah, *Man lā yaḥḍuruhu*, vol. iv, p. 224 (males and females inherit equally through *walāʾ*, but note the reason given: because it is *luḥma ka-luḥmat al-nasab*, rather than because it is ordinary property); Ṭūsī, *Istibṣār*, vol. iv, nos. 79f, 652f and the commentaries thereto; id., *Mabsūṭ*, vol. iv, p. 95; id., *Nihāya*, pp. 547f (contradictory doctrines due, according to Ṭūsī, to *taqiyya*: that the children of the manumitter inherit *walāʾ* regardless of sex is *al-aẓhar min madhhab aṣḥābinā*, but the *mukhālifūn* say that the tie can only pass to males); cf. also Ḥillī, *Sharāʾiʿ*, vol. iv, p. 37.

67 Sarakhsī, *Mabsūṭ*, vol. viii, p. 83; Saḥnūn, *Mudawwana*, part viii, p. 88; Shīrāzī, *Tanbīh*, part ii, p. 114; Ibn Qudāma, *Mughnī*, vol. vi, no. 4962; Ibn al-Murtaḍā, *Baḥr*, vol. v, pp. 230f; Hawsamī *Ibāna* (D. 224), fol. 125b.

68 Saḥnūn, *Mudawwana*, part viii, p. 77; Sarakhsī, *Mabsūṭ*, vol. viii, p. 86; Ibn Qudāma, *Mughnī*, vol. vi, no. 4972; Hawsamī, *Kitāb al-kāfī*, Ambrosiana, H. 137, fol. 129a; Ibn Rushd, *Bidāya*, vol. ii, p. 399, all with reference to a tradition in which ʿUmar awards the status of heir to the son of a patroness (Zubayr), all while assigning responsibility for the freedman's blood-money to her agnates (respresented by ʿAlī).

69 Cf. Ibn Ḥazm, *Muḥallā*, vol. ix, pp. 300f.

70 *Walāʾ* is a *shuʿba min al-riqq*, as ʿAlī reputedly put it (Ibn Qudāma, *Mughnī*, vol. vi, no. 4934); cf. also Sarakhsī, *Mabsūṭ*, vol. vii, p. 83, vol. xxx, p. 39 (*athar min āthār al-mulk*, *juzʾ min al-mulk*).

71 Sarakhsī, *Mabsūṭ*, vol. viii, p. 83.

72 Ibn Qudāma, *Mughnī*, vol. vi, no. 4934; Ibn al-Murtaḍā, *Baḥr*, vol. iv, p. 228.

73 Thus for example Baghdādī, *Ishrāf*, vol. ii, p. 307; Sarakhsī, *Mabsūṭ*, vol. xxx, p. 45; Ibn al-Murtaḍā, *Baḥr*, vol. iv, p. 231.

74 Ḥillī, *Sharāʾiʿ*, vol. iv, p. 35; Sharīf al-Murtaḍā, *Intiṣār*, p. 168.

75 Ṭūsī, *Tahdhīb*, vol. viii, no. 802; Ibn Bābūyah, *Muqniʿ*, fol. 19b.

76 Ḥillī *Sharāʾiʿ*, vol. iv, p. 39, but with a different reason.

77 See the references given below, note 115.

78 *ʿAlā sabīl al-tabarruʿ* as opposed to *bi-wājib* (Sharīf al-Murtaḍā, *Intiṣār*, p. 168; cf. Ḥillī, *Sharāʾiʿ*, vol. iv, p. 38: *lā walāʾ biʾl-ʿitq al-qahrī*).

79 He who is forced to free a slave, for example in expiation of unintentional homicide or in fulfilment of vows, cannot ask for services, be they minor or major; the same is true of the manumitter who frees his slave *liʾllāh khāliṣan lahu*, or in other words what non-Ibāḍīs call *sāʾibatan* (Basyānī, *Mukhtaṣar*, pp. 237f). For the slave who has purchased his own freedom, see below, p. 86.

80 Ṭabarī, *Tafsīr*, vol. viii, pp. 275f, citing Qatāda; Bayḍāwī, *Anwār*, vol. i, p. 273 (both ad 4:37). The information could be inspired by the Qur'ānic mention of a *naṣīb*. On the other hand, passages suggesting that *ḥalīf*s would install each other as universal heirs do not say

whether or in what way their arrangements would be affected by the presence of heirs (e.g. several traditions in Ṭabarī and the story in *Aghānī*, vol. x, p. 28).
81 Kaser, *Privatrecht*, vol. II, pp. 508f, 522; cf. above, Chapter 3, pp. 36f.
82 Kaser, *Privatrecht*, vol. II, p. 509. But if the freedman left less than 100 *aurei*, the patron was only excluded by descendants.
83 Kaser, *Privatrecht*, vol. II, p. 522.
84 Ibn Saʿd, *Ṭabaqāt*, vol. III, p. 86, on Sālim, the *mawlā* of Abū Ḥudhayfa.
85 Kaser, *Privatrecht*, vol. II, pp. 139ff; cf. pp. 497f.
86 Cf. G. La Pira, 'Precedenti provinciali della riforma giustinianea del diritto di patronato', *Studi Italiani di Filologia Classica* 1929, pp. 146ff; Harada 'Verzicht'; add now the papyrus published by S. Daris, 'Note sui liberti', *Studia Papyrologica* 1979, p. 10. All the papyrological examples date from the third century.
87 Thus both La Pira and Harada (though only the latter insists on the connection between this practice and *paramonē*, cf. 'Verzicht', pp. 143f).
88 Cf. above, Chapter 5, p. 68.
89 Cf. above, p. 81.
90 Cf. above, note 79, where the Ibāḍī manumitter who frees his slave *li'llāh khāliṣan lahu* renounces service; that *walā'* frequently meant more than a title to succession is also suggested by the trade in it.
91 They only retained their honorary rights (Kaser, *Privatrecht*, vol. ii, p. 142).
92 Cf. Ibn Masʿūd in Ibn Qudāma, *Mughnī*, vol. VI, no. 4938 (*al-sā'iba yaḍaʿu mālahu ḥaythu shā'a*); similarly Masrūq in ʿAbd al-Razzāq, *Muṣannaf*, vol. IX, no. 16,373. For a *sā'iba* freedman who wills away his entire estate, see *ibid.*, no. 16,234 (where Shaʿbī objects); Ibn Ḥazm, *Muhallā*, vol. IX, p. 317 (where the patroness successfully contests the will); for another example, see Ibn Saʿd, *Ṭabaqāt*, vol. III, p. 86 (Sālim, *mawlā* of Abū Ḥudhayfa). Note that in Ibāḍī law, where the manumitter has no title to succession, the freedman may dispose of his entire estate by will on a par with the *sā'iba* freedman (Aṭfayyish, *Sharḥ*, vol. VIII, p. 393).
93 Cf. Bonfante, *Corso*, vol. I, p. 180.
94 Taubenschlag, 'Rezeption', p. 237; id., 'Droit local', p. 520.
95 Harada, 'Verzicht', pp. 151ff.
96 P. Oxy. IV, 706. Given that the governor explicitly based his decision on the *astikoi nomoi*, he hardly awarded paramonar services/*operae* to the manumitter on the simple ground that an Egyptian freedman should not be better off than a Roman one, as Seidl suggests (*Rechtsgeschichte Ägyptens*, p. 133). Presumably, the freedman could not prove that the manumitter had renounced all further claims.
97 P. Oxy. 1205, discussed by Harada, 'Verzicht', pp. 137, 150ff; P. Meyer Jur. Pap. 8, discussed by Taubenschlag, 'Rezeption', p. 237n.
98 As in BGU I, 96; PSI IX, 1040; and P. Daris inv. no. 46; cf. Harada, 'Verzicht', pp. 142, 151; Daris, 'Note', pp. 9f.
99 C. 6,4,3, adduced by Taubenschlag, 'Droit local', p. 520n (those who are freed by [monetary] agreements with their masters are indeed subject to the full patronate); C. 6,3,8, adduced by La Pira, 'Precedenti', p. 148n (the *suis nummis emptus* is not freed of the patronate).
100 Cf. Harada, 'Verzicht', p. 143.
101 Cf. above, chapter 5, p. 66.
102 The freedman of P. Oxy. IV, 706 clearly *believed* that he had purchased freedom not only from slavery, but also from further service (cf. La Pira, 'Precedenti', p. 153), viz. one *could* purchase one's freedom from both, though Harada seems to doubt it ('Verzicht', p. 141).
103 W. W. Buckland, *The Roman Law of Slavery*, Cambridge 1908, pp. 636ff.
104 Buckland, *Slavery*, p. 640; Bonfante, *Corso*, vol. I, p. 177.
105 Cf. above, note 99.
106 Kaser, *Privatrecht*, vol. II, p. 141[30] (C. 6,4,4). Buckland disputed this, but with reference to earlier sources which scarcely rule out innovation on behalf of Justinian (*Slavery*, p. 640 and note 11 thereto).
107 Cf. above, Chapter 5.
108 ʿAbd al-Razzāq, *Muṣannaf*, vol. IX, nos. 16,158–9, 16,218; Ibn Qudāma, *Mughnī*, vol. VI, no. 4943. Qatāda is here credited with the view that the *mukātab* gets his own *walā'* unless the manumitter explicitly reserves it (a view loosely credited to the Prophet in no. 16,159),

though the *mukātab* himself may also take the precaution of expressly stipulating that it should pass to him.

109 ʿAbd al-Razzāq, *Muṣannaf*, vol. IX, no. 16,217 (the *walāʾ* over the slave freed by *kitāba* or *qiṭāʿa* passes to the manumitter if nothing has been stipulated, but the freedman may stipulate that it should pass to him. The *aw* of note 2 should be substituted for the *wa* of the text); Ibn Qudāma, *Mughnī*, vol. VI, no. 4943, reports a more radical view.

110 Ibn Qudāma, *Mughnī*, vol. VI, no. 4943 (there is no *walāʾ* over the *mukātab*).

111 Ibn Qudāma, *Mughnī*, vol. VI, no. 4943 (the *mukātab* may stipulate the *walāʾ* should pass to him).

112 Mālik explicitly points out that it is *not* allowed for a slave to buy his freedom on condition that he can become the client of whoever he wants (*Muwaṭṭaʾ*, part ii, p. 143).

113 'People refused to follow him', as Maʿmar says of Qatāda in ʿAbd al-Razzāq, *Muṣannaf*, vol. IX, no. 16,159 (similarly 16,219).

114 If a slave buys himself, he is freed on acceptance of the offer and no *walāʾ* arises according to some, though the correct view is that the manumitter gets it (Ibn al-Murtaḍā, *Baḥr*, vol. IV, p. 228). Hādī recommended that the manumitter by *kitāba*, and indeed any manumitter, expressly reserve the *walāʾ*, though it would pass to him anyway (Hawsamī, *Kāfī*, fol. 127b).

115 'As for the *mukātab* who is freed by payment or the slave who buys his own freedom from his master, no *walāʾ* is established over them in our view unless it has been stipulated; but in their view it is' (Ṭūsī, *Mabsūṭ*, vol. IV, p. 71). Since any condition can be inserted in the *kitāba*, the manumitter is free to reserve the *walāʾ* (*id.*, *Nihāya*, p. 551). But just as the manumitter may reserve the *walāʾ*, so the *mukātab* may stipulate that nobody is to have *walāʾ* over him (*id.*, *Tahdhīb*, vol. VIII, no. 985). Ṭūsī thus endorses Qatāda's doctrine.

116 Abū Ghānim explicitly points out that the Ibāḍīs do not disagree with the *qawm* (the non-Ibāḍīs) over the question of the *mukātab*'s *walāʾ*, which goes to the former master (*Mudawwana*, vol. II, p. 183), but Basyānī differs: 'he who frees a slave by *kitāba*. . .does not become his patron because *walāʾ* only arises on manumission and he has not manumitted: he has merely sold him [the slave] to himself. So he [the slave] is free and gets his own *walāʾ* (Basyānī, *Mukhtaṣar*, p. 240).

117 Ḥillī, *Nukat*, fol. 332b; Ibn Qudāma, *Mughnī*, vol. VI, no. 4943.

118 The rule, attributed to the Prophet, that *al-walāʾ li-man aʿtaqa* is taken by the majority to mean that the manumitter acquires *walāʾ* no matter how the manumission took place.

119 Cf. Ṭūsī, Basyānī and Abū Thawr (above, notes 115–17). But the Zaydīs who held that no *walāʾ* arose over the slave who purchased himself argued that this was because he was not in the manumitter's ownership when freed (above, note 114; the argument is scarcely correct).

120 Cf. Basyānī, *Mukhtaṣar*, p. 237; Ḥillī, *Sharāʾiʿ*, vol. III, p. 108; Bonfante, *Corso*, vol. I, p. 175; W. W. Buckland, *A Text-Book of Roman Law from Augustus to Justinian*[3], ed. P. Stein, Cambridge 1966, p. 88. The fact that Imāmīs and Ibāḍīs share this recommendation suggests that it is old; and given that all Muslim lawyers tended to moralise legal relationships, it is odd that only they have it. Both points could be taken to suggest foreign origin, but this is clearly feeble evidence.

121 Cf. Bonfante, *Corso*, vol. I, pp. 174f (the freedman could not take legal action against the manumitter without the praetor's permission, he could not be forced to give evidence against him in court nor could the patron be forced to give evidence against him; the patron had the right to *ingrati accusatio*, and so forth. Most of these rights persisted even when the patronate (viz. the right to succession) was renounced).

122 It may be added that there is no trace in Islamic law of the view that slaves freed by testament were freed of the patronate, as was the case in classical Roman law according to some. But then it is not certain that *liberti orcini* were freed of it in classical law (it is denied by La Pira, 'Precedenti', p. 151n), and they certainly were not freed of it in that of Justinian (Kaser, *Privatrecht*, p. 141[30]).

123 Kaser, *Privatrecht*, vol. II, p. 141[30].

124 Kindī, *Governors and Judges*, pp. 317f.

125 Cf. above, note 75.

126 Cf. ʿAbd al-Razzāq, *Muṣannaf*, vol. IX, no. 17,852: Muʿāwiya said that if people refuse to pay blood-money for their clients, the state will pay it and claim the *walāʾ*'; ʿAṭāʾ added that

if both the patrons and the community at large refuse to pay, he becomes a client of the victim (whose kinsmen will thus get the blood-money in the form of his estate).

127 Cf. *Exodus*, 21:26f; *Babylonian Talmud*, *Kiddushin*, fols. 24b–25a.

128 It is not attested in connection with stipulations of celibacy or the prostitution of slavegirls.

129 Buckland, *Slavery*, p. 609.

130 Cf. Mendelsohn, *Slavery*, p. 50. For her attestation in Nestorian law, see Ishoʿbokht in Sachau, *Syrische Rechtsbücher*, vol. III, p. 116 = 117). Taubenschlag assumed Ishoʿbokht to owe this rule to the Muslims for the simple reason that it applies in Islamic law too ('Syrische Rechtsbücher', p. 562). But it seems considerably more likely that this was a legal practice which had prevailed throughout the Near East since Hammurabi's time; we are hardly to take it that Justinian also owed it to the Muslims.

131 As mentioned already, *walāʾ* in their view arises whenever slavery gives way to freedom regardless of the circumstances in which it does so, and thus also on manumission by *istīlād*, though this is not always explicitly stated (Sarakhsī, *Mabsūṭ*, vol. VIII, p. 81; Shīrāzī, *Tanbīh*, part ii, p. 113; Khalīl, *Sommario*, vol. II, pp. 786f; Ibn Qudāma, *Mughnī*, vol. VI, no. 4945; Naḥwī, *Tadhkira*, fol. 224a; I have no Nāṣirī statement on this point, but there is nothing to suggest that they disagreed).

132 ʿĀmilī, *Miftāḥ*, vol. VI, p. 198 (where the *umm walad* is called a *mustawlada*).

133 Ṭūsī, *Mabsūṭ*, vol. VI, p. 71.

134 Cf. above, Chapter 3, note 27; above, note 58. See also Ṭūsī, *Mabsūṭ*, vol. IV, p. 70, where it is stated that conversion does not give rise to clientage *ijmāʿān illā Isḥāq*. This Isḥāq is not an Imāmī, as one might expect, but the semi-Ḥanbalite and semi-Shāfiʿite Isḥāq b. Rāhūyah. Unlike Sarakhsī, Ṭūsī did not know that the Qāsimī Zaydīs also accepted *walāʾ al-islām* (cf. Sarakhsī, *Mabsūṭ*, vol. VIII, pp. 91f, on the Rawāfiḍ).

135 ʿĀmilī, *Miftāḥ*, vol. VI, p. 198.

136 Duff, *Freedmen*, p. 79.

137 Cf. La Pira, 'Precedenti', p. 153.

138 Both Nuṣayb and Abū Maʿshar were *mukātabs* (cf. above, note 28). The freedman whose *walāʾ* was given away by Maymūna was also a *mukātab* according to Ibn Qudāma (*Mughnī*, vol. VI, no. 4936); and Qatāda is said to have permitted sale of *walāʾ* arising from *kitāba* as distinct from ordinary manumission (Ibn Abī Shayba, *Muṣannaf*, vol. XI, no. 11,669).

139 Numerous versions of the Barīra tradition are to be found in Ibn Abī Shayba, *Muṣannaf*, vol. XI, nos. 18,136–8; Ibn Saʿd, *Ṭabaqāt*, vol. VIII, pp. 256ff; ʿAbd al-Razzāq, *Muṣannaf*, vol. IX, nos. 16,161–4; Zurqānī, *Sharḥ*, vol. IV, pp. 90ff. All the classical collections of Prophetic Ḥadīth also cite at least one version. In this tradition ʿĀʾisha volunteers to buy a female *mukātab* by the name Barīra in order to free her, or to pay off the *kitāba* on her behalf, provided that she, ʿĀʾisha, gets the *walāʾ*; but though the owners are willing to part with Barīra, they insist on retaining the *walāʾ*. The Prophet settles the question by decreeing that the *walāʾ* always belongs to the manumitter, in this case ʿĀʾisha, or in other words that it can no longer be retained than it can be bought or sold. But in several versions he proceeds to make a speech, saying 'what is in the minds of people who make stipulations which are not in the book of God?', pronouncing such stipulations to be void and laying down that 'God's decree comes first and His stipulation is more binding'. Given that the book of God says nothing about *walāʾ*, the point of this speech is obscure. As has been seen, however, manumitters by *kitāba* were in the habit of reserving a right to part or all of the *mukatāb*'s estate, and the lawyers' response to such stipulations was precisely that 'God stipulated first', 'God's stipulations come before yours' (cf. above, Chapter 5, p. 71 and note 84 thereto). What Barīra's owners wished to retain would thus appear to have been an indefeasible right to part or all of her estate; and what the tradition condemns is both such stipulations and the trade in them: people have no right arbitrarily to lay down what rights should or should not arise from a manumission or to whom they should accrue.

140 Cf. above, note 79.

7. Conclusion

1 H. Delehaye (ed.), 'Passio sanctorum sexaginta', *Analecta Bollandiana* 1904, p. 302.

2 Cf. above, Chapter 4, note 37.

3 Cf. above, Chapter 4, note 116.

4 Cf. above, Chapter 3, p. 41.

5 Greek, Syriac and Coptic sources alike simply transliterate it (see for example P. Nessana III, 72; F. Nau, 'Notice historique sur le monastère de Qartamin', *Actes du XIV*[e] *Congrès internationale des Orientalistes*, part ii, Paris 1907, p. 95 = 84; A. Dietrich, *Arabische Briefe aus der Papyrussammlung der Hamburger Staats- und Universitäts-Bibliothek*, Hamburg 1955, p. 224).

6 *Encyclopaedia of Islam*[2], *s.v.* 'mawlā'. For the appearance of the patron's name next to that of the client in administrative records, see K. Morimoto, *The Fiscal Administration of Egypt in the Early Islamic Period*, Kyoto 1981, pp. 130f.

7 Cf. Crone, *Slaves on Horses*, Ch. 3.

8 That is Sarjūn b. Manṣūr (Crone, *Slaves on Horses*, note 358).

9 That it was an institution of Syrian origin is perhaps also suggested by the fact that the Syrians were particularly attached to it. One of the Companion traditions on the subject preserved by the Ḥanafīs invokes the opinion of ʿUmar I via a Syrian authority, Abū'l-Ashʿath al-Ṣanʿānī, a *tābiʿ* who settled in Damascus where he died in the reign of Muʿāwiya (Abū Yūsuf, *Ikhtilāf Abī Ḥanīfa wa-Ibn Abī Laylā*, ed. A.-W. al-Afghānī, Hyderabad 1358, p. 89; note how the version cited by Sarakhsī, *Mabsūṭ*, vol. VIII, p. 91, modifies the wording to bring it into accord with Ḥanafī doctrine). The classical tradition on *walāʾ al-islām* (*man aslama ʿalā yadayhi fa-huwa mawlāhu*) is also equipped with a Syrian *isnād*: the Prophet's words are transmitted by Tamīm al-Dārī, a Syrian Companion, to ʿAbdallāh b. Wahb or Mawhab, a *qāḍī* of Palestine in the reign of ʿUmar, who transmitted them to ʿAbd al-ʿAzīz b. ʿUmar, an Umayyad prince (see for example ʿAbd al-Razzāq *Muṣannaf*, vol. IX, no. 16,271). And it was a Syrian, Yaḥyā b. Ḥamza (a *qāḍī* of Damascus who died in 799), who improved on the *isnād* by inserting Qabīṣa b. Dhuʾayb between Tamīm al-Dārī and Ibn Mawhab (Ṭirmidhī, *Ṣaḥīḥ*, vol. VIII, p. 266). Yaḥyā b. Ḥamza also credited ʿUmar II with acceptance of *walāʾ al-islām* (Ṭaḥāwī, *Mushkil al-āthār*, vol. IV, p. 53; contrast Saḥnūn, *Mudawwana*, vol. VIII, p. 73, where ʿUmar II is credited with having rejected it). Muʿāwiya b. Yaḥyā al-Ṣadifī, another Damascene who was fiscal governor of Rayy for Mahdī, provided the tradition with a completely different Syrian *isnād* going back to the Prophet (Ibn Qudāma, *Mughnī*, vol. VI, no. 4975), and there was a third Syrian *isnād* for a slightly different version of it (*ibid.*). According to Abū Zurʿa, the Damascene scholar who died in 893, the tradition came from ʿAbd al- Azīz b. ʿUmar's *kitāb* and was valid: he did not himself know of a single scholar who rejected it! (Ibn Ḥajar, *Tahdhīb*, vol. VI, p. 47; for the many who did, see below, note 11).

10 In addition to the features discussed already, the patron's right to act as marriage guardian is undoubtedly an inference from his status of agnatic heir: the topic is not discussed in pre-classical law. The same is true of his eligibility for the custody of the client's children, discussed by the Mālikīs only.

11 *Walāʾ al-islām* is said to have been rejected already by Ḥasan al-Baṣrī (d. A.H. 110) (Ibn Abī Shayba, *Muṣannaf*, vol. XI, no. 11,631; Bukhārī, *Recueil*, vol. IV, p. 289; Ibn Qudāma, *Mughnī*, vol. VI, no. 4975); and Shaʿbī is credited with the maxim *lā walāʾ illā lī-dhi'l-niʿma* [*sc.* manumitter] which was in due course to be ascribed to the Prophet (Ibn Abī Shayba, *op. cit.*, vol. XI, no. 11,633; Shāfiī, *Umm*, vol. VII, p. 121; Saḥnūn, *Mudawwana*, vol. VIII, p. 73; Sarakhsī, *Mabsūṭ*, vol. VIII, p. 91, etc). Whether this information is correct or not is hard to say, but that concerning the next generation is presumably historical. Ibn Abī Laylā (d. A.H. 148) rejected *walāʾ* over converts, while Abū Ḥanīfa accepted it only if the convert made a separate agreement of *muwālāt* (Shāfiʿī, *loc. cit.*; compare ʿAbd al-Razzāq, *Muṣannaf*, vol. VI, nos. 9872–5; vol. IX, 16,160, 16,272, 16,275). The Syrian Awzāʿī (d. A.H. 157) similarly rejected it, though other Syrians did not (Siyāghī, *Rawḍ*, vol. V, p. 76; cf. above, note 9). In Medina Yaḥyā b. Saʿīd al-Anṣārī (d. A.H. 143) accepted it only in respect of converts in *dār al-ḥarb* (Ṭirmidhī, *Ṣaḥīḥ*, vol. VIII, p. 283; Saḥnūn, *Mudawwana*, vol. VIII, p. 73), and Mālik also considered *dhimmī* converts to be *mawālī* of the Muslims at large on a par with any other Muslim devoid of agnates (Saḥnūn, *loc. cit.*). But Rabīʿat al-Raʾy (d. A.H. 136) accepted it in respect of *dhimmī* and *ḥarbī* converts alike (Ṭaḥāwī, *Mushkil al-āthār*, vol. IV, p. 53; Ṭirmidhī, *Ṣaḥīḥ*, vol. VIII, p. 283), as did the Egyptian Layth b. Saʿd (d. A.H. 175), a pupil of the Medinese (Ṭirmidhī, *loc. cit.*). Shāfiʿī emphatically rejected it (*Umm*, vol. IV, pp. 55f. vol. VI, pp. 186f; vol. VII, p. 121), but Isḥāq b. Rāhūyah accepted it (Ibn al-Murtaḍā, *Baḥr*, vol. IV, p. 227; Ibn Qudāma, *Mughnī*, vol. VI, no. 4975; Baghdādī, *Ishrāf*, vol. II, p. 308), as did Ibn Ḥanbal according to some (Ibn

Qudāma, *loc. cit.*; Baghdādī *loc. cit.*; the Ḥanbalīs did not). Thereafter positions seem to have stabilised. The Imāmīs adopted the same position as the Ḥanafīs, the Qāsimīs the same as Yaḥyā b. Saʿīd, the Nāṣirīs that of the Sunnīs at large. For the Ibāḍīs, see above, Chapter 3, note 9.

12 Cf. Schacht, 'Foreign Elements', p. 128.

13 An impression one is apt to derive from Nallino, 'Considerazioni'; FitzGerald, 'Alleged Debt'.

14 Mitteis, *Reichsrecht und Volksrecht*, p. 62; id., 'Zwei griechische Rechtsurkunden aus Kurdistan', *Zeitschrift der Savigny-Stiftung für Rechtsgeschichte* 1915, p. 426.

15 Sachau, *Syrische Rechtsbücher*, vol. III, p. 8 = 9.

16 Cf. Mitteis, *Reichsrecht und Volksrecht*, p. 61.

17 Cf. above, Chapter 6, note 130.

18 Buckland, *Text-Book*, pp. 481f.

19 Cf. Schacht, *Introduction*, p. 9n; id., *Origins*, p. 264.

20 Cf. above, Chapter 4, p. 53.

21 The evidence is set out in Nallino, 'Affratellamento', where the conclusion is however somewhat negative.

22 Cf. the superb account by Maine, *Ancient Law*, London 1917, Ch. 6.

23 Maine, *Ancient Law*, pp. 102, 116.

24 A. S. Diamond, *Primitive Law Past and Present*, London 1971, pp. 254f, 259, with reference to African and other cattle-rearers.

25 Maine, *Ancient Law*, pp. 116f, 165, on later Germanic and Hindu law; L. Pospíšil, *Anthropology of Law, a Comparative Theory*, New York, San Francisco and London 1971, pp. 305ff, on to Kapauku Papuans.

26 Mitteis, *Reichsrecht und Volksrecht*, pp. 68f, 332ff, 372ff; Harrison, *Law of Athens*, pp. 149ff; Rädle, *Untersuchungen*, pp. 39, 128ff; H. Kreller, *Erbrechtliche Untersuchungen auf Grund der Graeco-Ägyptischen Papyrusurkunden*, Leipzig and Berlin 1919, pp. 178ff.

27 For two random examples, see M. Bloch, *Feudal Society*, London 1965, vol. I, pp. 132f, 141f; L. Mair, *African Societies*, Cambridge 1974, p. 58.

28 Kreller, *Erbrechtliche Untersuchungen*, pp. 179ff; M. San Nicolò, *Die Schlussklauseln der altbabylonischen Kauf- und Tauschverträge*[2], Munich 1974, pp. 160f; A. Skaist, 'Inheritance Laws and their Social Background', *Journal of the American Oriental Society* 1975, pp. 244ff.

29 Cf. E. W. West (tr.), *Pahlavi Texts*, part ii (= F. M. Müller (ed.), *The Sacred Books of the East*, vol. XVIII), Oxford 1882, pp. 183ff, where restrictions are placed on testamentary dispositions and gifts in death sickness.

30 H. J. Wolff, 'Rezeption der Beispruchsrecht ins byzantinische Reichsrecht?', *Syntaleia Vicenzo Arangio-Ruiz*, vol. I, Naples 1964.

31 Kreller, *Erbrechtliche Untersuchungen*, pp. 197f.

32 Sachau, *Syrische Rechtsbücher*, vol. III, p. 176 = 177; cf. above, Chapter 1, note 117.

33 Ibn Bābūyah, *ʿIlal al-sharāʾiʿ*, Najaf 1963, pp. 566f; Ṭūsī, *Tahdhīb*, vol. IX, no. 771.

34 For the various versions of this tradition see R. M. Speight, 'The Will of Saʿd b. a. Waqqāṣ: the Growth of a Tradition', *Der Islam* 1973; D. S. Powers, 'The Will of Saʿd b. Abî Waqqâṣ: a Reassessment', *Studia Islamica* 1983.

35 Coulson, *History*, pp. 65ff; cf. *id.*, *Succession*, pp. 213ff.

36 Powers, 'The Will of Saʿd'.

37 According to Coulson, the problem was the relationship between two systems of devolution, Qurʾānic and testamentary. But according to Powers, the Qurʾānic shares once applied to intestate succession alone, and the problem was the extent to which testators could disinherit close relatives in the absence of Qurʾānic limits.

38 Schacht, *Origins*, pp. 201f (tentatively); id., 'Modernism and Traditionalism', pp. 392ff (more dogmatically).

39 For valid criticisms of Schacht's argument, see Coulson, *History*, pp. 65ff; Powers, 'The Will of Saʿd', p. 37n. The account of the cultural origins of the limitation offered in Crone and Cook, *Hagarism*, pp. 149ff, is also wrong, partly for the reasons given by Powers ('The Will of Saʿd', p. 38n), and partly because it concentrates on the figure of one third rather than the rationale behind the rule in Islamic and provincial law.

40 Ṭūsī, *Istibṣār*, vol. III, part 2, no. 459; Kulīnī, *Kāfī*, vol. VII, pp. 7ff (five versions).

41 The tradition refers to the man who had no relatives at all, be they close or remote, and no

imām ẓāhir, according to Ṭūsī (*Istibṣār*, vol. IV, no. 459). This is clearly not correct. The tradition makes no reference to the presence of relatives or otherwise, and another tradition explicitly states that a man *who has children* may dispose of his property as he wishes as long as he is alive [be it by testament or otherwise], cf. Kulīnī, *Kāfī*, vol. VII, p. 8 (three versions). But Ṭūsī's comment is correct in terms of classical Imāmı law.

42 Ṭūsī, *Tahdhīb*, vol. IX, pp. 195f, no. 785; Kulīnī, *Kafī*, vol. VII, pp. 7f.

43 Ṭūsī is very embarrassed by the fact that the imams seem to be acting contrary to *sharīʿat al-islām* in his traditions (which explicitly state that they accepted such wills) and suggests various ways out; Kulīnī's tradition adds that the imam only took a third.

44 D. L. O'Leary, *A Short History of the Fatimid Khalifate*, London 1923, p. 133, without reference; Maqrīzī, *Ittiʿaẓ al-ḥunafāʾ*, ed. M. H. M. Aḥmad, Cairo 1971, vol. II, p. 33 (I owe this reference to D. S. Richards). The caliph (Ḥākim) refused to accept the will, letting the sons take the entire estate, but this was meant as a gesture of magnanimity, not as a statement on law.

45 ʿAbd al-Razzāq, *Muṣannaf*, vol. IX, nos. 16,375, 16,398.

46 Raddatz, *Stellung*, p. 49.

47 ʿAbd al-Razzāq, *Muṣannaf*, vol. IX, nos. 16,361–5. The *isnāds* are Iraqi.

48 Cf. Ibn Rushd, *Bidāya*, vol. II, p. 368.

49 ʿAbd al-Razzāq, *Muṣannaf*, vol. IX, no. 16,363, with reference to Qur. 8:42, on God's fifth.

50 *Ibid.*, no. 16,366.

51 Ibn Qudāma, *Mughnī*, vol. VI, no. 4670; Ibn Rushd, *Bidāya*, vol. II, p. 368; cf. ʿAbd al-Razzāq, *Muṣannaf*, vol. IX, nos. 16,371, 16,373f.

52 Ibn Qudāma, *Mughnī*, vol. VI, no. 4670; cf. ʿAbd al-Razzāq, *Muṣannaf*, vol. IX, no. 16,370.

53 Ibn Rushd, *Bidāya*, vol. II, p. 368.

54 Ibn Qudāma, *Mughnī*, vol. VI, no. 4670. The same view is implied in traditions in which slaves freed *sāʾibatan* will away their entire estates (cf. above Chapter 6, note 92). A tradition directed against *walāʾ al-islām* similarly allows a convert to dispose of his entire estate (Ibn Abī Shayba, *Muṣannaf*, vol. XI, no. 11,634, ascribed to Ḥasan al-Baṣrī).

55 Shaybānī, *Kitāb al-ḥujja*, vol. IV, pp. 241ff.

56 Ibn al-Murtaḍā, *Baḥr*, vol. V, p. 304; Hawsamī, *Kāfī*, fols. 151bf; id., *Ibāna* (D. 224), fol. 145a.

57 Ṭūsī, *Istibṣār*, vol. IV, nos. 459f.

58 Shammākhī, *Īḍāh*, vol. IV, p. 474.

59 Ibn Ḥazm, *Muḥallā*, vol. IX, p. 317; Ibn Rushd, *Bidāya*, vol. II, p. 368.

60 Coulson, *Succession*, p. 243; Shīrāzī, *Tanbīh*, part ii, p. 98.

61 Ibn Qudāma, *Mughnī*, vol. VI, no. 4670.

62 Ibn Ḥazm, *Muḥallā*, vol. IX, p. 317.

63 Saʿd b. Abī Waqqāṣ, who is ill in Mecca, tells the Prophet that he has no parents or children, or that his only legal heir is a daughter, asking how much he can bequeath. This is a somewhat implausible situation, given that Saʿd b. Abī Waqqās had 35 children and 11 wives in the course of his life (Ibn Saʿd, *Ṭabaqāt*, vol. III, pp. 137f), and that he always had agnates in his clan of Zuhra (a point noted by Nawawī cited by Zurqānī, *Sharḥ*, vol. IV, p. 62). Apparently, the tradition was once about another Saʿd. Some traditions link him with a certain Saʿd b. Khawla/Khawlā or Khawlī, a *ḥalīf* or *mawlā* or, we are told, two such persons, both of whom fit the situation in that such persons are likely to be devoid of agnates, and in that one is said to have died in Mecca, the other dying childless (Ibn Saʿd, *ibid.*, pp. 115, 408f). As a story about Saʿd b. Abī Waqqāṣ, the tradition is clearly spurious (contrast the version cited by Coulson, *Succession*, p. 214, where it *is* a story about him, though Coulson does not recognise him: here he has heirs whom he wishes to disinherit; Mālik is simply the *ism* of Abū Waqqās). Moreover, all versions are long and verbose, and all deal with several questions, whereas early traditions are brief and confined to a single point (several versions have the Prophet dispose of the question whether the limit applies when the purpose of the bequest is charitable).

64 Schacht was not entirely wrong as regards the Mālikīs however, for the Mālikīs hold all Muslims to be each others' heirs and restrict bequests to a third of the estate under all circumstances: the Muslims at large, represented by the Treasury, cannot be disinherited by the testator who leaves no relatives of his own (cf. Ibn Rushd, *Bidāya*, vol. II, p. 368). But it was hardly to the Umayyads that the Mālikīs owed this idea.

65 Thus also Coulson and Powers, their differences notwithstanding (cf. above, note 37).

66 Ibn Ḥazm, *Muḥallā*, vol. IX, p. 318; Ibn Rushd, *Bidāya*, vol. II, p. 368; cf. also Ṭūsī, *Tahdhīb*, vol. IX, no. 769: bequests of a quarter or fifth of the estate are preferred because bequests of a third harm the heirs.

67 Cf. Abū Ghānim, *Mudawwana*, vol. II, p. 153; Sharīf al-Murtaḍā, *Intiṣār*, p. 220; Ibn al-Murtaḍā, *Baḥr*, vol. V, pp. 305f.

68 Cf. Kreller, *Erbrechtliche Untersuchungen*, p. 182.

69 Schacht, *Origins*, pp. 201f; cf. Crone and Cook, *Hagarism*, p. 150, where the significance of this point has been misunderstood; Mitteis, *Reichsrecht und Volksrecht*, pp. 69, 372ff; Taubenschlag, 'Privatrecht', p. 113 and the note therto; id., 'Rezeption', pp. 285f (disputed by Wolff, 'Rezeption des Beispruchsrecht'), where slaves are manumitted with the consent of the heirs.

70 Marghīnānī, *Hidāya*, part iv, p. 232; Shafiʿī, *Umm*, vol. IV, p. 33; Khalīl, *Sommario*, vol. II, p. 795; Ibn Qudāma, *Mughnī*, vol. VI, no. 4543; Tūsī, *Nihāya*, p. 608; cf. id., *Istibṣār*, vol. III, part ii, nos. 463–7; Ibn al-Murtaḍā, *Baḥr*, vol. V, p. 306; Mu'ayyad, *Tajrīd*, fol. 111b; Abu Ghānim, *Mudawwana*, vol. II, pp. 191, 195; Shammākhī, *Īḍāh*, vol. IV, p. 474; Ibn Ḥazm, *Muḥallā*, vol. IX, p. 317.

71 P. Nesana III, 57.

72 See the literature cited above, Chapter 1, notes 48–9.

73 Kraemer, *Excavations at Nessana*, vol. III, p. 163.

74 M. A. Friedman, 'The Ransom-Divorce: Divorce Proceedings Initiated by theWife in Mediaeval Jewish Practice', *Israel Oriental Studies* 1976, pp. 303ff.

75 Cf. Linant de Bellefonds, *Traité de droit musulman comparé*, vol. II, pp. 419ff.

76 Friedman, 'Ransom-Divorce'; cf. id., 'Divorce upon the Wife's Demand as Reflected in Manuscripts from the Cairo Geniza', *The Jewish Law Annual* 1981, where further documents are edited and translated.

77 Friedman, 'Ransom-Divorce', pp. 301f; id., 'Divorce upon the Wife's Demand', pp. 104ff.

78 Friedman, 'Ransom Divorce', p. 302; E. Lipiński, 'The Wife's Right to Divorce in the Light of an Ancient Near Eastern Tradition', *The Jewish Law Annual* 1981, pp. 21ff.

79 Contrast the *qasāma* which, though fairly recognizable in its Iraqi version, is far less recognisable in its Medinese version than is manumission by *kitāba* (Crone, 'Jāhilī and Jewish law'; cf. also Crone and Cook, *Hagarism*, pp. 97ff).

80 Koschaker, *Rechtsurkunden*, pp. 43ff.

81 D. Daube, 'The Scales of Justice', *Juridical Review* 1951, p. 109 (an attempt to explain why this should be so).

82 Koschaker, *Rechtsurkunden*, pp. 46, 47n.

83 *Al-ʿitq lā yubaʿʿaḍu* (Hawsamī, *Ibāna* (D. 225), fol. 240a; Hawsamī, *Ifāda*, fol. 55a).

84 Cf. the striking example in Saḥnūn, *Mudawwana*, vol. VII, p. 85. Mālikī law decrees that a *mukātab* who defaults is re-enslaved, but the manumitter himself may not stipulate this, according to Saḥnūn, since it is up to the authorities to decide whether and when it is to happen.

85 Ibn Ḥazm, *Muḥallā*, vol. IX, p. 318.

86 Maine, *Ancient Law*, pp. 79f.

87 Cf. Coulson, *History*, pp. 113ff; id., *Succession*, Ch. 8.

88 For Sasanid law, see the example given in P. Crone, review of M. Macuch, *International Journal of Middle East Studies* 1983, p. 425.

Works cited

I. Papyri

When papyri are referred to in the form P. Oxy. III, 494, the Roman numeral refers to the volume of the publication in which the papyrus is to be found, the Arabic numeral to the number of the papyrus in that volume or publication.

P. Berlin 13,002 in A. Grohmann (ed. and tr.), 'Arabische Papyri aus den staatlichen Museen zu Berlin', *Der Islam* 1935.

BGU I, 96; II, 567 in Ägyptische Urkunden aus den königlichen [later *staatlichen*] *Museen zu Berlin, griechische Urkunden*, Berlin 1895–1981.

Brooklyn 5 in E. G. Kraeling (ed. and tr.), *The Brooklyn Museum Aramaic Papyri*, New Haven 1953.

P. Cair. B. É. ta'rikh no. 1900 in A. Grohmann (ed.), *Arabic Papyri in the Egyptian Library*, vol. i, Cairo 1934.

CPR 18, in *Corpus Papyrorum Raineri, Griechische Texte*, vol. i, ed. C. Wessely, Vienna 1895.

P. Daris inv. no. 46 in S. Daris, 'Note sui liberti' *Studia Papyrologica* 1979.

P. Dura 10 in M. I. Rostovtzeff and C. B. Welles (eds. and trs.), *A Parchment Contract of Loan from Dura Europos on the Euphrates* (= *Yale Classical Studies*, vol. ii), New Haven 1931.

P. Elephantine 3, 4 in O. Rubensohn (ed.), *Elephantine-Papyri*, Berlin 1907.

P. Köln II, 102; III, 157 in B. Kramer and others (eds. and trs.), *Kölner Papyri*, Opladen 1976–85.

P. Meyer Jur. Pap. 8 in P. M. Meyer (ed.), *Juristische Papyri*, Berlin 1920.

P. Nessana II, 1, 2, 11, 12 in L. Casson and E. L. Hettich (eds. and trs.), *Excavations at Nessana*, vol. ii, Princeton 1950.

P. Nessana III, 18, 56, 57, 72 in C. J. Kraemer, Jr., (ed. and tr.) *Excavations at Nessana*, vol. iii, Princeton 1958.

P. Oxy. III, 494; IV, 706; IX, 1205; XIX, 2238 in B. P. Grenfell, A. S. Hunt and others (eds. and trs.), *The Oxyrhynchus Papyri*, London 1898–1981.

P. Petrie I, 15, re-edited as III, 2 in *The Flinders Petrie Papyri*, ed. and tr. J. P. Mahaffy and J. G. Smyly, Dublin 1891–1905.

PSI IX, 1040; XII, 1263 in *Papiri greci e latini (Pubblicazioni della società italiana)*, Firenze 1912–79.

II. Muslim lawbooks

Ḥadith collections are listed in the next section except insofar as they are statements of school doctrine.

(a) Ḥanafī

Abū Yūsuf, Yaʿqūb b. Ibrāhīm, *Ikhtilāf Abī Ḥanīfa wa-Ibn Abī Laylā*, ed. A.-W. al-Afghānī, Hyderabad 1358.
Marghīnānī, ʿAlī b. Abī Bakr al-, *al-Hidāya*, Cairo n.d.
Qudūrī, Aḥmad b. Muḥammad al-, *Le statut personel en droit musulman hanéfite*, ed. and tr. G.-H. Bousquet and L. Bercher, [Tunis] 1952.
Sarakhsī, Muḥammad b. Aḥmad al-, *al-Mabsūṭ*, Cairo 1324–31.
Shaybānī, Muḥammad b. al-Ḥasan al-. *al-Jāmiʿ al-kabīr*, ed. A.-W. al-Afghānī, Cairo 1356.
Kitāb al-aṣl, ed. A.-W. al-Afghānī, Hyderabad 1966– .
Kitāb al-ḥujja ʿalā ahl al-Madīna, ed. A.-W. al-Afghānī, Hyderabad 1965–71.
Kitāb al-makhārij fīl-ḥiyal, ed. J. Schacht, Leipzig 1930.

(b) Mālikī

Baghdādī, ʿAbd al-Wahhāb al-, *al-Ishrāf ʿalā masāʾil al-khilāf*, Tunis n.d.
Ibn Rushd, Muḥammad b. Aḥmad, *Bidāyat al-mujtahid*, ed. M. S. al-Muḥaysin and Sh. M. Ismāʿīl, Cairo 1970–4.
Khalīl, *Sommario* = I. Guidi and D. Santillana (trs.) *Il "Muḫtasar" o sommario del diritto malechita*, Milan 1919.
Kharashī, Muḥammad b. ʿAbdallāh al-, *Sharḥ ʿalāʾl-mukhtaṣar*, Cairo 1307–8.
Mālik b. Anas, *al-Muwaṭṭaʾ*, Cairo n.d.
Saḥnūn, ʿAbd al-Salām b. Saʿīd, *al-Mudawwana al-kubrā*, Cairo 1323–4.
Zurqānī, Muḥammad b. ʿAbd al-Bāqī al-, *Sharḥ ʿalā muwaṭṭaʾ al-imām Mālik*, n. p. 1936.

(c) Shāfiʿī

Nawawī, Abū Zakariyyāʾ Yaḥyā al-, *Minhāj al-ṭālibīn*, ed. L. W. C. van den Berg, Batavia 1882–4.
Shāfiʿī, Muḥammad b. Idrīs al-, *Kitāb al-umm*, Būlāq 1321–6.
Shīrāzī, Ibrāhīm b. ʿAlī al-, *Kitāb al-tanbīh*, tr. G.-H. Bousquet, Alger [1949–52].
Shirbīnī, Muḥammad b. Aḥmad al-, *Mughnī al-muḥtāj*, [Cairo 1308].

(d) Ḥanbalī

Ibn Qudāma, ʿAbdallāh b. Aḥmad, *al-Mughnī*, ed. T. M. al-Zaynī, A. ʿA. al-Fāyid and ʿA. A. al-ʿAṭāʾ, Cairo 1968–70.
Le Précis de droit d'Ibn Qudāma, tr. H. Laoust, Beirut 1950.

(e) Imāmī

ʿĀmilī, Muḥammad al-Jawād b. Muḥammad al-Ḥusaynī al-, *Miftāḥ al-karāma fī sharḥ qawāʿid al-ʿallāma*, Cairo 1326.
Ḥillī, Jaʿfar b. al-Ḥasan al-, *Sharāʾiʿ al-islām*, ed. ʿA. M. ʿAlī, Najaf 1969.
Ḥillī, Jaʿfar b. Saʿīd al-, *Nukat al-nihāya*, in *al-Jawāmiʿ al-fiqhiyya*, Tehran 1276. (Unpaginated lithograph, cited in the foliation of the copy in the British Library.)
Ibn Bābūyah, Muḥammad b. ʿAlī, *ʿIlal al-sharāʾiʿ*, Najaf 1963.
Man lā yaḥḍuruhuʾl-faqīh, ed. H. M. al-Khursān, Tehran 1390.
al-Muqniʿ, in *al-Jawāmiʿ al-fiqhiyya*, Tehran 1276. (Unpaginated lithograph cited in the foliation of the copy in the British Library.)

Sharīf al-Murtaḍā, ʿAlī b. al-Ḥusayn al-, *al-Intiṣār*, Najaf 1971.
Ṭūsī, Muḥammad b. al-Ḥasan al-, *Kitāb al-istibṣār*, ed. H.M. al-Khursān, Tehran 1390.
Kitāb al-khilāf, [Tehran] n.d.
al-Mabsūṭ fī fiqh al-imāmiyya, ed. M. T. al-Kashfī, Tehran 1387.
al-Nihāya, Beirut 1970.
Tahdhīb al-aḥkām, ed. H. M. al-Khursān, Tehran 1390.

(f) Ismāʿīlī

Nuʿmān b. Muḥammad, *Daʿāʾ im al-islām*, ed. A. ʿA. A. al-Fayḍī, Cairo 1951–60.
Kitāb al-iqtiṣār, ed. M. W. Mirzā, Damascus 1957.

(g) Zaydī

Hawsamī, Abū Jaʿfar Muḥammad b. Yaʿqūb al-, *Kitāb al-kāfī*, MS Ambrosiana, H. 137. (Cf. Sezgin, *Geschichte*, vol. I, p. 571, nos. 15–16, where this manuscript has been omitted.)
Kitāb sharḥ al-ibāna, MS Ambrosiana, D. 224.
Sharḥ al-ibāna, MS Ambrosiana, D. 225.
al-Juzʾ al-thānī min sharḥ al-ibāna fī'l-fiqh, MS Ambrosiana, E. 262. (Cf. Sezgin, *Geschichte*, vol. I, p. 567. Its title notwithstanding, this work is a straightforward exposition of Nāṣirī fiqh, with frequent reference to Qāsimī and other legal opinion, not a commentary from which the text of Nāṣir's *Ibāna* can be reconstituted.)
Ḥawsamī, Abū'l-Qāsim Ḥusayn b. ʿAlī Ibn Tāl al-, *Kitāb al-ifāda*, MS British Library, Or. 4031. (Cf. Sezgin, Geschichte, vol. I, p. 570, no. 14).
Ibn al-Murtaḍā, Aḥmad b. Yaḥyā, *Kitāb al-baḥr al-zakhkhār*, Cairo and Baghdad 1947–9.
al-Mu'ayyad bi'llāh, Aḥmad b. al-Ḥusayn, *al-Tajrīd*, MS Ambrosiana, G. 7. (Cf. Sezgin, *Geschichte*, vol. I, p. 570.)
Naḥwī, al-Ḥasan b. Muḥammad al-, *al-Tadhkira al-fākhira fī fiqh al-ʿitra al-ṭāhira*, MS British Library, Or. 3809. (Cf. C. Brockelmann, *Geschichte der arabischen Literatur*[2], vol. II, Leiden 1949, p. 237.)
Siyāghī, al-Ḥusayn b. Aḥmad al-, *Kitāb al-rawḍ al-naḍīr*, completed by ʿAbbās b. Aḥmad al-Ḥasanī, Cairo 1347–49.

(h) Ibāḍī

Abū Ghānim Bishr b. Ghānim al-Khurāsānī, *al-Mudawwana al-kubrā*, ed. M. Aṭfayyish, Beirut 1974.
Abū Isḥāq Ibrāhīm b. Qays al-Hamdānī, *Kitāb mā lā yasaʿu jahluhu*, MS British Library, Or. 3744. (Cf. C. Rieu, *Supplement to the Catalogue of Arabic Manuscripts in the British Museum*, London 1894, vol. II, p. 762; J. Schacht, 'Bibliothèques et manuscripts abadites', *Revue Africaine* 1956, p. 383, where what is doubtless the same work is entitled *Mukhtaṣar al-khiṣāl*.)
Aṭfayyish, Muḥammad b. Yūsuf, *Sharḥ al-nīl wa-shifāʾ al-ʿalīl*, vol. VIII, Cairo 1343.
Basyānī, ʿAlī b. Muḥammad al-, *Kitāb mukhtaṣar al-Basyawī [sic]*, ed. ʿA. Q. ʿAṭāʾ and M. Z. Zarqā, printed for the Ministry of the National Heritage, Sultanate of Oman, n.p., n.d.
Shammākhī, ʿĀmir b. ʿAlī al-, *Kitāb al-īḍāḥ*, Beirut 1971.

(i) Other

Ibn Ḥazm, ʿAlī b. Aḥmad, *al-Muḥallā*, ed. M. M. al-Dimashqī, Cairo 1347–52.
H.-P. Raddatz (ed.), 'Frühislamisches Erbrecht, nach dem Kitāb al-farā'iḍ des Sufyān aṯ-Ṯaurī. Edition und Kommentar', *Die Welt des Islams* 1971.

III. Other works

When references are given in the form 'p. 1 = 6', the first figure refers to the text and the second to the translation. When they are given in the form 'p. 40⁷', the main figure refers to the page and the superscript to either the line (in the case of texts) or the note on that page (in the case of modern works). Superscripts are also used to indicate the edition used (e.g. *Arabs in History*[4]). The form '40:7' is used in connection with the Qur'ān and, where possible, poetry: the first figure refers to the sura or poem, the second to the verse within that sura or poem.

All references to the *Zeitschrift der Savigny-Stiftung für Rechtsgeschichte* are to the *Romanistische Abteilung* of that periodical. All references to the Qur'ān are to the Flügel edition.

ʿAbbās b. Mirdās, *Dīwān*, ed. Y. al-Jubūrī, Baghdad 1968.
ʿAbd al-Razzāq b. Hammām al-Ṣanʿānī, *al-Muṣannaf*, ed. Ḥ.-R. al-Aʿẓamī, Beirut 1970–2.
Abū Dāwūd Sulaymān b. al-Ashʿath, *Saḥīḥ sunan al-muṣṭafā*, Cairo 1348.
Abū Ghānim, see above, II (h).
Abū Ḥanīfa Nuʿmān b. Thābit (attrib.), *al-Musnad*, ed. Ṣ. al-Ṣaqqā, Aleppo 1962.
Abū Isḥāq, see above, II (h).
Abū Tammām, Ḥabīb b. Aws, *Hamasae carminae cum Tebrisii scholiis*, ed. G. Freytag, Bonn 1828.
Abū Yūsuf, see above, II (a).
Adams, B., *Paramoné und verwandte Texte*, Berlin 1964.
Aghānī, see Iṣbahānī.
Akhṭal, Ghiyāth b. Ghawth al-. *Shiʿr*, ed. F.-D. Qabāwa, Aleppo [1970]–71.
ʿĀmir b. Ṭufayl, see Lyall.
ʿAlqama b. ʿAbāda, *Dīwān*, ed. M. Ben Cheneb, Algiers 1925.
ʿĀmilī, see above, II (e).
Amos, S., *The History and Principles of the Civil Law of Rome*, London 1883.
Ankum, J. A., '"Utilitatis Causa Receptum". On the Pragmatic Methods of the Roman Lawyers', *Symbolae Iuridicae et Historicae Martino David Dedicata*, Leiden 1968.
ʿAntara b. Shaddād, *Dīwān*, tr. A. Wormhoudt, William Penn College 1974. See also Shalabī.
Aphthonius, see Rabe.
ʿĀrif al-ʿĀrif, *Kitāb al-qaḍā' bayna'l-badw*, Jerusalem 1933 = L. Haefeli (tr.), *Die Beduinen von Beerseba*, Luzern 1938.
Ashkenazi, T., *Tribus semi-nomades de la Palestine du Nord*, Paris 1938.
Aṭfayyish, see above, II (h).

Baars, W., and P. A. H. de Boer, 'Ein neugefundenes Fragment des syrisch-römischen Rechtsbuches', *Symbolae Iuridicae et Historicae Martino David Dedicata*, Leiden 1968.
Babakos, A. M., 'Adoption von Freigelassenen im alt-griechischen Recht', *Syntaleia Vicenzio Arangio-Ruiz*, Naples 1964.
'Le droit de famille appliqué a l'île de Calymnos au Iᵉʳ siècle après J. C.', *Revue Internationale des Droits de l'Antiquité* 1964.

'Zur angeblichen Freilassung mit anschliessender Adoption in Kalymna', *Zeitschrift der Savigny-Stiftung für Rechtsgeschichte* 1963.
Babylonian Talmud.
Badian, E., *Foreign Clientelae*, Oxford 1958.
Baghdādī, see above II (b).
Baillie, N. B. E., *A Digest of Moohumudan Law*, London 1875–87.
Bakrī, Abū ʿUbaydallāh b. ʿAbd al-ʿAzīz al-, *Kitāb muʿjam mā istaʿjam*, ed. F. Wüstenfeld, Göttingen and Paris 1876–7.
Balādhurī, Aḥmad b. Yaḥyā al-, *Ansāb al-ashrāf*, vol. I, ed. M. Ḥamīdullāh, Cairo 1959; vol. IV a, ed. M. Schloessinger and M. J. Kister, Jerusalem 1971; vol. V, ed. S. D. F. Goitein, Jerusalem 1936.
Kitāb futūḥ al-buldān, ed. M. J. de Goeje, Leiden 1866.
Bamberger, B. J., *Proselytism in the Talmudic Period*[2], New York 1968.
Bāqillānī, Muḥammad b. al-Ṭayyib al-, *Kitāb al-tamhīd*, ed. M. M. al-Khuḍayrī and M. A.-H. Abū Rīdah, Cairo 1947.
Basyānī, see above, II (h).
Bayḍāwī, ʿAbdallāh b. ʿUmar al-, *Anwār al-tanzīl wa-astrār al-taʾwīl*, Istanbul n. d.
Bayhaqī, Aḥmad b. al-Ḥusayn al-, *Kitāb al-sunan al-kubrā*, Hyderabad 1344–55.
Becker, C. H., *Beiträge zur Geschichte Ägyptens under dem Islam*, Strassburg 1902–3.
Islamstudien, Leipzig 1924–36.
'Zur Entstehung der Waqfinstitution', *Der Islam* 1911.
Beeston, A. F. L., 'Kingship in Ancient Arabia', *Journal of the Economic and Social History of the Orient* 1972.
Berchem, M. van, *La propriété territoriale et l'impôt foncier sous les premiers califes*, Geneva 1896.
Berg, L. W. C. van den, *De contractu 'do ut des' iure mohammedano*, Leiden and Batavia 1868.
Bergh, S. van den, *Averroes' Tahafut al-tahafut*, London 1954.
Bergsträsser, G., 'Anfänge und Charakter des juristischen Denkens im Islam', *Der Islam* 1925.
Bevan, A. A., (ed.), *The Naḳaʾiḍ of Jarīr and al-Farazdaḳ*, Leiden 1905–12.
Bloch, M., *Die Freilassungsbedingungen der delphischen Freilassungsinschriften*, Strassburg 1914.
Bloch, M., *Feudal Society*, London 1965.
Blunt, A., *Bedouin of the Euphrates*, London 1879.
Bonfante, P., *Corso di diritto romano*, vol. I, Rome 1925.
Bousquet, G.-H., 'Le mystère de la formation et des origines du fiqh', *Revue Algérienne, Tunisienne et Marocaine de Législation et de la jurisprudence* 1947.
Brown, P., 'Understanding Islam', *The New York Review of Books*, February 22, 1979.
Bruns, K. G., and E. Sachau (eds. and trs.), *Syrisch-römischen Rechtsbuch*, Leipzig 1880.
Brunschvig, R., 'Considérations sociologiques sur le droit musulman ancien', *Studia Islamica* 1955.
'Herméneutique normative dans le judaïsme et dans l'Islam', *Atti della Accademia Nazionale dei Lincei* (Rendiconti, vol. xxx, Rome) 1975.
'Métiers vils en Islam', *Studia Islamica* 1962.
'Polémiques médiévales autour du rite de Malik', *al-Andalus* 1950.
'Un système peu connu de succession agnatique dans le droit musulman', *Revue de Droit Français et Étranger* 1950.
Buckland, W. W., *The Roman Law of Slavery*, Cambridge 1908.
A Text-Book of Roman Law from Augustus to Justinian[3], ed. P. Stein, Cambridge 1966.

Bukhārī, Muḥammad b. Ismā'īl al-, *Le recueil des traditions mahométanes*, ed. L. Krehl and T. W. Juhnboll, Leiden 1862–1908.
Bulsara, S. J., (tr.), *The Laws of the Ancient Persians*, Bombay 1937.
Burckhardt, J. L., *Notes on the Bedouins and Wahábys*, published by the Association for Promoting the Discovery of the Interior of Africa, London 1830.
Bussi, E., *Ricerche intorno alle relazioni fra retratto bizantino e musulmano*, Milan 1933.

Calderini, A., *La manomissione e la condizione dei liberti in Grecia*, Milan 1908.
Cameron, A., *Agathias*, Oxford 1970.
Cameron, A., 'Inscriptions relating to Sacral Manumission and Confession', *Harvard Theological Review* 1939.
Carusi, E., *Diritto e filologia*, Bologna 1925.
Caskel, W., 'Ein missverständniss in den Mufaḍḍalīyāt', *Oriens* 1954.
Casson and Hettich, *Nessana*, see above, I.
Chabot, J.-B., (ed. and tr.), *Synodicon Orientale ou Recueil de Synodes Nestoriens (= Notices et extraits de manuscripts de la Bibliothèque Nationale*, vol. XXXVII), Paris 1902.
Chehata, C., *Essai d'une théorie générale de l'obligation en droit musulman hanéfite*, Paris 1969.
Chelhod, J., 'Le droit intertribal dans les hauts plateaux de Yémen', *al-Bahit, Festschrift Joseph Henninger*, Bonn 1976.
Christophilopoulos, A., 'Zu Nessana Inv. Nr. 14', *Zeitschrift der Savigny-Stiftung für Rechtsgeschichte* 1947.
Clark, D. L., *Rhetoric in Greco-Roman Education*, New York 1957.
Clarke, M. L., *Higher Education in the Ancient World*, London 1971.
Claus, H., *Ho Skholastikos*, Cologne 1965.
Cohen, B., *Jewish and Roman Law*, New York 1966.
Collinet, P., *Histoire de l'école de droit de Beyrouth*, Paris 1925.
Collitz, H., (ed.), *Sammlung der griechischen Dialektinschriften*, Göttingen 1884–1915.
Conrad, L. I., 'Portents of the Hour: Ḥadīth and History in the First Century A.H.', paper presented at the Colloquium on Qur'ān and Ḥadīth, Cambridge 1985.
Cook, M. A., *Early Muslim Dogma*, Cambridge 1981.
'Eschatology, History and the Dating of Traditions', paper presented at the Third International Colloquium on 'From Jāhiliyya to Islam', Jerusalem 1985, to appear in *Jerusalem Studies in Arabic and Islam*.
'Magian Cheese: an Archaic Problem in Islamic Law', *Bulletin of the School of Oriental and African Studies* 1984.
'Monotheist Sages' (forthcoming).
Coulson, N. J., *A History of Islamic Law*, Edinburgh 1964.
Succession in the Muslim Family, Cambridge 1971.
Crone, P., 'Islam, Judeo-Christianity and Byzantine Iconoclasm', *Jerusalem Studies in Arabic and Islam* 1980.
'Jāhilī and Jewish Law: the *Qasāma*', *Jerusalem Studies in Arabic and Islam* 1984.
Meccan Trade and the Rise of Islam, Princeton 1987.
review of M. Macuch in *International Journal of Middle East Studies* 1983.
Slaves on Horses, the Evolution of the Islamic Polity, Cambridge 1980.
'Weber, Islamic Law and the Rise of Capitalism', forthcoming (in German) in W. Schluchter (ed.), *Max Weber's Studie über den Islam*.
and M. Cook, *Hagarism the Making of the Islamic World*, Cambridge 1977.
and M. Hinds, *God's Caliph, Religious Authority in the First Centuries of Islam*, Cambridge 1986.

Daiber, H., *Aetius Arbus, die Vorsokratiker in arabischer Uberlieferung*, Wiesbaden 1980.
Dandamayev, M., 'The Economic and Legal Character of the Slave's Peculium in the Neo-Babylonian and Achaemenid Periods' in D. O. Edzard (ed.), *Gesellschaftsklassen im alten Zweistromland und in den angrenzenden Gebieten*, Munich 1972.
Daoualibi, M., *La jurisprudence dans le droit islamique*, Paris 1941.
Dareste, R., B. Houssoulier and T. Reinach (eds. and trs.), *Recueil des inscriptions juridiques grecques*, ser. ii, Paris 1898.
Daris, see above, I.
Daube, D., 'Rabbinic Methods of Interpretation and Hellenistic Rhetoric', *Hebrew Union College Annual* 1949.
'The Scales of Justice', *Juridical Review* 1951.
Delehaye, H., (ed.), 'Passio sanctorum sexaginta', *Analecta Bollandiana* 1904.
Dhū'l-Rumma Ghaylān b. ʿUqba, *Dīwān*, ed. C. H. H. Macartney Cambridge 1919.
Diamond, A. S., *Primitive Law Past and Present*, London 1971.
Dickson, H. R. P., *The Arab of the Desert*, London 1949.
Dietrich, A., *Arabische Briefe aus der Papyrussammlung der Hamburger Staats- und Universitätsbibliothek*, Hamburg 1955.
Dilger, K., 'Orientalistik und Rechtswissenschaft', *Deutscher Orientalistentag* 1975 (= *Zeitschrift der Deutschen Morgenländischen Gesellschaft* 1977, supplement no. 3).
Doughty, C. M., *Travels in Arabia Deserta*, London 1936 (first published 1888).
Duff, A. M., *Freedman in the Early Roman Empire*², Cambridge 1958.

Emilia, A. d', 'Roman and Muslim Law', *East and West* 1953.
Encyclopaedia Judaica, Jerusalem 1971–2.
*The Encyclopaedia of Islam*¹, Leiden 1913–38.
*The Encyclopaedia of Islam*², Leiden and London 1960– .
Enger, M., (ed.), *Maverdii constitutiones politicae*, Bonn 1853.
Ess, J. van, *Das Kitāb al-Nakt des Naẓẓām und seine Rezeption im Kitāb al-futyā des Ǧāḥiẓ*, Göttingen 1972.
Ettinghausen, R., *Arab Painting*, Cleveland 1962.

Falenciak, J., 'Note on P. Colt Inv. Nr. 13,306 – Release from *Paramonē*', *Journal of Juristic Papyrology* 1948.
Farazdaq, Tammām b. Ghālib al-, *Dīwān*, ed. and tr. R. Boucher, Paris 1870.
Fattal, A., *Le statut légal des non-musulmans en pays d'Islam*, Beirut 1958.
Finely, M. I., 'The Servile Statuses of Ancient Greece', *Revue Internationale des Droits de l'Antiquité* 1960.
FitzGerald, S. V., 'The Alleged Debt of Islamic to Roman Law', *The Law Quarterly Review* 1951.
Foster, B. R., 'Agoranomos and Muḥtasib', *Journal of the Economic and Social History of the Orient* 1970.
Fraenkl, S., 'Das Schutzrecht der Araber' in C. Bezold (ed.), *Orientalistische Studien Theodor Nöldeke gewidmet*, vol. 1, Giessen 1906.
Friedman, M. A., 'Divorce upon the Wife's Demand as Reflected in Manuscripts from the Cairo Geniza', *The Jewish Law Annual* 1981.
'The Ransom Divorce: Divorce Proceedings Initiated by the Wife in Medieval Jewish Practice', *Israel Oriental Society* 1976.

Gaius, *Institutes*, ed. and tr. F. de Zulueta, Oxford 1946–53.
Gatteschi, D., *Manuale di diritto pubblico e privato ottomano*, Alexandria 1865.

Gaudefroy-Demombynes, M., 'Un magistrat musulman: le mohtasib', *Le Journal des Savants* 1947 (review of E. Tyan).
'Sur les origines de la justice musulmane', *Mélanges syriens offerts à René Dussaud*, Paris 1939.
Girard, P. F., *Textes de droit romain*[6], ed. F. Senn, Paris 1937.
Goitein, S. D., 'A Turning Point in the History of the Muslim State', *Islamic Culture* 1949.
Goldziher, I., 'A muhammadán jogtudomány eredetéröl', *A Magyar Tudományos Akadémia*, Értehezéseh a nyelv-és széptudományok köréböl kötet XI, (Budapest) 1884.
(ed.), 'Der Dîwân des Ǵarwal b. Aus Al-Ḥuṭej'a', *Zeitschrift der Deutschen morgenländischen Gesellschaft* 1892.
'Fiḳh' in *Encyclopaedia of Islam*'.
'Die Handwerke bei den Arabern', *Globus* 1894.
Muhammedanische Studien, Halle 1889–90.
'Das Prinzip des *Istiṣḥāb* in der muhammedanischen Gesetzwissenschaft', *Wiener Zeitschrift für die Kunde des Morgenlandes* 1887.
'The Principles of Law in Islam' in H. S. Williams (ed.), *The Historians' History of the World*, London 1907, vol. VIII.
'Die Religion des Islams' in P. Hinneberg (ed.), *Die Kultur des Gegenwart*, vol. I, part iii, Berlin and Leipzig 1906.
review of C. H. Becker in *Deutsche Literaturzeitung* 1902–3.
review of Savvas Pacha in *Byzantinische Zeitschrift* 1893.
review of F. F. Schmidt in *Deutsche Literaturzeitung* 1911.
Goto, A., 'An Aspect of Arab Society of the Early Seventh Century', *Orient* (Tokyo) 1976.
Grabar, O., *The Formation of Islamic Art*, New Haven and London 1973.
Great Britain, Naval Intelligence Division, *A Handbook of Arabia*, [London] 1916–17.
Griffini, E., (ed.), *'Corpus Iuris' di Zayd Ibn ʿAlī*, Milan 1919.
Grohmann, see above, I.
Guest, R., 'Relations between Persia and Egypt under Islam up to the Fâtimid Period', *A Volume of Oriental Studies Presented to E. G. Browne*, Cambridge 1922.
Guidi and Santillana, see above, II (b), s.v. 'Khalīl'.
Guillaume, A., *The Traditions of Islam, an Introduction to the Study of the Hadith Literature*, Oxford 1924.
See also Ibn Hishām.

Haefeli, see ʿĀrif al-ʿĀrif.
Halm, H., *Die Ausbreitung der šāfiʿitischen Rechtsschule von den Anfängen bis zum 8./14. Jahrhundert*, Wiesbaden 1974.
Ḥamāsa, see Abū Tammām.
Hamdānī, al-Ḥasan b. Aḥmad al-, *al-Iklīl*, book x, ed. M.-D. al-Khaṭīb, n.p., n.d.
Ṣifat jazīrat al-ʿarab, ed. D. H. Müller, Leiden 1884–91.
Ḥamīdullāh, M., 'Influence of Roman Law on Muslim Law', *Journal of the Hyderabad Academy* 1943.
Muslim Conduct of State[2], Hyderabad 1945.
Hamilton, R. A. B., 'The Social Organization of the Tribes of the Aden Protectorate', *Journal of the Royal Central Asian Society* 1942.
Handbook of Arabia, see Great Britain.
Harada, K., 'Der Verzicht auf den Patronat und das Gesetz Justinians in C. 6, 4, 3', *Zeitschrift der Savigny-Stiftung für Rechtsgeschichte* 1938.

Hardy, M. J. L., *Blood Feuds and the Payment of Bloodmoney in the Middle East*, Beirut 1963.
Harrison, A. R. W., *The Law of Athens*, Oxford 1968.
Hartmann, R., review of J. Hatschek in *Orientalistische Literaturzeitung* 1923.
Hassam, A., 'Le droit musulman et le droit romain', *Archives d'Histoire du Droit Oriental* 1949, with observations by J. Wigmore appended.
Ḥassān b. Thābit, *Dīwān*, ed. H. Hirschfeld, Leiden and London 1910.
Ḥātim Ṭayyi', *Dīwān*, ed. and tr. F. Schulthess, Leipzig 1897.
Hatschek, J., *der Musta'min*, Berlin and Leipzig 1919.
Hawsamī, see above, II (g).
Hawting, G. R., 'The Dispute in Muslim Law about the Rights of a Divorced Woman during her "Waiting Period" ', paper presented at the Colloquium on Qur'ān and Ḥadīth, Cambridge 1985.
Heffening, W., *Das islamische Fremdenrecht*, Hannover 1925.
review of J. Hatschek in *Der Islam* 1923.
'Zum Aufbau der islamischen Rechtswerke' in W. Heffening and W. Kirfel (eds.), *Studien zur Geschichte und Kultur des nahen und fernen Ostens – Paul Kahle zum 60. Geburtstag*, Leiden 1935.
Hengstl, J., *Private Arbeitsverhältnisse freier Personen in den hellenistischen Papyri bis zu Diokletian*, Bonn 1972.
Henninger, J., 'Die Familie bei den heutigen Beduinen Arabiens und seiner Randgebiete', *Internationales Archiv für Ethnographie*, vol. 42, 1943.
'Pariastämme in Arabien', *Sankt Gabrieler Studien, Festschrift des Missionhauses Sankt Gabriel*, Vienna and Mödling 1939.
Hilali, T. al-, 'Die Kasten in Arabien', *Die Welt des Islams* 1940.
Ḥillī, see above, II (e).
Hinnells, J. R., *Zoroastrianism and the Parsees*, London 1981.
Honoré, A. M., 'The "Fragmentum Dositheaneum"', *Reveue Internationale des Droits de l'Antiquité* 1965.
Howard, I. K. A., '*Mutʿa* Marriage Reconsidered in the Context of the Formal Procedures for Islamic Marriage', *Journal of Semitic Studies* 1975.
Huber, C., *Voyage dans l'Arabie Centrale (Extrait du Bulletin de la Société de Géographie* 1884–5), Paris 1885.
Hugues, H., 'La justice française et le droit musulman en Algérie', *La France judiciaire* 1878–9.
'Les origines du droit musulman', *La France judiciaire* 1879–80.
Humphreys, S. C., *Anthropology and the Greeks*, London 1983.

Ibn ʿAbd Rabbih, Aḥmad b. Muḥammad, *Kitāb al-ʿIqd al-farīd*, ed. A. Amīn and others, Cairo 1940–65.
Ibn Abī Shayba, ʿAbdallāh b. Muḥammad, *Kitāb al-muṣannaf fi'l-aḥādīth wa'l-āthār*, ed. M. A. al-Nadwī, Bombay 1979–83.
Ibn al-Athīr, Majd al-Dīn al-Mubārak, *al-Nihāya fī gharīb al-ḥadīth*, ed. Ṭ. A. al-Zāwī and M. M. al-Ṭannāḥī, Cairo 1963–5.
Ibn Bābūyah, see above, II (e).
Ibn Ḥabīb, *Kitāb al-munammaq*, ed. Kh. A. al-Fāriq, Hyderabad 1964.
Ibn Ḥajar al-ʿAsqalānī, Shihāb al-Dīn Aḥmad, *al-Iṣāba fī tamyīz al-ṣaḥāba*, Cairo 1323–5.
Tahdhīb al-tahdhīb, Hyderabad 1325–7.
Ibn Ḥazm, see above, II (i).
Ibn Hishām, ʿAbd al-Malik, *Das Leben Muhammed's nach Muhammed Ibn Ishâk*, ed. F. Wüstenfeld, Göttingen 1858–60 = A. Guillaume (tr.), *The Life of Muhammad*, Oxford 1955.

Ibn Khallikān, Aḥmad b. Muḥammad, *Wafayāt al-aʿyān*, ed. I ʿAbbās, Beirut 1968–72.
Ibn Manẓūr, Muḥammad b. al-Mukarram, *Lisān al-ʿarab*, Būlāq 1307.
Ibn Muqbil, Tamīm b. Ubayy, *Dīwān*, ed. ʿA. Ḥasan, Damascus 1962.
Ibn al-Murtaḍā, see above, II (g).
Ibn Qudāma, see above, II (d).
Ibn Qutayba, ʿAbdallāh b. Muslim, *al-Maʿārif*, ed. M. I. ʿA. al-Ṣāwī, Beirut 1970.
Ibn Rushd, see above, II (b).
Ingrams, D., *A Survey of Social and Economic Conditions in the Aden Protectorate*, Eritrea 1949.
Ingrams, W. H., *A Report on the Social, Economic and Political Conditions of the Hadhramaut*, London, Colonial Office, 1937.
Iṣbahānī, Abū'l-Faraj ʿAlī b. al-Ḥusayn al-, *Kitāb al-aghānī*[3], Cairo 1927–72.

Jackson, B. S., *Theft in Early Jewish Law*, Oxford 1972.
Jacob, G., *Altarabisches Beduinenleben*[2], Berlin 1897.
Jāḥiẓ, ʿAmr b. Baḥr al-, *Kitāb al-ḥayāwān*, ed. ʿA.-S. Hārūn, Cairo 1937–47.
Rasāʾil, ed. H. al-Sandūbī, Cairo 1933.
Jastrow, M., *Dictionary of the Targumim, the Talmud Babli and Yerushalmi, and the Midrashic Literature*, London 1895–1903.
Jaussen, A., *Coutumes des arabes au pays de Moab*, Paris 1908.
Juda, J., *Die sozialen und wirtschaftlichen Aspekte der Mawālī in frühislamischer Zeit* (Inaugural-Dissertation), Tübingen 1983.
Juynboll, G. H. A., *Muslim Tradition*, Cambridge 1983.

Kaser, M., 'Die Geschichte der Patronatsgewalt über Freigelassene', *Zeitschrift der Savigny-Stiftung für Rechtsgeschichte* 1938.
Das römische Privatrecht[2], Munich 1971–5.
Kashshī, Muḥammad b. ʿUmar al-, *al-Rijāl*, ed. A. al-Ḥusaynī, Najaf n.d.
Khalīfa b. Khayyāṭ, *Kitāb al-ṭabaqāt*, ed. A. D. al-ʿUmarī, Baghdad 1967.
Khalīl, see above, II (b).
Kharashī, see above, II (b).
Kindī, Muḥammad b. Yūsuf al-, *The Governors and Judges of Egypt*, ed. R. Guest, Leiden and London 1912.
Kister, M. J., 'On Strangers and Allies in Mecca', paper presented at the Third International Colloquium on 'From Jahiliyya to Islam', to appear in *Jerusalem Studies in Arabic and Islam*.
'On the Wife of the Goldsmith from Fadak and her Progeny', *Le Muséon* 1979.
Koschaker, P., 'Bericht über den 5. internationalen Papyrologenkongress in Oxford', *Zeitschrift der Savigny-Stiftung für Rechtsgeschichte* 1938.
Über einige griechische Rechtsurkunden aus den östlichen Randgebieten des Hellenismus (= Abhandlungen der philosophisch-historischen Klasse der Sächsischen Akademie der Wissenschaften, vol. XLII), Leipzig 1931.
Kosegarten, J. G. L., (ed.), *The Hudsailian Poems*, London 1854.
Köprülü, F., 'L'institution de vakouf', *Vakıflar Dergisi* 1942.
Kraeling, see above, I.
Kraemer, C. J., 'The Colt Papyri from Palestine', *Actes du Vᵉ congrès internationale de papyrologie, Oxford 30 août–30 Septembre 1937*, Brussels 1938.
and N. Lewis, 'A Divorce Agreement from Southern Palestine', *Transactions and Proceedings of the American Philological Association* 1938.
see also above, I.
Kramer and Hagedorn, *Kölner Papyri*, see above, I.
Kreller, H., *Erbrechtliche Untersuchungen auf Grund der Graeco-Ägyptischen Papyrusurkunden*, Leipzig and Berlin 1919.
Kremer, A. von, *Culturgeschichte des Orients under den Chalifen*, Vienna 1875–7.

Krenkow, F., (ed. and tr.), *The Poems of Ṭufail Ibn Auf al-Ghanawī and aṭ-Ṭirimmāḥ Ibn Ḥakīm at-Ṭā'yī*, London 1927.
Kuhn, T. S., *The Structure of Scientific Revolutions*², Chicago 1970.
Kustas, G. L., *Studies in Byzantine Rhetoric*, Thessalonica 1973.

Labīd b. Rabī'a al-'Āmirī, *Dīwān*, ed. I. 'Abbās, Kuwait 1962; ed. and tr. C. Brockelmann, Leiden 1891.
Lambert, J., *Les operae liberti*, Paris 1934.
La Pira, G., 'Precedenti provinciali della riforma giustinianea del diritto di patronato', *Studi Italiani di Filologia Classica* 1929.
Landau-Tasseron, E., ' "The Sinful Wars": Religious, Social and Historical Aspects of *Ḥurūb al-Fijār*', *Jerusalem Studies in Arabic and Islam* 1986.
Lane, E. W., *An Arabic-English Lexicon*, London 1863–93.
Laoust, see above, II (d).
Lemerle, P., *Le premier humanisme byzantin*, Paris 1971.
Lewis, B., *The Arabs in History*⁴, London 1966.
(tr.), *Islam from the Prophet Muhammad to the Capture of Constantinople*, New York 1974.
Lichtenstädter, I., *Women in the Aiyâm al-'arab*, London 1935.
Liebermann, S., 'Roman Legal Institutions in Early Rabbinics and in the Acta Martyrum', *Jewish Quarterly Review* 1944–5.
Liebeschuetz, J. H. W. G., *Antioch: City and Imperial Administration in the Later Roman Empire*, Oxford 1972.
Linant de Bellefonds, Y., *Traité de droit musulman comparé*, Paris and the Hague 1965– .
Lipiński, E., 'The Wife's Right to Divorce in the Light of an Ancient Near Eastern Practice', *The Jewish Law Annual* 1981.
Lisān, see Ibn Manẓūr.
Luciani, J.-D., *Traité des successions musulmanes*, Paris 1890.
Lyall, C., (ed. and tr.), *The Dīwāns of 'Abīd b. al-Abraṣ, of Asad, and 'Āmir Ibn aṭ-Ṭufail, of 'Āmir b. Ṣa'ṣa'a*, Cambridge 1913.
(ed. and tr.), *The Mufaḍḍalīyāt*, Oxford 1918–21.
(ed. and tr.), *The Poems of 'Amr Son of Qamī'a*, Cambridge 1919.

Macuch, M., (ed. and tr.), *Das sasanidische Rechtsbuch 'Mātakdān I Hazār Dātistān', Teil II*, Wiesbaden 1981.
Madelung, W., *Der Imām al-Qāsim ibn Ibrāhīm und die Glaubenslehre der Zaiditen*, Berlin 1965.
'Shi'i Attitudes towards Women as Reflected in Fiqh' in A. L. al-Sayyid-Marsot (ed.), *Society and the Sexes in Medieval Islam*, Malibu 1979.
'The Sources of Ismā'īlī Law', *Journal of Near Eastern Studies* 1976.
Maḥmaṣānī, Ṣ. al-, *al-Awzā'ī*, Beirut 1978.
Maine, H., *Ancient Law*, London 1917.
Mair, L., *African Societies*, Cambridge 1974.
Mālik, see above, II (b).
Maltzan, H. Freiherr von, *Reise nach Südarabien*, Braunschweig 1873.
Maqrīzī, Aḥmad b. 'Alī al-, *Itti'āẓ al-ḥunafā'*, ed. M. H. M. Aḥmad, Cairo 1971.
Marghīnānī, see above, II (a).
Marrou, H. I, *A History of Education in Antiquity*, London 1956.
Marx, E., *Bedouins of the Negev*, Manchester 1967.
Marzubānī, Muḥammad b. 'Imrān al-, *al-Muwashshaḥ*, Cairo 1343.
Mendelsohn, I., *Slavery in the Ancient Near East*, New York 1949.
Mitteis, L., 'Antike Rechtsgeschichte und romanistisches Rechtsstudium', *Mitteilungen des Wiener Vereins der Freunde des humanistischen Gymnasiums* 1917.

Reichsrecht und Volksrecht in den östlichen Provinzen des römischen Kaiserreichs, Leipzig 1891.

'Über drei neue Handschriften des syrisch-römischen Rechtsbuchs' (reprinted from *Abhandlungen der Königlichen Preussischen Akademie der Wissenschaften*), Berlin 1905.

'Zwei griechische Rechtsurkunden aus Kurdistan', *Zeitschrift der Savigny-Stiftung für Rechtsgeschichte* 1915.

Montevecchi, O., *La papirologia*, Turin 1973.

Morand, M., *Études de droit musulman algérien*, Alger 1910.

Morimoto, K., *The Fiscal Administration of Egypt in the Early Islamic Period*, Kyoto 1981.

Mottahedeh, R., *Loyalty and Leadership in an Early Islamic Society*, Princeton 1980.

Mu'arrij al-Sadūsī, *Kitāb ḥadhf min nasab Quraysh*, ed. Ṣ. al-Munajjid, Cairo 1960.

Mu'ayyad, see above, II (g).

Mubarrad, Muḥammad b. Yazīd al-, *al-Kāmil*, ed. W. Wright, Leipzig 1867–92.

Musil, A., *Arabia Petraea*, Vienna 1907–8.

The Manners and Customs of the Rwala Bedouins, New York 1928.

Muslim b. Ḥajjāj, *al-Jāmiʿ al-ṣaḥīḥ*, Constantinople 1329–33.

Müller, H., *Die Gesetze Ḥammurabis und ihr Verhältnis zur mosaischen Gesetzgebung, sowie zu den XII Tafeln*, Vienna 1903.

Nābigha al-Dhubyānī, Ziyād b. Muʿāwiya, *Dīwān*, ed. and tr. H. Derenbourg, Paris 1869.

Nābigha al-Jaʿdī, ʿAbdallāh b. Qays, *Dīwān*, ed. and tr. M. Nallino, Rome 1953.

Naḥwī, see above, II (g).

Nallino, C. A., 'A proposito di alcuni studi sui diritti orientali' in his *Raccolta*, vol. IV (an abbreviated version of his 'Gli Studi di E. Causi').

'Considerazioni sui rapporti fra diritto romano et diritto musulmano' in his *Raccolta*, vol. IV.

'Intorno al divieto romano imperiale dell'affratellamento e ad alcuni paralleli arabi' in his *Raccolta*, vol. IV,

Raccolta di scritti editi e inediti, vol. IV, Rome 1942.

review of E. Carusi, in *L'Oriente Moderno* 1925.

'Gli studi di E. Carusi sui diritti orientali', *Rivista degli Studi Orientali* 1921–3.

'Sul libro siro-romano e sul presunto diritto siriaco' in his *Raccolta*, vol. IV.

Nallino, M., 'an-Nābiġah al-Ǵaʿdī e le sue poesie', *Rivista degli Studi Orientali* 1934.

Narshakhī, Muḥammad b. Jaʿfar, *Déscription de Boukhara*, ed. C. Schefer, Paris 1892 = *id.*, *The History of Bukhara*, tr. R. N. Frye, Cambridge Mass. 1954.

Nau, F., 'Notice historique sur le monastère de Qartamin', *Actes du XIV*[e] *Congrès internationale des Orientalistes*, part ii, Paris 1907.

Nawawī, see above, II (c).

Nicholas, B., *An Introduction to Roman Law*, Oxford 1962.

Nöldeke, T., *Die Gedichte des ʿUrwa Ibn Alward* (= *Abhandlungen des königlichen Gesellschaft der Wissenschaften zu Göttingen*, vol. XI), Göttingen 1863.

Nuʿmān, see above, II (f).

O'Leary, D. l., *A Short History of the Fatimid Khalifate*, London 1923.

Oppenheim, M. Freiherr von, *Die Beduinen*, vol. IV, part i, ed. W. Caskel, Wiesbaden 1967.

Partsch, J., 'Neue Rechtsquellen der nestorianischen Kirche', *Zeitschrift der Savigny-Stiftung für Rechtsgeschichte* 1909.

review of A. Calderini in *Archiv für Papyrusforschung* 1913.
review of E. Sachau in *Zeitschrift der Savigny-Stiftung für Rechtsgeschichte* 1907.
Payne-Smith, R., *Thesaurus Syriacus*, Oxford 1879–1901.
Pedersen, J., *Der Eid bei den Semiten*, Strassburg 1914.
Perikhanian, E., 'Iranian Society and Law' in E. Yarshater (ed.), *The Cambridge History of Iran*, vol. III, part ii, Cambridge 1983.
Peters, E. L., 'Some Structural Aspects of the Feud among the Camel-herding Bedouin of Cyrenaica', *Africa* 1967.
Philby, H. St. J. B., *The Heart of Arabia*, London 1922.
Pospíšil, L., *Anthropology of Law, a Comparative Theory*, New York, San Francisco and London 1971.
Powers, D. S., 'The Will of Saʿd b. Abî Waqqâṣ: a Reassessment', *Studia Islamica* 1983.
Pretzl, O., 'Die frühislamische Atomenlehre', *Der Islam* 1931.
Procksch, O., *Über die Blutrache bei den vorislamischen Arabern*, Leipzig 1899.

Qays b. al-Khaṭīm, *Dīwān*, ed. and tr. T. Kowalsi, Leipzig 1914.
Qudūrī, see above II (a).
Quintillian, *Institutio Oratio*, ed. and tr. H. E. Butler, London 1921–2.
Quṭāmī, ʿUmayr b. Suḥaym al-, *Dīwān*, ed. J. Barth, Leiden 1905.

Rabe, H., (ed.), *Aphthonii Progymnasmata* (*Rhetores Graeci*, vol. x), Leipzig 1926 = R. Nadeau (tr.), 'the Progymnasmata of Aphthonius', *Speech Monographs* (Ann Arbor, Michigan) 1952.
Rabinowitz, J. J., 'Brooklyn 5 and Manumission with Paramone in Greece' in his *Jewish Law, its influence on the Development of Legal Institutions*, New York 1956.
Raddatz, H.-P., *Die Stellung und Bedeutung des Sufyān aṯ-Ṯaurī (gest. 778)*, Bonn 1967.
see also above, II (i).
Rädle, H., *Untersuchungen zum griechischen Freilassungswesen*, Munich 1969.
Raswan, C. R., *The Black Tents of Arabia*, London 1953.
Rathjens, C., 'Tâghût gegen scherî'a', *Jahrbuch des Lindenmuseums* 1951.
Reinert, W., *Das Recht in der altarabischen Poesie* (Inagural-Dissertation), Cologne 1963.
Reland, H., *Dissertationes Miscellaneae*, trajecti ad Rhenum 1706–8.
Rescher, O., 'Die Qaçîden des ʿAmr b. Kulthûm' in his *Orientalistische Miszellen*, vol. II, Constantinople 1926.
Robertson Smith, W., *Kinship and Marriage in Early Arabia*², London 1903.
Rosenthal, F., *Gambling in Islam*, Leiden 1975.
Rostovtzeff and Welles, see above, I.
Rubensohn, see above, I.

Sachau, E., 'Muhammedanisches Erbrecht nach der Lehre der Ibaditischen Araber von Zanzibar und Ostafrika', *Sitzungsberichte der Königlichen Preussischen Akademie der Wissenschaften zu Berlin* 1894.
Muhammedanisches Recht nach schafiitischer Lehre, Stuttgart and Berlin 1897.
(ed. and tr.), *Syrische Rechtsbücher*, Berlin 1907–14.
Saḥnūn, see above, II (b).
Said, E. W., *Orientalism*, London 1978.
Samuel, A. E., 'The Role of Paramone Clauses in Ancient Documents', *Journal of Juristic Papyrology* 1965.
San Nicolò, M., review of A. Grohmann in *Zeitschrift der Savigny – Stiftung für Rechtsgeschichte* 1935.
*Die Schlussklauseln der altbabylonischen Kauf- und Tauchsverträge*², Munich 1974.

Santillana, D., *Code civil et commercial Tunisien, avant projet discuté et adopté*, Tunis 1899.

'Il libro di Zayd b. ʿAli e il sistema zaydita', *Rivista degli Studi Orientali* 1919–20 (review of E. Griffini).

Istituzioni di diritto musulmano malichita, Rome 1926–38.

review of M. Fathy in *Rivista degli Studi Orientali* 1916–18.

Sarakhsī, see above, II (a).

Savvas pacha, *Le droit musulman expliqué*, Paris 1896.

Études sur la théorie du droit musulman, vol. 1, Paris 1892.

Schacht, J., 'Droit byzantin et droit musulman', *Accademia Nazionale dei Lincei, Fondazione Allesandro Volta, Atti dei Convegni*, no. 12, Rome 1957.

'Foreign Elements in Ancient Islamic Law', *Mémoires de l'Académie Internationale de Droit Comparé* 1955.

An Introduction to Islamic Law, Oxford 1964.

'The Law' in G. E. von Grunebaum (ed.), *Unity and Variety in Muslim Civilization*, Chicago 1955.

'Modernism and Traditionalism in a History of Islamic Law', *Middle Eastern Studies* 1965 (review of N. J. Coulson).

The Origins of Muhammadan Jurisprudence, Oxford 1950.

'Pre-Islamic Background and Early Development of Jurisprudence' in M. Khadduri and H. J. Liebesny (eds.), *Law in the Middle East*, vol. 1, Washington 1955.

'Remarques sur la transmission de la pensée grecques aux arabes', *Hisoire de la Médicine* 1952.

review of E. Tyan in *Orientalia* 1948.

'Vom babylonischen zum islamischen Recht', *Orientalistische Literaturzeitung* 1927.

Scheltema, H. J., *L'enseignement de droit des antecesseurs*, Leiden 1970.

'The Nomoi of Iulianus of Ascalon', *Symbolae ad Jus et Historiam Antiquitatis Pertinentes Julio Christiano van Oven Dedicatae*, Leiden 1946.

Schmidt, F. F., 'Die Occupatio im islamischen Recht', *Der Islam* 1910 (also published as a book in Strassburg in the same year).

Schram-Nielsen, E., *Studier over Erstatningslæren i Islamisk Ret*, Copenhagen 1945.

Schulz, F., *History of Roman Legal Science*, Oxford 1946.

Schwabe, M., 'Writ of Manumission among Papyri in Auja al-Hafir in Southern Palestine', *Magnes Anniversary Book*, Jerusalem 1938 (in Hebrew).

Seidl, E., *Rechtsgeschichte Ägyptens als römischer Provinz*, Sankt Augustin 1973.

Selb, W., 'Sententiae syriacae', *Zeitschrift der Savigny-Stiftung für Rechtsgeschichte* 1968.

Zur Bedeutung des syrisch-römischen Rechtsbuches, Munich 1964.

Sezgin, F., *Geschichte des arabischen Schrifttums*, vol. 1, Leiden 1967.

Shāfiʿī, see above, II (c).

Shalabī, ʿA.-M. ʿA.-R., (ed.), *Sharḥ Dīwān ʿAntara b. Shaddād*, Cairo n.d.

Shammākhī, *Īḍāḥ*, see above, II (h).

Shammākhī, Aḥmad b. Saʿīd al-, *Kitāb al-siyar*, Cairo n.d.

Sharīf al-Murtaḍā, see above, II (e).

Shaybānī, see above, II (a).

Shīrāzī, see above, II (c).

Shirbīnī, see above, II (c).

Shivtiel, A., W. Lockwood and R. B. Serjeant, 'The Jews of Ṣanʿa'' in R. B. Serjeant and R. Lewcock (eds.), *Ṣanʿā', an Arabian Islamic City*, London 1983.

Shuqayr, Naʿūm Bak, *Ta'rīkh Sīnā*, Cairo n.d. [preface dated 1916].

Simon, D., *Untersuchungen zum justinianischen Zivilprozess*, Munich 1969.

Siyāghī, see above, II (g).

Skaist, A., 'Inheritance Laws and their Social Background', *Journal of the American Oriental Society* 1975.
Snouck Hurgronje, C., *Mekka in the Latter Part of the 19th Century*, Leiden and London 1931.
Selected Works, ed. G.-H. Bousquet and J. Schacht, Leiden 1957.
Verspreide Geschriften, vol. II, Bonn and Leipzig 1923.
Soden, W. von, 'Muškenum und die Mawālī des frühen Islam', *Zeitschrift für Assyriologie* 1964.
Speight, R. M., 'The Will of Saʿd b. a. Waqqāṣ: the Growth of a Tradition', *Der Islam* 1973.
Sperber, D., 'On the Office of the Agoranomos in Roman Palestine', *Zeitschrift der Deutschen Morgenländischen Gesellschaft* 1977.
'on the term *Heshbon*', *Tarbiz* 1969–70 (in Hebrew with English summary).
Steinwenter, A., 'Eine Ehescheidung aus dem Jahre 689', *Zeitschrift der Savigny-Stiftung für Rechtsgeschichte* 1943.
'Rhetorik und römischer Zivilprozess', *Zeitschrift der Savigny-Stiftung für Rechtsgeschichte* 1947.
'Utilitas publica – utilitas singulorum', *Festschrift P. Koschaker* Weimar 1939, vol. I.
'Was beweisen die Papyri für die praktische Geltung des justinianischen Gesetzgebungswerkes?', *Aegyptus* 1952.
Strothmann, R., 'Das Problem der literarischen Persönligkeit Zaid b. ʿAlī', *Der Islam* 1923.

Ṭabarī, Muḥammad b. Jarīr al-, *Tafsīr*, ed. M. M. Shākir and A. M. Shākir, Cairo 1954– .
Taʾrīkh al-rusul waʾl-mulūk, ed. M. J. de Goeje and others, Leiden 1879–1901.
Ṭaḥāwī, Aḥmad b. Muḥammad al-, *Mushkil al-āthār*, Hyderabad 1333.
Tāj, see Zabīdī.
Ṭarafa b. ʿAbd, *Dīwān*, ed. and tr. M. Seligsohn, Paris 1901.
Taubenschlag, R., 'Il diritto provinciale nel libro siro-romano' in his *Opera Minora*, vol. I,
'Le droit local dans les Digesta et Responsa de Cervidius Scaevola' in his *Opera Minora*, vol. I,
'Geschichte der Rezeption des römischen Privatrechts in Ägypten' in his *Opera Minora*, vol. I.
The Law of Greco-Roman Egypt in the Light of the Papyri[2], Warsaw 1955.
'The Legal Profession in Greco-Roman Egypt' in his *Opera Minora*, vol. II.
'The Legislation of Justinian in the Light of the Papyri' in his *Opera Minora*, vol. II.
Opera Minora, Warsaw 1959.
'Das römische Privatrecht zur Zeit Diokletians' in his *Opera Minora*, vol. I.
'Das Sklavenrecht im Lichte der Papyri' in his *Opera Minora*, vol. II.
'Syrische Rechtsbücher' in his *Opera Minora*, vol. I.
Thaʿālibī, ʿAbd al-Malik b. Muḥammad al-, *Thimār al-qulūb*, ed. M. A.-F., Ibrāhīm, Cairo 1963.
Theophanes, *Chronographia*, ed. C. de Boor, Leipzig 1883–5.
Thomas, B., *Arabia Felix*, London 1932.
Ṭirimmāḥ, see Krenkow.
Tirmidhī, Muḥammad b. ʿIsā al-, *al-Ṣaḥīḥ*, Cairo 1931–4.
Ṭūsī, see above, II (e).
Tyan, E., *Institutions du droit public musulman*, vol. I, Paris 1954.

Udovitch, A. L., *Partnership and Profit in Medieval Islam*, Princeton 1970.

Vasiliev, A. A., *History of the Byzantine Empire*, Madison and Milwaukee 1964 (first published 1928).

Vocabularium Iurisprudentiae Romanae, iussu Instituti Savigniani compositum, Berlin 1903–85.

Volterra, E., *Diritto romano e diritti orientali*, Bologna 1937.

Vööbus, A., *History of the School of Nisibis* (= CSCO, subsidia, vol. XXVI), Louvain 1965.

Wakīʿ, Muḥammad b. Khalaf, *Akhbār al-quḍāh*, ed. ʿA.-ʿA. M. al-Marāghī, Cairo 1947–50.

Wallin, G. A., *Travels in Arabia (1845 and 1848)*, Cambridge 1979.

Wāqidī, Muḥammad b. ʿUmar al-, *Kitāb al-maghāzī*, ed. M. Jones, London 1966.

Watt, W. M., *Islam and the Integration of Society*, London 1966.

Welles, C. Bradford, 'Manumission and Adoption', *Revue Internationale des Droits de l'Antiquité* 1949 (= *Mélanges Fernand de Visscher*, vol. II).

Wellhausen, J., (ed. and tr.), 'Letzter Teil der Lieder der Hudhailiten' in his *Skizzen und Vorarbeiten*, vol. I, Berlin 1884.

'Medina vor dem Islam' in his *Skizzen und Vorarbeiten*, vol. IV, Berlin 1889.

Die religiös-politischen Oppositionsparteien im alten Islam, Berlin 1901.

Reste Arabischen Heidentums, Berlin 1887.

Wenger, L., *Römische und antike Rechtsgeschichte*, Graz 1905.

Wensinck, A. J., 'Die Entstehung der muslimischen Reinheitsgesetzgebung', *Der Islam* 1914.

West, E. W., (tr.), *Pahlavi Texts*, part iii (= F. M. Müller (ed.), *The Sacred Books of the East*, vol. XVIII), Oxford 1882.

Westermann, W. L., 'The Paramone as General Service Contract', *Journal of Juristic Papyrology* 1948.

'Two Studies in Athenian Manumission', *Journal of Near Eastern Studies* 1946.

Wigmore, see Hassam.

Wilcken, U., 'Papyrus-Urkunden', *Archiv für Papyrusforschung* 1913.

'Urkundenreferat', *Archiv für Papyrusforschung* 1941.

Wilkinson, J., 'Bayāsirah and Bayādīr', *Arabian Studies*, vol. I, Cambridge 1974.

'Ibāḍī Ḥadīth: an Essay on Normalization', *Der Islam* 1985.

Wissowa, G., (ed.), *Pauly's Realencyclopädie der classischen Alterthumswissenschaft*², Stuttgart 1893– .

Wolff, H. J., 'Der byzantinische Urkundenstil Ägyptens im Lichte der Funde von Nessana und Dura', *Revue Internationale des Droits de l'Antiquité* 1961.

'Rezeption der Beispruchsrecht ins byzantinische Reichsrecht?', *Syntaleia Vicenzo Arangio-Ruiz*, vol. I, Naples 1964.

'Das Vulgarrechtsproblem und die Papyri', *Zeitschrift der Savigny-Stiftung für Rechtsgeschichte* 1974.

'Zur Romanisierung des Vertragsrecht der Papyri', *Zeitschrift der Savigny-Stiftung für Rechtsgeschichte* 1965.

Yāqūt b. ʿAbdallāh, *Muʿjam al-buldān*, ed. F. Wüstenfeld, Leipzig 1866–73.

Zabīdī, Muḥammad b. Muḥammad al, *Tāj al-ʿarūs*, Būlāq 1306–7.

Zimmermann, F. W., '*Kalām* and the Greeks', paper read at the tenth congress of the Union Européenne des Arabisants et Islamisants, Edinburgh 1980.

Zulueta, F. de, 'De Patrociniis Vicorum', in P. Vinogradoff (ed.), *Oxford Studies in Social and Legal History*, vol. I, Oxford 1909.

Zurqānī, see above, II (b).

Index

ʿAbd al-Qays, 57f
ʿAbd al-Razzāq b. Hammām al-Ṣanʿānī, 26f
ʿabīd, see slaves
Abū ʿAṣim al-Nabīl, 22
Abū Ghānim, 21
Abū Ḥanīfa, 20, 41, 122[39]
Abū Ḥudhayfa, 68
Abū Thawr, 122[29]
Abū Yūsuf, 20, 26, 122[39]
agnates, agnatic succession, 36, 40, 79f, 99
agoranomos, 11, 107f
al-aḥkām al-khamsa, 11
Alexandria, 12
alimony, 67, 70f
B. al-ʿAmm, 48f, 89
ʿAmmār b. Yāsir, 68
Amos, 1f
Antioch, 13
Aphthonius, 10
apolyein, apolysis, 66, 72f, 85
ʿāqila, 37; *see also* blood-money
Arabia
  customary law of, 2, 5, 92, 93, 96f
  legal schools of, 20, 22, 23
  status of non-tribesmen in, 44f, 45–51, 56–63
Asāwira, 54, 89
Ascalon, 15
aṣīl, 44
Athanasius, 13
Athens, *see* Greek law
Awzāʿī, 22

banū'l-ʿamm, 48f
Barīra tradition, 88
Basra, legal schools of, 20, 21, 23
Bayhaqī, 27
Becker, 3, 5, 7, 11, 15
Beirut, 12f, 103
Berg, van den, 2
Bergh, van den, 11
Bergsträsser, 5, 11
blood-money
  between client and patron in Islamic law, 37, 39f, 44; denial of the obligation, 62; refusals to pay, 87
  for *ḥalīf* and *jār*, 52
  for foreign woman in Arabia, 134[99]
  for slaves and freedmen, in modern Arabia, 47; in pre-Islamic Arabia, 61f
Bousquet, 5
brothers, brotherhood, 45, 49, 93
Brown, 17
Brunschvig, 11, 82
Bukhārī, 25, 33
Burckhardt, 47
Bussi, 5, 114[53]

Caesarea, 12f, 15
Carusi, 5, 120[142]
celibacy, 71f, 87
changing patrons, 32f, 81
Cicero, 9
clerk of court, 118[113]
clientage
  collective vs individual, 43f, 45–9, 56–63
  contractual (*walāʾ al-muwālāt*), 38–40, 81, 90f; *see also* changing patrons
    by conversion (*walāʾ al-islām*), 36, 38, 90f
  see also patronate
common link, 28f
Constantinople, 13
Constitution of Medina, 32
  mawālī in 136[141]
converts, 35f
  as illegal immigrants, 125[7]
  see also clientage
Coulson, 94, 96, 123[59], 124[66], 125[78]
custody (*ḥaḍāna*), 37, 38, 39, 155[10]

daʿī, 60
dating of traditions, 29–31
Daube, 11, 98
Dāwūd b. Khalaf, 22
dhawū'l-arḥām, non-agnatic relatives, 23, 37, 79f
*dhimmī*s, 35f, 38
divorce, 97
diya, *see* blood-money
Doughty, 47–9
Dura Europos, 65

earnest-money, 93
Egypt, 12, 13, 20, 64, 65
Elephantine, 65
Enger, 2

fatwās, 19, 103,
fiqh, 102, 103, 115[65]
FitzGerald, 5, 6, 102–6
Foster, 107
freedmen in Arabia, 46–9, 56, 58–63

Gatteschi, 1f
Gaudefroy-Demombynes, 107
Gaza, 89
GHLẒ, 143[64], 145[99]
Goldziher, 3, 5, 6, 7f, 10, 11, 31, 102–6
Greek law, 36, 92, 142[51]
  freedmen and foreigners in, 35f
Griffini, 5
guardianship
  Roman, 77f, 120[138]; and Islamic, 112[25]
  marriage-, 37, 38, 39, 155[10]
  see also custody

Hadawīs, 20
Ḥadīth, 23–34
Hajar, 57, 89
hajīn, 59f, 62
ḥalīf, 49, 51–6, 84, 89, 93
Hammurabi, 87
Ḥamrā', 54, 89
Ḥanafīs, 20, 23, 26
B. Ḥanīfa, 50
Ḥanbalīs, 22, 23
Harada, 85f
Ḥasan al-Baṣrī, 24, 25
Hassam, 5, 6
Hatschek, 112[31]
Heffening, 3, 5, 6, 8
Hermagoras, 10
ḥilf, 51, 53–5, 67, 136[141]; *see also ḥalīf*
Hugues, 2, 102f

Ibāḍīs, 21, 23
  and succession by *walā'*, 36
Ibn ʿAbbās, 24, 33
Ibn Abī Shayba, 27
Ibn Bābūyah, 26
Ibn Ḥanbal, 22, 25, 33
Ibn Ḥazm, 22, 27
Ibn Judʿān, 67
Ibn Masʿūd, 24
Ibn al-Muqaffaʿ, 118[113]
Ibn Qudāma, 27
Ibrāhīm al-Nakhaʿī, 23f, 25
ijmāʿ, 11, 104
ʿilla, 96, 105
Imāmī law, 21, [23], 25f
  archaisms of: contractual clientage, 38; contractual freedom for manumitters, 98; no agnatic imprint, 80, 99; no patronate if renounced, 81; no patronate unless manumission is gratuitous, 83f, 86; stipulations of re-enslavement, 73
immutability of Islamic law, 18f
interpretatio prudentium, 11, 103
Iraq
  legal schools of, 20f, 23
  no Roman law in, 10, 12
  Roman law supposedly transmitted via, 8, 10
Isḥāq b. Rāhuyah, 122[29]
Ishoʿbokht, 12, 92, 94, 118[114], 140[4], 154[130]
istiḥsān, 23
Ismāʿīlīs, 21 [23]
istiṣḥāb, 11, 105
istiṣlāḥ, see *maṣlaḥa*
Ithnā-ashʿarīs, *see* Imāmī law

jār, 49, 51–6
Jews of Arabia, 50, 56f
Jewish law
  freedmen and proselytes in, 35, 62, 64
  influence on Islamic law, 3, 11, 87, 92, 103–5, 117[108], 118[111]
  Roman law transmitted via, 2, 11, 103, 104
Justinian, 13, 93, 99, 105, 119[117], 147[1]
  and the Roman patronate, 84–8, 92, 153[122]

Kalām, 9
Khalīfat Allāh, 15
Khārijites, *see* Ibāḍīs
Khiraqī, 22, 27
khulʿ, 97
khuwwa, 46, 56
kinship, fictitious and metaphorical, 48
kitāba, 64, 69–76, 88, 109, 158[79]
  supposedly in the Qur'ān, 145[100]
  see also mukātab
Koschaker, 67, 76, 98
Kremer, von, 1, 2, 11

kubr, 81–3
Kufa, schools of, 20f, 23
Kulīnī, 21

Lammens, 5
Latini Iuniani, 88
Layth b. Saʿd, 22
legitima aetas, 11, 112[25]
Lex Fufia Caninia, 119[117]
Libanius, 9, 10
libera testamenti factio, 85, 94
liberti orcini, 153[122]

madhhabs, *see* schools
Maine, 99
Mālik b. Anas, 22, [26]
Mālikīs, 22, 23, 26
Maʿmar b. Rāshid, 26
manumission
  conditional, 65–76
  documents of, 109, 141[16]
  with adoption, 64f, 67, 68
  with *paramonē*, 64–76, 109f
  without further service, 46, 67, 68, 88
  without *walā*ʾ, 38, 68, 88; *see also sāʾiba*
    see also kitāba; tadbīr
Marghinani, 26
marriage guardianship, *see* guardianship
maṣlaḥa, 11, 104f
mawlā, mawālī
  in historical sources, 41
  meanings of the term, 49, 71; beyond translation, 90
  in poetry, 55f
  upper and lower, 40
Mecca, 20, 22, 49
Medina, schools of, 20, 22f
  and agnatic succession, 79f
metics, 35
Mitteis, 4, 5
Morand, 3f, 5, 11
Muʿāwiya and the patronate, 91
muḥtasib, 11, 107f
mukātab, 73–6
  escapes *walā*ʾ, in Imāmī and Ibāḍī law, [83f], 86, 126[9]; in pre-classical law, 86
  sale of *walā*ʾ associated with, 88
  see also kitāba
muṣannaf, 26
muškenum, 139[1]
musnad, 26
mutilation of slaves, 83, 87

Nallino, 4, 5f, 10, 11, 12, 14, 17
Nāṣir al-Uṭrūsh, 20
Nāṣirīs, 20
Negev, 5, 14
Nessana papyri, 5, 8, 14, 65, 73, 97
Nestorians, 10, 65, 87, 92
niṣāb, 118[108]
Nisibis, 10
non-Muslim freedmen, 83
North Africa, 20, 22
Nuʿmān, Qāḍī, 21

oath, defensive, 106
obsequium, 77, 87
operae, labour services, 69, 77f, 85, 86, 152[96]
opinio prudentium, 11, 103f

paramonē
  in antiquity, 64–7
  in Arabia, 67f
  influences the Roman patronate, 78, 84, 85f
  in Islam, 68–76
  as legal *koinē*, 92f
paterfamilias, 77
patria potestas, 77, 139[186]
patronate
  Islamic (*walā*ʾ), exchanges of, 32f; history of, 89–91; legal incidents of, 36–40; loss of, 87; nature of, 40, 78–83; purchase of freedom from, 85f; renunciation of, 81, 84f, 110; sale and gifts of, 31f, 40, 80f, 82, 87f; succession to, 81–3, 84, 110; succession by, 36–9, 78–80, 84; Syrian attachment to, 155[9]
  Roman, 77f, 84–8; transmission of, 90f
  see also clientage
peregrine law, *see* provincial law
Persian (Iranian, Sasanid, Zoroastrian) law, 11, 64, 94, 99, 113[36]
Powers, 94, 96
presumptions, 105
Pretzl, 8
prostitution of slavegirls, 87
provincial law (peregrine law; *Volksrecht*), 1, 4, 14f, 92
  as legal *koinē*, 92–8
  Roman law transmitted via, 91f

qasāma, 23, 158[79]
Qāsim b. Ibrāhīm, 20
Qāsimīs, 20
qiṭāʿa, 86
qiyās, 23
Quintilian, 9

Rabīʿ b. Ḥabīb, 21
raʾy, 11, 103f
re-enslavement, 65, 67, 73, 141[20]
Reland, 1
renunciation of *walā*ʾ, *see patronate; sāʾiba*

resolutive and suspensive conditions, 65
responsa prudentium, 11, 104
rhetoric, 8–11
Rome, 13
Roman law
in Egypt and Syria, 12–15
in Iraq, *see* Iraq
in Islam, *a priori* case for, 1f; earlier studies of, 1–12, 102–8; elusive nature of, 2f, [100f]; transmission of, 2, 8–11, 12, [16], 91f; *see also* Jewish law; provincial law

sabab, 37, 80
Sachau, 4, 17
Saʿd b. Abī Waqqāṣ, 157[63]
sāʾiba, 67, 68, 81, 85, 151[79], 157[54]
sale and gifts of *walāʾ*, *see* patronate
Sālim b. Maʿqil, 67
Salmān al-Fārisī, 143[53]
ṣamīm, *ṣarīḥ*, 59–62
Samuel, 67, 76
Santillana, 2, 3f,
Sarakhsī, 26, 27
ṣarīḥ, *see ṣamīm*
Sarjūn b. Manṣūr, 128[1], 155[8]
Sasanid law, *see* Persian law
Savvas Pacha, 102, 115[63]
Schacht, 7–12, 15f, 29f, 31, 34, 94, 96, 107f, 123[59], 151[59]
Schmidt, 3, 5
Scholia Sinaitica, 13
schools, legal, 19–23
Schulz, 13
Selb, 14, 119[119]
servilis cognatio, 147[1]
Shāfiʿī, 22, 24f, 26
Shafiʿīs, 22, 23
Shaybānī, 20, 24, 25, 26, 122[39]
Shīʿites, *see* Imāmīs, Ismāʿīlīs, Zaydīs
Sidon, 13
slaves in Arabia, 46, 50, 58–63
Snouck Hurgronje, 3
Spain, 20, 22
Sperber, 108
statuliber, 75
succession
to freedmen in Arabia, 62
between *ḥalīfs*, 53, 84, 93
pacts of, 78, 90, 93
testamentary, in the pre-Islamic Near East, 93f; in Islam, 94–7
by and to *walāʾ*, *see* patronate
Sufyān al-Thawrī, 20, 95, 122[39]
Ṣuhayb b. Sinān, 67
suis nummis emptus, 86
Sunnī law, 23
Syria
transmission of Roman law via, 8, 12, 91, [92]; role of bureaucrats in, [13], 90f, 92
schools of, 20, 22, 23
and Umayyad legislation, 16, 91
Syro-Roman lawbook, 10, 12, 13, 14, 113[39]

Ṭabarī, 23
tadbīr, 75, 109f
ṭalab al-ʿilm, 25
tasyīb, see *sāʾiba*
Taubenschlag, 85f, 118[114], 154[130]
theft in Jewish and Islamic law, 11
Timothy, 12
tribal commonwealth, 44f, [50f]
reshuffles of, 89, 91
Ṭūsī, 21, 26, 87, 126[27], 151[58]
Tyan, 56, 107

ʿulamāʾ (scholars), 3, 15, 18, 91
ʿUmar II, 16
ʿUkl, 50f
Umayyad art, 17
Umayyad law, 8, 15f, 18f
umm walad, 87, [93]
utilitas publica, 11, 105

Virgil, 14

waqf, cultural origins of, 4, 11, 113[36]
walāʾ, *see* clientage; patronate
al-walad liʾl-firāsh, 10f, 106
Wigmore, 5, 6
wills, *see* succession, testamentary
women's *walāʾ*, 82f
'worn coins', 8, 17
written and unwritten law, 104

Yamāma, 50
Yathrib, 50, 56f
Yāsir, 68
Yemen, the, 20, 22

Ẓāhirīs, 22
Zayd b. ʿAlī, 20, 25
Zayd b. Ḥāritha, 67
Zaydīs, 20, 21, [23]
Zoroastrian law, *see* Persian law
Zoroastrianism, conversion to, 125[1]
Zufar b. Hudhayl, 122[29]